FLEXIBLE WORK AND THE FAMILY

CONTEMPORARY PERSPECTIVES IN FAMILY RESEARCH

Series Editor: Sampson Lee Blair

Recent Volumes:

Volume 1:	Through the Eyes of the Child Re-visioning Children as Active Agents of Family Life – Edited by Michael Abrams, Johnson Matthey, B. A. Murrer, Felix M. Berardo, and Constance L. Shehan, 2000
Volume 2:	Families, Crime and Criminal Justice Charting the Linkages – Edited by Greer Litton Fox and Michael L. Benson, 2000
Volume 3:	Minding the Time in Family Experience Emerging Perspectives and Issues – Edited by Kerry Daly, 2001
Volume 4:	Intergenerational Ambivalences New Perspectives on Parent–Child Relations in Later Life – Edited by Karl A. Pillemer and Kurt K. Luscher, 2003
Volume 5:	Families in Eastern Europe – Edited by Mihaela Robila, 2004
Volume 6:	Economic Stress and the Family – Edited by Sampson Lee Blair, 2012
Volume 7:	Visions of the 21st Century Family: Transforming Structures and Identities – Edited by Patricia Neff Claster and Sampson Lee Blair, 2013
Volume 8A:	Family Relationships and Familial Responses to Health Issues – Edited by Jennifer Higgins McCormick and Sampson Lee Blair, 2014
Volume 8B:	Family and Health: Evolving Needs, Responsibilities, and Experiences – Edited by Sampson Lee Blair and Jennifer Higgins McCormick, 2014
Volume 9:	Violence and Crime in the Family: Patterns, Causes, and Consequences – Edited by Sheila Royo Maxwell and Sampson Lee Blair, 2015
Volume 10:	Divorce, Separation, and Remarriage: The Transformation of Family – Edited by Giovanna Gianesini and Sampson Lee Blair 2017
Volume 11:	Intimate Relationships and Social Change: The Dynamic Nature of Dating, Mating, and Coupling – Edited by Christina L. Scott and Sampson Lee Blair 2018
Volume 12:	Fathers, Childcare and Work – Edited By Arianna Santero and Rosy Musumeci, 2018
Volume 13:	The Work–Family Interface: Spillover, Complications, and Challenges – Edited by Sampson Lee Blair and Josip Obradović, 2018
Volume 14:	Childbearing and the Changing Nature of Parenting: The Contexts, Actors, and Experiences of Having Children – Edited by Rosalina Pisco Costa and Sampson Lee Blair, 2019
Volume 15:	Transitions into Parenthood: Examining the Complexities of Childrearing – Edited by Sampson Lee Blair and Rosalina Pisco Costa
Volume 16:	Chinese Families: Tradition, Modernisation, and Change – Edited by Man-Yee Kan and Sampson Le Blair
Volume 17:	Aging and the Family: Understanding Changes in Structural and Relationship Dynamics – Edited by Patricia Neff Claster and Sampson Lee Blair
Volume 18:	Families in Nigeria: Understanding their Diversity, Adaptability, and Strengths – Edited by Olufemi Adeniyi Fawole and Sampson Lee Blair
Volume 19:	Facing Death: Familial Responses to Illness and Death – Edited by Christina L Scott, Heidi M Williams, and Siri Wilder
Volume 20:	The Justice System and the Family: Police, Courts, and Incarceration – Edited by Sheila Royo Maxwell and Sampson Lee Blair

EDITORIAL BOARD

CONTEMPORARY PERSPECTIVES IN FAMILY RESEARCH VOLUME 21

FLEXIBLE WORK AND THE FAMILY

EDITED BY

ANJA-KRISTIN ABENDROTH
Bielefeld University, Germany

and

LAURA LÜKEMANN
Bielefeld University, Germany

emerald PUBLISHING

United Kingdom – North America – Japan
India – Malaysia – China

Emerald Publishing Limited
Howard House, Wagon Lane, Bingley BD16 1WA, UK

First edition 2023

British Library Cataloguing in Publication Data
A catalogue record for this book is available from the British Library

ISBN: 978-1-80455-593-4 (Print)
ISBN: 978-1-80455-592-7 (Online)
ISBN: 978-1-80455-594-1 (Epub)

ISSN: 1530-3535 (Series)

Printed and bound by CPI Group (UK) Ltd, Croydon, CR0 4YY

ISOQAR certified Management System, awarded to Emerald for adherence to Environmental standard ISO 14001:2004.

ISOQAR REGISTERED
Certificate Number 1985
ISO 14001

INVESTOR IN PEOPLE

CONTENTS

LIST OF TABLES AND FIGURES

Tables

Figures

Appendix

ABOUT THE CONTRIBUTORS

Ayhan Adams is a Research Assistant at Osnabrück University. His research interests include work–family interference and related life course decisions, behavioral dynamics in couples, and flexibilization of work with a broader focus on gender differences. His Ph.D. project examines the interrelatedness between support in couple relationships and work–family conflicts.

Laura den Dulk, PhD, is a Professor of Public Administration in Employment, Organization and Work-Life Issues at Erasmus University Rotterdam, the Netherlands. Her research interests focus on the work–life interface, workplace practices, and social policies in different national contexts.

Ines Entgelmeier, is a Research Assistant at the Federal Institute for Occupational Safety and Health (BAuA), where she works in the project "Working Time Reporting for Germany" and a PhD student at the Department of Sociology at the University of Bielefeld. In her doctoral thesis, she looks at the relation between the occupational use of ICT and working from home with regard to positive and negative forms of a dissolution of boundaries between working and private life. She examines whether these work arrangements are accompanied by better possibilities of reconciliation, additional work and psychological stress with a focus on gender-specific differences.

Katrin Golsch is a Professor of Sociology at Osnabrück University. Her research spans multiple topics in social inequality, youth, family, labor market research and quantitative social research methods and longitudinal data analysis. Currently, she is interested in the flexibilization and digitalization of work, work–family conflicts and social support among couples.

Hilpi Kangas, PhD, is a University Teacher at the University of Vaasa, Department of Management, Finland. Her research interests lie on leadership in challenging situations, trust and hybrid work. She has published her research in international journals including *Leadership, Human Resource Development International* and *Journal of Global Mobility*.

Samu Kemppinen is a Project Researcher at the University of Vaasa, Department of Management, Finland. He is an Expert in Statistical Methodology, and his research interests focus on employee well-being and remote work.

Melissa Rector LaGraff is a Research Associate for the Social Work Office of Research and Public Service at the University of Tennessee, Knoxville. She received her B.S. in Human Ecology and her M.S. and Ph.D. in Child and Family Studies from the University of Tennessee, Knoxville. Prior to her doctoral studies, she was a County Director and Family & Consumer Sciences Agent with University of Tennessee Extension. In addition to conducting program evaluation research, her research examines how parental work experiences influences parenting decisions and behaviors as well as how to improve family functioning through family policies and parenting education. She is a Certified Fair Play Method Facilitator.

Liisa Mäkelä is a Professor (Human Resource Management) at the University of Vaasa, Department of Management, Finland and a Senior researcher in Finnish Institute for Occupational Health. Her research interests focus on the future of work, employee well-being and work–life balance. Leadership, international mobility and gender issues are also part of her areas of interest. She has published her research in international journals including *Human Resource Management and Gender, Work and Organization*, and as book chapters.

Alexandra Mergener, Dr. phil., is a Senior Researcher in the department "Qualifications, Occupational Integration and Employment" at the German Federal Institute for Vocational Education and Training (BIBB). Her areas of expertise cover changes in work, occupations and qualifications, forms and effects of flexible working, and labor market inequality. She completed her PhD at the department for empirical social research and methodology at the University of Trier, researching the hiring chances of foreign skilled workers on the German labor market. Her current research projects explore access and use of Working from Home and its relation to occupational tasks, social needs, risk of overeducation, commuting behavior, and Life-Work Integration focusing on gender- and family-specific differences. Her research has been published among others in *New Technology, Work and Employment, Social Science Research, Social Science Computer Review,* or *Journal of International Migration and Integration.*

Samantha Metselaar, MSc, is a PhD Candidate at Erasmus University Rotterdam, Department of Public Administration and Sociology, the Netherlands. Her research includes the consequences of time/spatial flexibility for employee well-being and performance, the role of leadership and boundary management.

Heini Pensar is a Project Manager and a Ph.D. candidate in Human Resource Management at the University of Vaasa, School of Management. Her research relates to work well-being, work–life balance and recovery from work, and more specifically how those are constructed in remote and hybrid working models.

Aneesa F. Qadri is a Doctorate Student in Sociology at the University of Oxford. Her research analyses the role of intersecting structural and institutional changes in extending gender equality in domestic and non-domestic spheres across the life course. She predominantly works with household panel survey data. Apart from her doctoral research, previously she has also aided a project exploring gender inequality in time use within her department. Prior to studying at Oxford, she earned a Bachelor of Science in Politics and International Relations and a Master of Science in Policy Analytics at The University of Exeter.

Mareike Reimann, PhD, is a Postdoctoral Researcher at the Faculty of Sociology at Bielefeld University, Germany. She is currently responsible for the project "Changed working conditions and quality of life in digitalized work environments" in cooperation with the Federal Institute for Occupational Safety and Health" and the project "How can working from home succeed? Fair solutions in the view of employees and employers" funded by the Federal Ministry of Labour and Social Affairs. Her main research interests cover the topics health, well-being and work–life interface of employed persons. She also focusses on the design and perception of employment relationships and involved demands and gratifications depending on heterogeneous employee and employer expectations, as well as changed working conditions in the course of the digitalization of work.

Timothy Rinke is a Research Assistant at the Institute Work and Qualification at the University of Duisburg-Essen. His research interests lie in the field of sociology of work with a special focus on working time and organization as well as the associations between organizational structures and social inequalities. The research projects in which he is involved as well as his empirical doctoral thesis are located in this area.

Antje Schwarz is a Graduate Student of Sociology and a Student Research Assistant in the project "Flexibility in digitalized working worlds: Use and implications of telework and digital work communication" funded by the German Research Foundation at Bielefeld University. Her research interests focus on flexibilization and digitalization of work, reconciliation in different organizational cultures and research on welfare state regimes.

Heidi E. Stolz, PhD, is a Professor of Child and Family Studies at the University of Tennessee, where she also serves as a Faculty Fellow for the Engaged Online Course Initiative. Her research and teaching interests center on family wellness, family interaction, and family financial literacy, and she is excited to offer a variety of fully online asynchronous courses on these topics. She is a member of the National Council on Family Relations. She enjoys taking students on study abroad to Scandinavia, both virtually and in real life.

Brenda Vermeeren, PhD, is an Associate Professor at the Department of Public Administration and Sociology, Erasmus University Rotterdam, the Netherlands. She is also a Senior Advisor at ICTU-InternetSpiegel (a program of the Dutch Ministry of the Interior and Kingdom Relations).

FOREWORD

With the availability of information and communication technologies (ICTs) and the extension of digital infrastructures, employees increasingly have more control over when and where they work. Moreover, due to the global COVID-19 pandemic, which for many meant a shift to working from home to reduce the spread of the virus, more workers and employers than ever before experienced such flexibility. *Flexiplace* arrangements (also referred to as teleworking, working from home, or remote working) and *flexitime* (flexible starting/finishing times and the option to interrupt work as needed to attend to other responsibilities) offer employees more leeway in work location as well as in scheduling tasks during the traditional work week. These two forms of flexible work are the main focus this volume.

The consequences of work flexibility on an employee's family life are currently being debated: Does such flexibility help to better align the competing demands of work and family,[1] or does it harm family well-being by allowing work to invade the employee's personal sphere? According to *resource perspectives*, work flexibility allows employees to respond to predictable and unpredictable family needs. In turn, relationship quality in families and women's careers might be sustained despite work and family obligations, and men might experience additional opportunities to become more involved in care and household tasks. In contrast, *demand perspectives* suggest that flexible working increases the likelihood that work will invade the employee's family sphere. The timing and location of work may not be clearly set or separated, thus blurring work–life boundaries, and/or employers might use flexible work in their own interests to realize high work demands.

Regarding the implications of flexitime and flexiplace for employees' families, the research findings have been inconsistent, suggesting that there is no uniform relationship. This volume aims to contribute a more nuanced understanding of the interrelation of flexible work and the family. The contents are divided into three sections. The first section, "Flexible Work and the Family During the COVID-19 Pandemic," provides insights into the relationship between work and family while working from home during the pandemic. The authors not only suggest that the implications of flexible working are context-dependent but also point to the various facilitators and barriers present in the work and family spheres. The second section, "Gender, Parenthood, and Status-Specific Patterns of Flexible Work and the Family," acknowledges and emphasizes group differences when it comes to the ways in which flexible work is experienced. Moreover, it provides some evidence that these patterns have been sustained during the pandemic. In the third section, "Linked-Lives Perspective on Flexible Work and the Family," the contributing authors go beyond the individual experiences of work–family conflict or balance and discuss the implications of work flexibility for patners' well-being and parenting behavior.

Throughout this volume, the research on the interrelationships of flexible work and the family represents contexts from different countries, including Finland, Germany, the Netherlands, the United Kingdom, and the United States, thus revealing a broad spectrum of similarities and differences.

Section 1: Flexible Work and the Family During the COVID-19 Pandemic

The first three chapters provide insights into the work–family balance and work–family conflicts experienced by employees who were working from home during the COVID-19 pandemic. They offer lessons learned about potential facilitators and barriers with regard to flexible working arrangements that could help employees to better align their work and family demands. In "When Home Becomes the Workplace: Work–Life Balance Experiences During the COVID-19 Pandemic", Samantha Metselaar, Laura den Dulk, and Brenda Vermeeren applied a mixed-methods design to study how Dutch government employees perceived their work–life balance during the pandemic as compared with the pre-pandemic situation, as well as how to explain differences in what these employees were experiencing. The results indicate that the combined demands and resources at work, at home, and at the personal level shaped whether working from home facilitated work–life balance. In particular, respondents' control over their boundary management and strategies helped them distinguish between different roles across their life domains and were important in their achieving a satisfactory work–life balance. Family demands, such as care responsibilities and homeschooling, were found to hinder an individual's ability to achieve such balance but only in the absence of coping resources, such as sharing a task with a partner. Working parents reported experiences of family enrichment, since working entirely from home gave them more time to spend with their partners and children.

In "Working from Home During the COVID-19 Pandemic: Lessons Learned About the Relationship Between Flexible Work and Work–Family Conflict", Mareike Reimann used a sample of employees who worked from home taken from German linked employer–employee data, collected in spring 2021, and shows that pronounced caring obligations were associated with more work–family conflicts. However, temporal flexibility, job autonomy, and the existence of fixed rules and a supportive supervisor were identified as workplace facilitators that contributed to fewer work–family conflicts among the employees working from home irrespectively of family obligations. Autonomy was even more beneficial for individuals who cared for other relatives, since it was associated with fewer work–family conflicts.

In "Working Remotely During the COVID 19-Pandemic: Work and Non-Work Antecedents of Work–Life Balance Development," Liisa Mäkelä, Heini Pensar, Samu Kemppinen, and Hilpi Kangas used longitudinal data from a multinational company in Finland that were collected in May/June 2020 and December 2020.

In studying remote workers' work–life balance, these authors showed that time saved by not having to commute facilitated a better work–life balance. Investigating how work–life balance has changed over time during the pandemic, they noted a general reduction in work–life balance, which could be explained by an increase in the employees' quantitative workload. Beyond the initial differences in the experiences of work–life balance – that is, less work–life balance among mothers at the beginning of the pandemic, the decreases reported during the pandemic did not differ by gender or number of children in the household.

Section 2: Gender, Parenthood, and Status-Specific Patterns of Flexible Work and the Family

Whereas previous research has identified gender, parenthood, and status-specific patterns in the use of work from home, two of the chapters investigate these patterns to determine variation in the implications of flexible work for work-to-family conflicts and improvements in the temporal alignment of work and private life. In "Does Telework Mediate the Impact of Occupational Status on Work-to-Family Conflicts? An Investigation of Conditional Effects of Gender and the COVID-19 Pandemic", Antje Schwarz, Ayhan Adams, and Katrin Golsch used data from two waves (2017–2020) of the German Family Panel. The results showed that work-to-family conflicts among parents did not change during the pandemic but that work-to-family conflicts were in general higher among parents who telework and who have a higher status. In general, the conflict-enhancing implications of telework seemed to be more pronounced for mothers than for fathers. Stronger conflicts among higher-status employees were also found to be mediated by telework, especially for mothers before and during the pandemic.

In "Does Working from Home Improve the Temporal Alignment of Work and Private Life? Differences Between Telework and Informal Overtime at Home by Gender and Family Responsibilities", Alexandra Mergener, Ines Entgelmeier, and Timothy Rinke found that formally recognized telework is more likely to be a resource that contributes to a temporal alignment of work and private life when compared with informal overtime at home. They also identified the gender- and parenthood-specific implications of telework. Based on their results using data from the German BIBB/BAuA Employment Survey 2018, these researchers concluded that mothers did not benefit from telework during regular working hours in particular; however, when they worked informal overtime at home, their temporal alignment of work and private life was found to be worse than that for the other groups studied.

Section 3: Linked-Lives Perspective on Flexible Work and the Family

The two final chapters contribute a linked-live perspective on the implications of flexible work for the family. Whereas previous research focused mainly on the importance of flexible working in terms of the individual employee's experiences of work–family conflict or balance, these researchers investigated the meaning of flexible working for other family members. In "Individual and Cross-partner Transitions to Flexitime and Teleworking and Cognitive Subjective Well-Being,"

Aneesa F. Qadri used British Understanding Society data from 2009 to 2019 to investigate transitions to flexitime and teleworking by employees and how it affected their subjective well-being and that of their partners. Fathers' transitions to teleworking were found to increase their likelihood of reporting higher levels of satisfaction with their amount of leisure time, and flexitime fostered their female partners' satisfaction with leisure time. Mothers' transitions to flexitime and flexiplace positively impacted their own satisfaction with leisure time but not that of their partners.

In "Workplace Flexibility, Work–Family Guilt, and Working Mothers' Parenting Behavior" Melissa Rector LaGraff and Heidi E. Stolz looked at a sample of US working mothers to show that flexible working was positively associated with positive parenting, positive reinforcement, and warmth behaviors. Work–family guilt did not mediate these relationships but was negatively associated with workplace flexibility. The authors concluded that policies that promote flexible work arrangements could also promote positive family outcomes as well as reduce feelings of guilt related to employees' work and family life.

ACKNOWLEDGMENTS

We want to thank Blair Sampson editor of CPFR, as well as CPFR-support team, helping us to bring together this volume on flexible work and the family. We also want to thank all scholars who agreed to and took the time to review submitted manuscripts, and providing valuable feedback to the authors. This volume of CPFR developed as part of the project "Flexibility in Digitalized Working Worlds: Use and Implications of Telecommuting and Digital Work Communication Across European Countries" which is part of the interdisciplinary DFG priority programme "Digitalisation of Working Worlds" (SPP 2267).

NOTE

1. In this context, the term "family" refers to individuals who live together in the same household with their own or adoptive children, partners, or relatives.

SECTION 1

FLEXIBLE WORK AND THE FAMILY DURING THE COVID-19 PANDEMIC

CHAPTER 1

WHEN HOME BECOMES THE WORKPLACE: WORK–LIFE BALANCE EXPERIENCES DURING THE COVID-19 PANDEMIC

Samantha Metselaar, Laura den Dulk and Brenda Vermeeren

ABSTRACT

The COVID-19 pandemic has highlighted the relevance of the intersections between work and personal life. Measures introduced to slow the spread of COVID-19 have included an increase of working from home and the temporary closure of schools and child-care facilities, leading to a lighter workload for some and a heavier workload for others. These consequences are likely to affect employees' work–life balance (WLB), although the impact may differ across groups of employees depending on the nature of their work, family and personal demands and resources. This mixed-method study examined how Dutch government employees perceive their WLB during the pandemic and how differences in what employees are experiencing can be explained. In May/June 2020, an online survey (N = 827) and an interview study (N = 17) were conducted at a government organization whose employees were obliged to work from home partly or exclusively. Results indicate that demands changed when working entirely from home and resources became more important to maintain WLB satisfaction. Being able to manage boundaries across life domains and find a new routine also appeared to be crucial for WLB satisfaction.

Flexible Work and the Family
Contemporary Perspectives in Family Research, Volume 21, 3–30

Published under exclusive licence by Emerald Publishing Limited
ISSN: 1530-3535/doi:10.1108/S1530-353520230000021001

Keywords: Work–life balance; working from home; JD-R; boundary management; COVID-19; public sector

INTRODUCTION

The COVID-19 pandemic has rapidly changed the way people work. Efforts to slow the spread of the virus included national lockdowns that required any employee who could reasonably do so to work from home. Schools and child-care facilities also closed temporarily, and measures were introduced to foster social distancing. As a result, families across the globe saw their homes become their place of work, their children's schoolroom, and their social sanctuary (Anderson & Kelliher, 2020; Hjálmsdóttir & Bjarnadóttir, 2021). Working parents had to juggle care responsibilities and homeschooling with their jobs, posing additional challenges to their WLB (TNO, 2021).

Even before the COVID-19 pandemic, a growing number of employees had the option of working from home (Allen et al., 2015). In the Netherlands, for example, more than a third of the labor force worked from home. In most cases, however, this was incidental, on average one day a week (CBS, 2021). For several decades, working from home has been viewed as a means to achieve a better WLB or to reduce work–family conflict (Anderson & Kelliher, 2020; Hill et al., 2008), even though findings have been inconclusive so far (Allen et al., 2015; Kelliher & De Menezes, 2019). On the one hand, working from home reduces commuting time and may give employees more control over their work schedules, allowing them to better align responsibilities from different life domains and increase their WLB satisfaction (Gajendran & Harrison, 2007). On the other hand, working from home leads to blurred boundaries, making it more likely that work will creep into the personal domain or vice versa. This can lead to a situation in which *"there is too much overlap between jobs and personal lives"* (Kossek, 2016, p. 259). Boundary blurring may also increase work pressure (Demerouti et al., 2014) or work intensification (Kelliher & Anderson, 2010), as it may be harder for people to disconnect from work. During the COVID-19 pandemic, employees who were forced to work entirely from home struggled with boundary blurring to a greater extent, whether they were working parents or employees without child-care responsibilities. Their predicament makes clear that more research is needed to shed light on the conditions under which working from home increases or diminishes WLB satisfaction (Allen et al., 2015; Kelliher & De Menezes, 2019).

In this explorative chapter, we examine how government employees working entirely from home during the COVID-19 pandemic experienced their WLB. By exploring a unique set of circumstances caused by the COVID-19 pandemic, and based on both survey and interview data, we aim to improve our knowledge of the relationship between working from home and WLB satisfaction. The data for this chapter were collected shortly after the beginning of the first lockdown in the Netherlands, allowing respondents to reflect on their pre-COVID-19 situation and compare their WLB experiences before and while working entirely from home. These comparisons help us to better understand how the context of working entirely from home shapes WLB experiences and why employees have differing experiences.

The consequences of working entirely from home for WLB satisfaction may depend on exposure to demands and access to resources across life domains (Glavin & Schieman, 2012). When working from home is involuntary and schools and child-care facilities close at the same time, the demands may increase and working parents with children in particular may find it difficult to maintain a satisfactory WLB. Employees who have sufficient resources may be better able to adjust to working entirely from home and maintain a satisfactory balance between their work and their personal/family life. Boundary management may allow employees to mitigate the negative consequences of boundary blurring (Kossek & Lautsch, 2012), especially for those who were unused to working from home before the pandemic. However, when employees lack resources, working from home can negatively affect their WLB. Using Bakker and Demerouti (2007) job demands-resources (JD-R) model and boundary theory (Allen et al., 2014), we explore whether differences in WLB experiences are contingent on exposure to demands and access to resources in the work, family and personal domain. We thereby address the following research question: how do employees working at a government organization in the Netherlands experience their WLB satisfaction during working from home entirely, as opposed to the pre-COVID-19 situation, and how can we explain the diversity in experiences?

The contribution of this chapter is fourfold. First, research findings on the relation between working from home and WLB are inconclusive so far and little is known about the conditions that shape WLB experiences when working from home. Theoretically, we aim to increase our knowledge on how to explain differences in WLB experiences by looking at different conditions across life domains, not only in relation to the work context but also the home situation, family demands and resources, personal resources, and boundary management. Second, the transition to working entirely from home during the COVID-19 pandemic offers us a unique and extreme set of circumstances for examining WLB experiences. While private organizations may deviate from policy by allowing their employees to come to the office, working from home was strictly enforced in government organizations. As a result, employees working in various types of jobs and with different home lives were forced to work from home (Fukumura et al., 2021), including those who had not been allowed to work from home before or who did not wish to work from home because their home situation was unsuitable, or they preferred to work at the office. Most research on the impact of teleworking and working from home is based on high-educated knowledge workers who choose to work from home (Beauregard et al., 2019). The diverse group of employees in this study allows us to examine such factors as the nature of the job and the home situation, potentially increasing our knowledge of the conditions that explain differences in their WLB experiences. Third, scholars have so far argued that after a certain threshold, working from home or teleworking is no longer beneficial (Beauregard et al., 2019; Gajendran & Harrison, 2007). In particular, when working extensively from home is combined with heavy care responsibilities in the family domain, employees are more likely to experience work–life conflict (Golden & Veiga, 2005). The unique data collection of this chapter makes it possible to explore the consequences of working extensively from home. Fourth, as far as we are aware, there have been few mixed-method studies in this field. Nonetheless, a mixed-method approach can better capture WLB experiences of employees who work entirely from home. It allows us to identify the mechanisms behind the quantitative findings by using qualitative data derived from the same sample of employees.

In the next section, we present a theoretical framework for the relationship between working entirely from home and WLB satisfaction. We then explain our approach to data collection and the methods that we used. Next, we present our quantitative findings and follow this with a qualitative analysis to identify the mechanisms behind these findings. We end our chapter with a discussion and our conclusions, as well as a review of our chapter's limitations and practical implications.

THEORETICAL FRAMEWORK

WLB Satisfaction

A term widely used in both the academic literature and real-world practice, WLB has attracted growing interest over the years as people have increasingly attempted to combine their work and personal lives. Overall, when employees are able to achieve a satisfactory WLB, they are more likely to experience positive work-related outcomes (e.g., performance, job satisfaction and lower turnover intentions) as well as family-related outcomes (e.g., family performance and family satisfaction). Evidence suggests that WLB satisfaction can have a direct effect on these outcomes, but balance satisfaction can also facilitate the accumulation of additional resources such as self-belief and affective commitment (Kim, 2014). These additional resources may then result in enhanced performance and higher levels of employee well-being. Having a satisfactory WLB is therefore an important spill in fostering beneficial outcomes for both employees and organizations (Brough et al., 2020).

However, there has been some debate about the concept WLB and different views have emerged. Some definitions of WLB start by acknowledging that individuals fulfil multiple roles across different life domains (Kalliath & Brough, 2008): employee, mother, father, caregiver, friend and so on. The individuals concerned, or others, imbue these roles with different expectations and responsibilities (Fuegen et al., 2004; Graham et al., 2004; Jang & Zippay, 2011). Several scholars have defined WLB as the absence of conflict between these different life roles (e.g., Clark, 2000; Duxbury & Higgins, 2001; Frone, 2003). Conflict occurs when time and energy spent in one domain make it difficult to meet expectations and demands in other domains (Chen et al., 2009), meaning that different life roles are incompatible to some degree (Byron, 2005; Reynolds, 2005). Role conflict can therefore be regarded as a negative spillover. Scholars also argue that different life domains can facilitate one another. These processes are often referred to as work–life enrichment (i.e., positive spillover). Resources gained in one domain can facilitate role fulfilment in other domains (Carlson et al., 2006).

Other early conceptualizations of WLB mention an equal distribution of resources (e.g., time and energy) across work, family and other life roles (see for example Greenhaus et al., 2003; Kirchmeyer, 2000). The equality approach has, however, received criticism as it fails to account for individual preferences regarding the importance of different life domains (Brough et al., 2020).

More recently, scholars have argued that WLB is a global construct that concerns an overall perception of the work–life interface. These approaches differ from spill over approaches (such as conflict and enrichment) in that they do not refer to cross-domain processes or specific directions (Wayne et al., 2017). From a global perspective, WLB can be understood as an individual's ability to fulfil roles and meet commitments in different domains (Hill et al., 2001). Balance satisfaction refers to contentment with the combination of roles in different domains, rather than how these domains conflict or facilitate one another (Grawitch et al., 2013). In this chapter, we are interested in WLB satisfaction as it offers a more integrative approach of the work–life interface (Brough et al., 2020; Wayne et al., 2017), including individual preferences and priorities. Hence, using Valcour's conceptualization, WLB satisfaction is defined as *"an overall level of contentment resulting from an assessment of one's degree of success at meeting work and family role demands"* (2007, p. 1512). Valcour's (2007) definition implies that there is no optimal division between work and personal life that suits all employees, as an overall level of contentment proceeds from an individual's subjective evaluation (Annink, 2017). This evaluation is based on their expectations, experiences, or wishes and can be shaped by the social context (Wayne et al., 2017). In this chapter, we explore conditions, i.e., demands and resources, that either contribute to or hinder the ability to acquire a satisfactory balance between work and personal life.

Working from Home and WLB Satisfaction

Many authors have focused on the relationship between working from home and WLB satisfaction. Some have argued that working from home can be beneficial for WLB satisfaction because employees swap commuting time for more time spent on their personal lives (Tremblay & Thomsin, 2012). Moreover, working from home allows them to better align work and personal life, as it is likely to enhance temporal flexibility (Palumbo, 2020).

When home becomes the workplace, however, the beneficial effect on WLB satisfaction may be diminished. Scholars argue, for example, that working from home may foster work intensification, not only by increasing the number of work hours but also because of boundary blurring (Kelliher & Anderson, 2010), making it more difficult to disconnect from work. Working from home may also induce an involuntary overlap between activities in different life domains, such as work tasks and child-care responsibilities, potentially threatening the employee's ability to successfully balance work and personal life (Palumbo, 2020).

Working from home can therefore give rise to both positive and negative processes. Some researchers have found a positive relationship between working from home and WLB satisfaction, while others have found a negative relationship between the two constructs (Kelliher & De Menezes, 2019). The literature to date has therefore been inconclusive. More research is needed to examine why working from home unfolds positively for some and negatively for others. To increase our knowledge of this issue, it is important to explore the conditions that may play a role (Allen et al., 2015; Kelliher & De Menezes, 2019).

The Job-Demands Resources Model

The JD-R model (Bakker & Demerouti, 2007) can help us to identify conditions that may be important in the relationship between working from home and changes in WLB satisfaction. According to the JD-R model, conditions can be divided into demands and resources. We look first at *demands*: *"Demands refer to those physical, psychosocial, or organizational aspects that require sustained physical and/or mental effort and are, therefore, associated with certain physiological and/or psychological costs"* (Bakker & Geurts, 2004, p. 348). Examples of job demands are work pressure and task interdependency. Due to the COVID-19 pandemic, many employees saw an increase in their work demands (Craig & Churchill, 2021). They may have been assigned additional tasks or have had to adopt other, more time-consuming ways of doing their job to ensure the continuity of task accomplishment while working from home, possibly resulting in changes in WLB satisfaction. The latter may also apply to employees with a higher task interdependency. Task interdependency requires a higher degree of information exchange and interaction between employees. When working entirely from home, however, employees are physically far away from one another, possibly hampering the accomplishment of tasks that require multiple employees to work together simultaneously. Task interdependency can therefore become a more pronounced demand, whereas working entirely from home may be less problematic for less interdependent tasks (Beauregard et al., 2019). Task interdependency may therefore also affect WLB satisfaction during working from home entirely as opposed to the pre-COVID-19 situation.

Although the JD-R model focuses on the work domain (Xanthopoulou et al., 2007), demands and resources in the family domain can also play an important role with respect to WLB satisfaction. The temporary closure of schools and child-care facilities to slow the spread of COVID-19 may, for example, have increased child-care responsibilities for working parents, resulting in higher demands in the family domain (Del Boca et al., 2020). The increasing demands in the family domain may hinder the ability to successfully combine work and personal life, causing a shift in WLB satisfaction.

However, demands in both the work and family domain are not necessarily negative, but they can have a diminishing effect on outcomes when employees do not have sufficient *resources* to deal with them (Bakker & Demerouti, 2007): *"Resources refer to those physical, psychological, or organizational aspects that may be functional in meeting task requirements (i.e., demands)"* (Bakker & Geurts,

2004, p. 348). Again, we can distinguish between resources in the work domain and resources in the family domain. Examples of important resources in the work domain are autonomy (Bakker & Demerouti, 2007; Valcour, 2007) and supervisory support (Abendroth & Den Dulk, 2011). Previous research indicates that spousal support can be an important resource at home (Abendroth & Den Dulk, 2011). In addition, family flexibility can be marked as a resource in the family domain. This refers to the ability to adapt to necessary or desired domain activities (Matthews & Barnes-Farrell, 2010), which may help in maintaining a good balance between work and personal life. In addition, the presence of resources may mitigate the potential negative effects of demands across different life domains (Bakker & Demerouti, 2007).

We can also identify personal resources in the JD-R model (Xanthopoulou et al., 2007). Working extensively from home may, for example, require a high degree of self-regulation, defined as *"a process of managing the self"* (Baumeister & Vonasch, 2015, p. 4). This process can facilitate a person's ability to avoid distractions and to focus on the tasks at hand (Allen et al., 2015). This, in turn, may allow that person to successfully meet demands in both the work and the personal domain. Lower levels of self-regulation, on the other hand, may result in cognitive overload (Iyengar & Lepper, 2000), which can make it more difficult to accomplish tasks in one domain without being distracted by impulses in another (Allen et al., 2013). Employees with lower levels of self-regulation may struggle with working from home effectively (Raghuram et al., 2003) threatening WLB satisfaction.

Boundary Management

The increased intertwining of work and personal/family life may also highlight the importance of boundary management. Boundary management can be defined as the strategies employees use to define the boundaries between work and personal life that demarcate one from the other (Kossek & Lautsch, 2012). We can distinguish between physical boundaries (for example a separate place to work), temporal boundaries (such as set work hours) and psychological boundaries (using thoughts, emotions, or behaviors to disconnect from work or personal life mentally). Individuals deal with these boundaries on a continuum ranging from segmentation to integration (Nippert-Eng, 1996). Some individuals prefer to segment different life domains, for example by closing the door of their home office, turning off their cellphone after work, or only attending to personal matters during breaks or leisure time. Others prefer to integrate these domains, for example by taking on work-related tasks during leisure time and vice versa (Kreiner et al., 2009). Integrated boundaries are often associated with more interruptions, especially when there is a close connection between different domains. Segmented boundaries ward off interruptions, with time and attention being devoted to a single domain or role to protect the flow of that domain or role and to avoid fragmentation (Ashforth et al., 2000).

Boundary management can help in managing demands arising in different life domains either by integrating or by segmenting the roles associated with those demands. So far, most research indicates that employees experience a better WLB when they segment work and personal life (Allen et al., 2014). However, it is also argued that boundary management preferences play a role in effectively shaping the boundaries between work and personal life (Kossek & Lautsch, 2012; Kreiner, 2006). When employees work entirely from home, however, it may be more challenging to shape boundaries as they would prefer, especially for those who favor segmentation over integration (Allen et al., 2021). Employees who do succeed in managing boundaries may be better able to achieve a satisfying WLB.

Summarizing, working entirely from home during a lockdown is likely to result in higher exposure to demands at work and at home for many employees. Resources in different life domains, personal resources, and boundary management strategies, then play a more important role in helping them to deal with these demands. Hence, changes in WLB satisfaction due to working from home entirely may be contingent on the presence of demands and resources.

METHOD

Empirical Setting

This chapter examines WLB experiences among employees working in a Dutch government organization. The organization has many employees across the country who are very diverse in terms of educational background and job grade (e.g., project managers, innovation managers, purchase employees and administrative workers). Pre-COVID, some employees worked at a designated office while others traveled around the country for their work. They were familiar with the concept of time-spatial flexibility. Although working from home was not new for most of them, the COVID-19 pandemic meant that they spent many more hours doing so. It is worth mentioning again here that employees had no choice in this matter: working from home became mandatory for everyone, even those whose jobs did not typically allow them to do so, those whose household situation was unsuitable for working from home, and those who simply preferred to work at the office.

Data for this chapter was collected in May/June 2020. During this period, the Netherlands was in lockdown for about two months. In addition to working from home, schools and child-care facilities were closed, except for children whose parents worked in essential occupations. Public gatherings and social events were prohibited, effectively closing bars, restaurants, gyms and other venues and facilities De Voogd (2020).

Procedure and Respondents

Our research consisted of an online cross-sectional survey and an interview study. Our aim in the survey was to identify differences between groups with respect to their WLB satisfaction. The goal of the interview study was to illuminate the mechanisms that lay behind these differences.

Firstly, the survey, consisted largely of Likert-type and categorical questions meant to elicit information about WLB satisfaction and demands and resources at work (work pressure, task interdependency, autonomy and supervisory support for WLB), at home (family flexibility and child-care responsibilities) and at a personal level (self-regulation and boundary management strategies). We also included background information (gender, age and level of education). The survey was sent to all 2024 employees working across different departments of the government organization with a view to capturing workforce diversity. A total of 1,086 employees responded by answering at least one survey question. After we removed respondents who did not provide information on all our key variables, the sample consisted of 827 respondents (response rate = 41%).

Secondly, we conducted interviews with 17 employees drawn from the same sample. To continue capturing workforce diversity in the interview study, we selected the interviewees from nine separate teams in different departments. Respondents varied among others in gender, job title and child-care responsibilities (see Table 1.1). We began the interviews by asking respondents to describe the nature of their job. We then asked them about their experiences with working from home, followed by more specific questions about WLB experiences. Most respondents automatically compared their pre- and post-pandemic WLB. If not, we asked them whether their WLB experiences had changed since the start of the lockdown. We then asked follow-up questions for a broader understanding of demands and resources that may play a role in WLB experiences.

All interviews lasted approximately 60 minutes and were recorded and transcribed. We then cycled through multiple readings and different levels of coding for each transcript. These activities were informed by our focus on WLB experiences and characteristics that we could mark as possible demands or resources.

Table 1.1. Overview of Respondents in the Interview Study.

	Gender	Job Title	Childcare Responsibilities
Respondent 1	Male	Coordinator	Yes
Respondent 2	Female	Administrative employee	No
Respondent 3	Male	Communication advisor	No
Respondent 4	Male	Communication advisor	Yes
Respondent 5	Male	Project-assistant	Yes
Respondent 6	Male	Project manager	Yes
Respondent 7	Male	Portfolio manager	No
Respondent 8	Male	Portfolio manager	No
Respondent 9	Female	Purchasing employee	Yes
Respondent 10	Male	Consultant	Yes
Respondent 11	Male	Maintenance and control	No
Respondent 12	Female	Project-assistant	No
Respondent 13	Male	Project manager	No
Respondent 14	Female	Coordinator	Yes
Respondent 15	Female	Administrative employee	No
Respondent 16	Male	Quality manager	Yes
Respondent 17	Female	Innovation manager	No

Survey Measures

We measured *changes in work–life balance satisfaction* by asking respondents to compare their situation during COVID-19 – with their pre-COVID situation, querying whether they were less, more or equally satisfied with their WLB since COVID-19 on a scale ranging from 1 (a lot less satisfied) to 5 (a lot more satisfied). To facilitate analysis, we recoded this variable into three categories representing the three groups: less satisfied with WLB than before (= reference category), equally satisfied with WLB, and more satisfied with WLB. We then measured several demands and resources, thereby exploring possible indicators that may explain the differences in WLB satisfaction.

Demands and Resources

Work

Work pressure was measured using five items based on Karasek and Theorell (1990), for instance "does your job require that you work very hard?" ($\alpha = 0.75$).

Task interdependency was measured using three items taken from the Dutch translation of the work design questionnaire (WDQ) (Gorgievski et al., 2016; Morgeson & Humphrey, 2006). An example item is "my job cannot be done unless others do their work" ($\alpha = 0.75$).

Autonomy was measured using three items that were also derived from the WDQ (Gorgievski et al., 2016; Morgeson & Humphrey, 2006), for instance "my job allows me to make a lot of decisions on my own." In addition, we added an item about the ability to determine one's own work hours: "my job allows me to decide at what times I work" ($\alpha = 0.81$).

Supervisory support for WLB was measured by using the short form of the FSSB scale developed by Hammer et al. (2013). An example item is "my supervisor makes me feel comfortable talking to him/her about my conflicts between work and non-work" ($\alpha = 0.88$).

Home

Family flexibility ability (FFA) was measured using three items from the FFA scale developed by Matthews and Barnes-Farrell (2010), for instance "if the need arose, I could work late without affecting my family and personal responsibilities" ($\alpha = 0.82$).

We also asked whether respondents had *child-care responsibilities* for children living at home. When respondents indicated this was indeed the case, we asked for the age of their child or children. We then converted this into a new variable: children younger than 12 (yes/no).

Personal

The degree of *self-regulation* was measured using seven items derived from the scale developed by Tangney et al. (2004), for instance "I am able to work effectively toward long-term goals" ($\alpha = 0.70$).

We also measured several *boundary management* behaviors, more specifically the following: "I work in a separate place at home (for example a home office or a study)," "when I am working, I make it clear to my family/friends/roommates that I do not want to be disturbed," "I do not engage in domestic labor or other personal related tasks until the working day is over," "in the evenings or on weekends, I rarely check my work e-mail," and "I interrupt my working day for a walk or exercise."

With respect to our control variables, gender was added as a covariate. Because women still carry most of the responsibility for domestic work, it is more difficult for them to achieve a satisfactory WLB (Rothbard & Dumas, 2006; Valcour, 2007). Another covariate was age, since life satisfaction generally increases as one gets older (Argyle, 2001). We divided age into four categories (1 = 15–23 years, 2 = 26–40 years, 3 = 41–55 years and 4 = older than 55 years). Subsequently, a dummy variable was created (0 = 40 or younger, 1 = older than 40). The third covariate was level of education. Employees with a higher level of education often have more experience with working from home and are employed in jobs that are more sensitive to work–life interference (Milliken & Dunn-Jensen, 2005). Level of education was subdivided into seven classes (1 = primary education, 2 = lower general secondary education, 3 = higher general secondary education, preparatory scientific education 4 = lower vocational education, 5 = higher vocational education, 6 = scientific education and 7 = doctorate/PhD. A dummy variable was created by dividing these categories in lower educated (1 to 4) and higher educated (5 to 7) employees. We also controlled for experience with working from home before COVID-19. We asked how many hours respondents worked from home before they were obliged to work from home and divided this amount by the total number of work hours during the week to get a more meaningful measure. Finally, we added a covariate measuring the feasibility of carrying out work duties from home (1 = all work duties can be carried out from home and 5 = none of the work duties can be carried out from home). This variable was then reverse coded.

RESULTS

Analysis

The purpose of this chapter was to explore differences in WLB experiences. We therefore first report on descriptive statistics, distinguishing between the three groups (i.e., less satisfied with WLB, equally satisfied with WLB and more satisfied with WLB). Next, we describe the outcomes of multinomial logistic regression (MLR), used to examine possible demands and resources that may explain the variation in WLB experiences. By using maximum likelihood estimation, MLR allows us to evaluate the relative probability of being less satisfied, equally satisfied or more satisfied with WLB (Starkweather & Moske, 2011), based on the independent variables (i.e., the presence of demands and resources).

Descriptive Statistics

Descriptive statistics show that about 27% of the respondents are less satisfied with their WLB than before they worked entirely from home, 27% are equally satisfied and about 46% are more satisfied (see Table 1.2). With respect to the differences

Table 1.2. Descriptive Statistics Per Group.

	Less Satisfied (27%)		As Satisfied (27%)		More Satisfied (46%)	
	Mean	SD	Mean	SD	Mean	SD
Work pressure (1–4)	2.39	0.52	2.17	0.44	2.21	0.49
Task interdependency (1–5)	3.71	0.71	3.56	0.74	3.55	0.74
Autonomy (1–5)	3.83	0.75	4.01	0.63	3.93	0.78
Supervisory support for WLB (1–5)	3.39	0.67	3.38	0.72	3.39	0.76
FFA (1–5)	3.42	1.02	3.86	0.83	3.88	0.83
Children under twelve (0–1)	0.43	0.50	0.26	0.44	0.25	0.43
Self-regulation (1–5)	3.47	0.61	3.75	0.56	3.76	0.55
Separate workplace (1–5)	3.15	1.61	3.71	1.44	3.43	1.65
Making clear not to disturb (1–5)	3.56	0.95	3.61	0.98	3.74	0.92
Not engaging in domestic labor (1–5)	2.62	1.09	2.88	0.99	2.76	1.05
Not checking e-mail (1–5)	3.07	1.36	3.17	1.19	3.20	1.30
Interrupting work for a walk/exercise (1–5)	2.85	1.23	2.99	1.13	3.09	1.21
Male (0–1)	0.65	0.48	0.76	0.43	0.62	0.49
Age (0–1)	0.69	0.46	0.82	0.39	0.81	0.40
Level of education (0–1)	0.77	0.42	0.70	0.46	0.74	0.44
Working from home before COVID-19 (% of actual work hours)	20.00	13.81	24.83	19.44	24.27	16.32
Feasibility to carry out work duties from home (1–5)	4.17	0.67	4.19	0.64	4.39	0.59

between the three groups, descriptive statistics indicate that respondents who are equally or more satisfied with their WLB in general score lower on demands and higher on resources than respondents who are less satisfied. Remarkably, we do not see any differences between the three groups when it comes to the amount of supervisory support respondents receive. Descriptive statistics also revealed similarities between the equally-satisfied and more-satisfied groups. We assessed these differences in greater detail using MLR.

MLR Analysis

Before interpreting the MLR results, we assessed the overall fit of the model. The overall fit yielded 54% correct classifications, which can be marked as a reasonable result (see Table 1.3). The criterium for classification accuracy was also satisfied, with the overall case classification being more than 25% higher than the proportion by chance rate (PCC).[1] The classification statistics show which group memberships

Table 1.3. Classification Statistics.

	Predicted			
Observed	Less Satisfied	As Satisfied	More Satisfied	Percent Correct
Less satisfied	106	15	106	46,7%
As satisfied	32	51	141	22,8%
More satisfied	49	40	287	76,3%
Overall percentage	22,6%	12,8%	64,6%	53,7%

were predicted by our model. In this case, the model correctly predicted approximately 47% of the respondents who were less satisfied with their WLB than before (i.e., 106 of the 227 respondents who were less satisfied with their WLB). The model was especially suitable for predicting which respondents would be more satisfied with their WLB than before, with an accuracy of 76%. The classification scores indicated, however, that it was harder to predict which respondents were equally satisfied with their WLB. Of the 224 respondents in the equally-satisfied group, the model predicted that 141 would be *more* satisfied, resulting in an accuracy of only 23%. This may also indicate the difficulty of distinguishing between those who are equally satisfied and those who are more satisfied.

The results of the MLR indicate that there are several significant differences between our covariates if we compare respondents who are less satisfied (= reference group) with respondents who are equally satisfied or more satisfied with their WLB than before they began working entirely from home. With respect to work demands and resources, Table 1.4 shows that work pressure matters for changes in WLB satisfaction. Respondents with less work pressure are more likely to be in the group that is equally or more satisfied with their WLB. In other words, for

Table 1.4. Multinomial Logistic Regression Model: Changes in Work–Life Balance Satisfaction (Reference Category = Less Satisfied with Work–Life Balance).

	Work–Life Balance Satisfaction					
	As Satisfied			More Satisfied		
	B	S.E.	OR	B	S.E.	OR
Intercept	−2,895	1.418		−4.379	1.268	
Work pressure	−0.949**	0.234	0.387	−0.606**	0.201	0.546
Task interdependency	−0.130	0.148	0.878	−0.221	0.133	0.802
Autonomy	0.254	0.146	1.289	0.078	0.125	1.081
Supervisory support for WLB	−0.194	0.147	0.824	−0.129	0.131	0.879
Family flexibility ability	0.300*	0.126	1.349	0.339**	0.110	1.404
Children younger than 12	−0.332	0.240	0.718	−0.361	0.214	0.697
Self-regulation	0.634**	0.189	1.885	0.630**	0.167	1.877
Separate workplace at home	0.223**	0.067	1.250	0.110	0.059	1.116
Making clear not to disturb	−0.014	0.116	0.986	0.159	0.106	1.172
Not engaging in domestic work	0.162	0.109	1.176	−0.013	0.097	1.013
Not checking e-mail	0.043	0.082	1.044	0.080	0.073	1.084
Interrupting work for a walk or exercise	0.080	0.087	1.083	0.141	0.078	1.152
Male	0.420	0.233	1.522	−0.088	0.198	0.916
Age	0.450	0.255	1.569	0.518*	0.222	1.679
Educational level (lower)	−0.205	0.240	0.815	0.027	0.221	1.028
Working from home before COVID-19	0.012	0.007	1.012	0.009	0.006	1.009
Feasibility to carry out work duties from home	−0.092	0.162	0.912	0.379*	0.150	1.460
Cox & Snell R^2	0.182					
Nagelkerke R^2	0.207					
McFadden R^2	0.094					
N	827					

every one unit increase in work pressure, the odds of being in the equally satisfied or more satisfied group decreases (the odds ratios were 0.387 and 0.546, respectively). No significant differences were found with respect to task interdependency, nor did autonomy and supervisory support for WLB reveal any differences between the three groups.

Family flexibility, one of the resources at home, appears to be important for WLB satisfaction: respondents with a higher degree of flexibility are more likely to be in the group that is equally or more satisfied with their WLB compared with respondents with little flexibility (the odds ratios were 1.349 and 1.404 respectively). Remarkably, we did not find significant differences between the three groups with respect to child-care responsibilities.

In terms of personal resources, the results highlight the importance of self-regulation when it comes to WLB satisfaction. Respondents who reported a higher level of self-regulation were more likely to be equally satisfied or more satisfied than before they worked entirely from home (the odds ratios were 1.885 and 1.877 respectively). Boundary management that takes the form of a separate workplace is also related to WLB satisfaction. Results indicate that respondents with a separate workplace at home are more likely to be in the group whose WLB satisfaction is the same as before the lockdown, with the probability of being in this group increasing by a factor of 1.250. This may be an indication that these respondents maintain a pattern while working entirely from home that is similar to their pre-COVID situation, so that there are no noteworthy changes in their WLB experiences. Other indicators of boundary management were not significant. With respect to our control variables, results showed that respondents in a higher age category are more likely to be in the more-satisfied group (the odds ratio was 1.651). We also found that respondents who's work duties are more feasible to be carried out from home are more likely to be in the group that is more satisfied with WLB (with an odds ratio of 1.460), indicating that the nature of the job matters for changes in WLB satisfaction. No significance differences were found for gender and level of education. Experience with working from home before employees were obliged to work from home entirely yielded no significant differences between groups either.

In summary, the MLR analysis did provide more insight into the demands and resources that may explain variation in WLB experiences. Respondents with higher demands, such as work pressure, are more likely to be less satisfied with their WLB, while respondents with lower demands and sufficient resources, such as FFA and self-regulation, are more likely to be more satisfied with their WLB than before. However, this was not the case for all demands and resources in the model, for example when it comes to task interdependency and child-care responsibilities. In the next section, we use qualitative data to shed a light on the mechanisms that may be at play here.

Interview Study

In exploring WLB experiences of employees in the interview study, we found that most respondents were less satisfied with their WLB than before the COVID-19 lockdown. Fewer than a third were more satisfied with their WLB, and a small group did not report any differences in WLB satisfaction. Results of the interview study indicate that an especially relevant factor for WLB experiences is the combined demands and resources at work, at home and at the personal level. In the following sections, we attempt to capture this intertwinement of demands and resources.

WORK DEMANDS AND RESOURCES

The respondents held jobs of various natures. Some respondents – for example those responsible for organizing social events – saw a decline in their work because of COVID-19, resulting in feelings of dissatisfaction and dullness. Other respondents, for example project managers, had jobs that mainly involve establishing and maintaining social relationships to foster collaboration and to achieve results. These respondents indicated that it was much harder to do their job (demands), as they found it more difficult to maintain social relationships digitally. They described feeling as if they were unable to do their job well, or they mentioned that it takes more time to complete tasks than before they worked entirely from home, resulting in a higher perceived work pressure.

> My role as a project manager…is to resolve irritations by giving people the space to speak up and by paying attention to the small details that sometimes help you collaborate closely along the way. And that is not possible now. It's just not possible. … You just need so much more time to do your job that at some point it gets tight. I don't have the time…to talk to enough people, to manage enough. On the contrary. (R13)

In other words, respondents felt that some activities went much faster in the office than digitally, from home.

Some jobs also involve extensive deliberation or checking by others. Respondents in these jobs depend on others to get their work done. Task interdependency appears to be a more pronounced work demand when working entirely from home. Respondents indicated that it is more difficult to see whether colleagues are available. This was less problematic before the lockdown because employees saw one another in the office regularly. Some respondents also said that such circumstances not only influence the workflow but also determine when they work, rather than being able to control their own work hours. *"…It's frustrating. You're out for a walk with your kids and then they* [colleagues] *suddenly start calling you."* (R6)

The respondents described above often indicated that they are less satisfied with their WLB than before the lockdown. Their experience is, in the first place, driven by changes in the work domain. The data indicate that respondents who depend on others to perform their job do not always have sufficient resources, such as accessible colleagues or face-to-face conversations, to meet work demands adequately. Respondents who depend on others appear to have more difficulty working entirely or almost entirely from home because of COVID-19. The negative impact of task interdependency can, however, be overcome if collaboration between colleagues is well organized. Some respondents, for example, described fellow team members as being well attuned. They know they can rely on one another, and collaboration often went smoothly as a result. Task interdependency was therefore less of a barrier for these employees.

> Fortunately, we have a team that has been running for a few years. So, we know each other through and through. We have also invested a lot in our collaboration. So yes, half a word is enough … (R14)

Some jobs, on the other hand, are much more stand-alone in nature, for example administrative jobs that involve controlling and processing invoices. This does not mean that the relevant respondents do not have to consult colleagues, but they can generally do their work independently (i.e., their tasks are sequential rather than interdependent). As a result, they had more control over their schedule than respondents who depend more on others to do their job. Some of them also indicated that they could do their work even better at home because they were not being distracted by colleagues. The respondents in question are therefore often more satisfied with their WLB.

> My work requires concentration. I don't need anyone else for that. I don't want to be disturbed; I want to compare [documents]. Only when I am finished, I need someone else to do a second check. (R1)

To briefly summarize our findings regarding the work domain, respondents who work under more pressure and respondents whose work involves higher amounts of task interdependency are generally less satisfied with their WLB than respondents whose jobs are much more stand-alone. The same goes for respondents who saw a decline in their work demands, resulting in feelings of dissatisfaction and dullness, compared with respondents who did not experience any changes in their work other than the location. We also saw that two main conditions influence the extent to which such characteristics result in less WLB satisfaction: collaboration and control over work hours. These resources can help to cope with demands at work. For example, task interdependency does not necessarily have to lead to less WLB satisfaction if the employee has the resources to handle these dependencies (e.g., close collaboration with colleagues). This may explain why our MLR did not reveal any differences between groups in terms of task interdependency.

HOME DEMANDS AND RESOURCES

The combination of demands and resources at home also plays an important role in WLB satisfaction when working entirely from home. Child-care responsibilities are the most pronounced in the data in this context. The associated demands (such as home schooling and caregiving duties) were sometimes incompatible with work. The work domain and the personal domain pulled at the respondents in question simultaneously, resulting in conflict between those domains. These respondents were often less satisfied with their WLB because they did not have enough resources to deal with these demands. In some cases, partners did not work at home, meaning that the respondents had to take on domestic responsibilities by themselves. What is striking is that these respondents were not in control when it came to scheduling their workdays. In other words, they lacked the flexibility, mainly at home, to deal adequately with demands. For these respondents, the day felt very long and exhausting.

> My wife works at the hospital, so I am alone with two young children. They demand your attention the entire day. So, I cannot concentrate on my work the way I used to when I still worked in the office. ... So, it [work-life balance] is non-existent. At the moment there is no balance at all because I start working early in the morning and the children are there then too. It goes on all day, until 10 p.m., and then I'm completely drained and I just go to bed. (R6)

Some respondents indicated that their supervisor plays an important role for employees who have to combine their work demands with child-care responsibilities and are thus experiencing difficulties working entirely from home. One respondent, for example, mentioned that *"...he [the supervisor] tells these people to take it down a notch, to work a little bit less"* (R7). Respondents who are struggling with working from home can sometimes count on support from their supervisor.

> He [the supervisor] knows that some employees have children at home. And so, he says if you need to take your little one out, just do it. So those employees work until 1:30 p.m. and that's totally fine. (R9)

On the other hand, there were respondents with child-care responsibilities who reported a richer family life because they had more time to spend with family. Child-care in this case was a source of enrichment rather than conflict. Taking a closer look, we see that these respondents have sufficient resources to deal with child-care responsibilities, unlike respondents with lower WLB satisfaction. They may have a partner with whom they can divide up the tasks.

> We [my partner and I] take it in shifts. When it's my shift, I look after the children and help them with their homework, and then we switch. And that works quite well actually. We found an adequate structure (R7).

Furthermore, instead of time spent commuting, these respondents can spend this time with their family. Some respondents who described their family life as richer did not face demands such as home schooling, for example because their children were older or their partner was able to take care of younger children. These respondents, many of them male, worked traditional hours during the day and did not do any household or child-care tasks then. They were able to spend more time with their family before and after work, however.

> It suits me fine and it's also more fun. We see each other more often; the children are of course also at home. We have a lot more family-time now... It's a bit more intense because we're condemned to being at home. What has changed is that I'm no longer off in [city name]. ...That makes it just that little bit more pleasant and convivial and better. (R1)

> Before, I didn't see my son in the mornings and I came home at 5:45 p.m., then we would have dinner and after an hour he would go to bed. And now, and that is partly because he does not go to school [homeschooling], but even if he did go to school, I see so much more of him. So, you get so much in return. And that not only applies to my son, but also to my husband. I also see my husband a lot more. (R14)

In other words, for some respondents working from home and not commuting cleared more time to spend with family, enriching family life and thus increasing their WLB satisfaction. This was especially true for those with jobs suitable for working from home. It appears, for example, that respondents who referred to a richer family life also did not have to deal with changes at work. Moreover, most respondents in this group had a partner who could take on some or all of the child-care tasks, or their children were older. This was more often not the case for respondents who were less satisfied with their WLB. As described at the beginning of this section, they found it more challenging to combine their work with child-care responsibilities such as homeschooling, especially when their jobs involved task interdependency and/or a heavier workload. Unlike the respondents who felt more satisfied with their WLB, these respondents had little control over their workday. On the contrary, they were controlled by demands at work and demands at home.

We see, then, that respondents with child-care responsibilities (including homeschooling) are not necessarily less satisfied with their WLB. This may explain why our quantitative data did not reveal any differences between the three groups. The interview study suggests that access to resources for dealing with child-care responsibilities (and work demands) is decisive in mitigating the impact of those demands on WLB satisfaction.

Personal Resources

Two Faces of Commuting

As we have seen, the absence of commuting time means more time for other things, such as a family life or sports activities. This certainly applies to respondents who had to travel a lot to different locations across the country, or those who had a long commute in general. However, there are also respondents who indicated that commuting time provided a natural transition between work and personal life. Traveling from one place to another allowed them to leave work or their personal life behind and to redirect their focus to the other domain. In other words, commuting time created a boundary between work and personal life.

> When I still lived in [city name], I always cycled home. It took only five minutes, but I had that transition. A literal transition from work to home. Now I can go downstairs, but it's not the same. It's more intertwined now (R3).

Commuting offered these respondents a way of marking the transition between different life domains. For example, it determined when they could stop working and helped them to make the switch, psychologically and otherwise, to the personal domain.

> What bothers me sometimes…when I know that I still have quite a bit of work to do, but it's 6 p.m. and I just want to relax…then I still feel like 'I can also just continue working.' Normally, you have that moment on the train when you can put your day into perspective and end your workday. (R16)

Role Blurring and Boundary Management

With work and personal life intersecting at the same location, some respondents had trouble making a distinction between domains. One key element that came to the fore in several interviews is related to boundary blurring. Respondents, for example, said that their work and personal lives were continuously encroaching on one another, making it harder for them to distance themselves from work.

> Well, I am glad that my husband tells me when I've done enough and should stop working. It's much harder now that I don't go to the office in the morning and come back home in the evening. It's much more blurred. (R2)

Blurred boundaries thus make it harder to determine when the workday is done and personal life begins. They can be challenging for employees because they can simply keep working. This tendency is aggravated by the absence of clear work hours. Although respondents from all groups indicated that boundaries were blurred, those who had specific boundary management tools in place are often more satisfied with their WLB. They may, for example, have a separate workplace, which can be viewed as a spatial strategy. This is in line with our quantitative findings, where we saw that respondents with a separate workplace were more likely to be either equally satisfied or more satisfied with their WLB. A separate workplace at home seems to help in setting boundaries between work and personal life, as indicated by the following quotation: *"I put my computer in a separate space, so I can view that as my office"* (R10). It should be noted, however, that not all respondents had a separate workplace at home. Those who did not were generally less satisfied with their WLB, as work and personal life were much more blurred. It was also harder for them to disconnect from work.

Related to temporal strategies, respondents indicate that they can balance their work and personal life by making firm agreements or by sticking to a (tight) schedule. Respondents who experienced a decline in WLB satisfaction also mentioned that such boundary management tools helped them to reduce the negative experiences.

> At home, we at least have agreements about when I work and when I don't. I also make that clear in my calendar. So, if I have to help my children with their homework in the morning, it says so in my calendar. And when I'm working, I do sit in a separate room with the door closed and then I do in fact work. I need that, those agreements at home. (R16)

When it comes to managing boundaries between work and personal life, many roads lead to Rome. In other words, there are various ways to achieve a good WLB using different boundary management strategies. The literature shows that people can apply different strategies on a continuum from segregating to integrating different life domains (Ashforth et al., 2000). Preferences for certain strategies also vary among employees (Kossek & Lautsch, 2012). Some respondents, for example, prefer to keep traditional hours and attend to their personal life before and after those hours. There are also respondents, however, who prefer to switch between work and personal activities during the day.

> And it gives you space, the great thing is that you have the flexibility to switch on the washing machine, to do something in between. It's very practical, quickly unload the dishwasher and so on. The variation makes it very pleasant. (R1)

The data do not show, then, that respondents who integrate work and personal life are more satisfied with their WLB than those who keep work and personal life separate, or vice versa. This finding is confirmed in our MLR, where we did not find any differences in boundary management behaviors. Two factors appear to be important. The first is whether respondents have control over how they organize their workday themselves and their own boundary management strategies. Earlier on, we saw that some respondents are controlled by their work or by home demands and are therefore not (fully) in control of when they work and when they attend to personal matters. The second important factor is whether respondents have strategies in place to help them distinguish between different roles across life domains. They can also achieve this by integrating different life domains, by establishing some kind of "integrated pattern." The latter means that employees switch between work and personal life during the day, but that they try to maintain a structure, for example by sticking to a schedule. The degree of self-regulation plays an important role in such cases. We elaborate on this finding in the next section.

Self-Regulation

Several respondents described themselves as lacking the ability to self-regulate. They preferred to work at the office, for example, because all the distractions at home kept them from focusing on their work. This was especially true for people who did not have a separate workplace. Their inability to concentrate was sometimes aggravated by their being almost entirely house-bound, since the COVID-19 measures had also restricted many other outside activities (e.g., visiting a restaurant or a museum).

> It's exhausting and there are more distractions at home. You're at home all the time, so you rarely see anything else, and you hardly get any stimuli during the day … But yes, you notice more things in your house that distract you…the house has never been cleaner, I suppose. (R12)

There are also respondents, however, who said they were able to concentrate on the tasks at hand. These respondents were often better able to adequately manage boundaries between work and personal life (either by integrating or segregating different domains). For example, they managed to develop a certain work schedule or rhythm in which there was sometimes room to switch back and forth between work and personal life.

> I log in at 7 a.m. sharp and I shut down my computer at 4:30 p.m. sharp. So, the discipline I was so afraid of lacking…it turned out I have it. (R14)

Respondents who lack self-regulation, on the other hand, tended to work longer hours or were unable to work a full day. All in all, respondents with a better ability to self-regulate were generally more satisfied with their WLB than those who lacked self-regulation. This may explain our quantitative findings, in which self-regulation was found to be an important factor in the probability of a respondent being more satisfied with WLB.

To summarize our findings, respondents used different strategies to manage boundaries between work and personal life. Some tried to keep work and personal life as separate as possible, for example by working in a separate workspace and sticking to a tight schedule (much as they did when they worked in the office).

Others preferred to alternate between work and personal life. It is not the strategy as such, however, but the ability to develop new (temporal) routines, either by segregating or integrating different life domains, and to carve out a separate workspace at home that appear to contribute in general to a higher level of WLB satisfaction.

Being in control is another important resource for WLB satisfaction. Our data show that some respondents were unable to schedule their workday or find a new routine that works for them. They were controlled by demands in the work and/or life domain and it was harder for them to manage boundaries between the two adequately.

The final critical resource is self-regulation, which helps respondents to achieve the desired balance and to structure the working day to their satisfaction.

DISCUSSION

This study combined a survey and interviews to explore differences in WLB satisfaction during the first COVID-19 pandemic lockdown in the Netherlands. In this unique situation, employees were obliged to work from home. Some had already worked from home before the pandemic, whereas others had not because they preferred not to or were not permitted to do so. As a result, the employees now compelled to work from home were a diverse group. Moreover, during the lockdown, schools were closed, and social gatherings were prohibited. Hence, the pandemic affected both the work and the family domains. The aim of this chapter was to explore how government employees in the Netherlands experienced their WLB satisfaction while working entirely from home and how differences in their experiences can be explained. To understand how these differences relate to working entirely from home under COVID-19 restrictions, we asked our respondents to compare their pre-COVID situation with their experience during the first lockdown.

Remarkably, experience with working from home before employees were obliged to work from home entirely did not account for significant differences in WLB satisfaction. This may indicate that there are employees, who used to work from home to a greater extent but struggled with working from home entirely. At the same time, there are employees who experienced that they were able to work from home effectively, while they did not or barely work from home before COVID-19.

The necessity of working entirely from home caused a shift in demands across different life domains. Empirical evidence indicates that the nature of the job is an important starting point for working from home effectively. Our qualitative analysis showed that task interdependency sometimes leads to less WLB satisfaction because colleagues are not always accessible, making it harder and more time-consuming to accomplish one's work, close collaboration within teams can mitigate this and serves as an important resource in this regard. Similarly, child-care responsibilities can negatively affect WLB satisfaction when coping resources are insufficient. This finding highlights the notion that family demands, such as care responsibilities and homeschooling, can hinder an individual's ability to achieve a satisfactory WLB (Brough et al., 2020). Sufficient resources are important to mitigate the negative consequences of fulfilling different work and family roles. However, when tasks can be shared with a partner, child-care responsibilities do not have to result in less WLB satisfaction. Although working parents sometimes faced difficulties with respect to combining conflicting demands from the work and family domain, they also spoke about work–life enrichment, as working entirely from home gave them more time to spend with their partner and children.

Moreover, our findings indicate that having a partner can be helpful in managing boundaries between work and personal life because a partner can help an employee to disconnect from work (by saying "enough is enough"). In addition, the ability to manage boundaries based on personal preferences can be seen as a relevant resource for achieving a satisfactory WLB. Our findings reveal two crucial factors: to be able to control boundary management strategies and to find a new routine which enables managing demands from different life domains. Hence, when employees are enabled to act on their preferred strategies, boundary management can become an important personal resource to foster WLB satisfaction (Kossek & Lautsch, 2012). This finding highlights the importance of boundary control in relation to WLB satisfaction. Our results also indicate that self-regulation is an important personal resource for working from home effectively and avoiding distractions (Allen et al., 2015). Self-regulation can assist employees in organizing the workday when working from home. Previous research has shown that structuring behaviors like these are beneficial for work–life outcomes (Raghuram & Wiesenfield, 2003).

All in all, this chapter highlights the interrelatedness of demands and resources. Whereas previous studies on teleworking and WLB satisfaction have been inconclusive or show that teleworking has minimal effects (Allen et al., 2015), this chapter suggests that a constellation of factors comes into play, rather than a single demand or resource. This also means that the impact of a specific condition on WLB satisfaction is contingent on the presence of other demands and resources. In line with the JD-R model, our results also show that both demands and resources can reinforce one another (Bakker & Demerouti, 2007).

Moreover, new perspectives on the work–life interface have emerged, focusing on the conditions under which and the processes that lead to interaction between work and personal life (see for example Ten Brummelhuis & Bakker, 2012). This chapter has shed light on some of these conditions and processes, by identifying a constellation of demands and resources arising from the work domain, the family domain as well as personal resources. Heavy demands and insufficient resources lead to conflict between work and personal life, which in turn reduces WLB satisfaction. In contrast, sufficient resources to cope with demands can lead to enrichment (e.g., more time with family) and, consequently, greater WLB satisfaction (Wayne et al., 2017). It is important to take these underlying processes into account when examining WLB satisfaction in relation to working from home.

Limitations

This chapter showed that there are several demands and resources that play an important role in WLB satisfaction when working entirely from home. Nevertheless, the mechanisms put forward in this chapter are not exhaustive, as they may encompass other demands and resources. The literature, for example, suggests that supervisory support (Hammer et al., 2009) can be important for WLB satisfaction. Our findings indicate that certain specific forms of support (e.g., telling employees to take on less work) can help in creating a better balance between work and personal life. Our data has limited information on leadership, however, leaving it to future research to examine the role of leadership in similar circumstances in more detail.

Second, there are indications in our data that employees who were sceptic toward working from home before, started to appreciate it during the first lockdown. Others, however, learned that it is better for them to work at the office (most of the time). Our data on attitudes toward working from home is however too limited to fully analyze the impact on changes in WLB satisfaction.

A third limitation is that the data for this chapter were collected during the first COVID lockdown. As mentioned earlier, it can take time to adjust to a new situation and to develop new routines. The timing of the data collection may therefore have affected the results. During the first lockdown, for example, people may have thought that the restrictions meant to slow the spread of the virus were only temporary. However, we have been dealing with COVID-19 restrictions for a great amount of time, including working from home as much as possible. People may have adapted to their new situation over time, resulting in positive outcomes such as a better WLB, but this does not have to be the case for everyone. The extent to which adaptation occurs may also be contingent on personal characteristics, the degree of control, and the course of the COVID-19 pandemic (Eby et al., 2016). It is therefore important to monitor the outcomes of working entirely (or almost entirely) from home, as they may change over time.

Fourth, the pandemic impacted other aspects of life beyond the work and family domain. Our findings, for example, indicate that it became harder to set boundaries between domains because the scope for engaging in social/non-work activities was curtailed. After all, COVID-19 put social lives on hold as well. There are also indications in our data that these constraints resulted in less work–life enrichment for singles who live alone. Singles who live alone were more likely to enter a figurative void where there were very few possibilities to detach from work (i.e., to be active in the life domain). When people are unable to fulfill their social roles (e.g., as a friend, an aunt) or meet their need to recover from work by engaging in social activities, such as going to the theater or a restaurant, their WLB satisfaction may be affected. Our chapter focused on the combination of work and personal/family life, however, and less on the social domain and leisure activities. Future research could examine the role of the social domain within WLB experiences, especially in circumstances such as the COVID-19 pandemic.

Practical Implications

Employees need time to adapt to working largely from home to achieve a satisfactory WLB (Beauregard et al., 2019; Gajendran & Harrison, 2007). This study indicates that boundary management is an important tool for achieving this. Results from both our quantitative data and qualitative analyses show that there is no one strategy for success. Both integration between and segregation of work and family or personal life can result in a satisfactory WLB. This result is in line with previous findings highlighting the importance of acting on preferences for integrating or segregating work and personal life, rather than following an imposed strategy (Kossek & Lautsch, 2012). Hence, in line with Kossek and Lautsch (2012), this chapter emphasizes the importance of control over boundary management. Organizations can step up by facilitating both integration and segregation of work and personal life. This may require a balancing act between fostering individual autonomy and organizational efforts to support successful boundary management. Organizations can, for instance, give employees autonomy over their work schedule. At the same time, it is important to create an organizational culture in which people feel free to fully disconnect from work when they leave the (home) office.

In addition, the qualitative data indicates that applying some form of structure, for example developing new schedules or routines that differentiate between work and non-work roles, can be conducive to WLB satisfaction when working entirely from home. This can also be accomplished when alternating between work and personal life. It may take time to develop these new routines, however, and to adjust to the new situation in general. In addition, scholars have argued that it is important to reflect regularly on the strategies used (Wessels et al., 2019), to determine whether they are still effective or need to be adjusted. One way to do this is to talk things over with household members and colleagues. Organizations can play a facilitating role, for example by organizing training sessions and workshops in which employees can discuss their routines and boundary management strategies with their colleagues and their supervisor.

In a situation where working parents are facing both work demands and childcare responsibilities, organizations and supervisors can step in by temporarily easing the workload for these employees. With many social activities being prohibited, moreover, it is important for employees to seek out other activities that allow them to recover from work (e.g., sports) (Wepfer et al., 2018). Recovery time can not only help them detach from work but can also help them demarcate their work and their personal life. Organizations can play a role in this, for example by promoting sports or other non-work activities during or after work hours.

All in all, our research on working from home during the COVID-19 pandemic has given us a better understanding of how demands and resources, including boundary management strategies, affect WLB experiences. Working largely from home is likely to remain a common practice for many employees for the foreseeable future. Based on our analyses, we have provided practical suggestions aimed at helping employees adjust to working from home. In addition, we have stressed the importance of looking into the long-term effects of working extensively from home. Moreover, the exposure to demands and access to resources varies among employees, highlighting the need for tailored approaches from organizations and supervisors to help their employees in working from home successfully.

NOTE

1. The PCC was calculated by squaring and subsequently summing the proportion of cases for each group $(0.274^2 + 0.271^2 + 0.455^2) = 0.351$. $0.351 * 1.25 = 0.439$, which equals 43.9%. This is lower than the 54.3% correct classifications yielded by the model, thus demonstrating a satisfactory PCC.

REFERENCES

Abendroth, A. K., & Den Dulk, L. (2011). Support for the work-life balance in Europe: The impact of state, workplace and family support on work-life balance satisfaction. *Work, Employment and Society*, *25*(2), 234–256.

Allen, T. D., Cho, E., & Meier, L. L. (2014). Work-family boundary dynamics. *Annual Review of Organizational Psychology and Organizational Behavior*, *1*(1), 99–121.

Allen, T. D., Golden, T. D., & Shockley, K. M. (2015). How effective is telecommuting? Assessing the status of our scientific findings. *Psychological Science in the Public Interest*, *16*(2), 40–68.

Allen, T. D., Johnson, R. C., Kiburz, K. M., & Shockley, K. M. (2013). Work–family conflict and flexible work arrangements: Deconstructing flexibility. *Personnel Psychology*, *66*(2), 345–376.

Allen, T. D., Merlo, K., Lawrence, R. C., Slutsky, J., & Gray, C. E. (2021). Boundary management and work-nonwork balance while working from home. *Applied Psychology*, *70*(1), 60–84.

Anderson, D., & Kelliher, C. (2020). Enforced remote working and the work-life interface during lockdown. *Gender in Management: An International Journal*, *35*(7/8), 677–683.

Annink, A. (2017). Busyness around the business: A cross-national comparative research of the work-life balance of self-employed workers.

Argyle, M. (2001). *The psychology of happiness*. Routledge.

Ashforth, B. E., Kreiner, G. E., & Fugate, M. (2000). All in a day's work: Boundaries and micro role transitions. *Academy of Management Review*, *25*(3), 472–491.

Bakker, A. B., & Demerouti, E. (2007). The job demands-resources model: State of the art. *Journal of Managerial Psychology*, *22*(3), 309–328.

Bakker, A. B., & Geurts, S. A. (2004). Toward a dual-process model of work-home interference. *Work and Occupations*, *31*(3), 345–366.

Baumeister, R. F., & Vonasch, A. J. (2015). Uses of self-regulation to facilitate and restrain addictive behavior. *Addictive Behaviors*, *44*, 3–8.

Beauregard, T. A., Basile, K. A., & Canonico, E. (2019). Telework: Outcomes and facilitators for employees. In R. N. Landers (Ed.), *The Cambridge handbook of technology and employee behavior* (pp. 511–543). Cambridge University Press.

Brough, P., Timms, C., Chan, X. W., Hawkes, A., & Rasmussen, L. (2020). Work–life balance: Definitions, causes, and consequences. *Handbook of Socioeconomic Determinants of Occupational Health: From Macro-level to Micro-level Evidence*, 473–487.

Byron, K. (2005). A meta-analytic review of work-family conflict and its antecedents. *Journal of Vocational Behavior*, *67*(2), 169–198.

Carlson, D. S., Kacmar, K. M., Wayne, J. H., & Grzywacz, J. G. (2006). Measuring the positive side of the work–family interface: Development and validation of a work–family enrichment scale. *Journal of Vocational Behavior*, *68*(1), 131–164.

Centraal Bureau voor de Statistiek. (2021, 16 februari). *Werkzame beroepsbevolking: thuiswerken in 2019*. https://opendata.cbs.nl/#/CBS/nl/dataset/83258NED/table?dl=327E0

Chen, Z., Powell, G. N., & Greenhaus, J. H. (2009). Work-to-family conflict, positive spillover, and boundary management: A person-environment fit approach. *Journal of Vocational Behavior*, *74*(1), 82–93.

Clark, S. C. (2000). Work/family border theory: A new theory of work/family balance. *Human Relations*, *53*(6), 747–770.

Craig, L., & Churchill, B. (2021). Dual-earner parent couples' work and care during COVID-19. *Gender, Work & Organization*, *28*, 66–79.

Del Boca, D., Oggero, N., Profeta, P., & Rossi, M. (2020). Women's and men's work, housework and childcare, before and during COVID-19. *Review of Economics of the Household*, *18*(4), 1001–1017.

Demerouti, E., Derks, D., Lieke, L., & Bakker, A. B. (2014). New ways of working: Impact on working conditions, work–family balance, and well-being. In C. Korunka & P. Hoonakker (Eds.), *The impact of ICT on quality of working life* (pp. 123–141). Springer.

De Voogd, C. (2020). *The "Intelligent Lockdown" Gamble of the Netherlands* [Internet]. Institute Montaigne Blogs. [cited 2021 Oct 11]. Retrieved from https://www.institutmontaigne.org/en/analysis/europe-versus-coronavirus-intelligent-lockdown-gamble-netherlands

Duxbury, L., & Higgins, C. (2001). *Work-life balance in the new millenium: Where are we? Where do we need to go?* CPRN.

Eby, L. T., Mitchell, M., & Zimmerman, L. (2016). Work and family in times of crisis. In T. D. Allen & L. T. Eby (Ed.), *The Oxford Handbook of work and family* (pp. 417–430). Oxford University Press.

Frone, M. R. (2003). Work-family balance. In J. C. Quick & L. E. Tetrick (Eds.), *Handbook of occupational health psychology* (pp. 143–162). American Psychological Association.

Fuegen, K., Biernat, M., Haines, E., & Deaux, K. (2004). Mothers and fathers in the workplace: How gender and parental status influence judgments of job-related competence. *Journal of Social Science*, *60*(4), 737–754.

Fukumura, Y. E., Schott, J. M., Lucas, G. M., Becerik-Gerber, B., & Roll, S. C. (2021). Negotiating time and space when working from home: Experiences during COVID-19. *OTJR: Occupation, Participation and Health*, *41*(4), 223–231.

Gajendran, R. S., & Harrison, D. A. (2007). The good, the bad, and the unknown about telecommuting: Meta-analysis of psychological mediators an individual consequence. *Journal of Applied Psychology*, *92*(6), 1524–1541.

Glavin, P., & Schieman, S. (2012). Work–family role blurring and work–family conflict: The moderating influence of job resources and job demands. *Work and Occupations*, *39*(1), 71–98.

Golden, T. D., & Veiga, J. F. (2005). The impact of extent of telecommuting on job satisfaction: Resolving inconsistent findings. *Journal of Management*, *31*(2), 301–318.

Gorgievski, M., Peeters, P., Rietzschel, E. F., & Bipp, T. (2016). Reliability and validity of the Dutch translation of the Work Design Questionnaire. *Gedrag & organisatie*, *29*(3), 273–301.

Graham, C. W., Sorell, G. T., & Montgomery, M. J. (2004). Role-related identity structure in adult women. *Identity: An International Journal of Theory and Research*, *4*(3), 251–271.

Grawitch, M. J., Maloney, P. W., Barber, L. K., & Mooshegian, S. E. (2013). Examining the nomological network of satisfaction with work–life balance. *Journal of Occupational Health Psychology*, *18*(3), 276–284.

Greenhaus, J. H., Collins, K. M., & Shaw, J. D. (2003). The relation between work–family balance and quality of life. *Journal of Vocational Behavior*, *63*(3), 510–531.

Hammer, L. B., Kossek, E. E., Bodner, T., & Crain, T. (2013). Measurement development and validation of the family supportive behavior short-form (FSSB-SF). *Journal of Occupational Health Psychology*, *18*(3), 285–296.

Hammer, L. B., Kossek, E. E., Yragui, N. L., Bodner, T. E., & Hanson, G. C. (2009). Development and validation of multidimensional measure of family supportive supervisor behaviors (FSSB). *Journal of Management*, *35*(4), 837–856.

Hill, J. E., Grzywacz, J. G., Allen, S., Blanchard, V. L., Matz-Costa, C., Shulkin, S., & Pitt-Catsouphes, M. (2008). Defining and conceptualizing workplace flexibility. *Community, Work and Family*, *11*(2), 149–163.

Hill, E. J., Hawkins, A. J., Ferris, M., & Weitzman, M. (2001). Finding an extra day a week: The positive influence of perceived job flexibility on work and family life balance. *Family Relations*, *50*(1), 49–58.

Hjálmsdóttir, A., & Bjarnadóttir, V. S. (2021). "I have turned into a foreman here at home": Families and work–life balance in times of COVID-19 in a gender equality paradise. *Gender, Work & Organization*, *28*(1), 268–283.

Iyengar, S. S., & Lepper, M. R. (2000). When choice is demotivating: Can one desire too much of a good thing? *Journal of Personality and Social Psychology*, *79*(6), 995–1006.

Jang, S. J., & Zippay, A. (2011). The juggling act: Managing work-life conflict and work-life balance. *Families in Society*, *92*(1), 84–90.

Kalliath, T., & Brough, P. (2008). Work–life balance: A review of the meaning of the balance construct. *Journal of Management & Organization*, *14*(3), 323–327.

Karasek, R., & Theorell, T. (1990). *Health work-stress, productivity and the reconstruction of working life*. Basic Books.

Kelliher, C., & Anderson, D. (2010). Doing more with less? Flexible working practices and the intensification of work. *Human Relations*, *63*(1), 83–106.

Kelliher, C., & De Menezes, L. M. (2019). *Flexible working in organisations: A research overview*. Routledge.

Kim, H. K. (2014). Work-life balance and employees' performance: The mediating role of affective commitment. *Global Business and Management Research: An International Journal*, *6*(1), 3751.

Kirchmeyer, C. (2000). Work-life initiatives: greed or benevolence regarding workers' time? In C. L. Cooper & D. M. Rousseu (Eds.), *Trends in organizational behavior: Time in organizational behavior* (pp. 79–94). Wiley.

Kossek, E. E. (2016). Managing work-life boundaries in the digital age. *Organizational Dynamics*, *45*(3), 258–270.

Kossek, E. E., & Lautsch, B. A. (2012). Work–family boundary management styles in organizations: A cross-level model. *Organizational Psychology Review*, *2*(2), 152–171.

Kreiner, G. E. (2006). Consequences of work-home segmentation or integration: A person-environment fit perspective. *Journal of Organizational Behavior: The International Journal of Industrial, Occupational and Organizational Psychology and Behavior*, *27*(4), 485–507.

Kreiner, G. E., Hollensbe, E. C., & Sheep, M. L. (2009). Balancing borders and bridges: Negotiating the work-home interface via boundary work tactics. *Academy of Management Journal*, *52*(4), 704–730.

Matthews, R. A., & Barnes-Farrell, J. L. (2010). Development and initial evaluation of an enhanced measure of boundary flexibility for the work and family domains. *Journal of Occupational Health Psychology*, *15*(3), 330.

Milliken, F. J., & Dunn-Jensen, L. M. (2005). The changing time demands of managerial and professional work: Implications for managing the work-life boundary. In E. E. Kossek & S. J. Lambert (Eds.), *Work and life integration, organizational, cultural, and individual perspectives* (pp. 43–60). Lawrence Erlbaum.

Morgeson, F. P., & Humphrey, S. E. (2006). The Work Design Questionnaire (WDQ): Developing and validating a comprehensive measure for assessing job design and nature of work. *Journal of Applied Psychology*, *91*(6), 1321–1339.

Nippert-Eng, C. E. (1996). *Home and work. Negotiating boundaries through everyday life*. University of Chicago Press.

Palumbo, R. (2020). Let me go to the office! An investigation into the side effects of working from home on work-life balance. *International Journal of Public Sector Management*, *33*(6/7), 771–790.

Raghuram, S., Wiesenfield, B., & Garud, R. (2003). Technology enabled work: The role of self-efficacy in determining telecommuter adjustment and structuring behavior. *Journal of Vocational Behavior*, *63*, 180–198.

Reynolds, J. (2005). In the face of conflict: Work–life conflict and desired work hour adjustment. *Journal of Marriage and Family*, *67*(5), 1313–1331.

Rothbard, N. P., & Dumas, T. L. (2006). Research perspectives: Managing the work-home interface. In F. Jones et al. (Eds.), *Work-life balance: A psychological perspective* (pp. 71–89). Psychology Press.

Starkweather, J., & Moske A. K. (2011) Multinominal logisc regression. Lecture notes. Retrieved from http://bayes.acs.unt.edu:8083/BayesContent/class/Jon/Benchmarks/MLR_JDS_Aug2011.pdf

Tangney, J. P., Baumeister, R. F., & Boone, A. L. (2004). High self-control predicts good adjustment, less pathology, better grades, and interpersonal success. *Journal of Personality*, *72*(2), 271–324.

Ten Brummelhuis, L. L., & Bakker, A. B. (2012). A resource perspective on the work-home interface: The work-home resources model. *American Psychologist*, *67*(7), 545–556.

TNO. (2021). Zorgtaken maken verschil tussen ontspannen of gestreste corona-tijd. https://www.monitorarbeid.tno.nl/nl-nl/coronacrisis/blog-splitsen-zorgtaken/#

Tremblay, D. G., & Thomsin, L. (2012). Telework and mobile working: Analysis of its benefits and drawbacks. *International Journal of Work Innovation*, *1*(1), 100–113.

Valcour, M. (2007). Work-based resources as moderators of the relationship between work hours and satisfaction with work-family balance. *Journal of Applied Psychology*, *92*(6), 1512.

Wayne, J. H., Butts, M. M., Casper, W. J., & Allen, T. D. (2017). In search of balance: A conceptual and empirical integration of multiple meanings of work–family balance. *Personnel Psychology*, *70*(1), 167–210.

Wepfer, A. G., Allen, T. D., Brauchli, R., Jenny, G. J., & Bauer, G. F. (2018). Work-life boundaries and well-being: Does work-to-life integration impair well-being through lack of recovery? *Journal of Business and Psychology*, *33*(6), 727–740.

Wessels, C., Schippers, M. C., Stegmann, S., Bakker, A. B., Van Baalen, P. J., & Proper, K. I. (2019). Fostering flexibility in the new world of work: A model of time-spatial job crafting. *Frontiers in Psychology*, *10*, 1–13.

Xanthopoulou, D., Bakker, A. B., Demerouti, E., & Schaufeli, W. B. (2007). The role of personal resources in the job demands-resources model. *International Journal of Stress Management*, *14*(2), 121–141.

CHAPTER 2

WORKING FROM HOME DURING THE COVID-19 PANDEMIC: LESSONS LEARNED ABOUT THE RELATIONSHIP BETWEEN FLEXIBLE WORK AND WORK–FAMILY CONFLICT

Mareike Reimann

ABSTRACT

During the COVID-19 pandemic, working from home (WFH) has become the norm for many employees and their families in Germany. Although WFH has been suggested as a form of flexible work to foster work–life integration (especially for workers with greater care responsibilities), studies have also pointed to its risks when the boundaries between these two life spheres become blurred. To help disentangle these inconsistent findings in relation to work–family conflict, this study focuses on two main concerns: the relevance of additional forms of flexibility for those who work from home (i.e., temporal flexibility, job autonomy, fixed rules about availability) and the implications of WFH for employees' social relationships with co-workers and supervisors. Based on linked employer–employee data collected in the spring of 2021, the study examined work-to-family conflict (WFC) and family-to-work conflict (FWC) among a sample of 885 employees who worked from home. The results indicate that three factors – temporal flexibility, job autonomy, and fixed rules

Flexible Work and the Family
Contemporary Perspectives in Family Research, Volume 21, 31–67

Published under exclusive licence by Emerald Publishing Limited
ISSN: 1530-3535/doi:10.1108/S1530-353520230000021002

about availability as a way to set boundaries between work and family life – are important predictors of fewer work–family conflict. This equally applies to employees with caring obligations who overall experience more work–family conflicts while WFH. For those who cared for relatives, autonomy contributed even to fewer work–family conflicts. Supportive relationships with supervisors and co-workers are certainly directly beneficial when it comes to avoiding conflict, but they also reinforce the positive implications of flexible work, whereas poor relationships counteract the benefits of such flexibility. Thus, employers need to provide additional forms of flexibility to employees who work from home and should pay attention to social relationships among their employees as a way to support families and other individuals.

Keywords: Autonomy; COVID-19; supervisors; families; remote work; social support

1. INTRODUCTION

The COVID-19 pandemic has changed lives across the globe and has had a huge impact on many different aspects of people's daily lives. Families who have children and high care demands have been hit especially hard by the measures designed to protect against COVID-19 infections (Bujard et al., 2021; Müller et al., 2020). As social distancing became the main strategy to curb the spread of the virus, the option of WFH[1] received a considerable boost and became relevant for more workers than ever (Felstead & Reuschke, 2020). Despite the advantages of WFH with regard to infection protection (Alipour et al., 2021), scholars increasingly point to certain risks of WFH, such as social isolation (Lengen et al., 2020) and impaired health (Xiao et al., 2021). Empirical evidence for consequences of WFH that affect the work–family interface, however, is still inconsistent (Reimann et al., 2022; Schieman et al., 2021). To investigate the risks and benefits of flexible work for families, this research examined work–family conflict among employees in Germany who were WFH during the COVID-19 pandemic.

In terms of balancing work and family life responsibilities, work–family conflict has been identified as a form of inter-role conflict that occurs as part of the specific interplay between employees' work and family lives (Greenhaus & Beutell, 1985). Such conflict can occur in two directions – that is, *WFC*, when carrying out one's work role makes it more difficult to meet one's responsibilities in the family role, and FWC, when responsibilities in the home interfere with one's accomplishing work tasks (Gutek et al., 1991; Netemeyer et al., 1996). In this context, different dimensions of flexible work (e.g., flexiplace, flexitime, job autonomy) have long been suggested as a means of fostering work–life integration by allowing employees to adjust their work and family demands (Allen et al., 2013; Hill et al., 2010; Schieman & Glavin, 2008). Thus, it has been assumed that workers with greater family responsibilities (such as family caregivers or parents, especially mothers and single parents) would benefit considerably from the opportunity to work from home (Duxbury et al., 1994; Reimann et al., 2019;

Son & Bauer, 2010). As a type of *location flexibility*, WFH should operate as just such a resource and should therefore reduce work–family conflict. At the same time, however, scholars point out that WFH can risk blurring the boundaries between work and family lives and thus exacerbate such conflict (Ashforth et al., 2000; Kossek et al., 2006). Corresponding to these ambivalent ideas are the results of empirical research regarding WFH, which have also been inconsistent (for an overview, see Allen et al., 2015). Reports have indicated both positive and negative effects of WFH on work–family conflict, and these effects depend on many factors, including workplace culture (Abendroth & Reimann, 2018) and the intensity of WFH (Golden, 2006).

Before COVID-19 struck, WFH was not yet a widespread practice in Germany and its use was highly selective in terms of social groups, occupational positions, and economic sectors. For the most part, WFH was limited to a few days per month, which was a relatively small share of an employee's total working hours (Backhaus et al., 2019; Grunau et al., 2019), and the use of WFH was severely restrained for both employers and employees (Diewald, 2020; Lott & Abendroth, 2020). Thus, the typical drawback of existing studies was the highly selective and consequently small share of employees who worked from home. As employees who worked from home were often very similar in their family and work characteristics, their experiences of work–family conflict were likely to be comparably homogeneous as well. With the ongoing COVID-19 pandemic, the use of WFH has increased among many employees and their families and within many organizations, even among those who had not previously considered this option. In fact, in many instances, WFH has even been mandatory. Since WFH seems to have become more prevalent as a result of the pandemic, and since research has already indicated that both employees and employers wish to continue WFH once the pandemic is over, this form of flexible work will remain an important aspect of work and family processes (Erdsiek, 2021; Felstead & Reuschke, 2021).

This research aims to contribute to a better understanding of WFH during the COVID-19 pandemic, as well as to the general research on the interactions between flexible work and family life, in the following three ways:

First, this study investigates work–family conflict that exists in both directions – WFC and FWC – in order to further elucidate the permeability of family and work boundaries when family members work from home.

Second, this contribution asks whether the location flexibility provided by WFH is enough to help facilitate work–life integration. To illuminate the relevance of additional dimensions of flexible work, this contribution focuses on temporal flexibility, job autonomy, and the existence of fixed rules about availability as a way to measure boundary-setting possibilities. In addition, the study asks whether workers in families with greater care responsibilities – especially parents with young children and individuals who care for other dependent relatives – can especially benefit from additional flexibility opportunities.

Third, this study aims to determine whether supportive relationships with co-workers and supervisors can operate as resources to avoid work–family conflict when employees work from home and whether those relationships can enforce the benefits of flexible working. Employees who work from home are considered to be still embedded within social and organizational work processes with their co-workers and supervisors (Fay & Kline, 2012). Previous research has focused on the WFH situations of individual employees, not least because of the low prevalence of WFH. Although studies have confirmed that, overall, supportive relationships with supervisors and co-workers are important indicators of work–family conflict (Bakker et al., 2005; Beauregard, 2011; O'Driscoll et al., 2003), evidence is scarce when it comes to the implications of supervisors' and co-workers' WFH on employees' work–family conflict and whether these relationships encourage or exacerbate conflict.

To address these research questions, this study draws on cross-sectional German linked employer–employee data collected from February through May 2021. Thus, the empirical investigation will provide new insights into the work–family conflict experiences of employees after one year of the pandemic. Analyzing data from a heterogeneous sample of 885 employees from 18 organizations accounts for the clustering of employees in different organizations that might differ in terms of the conditions for WFH as well as for work–life integration in general.

2. WFH AND WORK–FAMILY CONFLICT: THE IMPORTANCE OF FLEXIBILITY

Before COVID-19 hit Germany, the option of WFH was of only marginal interest in political, societal, and scientific debates. In 2019, only 12 per cent of dependent employees worked from home from time to time, and instances of WFH were highly selective, its use being more likely among those in higher-level positions, in specific jobs or occupations, and in specific economic sectors (such as the information and communication sector); among men; and among those who were highly educated (Backhaus et al., 2019; Grunau et al., 2019; Mergener, 2020). In many organizations, WFH already existed as part of their family-friendly workplace policies as a way to improve work–life integration, although it was mostly enacted as a concession to privileged staff rather than being an option offered to all employees (Abendroth & Diewald, 2019; Marx et al., 2021). Moreover, employees who took advantage of this option were seen as being less committed to their work and less dedicated to their employer, which led to stereotyping and stigmatization (Chung & van der Horst, 2020; Konrad & Yang, 2012).

As in most other countries of the Global North, curbing the spread of COVID-19 in Germany during the first wave of the pandemic became a political and societal priority beginning in mid-March 2020 (for a detailed review, see, e.g., Buthe et al., 2020). In response to rigorous restrictions on personal contact, employers were obligated to offer WFH to as many employees as possible, and during the first few months of the pandemic about 25 per cent of the working population began WFH (Möhring et al., 2020). Relocating the workplace to employees' homes was important for maintaining productivity and protecting against the health risks posed by COVID-19 infection (Alipour et al., 2020). Scholars have described this situation as the "largest homeworking experiment in history" (Felstead & Reuschke, 2021, p. 2). However, the share of employees who worked from home varied greatly between sectors and between different organizations, ranging from almost none to 100 per cent (Erdsiek, 2021). Patterns that had existed previously remained the same on the individual level – that is, employees with higher education, higher income, and occupations in the service sector were more likely to switch to WFH during the pandemic (Hoenig & Wenz, 2021; Moehring et al., 2021). Though parents who were employed had to compensate for the lack of external childcare because of the need for home-schooling and because childcare facilities were closed (Kohlrausch & Zucco, 2020; Müller et al., 2020; Zoch et al., 2021b), empirical findings showed that such parents were not more likely to choose WFH and that the decision to work from home could be predicted based mostly on differences in job characteristics (Hipp & Bünning, 2021).

2.1. Work–Family Conflict

Among researchers who study the work–life interface, it is basically assumed that when individuals are engaged in different life spheres, they are also obligated to meet the different demands, values, and functions of those domains (Burkart, 2005; Parsons, 1949; Voydanoff, 2002). Inter-role conflicts (Kahn et al., 1964) are one of the most prominent subjects in the study of work–life integration, assuming that role requirements in one's various life domains compete for individual time and energy and may lead to conflict as one tries to reconcile these demands. Inter-role conflict that arises from the specific interaction of work and family demands are referred to as "work–family conflict" (Greenhaus & Beutell, 1985). These conflict may occur when participation in the work role makes meeting requirements in the family role more difficult – work-to-family conflict (WFC) (Greenhaus & Beutell, 1985) – or vice versa, family-to-work conflict (FWC) (Gutek et al., 1991; Netemeyer et al., 1996). A large body of literature has investigated the relevance of demands and resources in both the work life and the family life of employees as a way to explain workers' WFC and FWC experiences (for overviews, see, e.g., Bakker & Demerouti, 2017; Lesener et al., 2018; Michel et al., 2011). *Demands* are assumed to consist of aspects of work or family life that require physical or psychological effort that will increase the likelihood of conflict (Bakker & Demerouti, 2007; Frone et al., 1992; Voydanoff, 2004). *Resources* include those aspects of family or work life that either help a person handle certain demands or are directly effective in avoiding strain (Bakker et al., 2005).

2.2. Flexible Work and Work–Family Conflict

Flexible work may be considered as a job resource that allows for more individualized scheduling of work obligations and should consequently reduce a person's experiences of WFC and FWC (Allen et al., 2013; Hill et al., 2010; Schieman & Glavin, 2008). Flexible work is described as an opportunity to make decisions about where, when, and for how long the employee's time and effort is spent on work-related tasks (Hill et al., 2008). It can involve the location of one's work (*flexiplace*), the timing of one's work (*temporal flexibility* or *flexitime*) (Shockley & Allen, 2007), and the choices about what work one should do and how to do it (also known as *[job] autonomy*) (Baillien et al., 2011; Hackman & Oldham, 1976; Liu et al., 2005).

According to work–family border theory (Clark, 2000) and boundary management theory (Kossek, 2016), the ability to control the location and timing of one's obligations may allow work tasks to be flexibly coordinated with family requirements; therefore, different forms of flexible work should operate as resources that can mitigate or even prevent conflict between these two life spheres. Indeed, studies have indicated that flexibility with regard to the time and place of work is associated with less work–family conflict (Byron, 2005; Gallie & Russell, 2009; Nijp et al., 2012; Shockley & Allen, 2007) and that autonomy in particular is related to fewer conflict (Golden et al., 2006; Michel et al., 2011; Schieman & Young, 2013); in contrast, other studies have found no such relationship (Anderson et al., 2002; Mesmer-Magnus & Viswesvaran, 2006; Thomas & Ganster, 1995) or have even reported an increase in conflict (Felstead & Henseke, 2017).

This ambivalent role of flexible work applies especially to WFH, which is the most common form of location flexibility because it allows employees to transfer some or all of their work tasks to their home and thus be able to carry them out remotely instead of having to work on-site at the workplace (for an overview, see Allen et al., 2015). Meta-analyses have shown that WFH is significantly related to both lower WFC and lower FWC (Gajendran & Harrison, 2007), but other meta-analyses indicate higher levels of WFC when additional dimensions of flexible work are taken into consideration (Allen et al., 2013). The possible negative impacts of WFH are usually explained by an increased blurring of boundaries between the two life spheres. To avoid the blending of different roles, the transitions and shifts between work and family roles are important; however, when one works in the home, switching between roles makes such segmentation difficult (Ashforth et al., 2000; Kossek et al., 2006). In the case of WFH, the work and family domains share the same environment, with no physical barriers between the respective activities, so work tends to directly interfere with family life and vice versa. Such interference is common when there is no separate work space and when WFH takes place in the living room or the kitchen. The need to meet domestic responsibilities is an everpresent concern while one is trying to work and, conversely, the work area is always in sight during one's leisure time or while spending time with the children or a partner. This struggle may be especially evident during the COVID-19 pandemic, with everyone being at home most of the time. With children and/or a partner always present, the activities of other household members are likely to lead to more interruptions and thus to more conflict (Solís, 2016).

With the constant presence and availability of technological tools that are important for communication (e.g., smartphones, e-mail), the ability to separate work and family life is further constrained. Employees who work from home tend to set fewer boundaries when using these tools for work-related communication, even during non-working hours (Boswell & Olson-Buchanan, 2007; Olson-Buchanan & Boswell, 2006). The ability to control boundaries also depends on individual preferences with regard to role segmentation versus role integration, but it is also associated with emotional exhaustion (Piszczek, 2017). Having to manage boundaries more often may not only directly counteract the benefits of WFH but also may indirectly increase work–family conflict by depleting individual resources. Moreover, although WFH can help employees balance their work and family requirements, those who work from home may be expected to be available to accept more domestic obligations (e.g., Hammer et al., 2005), such as childcare, housework, or handling parcel deliveries or repair services. Although these additional responsibilities may not be a problem if they can be scheduled during work breaks, they are still likely to result in unplanned disruptions that disturb one's concentration or hamper work-related communications. Overall, these "micro–transitions" (Ashforth et al., 2000) between work and family roles can occur throughout the day, increasing inter-role interruptions and distractions and resulting in more opportunities for role conflict.

2.3. The Need for Additional Flexibility When Working from Home

Based on these ambiguous aspects of WFH, location flexibility alone seems insufficient as a way to avoid work–family conflict, so additional forms of flexible work will be required. Despite its flexibility potentials, WFH may be affected to the extent that it interacts with other dimensions of flexible work (Golden et al., 2006); however, the availability of these different dimensions varies between organizations as well as between individual employees (Kelly & Kalev, 2006; Stavrou, 2005). WFH arrangements may not be beneficial for everyone generally, and temporal flexibility, job autonomy, and rules for setting boundaries between work and family lives may be seen as resources for all employees. These other flexibility dimensions seem to be particularly important in making the best use of the WFH potentials. In contrast, if employees who work from home are not granted additional forms of flexibility, it is possible that WFH could even increase work–family conflict.

Though WFH offers flexibility in terms of one's work location, it does not always allow the employee to be flexible in terms of time or autonomy or to set availability boundaries between work and family times. For example, some employees may be required to log in to their computer terminals according to a specific time schedule, some may be bound to fixed daily or weekly tasks, and in some cases their work may be continuously monitored. When one works from home, it is important to have opportunities to interrupt the work when necessary and to arrange for tasks to be scheduled during times when it is quieter and there will be fewer interruptions. The greater one's ability to follow these principles, the less likely it is that work demands will interfere with the family situation, thus reducing the chances of WFC. Such measures are also be important when it comes to FWC; by postponing and rearranging their work tasks more flexibly, employees are able to deal with family issues more expeditiously and effectively, and family responsibilities will therefore interfere less with their work.

Moreover, as has become clear regarding the blurring of boundaries, fixed rules regarding one's availability can be important as well. At first sight, fixed rules may seem to contradict the flexibility argument, since individuals cannot schedule their work time around family life if they are required to be available for work at specific times. Then again, such rules define at which times those who work from home should be available so that their supervisors, co-workers, or customers can get in touch with them as needed – and at which time they do not have to be accessible and work time is over. Especially during lockdowns, one's sense of time is altered (Cellini et al., 2020), and fixed rules about availability are helpful for drawing lines between work and family life (Olson-Buchanan & Boswell, 2006) and thus avoiding conflict in both the WFC and the FWC directions.

In sum, additional flexibility seems to be of value when one works from home, and temporal flexibility, job autonomy, and fixed rules about availability should be deemed important for handling work and family demands and for reducing both WFC and FWC. As those forms of flexibility can be important for both WFC and FWC, hypotheses are more explorative regaining differences between the two directions of work–family conflict.

> *H1a.* Temporal flexibility, job autonomy, and fixed rules about availability are associated with lower levels of work–family conflict among employees WFH.

Although these three additional dimensions of flexible work arrangements should be beneficial for all employees who work from home, the degree of benefit may vary significantly between individuals, particularly depending on the family situation and one's family responsibilities. Overall, individuals with greater family responsibilities experience work–family conflict more strongly because the demands of family life are more likely to come into conflict with work obligations, and vice versa. Compared with workers who have no children, parents report higher levels of both WFC and FWC (Innstrand et al., 2010; Nomaguchi, 2009; Winslow, 2005). Having young children is especially associated with higher WFC and FWC because of the parents' time-consuming investments in care (Allen & Finkelstein, 2014; Gallie & Russell, 2009; Martinengo et al., 2010). During the COVID-19 pandemic, strict contact restrictions meant that parents had to compensate when external childcare was unavailable or uncertain or when they could not rely on support from family members outside the immediate household (C. Collins et al., 2020; Zoch et al., 2021b). Parents with young children (early school-age or younger) have time-sensitive demands within the family domain, since childcare is necessary throughout the day and the risks of blurring boundaries might be more significant than for individuals without such responsibilities. A similar point can be made for those working at home who must care for other dependent relatives, such as their parents or siblings. Studies carried out during the pandemic have already reported that parents experience difficulties in trying to satisfy the demands of both family and work lives, which leads to frustration in both spheres (Huebener et al., 2021; Möhring et al., 2021; Zoch et al., 2021a). Findings concerning the relationship between parents' dual demands and work–family conflict, however, have been inconsistent (Buschmeyer et al., 2021; Reimann et al., 2022; Schieman et al., 2021), and empirical evidence with regard to those who have care responsibilities other than childcare is lacking. Still, WFH along with the need to compensate for the lack of childcare outside the home was found to increase parents' FWC, especially for fathers (Reimann et al., 2022).

Thus, employees with younger children and those with other care responsibilities should especially benefit from additional forms of flexibility when they work from home, which leads to the following hypothesis:

> *H1b*. The association of all forms of flexibility with lower levels of work–family conflict is stronger for individuals with greater care responsibilities than for those without specific care requirements.

2.4. WFH and Relationships with Co-Workers and Supervisors

Now that the importance of different dimensions of flexibility for employees who work from home have been highlighted, the attention will be turned to the ways in which relationships with supervisors and co-workers are relevant to experiences of WFC and FWC, as well as how the benefits of flexibility may be either reinforced or mitigated by those relationships.

Relationships and interactions in the workplace are an important element in organizational life (Ferris et al., 2009), and among these, interpersonal relationships can act as direct resources for providing emotional and practical support (Bakker & Demerouti, 2007). These relationships are also indirectly relevant because they allow for the informal exchange of knowledge and information (Chiaburu & Harrison, 2008; Fay & Kline, 2011). Furthermore, support from supervisors plays a key role in the acceptance and administration of WFH arrangements (Lautsch et al., 2009). This role is important, since supervisors may have their own set of concerns associated with WFH that are not necessarily consistent with the attitudes of their employers and co-workers. Overall, supportive relationships with co-workers and supervisors are associated with fewer work–family conflict (Bakker et al., 2005; Beauregard, 2011; O'Driscoll et al., 2003). Moreover, prior research has indicated that, when one is WFH, it is the quality of the relationship that matters and not the frequency of interactions (Beauregard et al., 2013; Fay & Kline, 2011; 2012). Therefore, supportive relationships should generally operate as resources that could directly reduce work–family conflict experiences among employees who work from home. However, to understand the specific role of supervisors and co-workers when it comes to the individual experiences of work–family conflict among employees, it is important to see how WFH may alter work relationships and interactions (Dambrin, 2004).

Obviously, the nature of the communications with supervisors and co-workers changes when employees are working away from the office. Frequent face-to-face interactions are thought to facilitate the development of high-quality relationships (Barry & Crant, 2000), and despite the increased importance of digital communication technologies, face-to-face communication is still an important element within organizational processes (Reimann et al., 2020). WFH restricts regular face-to-face interactions between employees and their supervisors or co-workers, thereby forcing all parties to rely on electronic forms of communication, such as the telephone, e-mails, or digital communication platforms. The use of digital communication technologies offers temporal flexibility in that one can respond to such interactions at times that are convenient according to the individuals' schedules, but they also lack synchronicity and spontaneity (Golden, 2006). Exchanges with co-workers or supervisors who are also WFH or who are working on-site in the office are therefore less likely to contain the affective aspects of relationships that are necessary for forming supportive and good-quality relationships (Blau, 1964; Golden, 2006; Wayne et al., 1997). Similarly, WFH negatively affects the transfer of organizational information (Taskin & Bridoux, 2010). Moreover, the dependence on electronic forms of communication may make the coordination of work tasks more complicated and laborious, since direct feedback options are reduced and lively teamwork processes are made difficult (Knights & McCabe, 2003).

Because of the need for electronic communication and workers "not being there," employees may also be less visible to their co-workers and supervisors (Cooper & Kurland, 2002). From a supervisory perspective, this has implications for monitoring employees (Dambrin, 2004; van Dyne et al., 2007), but more importantly, it may lead to greater anonymity among the workforce. Employees may no longer be seen as individuals with personal characteristics (e.g., a mother with young children at home or a colleague who spreads good will in the office canteen) but instead may be viewed only as someone who is performing a professional function. Consequently, WFH might result in social and professional isolation (A. M. Collins et al., 2016; Kurland & Cooper, 2002), and research has shown that employees tend to socially distance themselves from those at the workplace because they experience less cohesiveness when nobody is around (Cohen & Bailey, 1997). This is important not only for the quality of social relationships, but also directly for the experience of WFC and FWC. As electronic interactions become more formalized and are focused on the exchange of very specific information (Taskin & Edwards, 2007), they are less likely to include critical discussions about sensitive topics, so that socio-emotional support for difficult issues may no longer be available (Wiesenfeld et al., 2001) and informal issues with regard to handling work and family responsibilities may be overlooked when communication is purely through electronic means (Golden, 2007).

Although evidence is lacking with regard to whether WFH by co-workers or supervisors is directly related to the individual employee's experiences of work–family conflict, one might reasonably infer the following two situations:

On the one hand, if more employees are WFH, and if the supervisor also works from home (Golden & Fromen, 2011), discussions about communication and interaction issues will be terser (Golden, 2007; Van der Lippe & Lippényi, 2020). Correspondingly, past research has shown that WFH did not harm co-worker relationships in general but it depended on the amount of time spent WFH – that is, the intensity of WFH (Gajendran & Harrison, 2007). Thus, it is important to consider WFH during the COVID-19 pandemic in particular, because in some cases the co-workers and supervisors are also all WFH. The situation might be more intense for direct supervisors, since they have a key position and are responsible for organizing the work, making final decisions, and mediating work and communication processes. Therefore, supervisors should be accessible, and their availability may be restricted if they are WFH.

On the other hand, positive implications are possible as well. If co-workers and supervisors work from home, they may have similar experiences with regard to the risks and benefits of WFH and will therefore better understand other employees' situations. Moreover, the more employees work at home, the more "normal" WFH becomes. This normalization might be particularly true during the COVID-19 pandemic, when a large proportion of workers work from home. If WFH is no longer reserved for a very specific minority but is a common practice among many employees, the individual is less likely to be stigmatized as someone whose performance or commitment is questionable. Consequently, the gap between those who work from home and those who work on-site at the workplace should shrink and invalidate the notion that those present at the workplace are in a more beneficial position. This new perspective should be mirrored in the quality and supportiveness of relationships with co-workers and supervisors. Therefore, it is not merely the number of co-workers and supervisors who work from home that might be a decisive factor when it comes to the experience of work–family conflict. Instead, the experience of conflict depends more on whether or not relationships with co-workers and supervisors are supportive, which leads to the following hypothesis:

> *H2*. The more supportive the relationships with co-workers and supervisors, the lower the levels of work–family conflict among employees WFH.

Finally, it can be suggested that supportive co-worker and supervisor relationships not only are directly relevant to the experience of WFC and FWC, but also foster the effects of flexibility. When relationships are supportive and of high quality, mutual trust is likely to be high (Grant-Vallone & Donaldson, 2001). In such cases, supervisors and co-workers may not be concerned about an employee's productivity during WFH (Bosua et al., 2013). Consequently, the supervisor might feel less obliged to constantly monitor employees, in turn allowing them more leeway (van Dyne et al., 2007). If one knows that supervisors and co-workers understand family demands, such as the need to care for children, employees need not fear being punished if they make use of flexibility opportunities. In contrast, if relationships are not supportive or of low quality, employees may be unable to profit from such flexibility, even if it is of a high degree. In this case, flexibility can be counteracted by poor work relationships. Therefore, relationships with supervisors and co-workers should moderate the association between different dimensions of flexible work and work–family conflict. The more supportive the relationships, the more likely it will be that temporal flexibility, job autonomy, and fixed rules about availability will help reduce work–family conflict, which led to the following moderation hypothesis:

> *H3*. The more supportive the relationships with supervisors and co-workers are, the more an employee's work flexibility is associated with lower levels of work–family conflict.

3. DATA AND METHODS

3.1. Data

The analyses were based on a cross-sectional, linked employer–employee data set that was collected as part of the study entitled "How can working from home succeed? Fair solutions in the view of employees and employers" in the context of COVID-19 research. The study was funded by the German Federal Ministry of Labor and Social Affairs (*Bundesministerium für Arbeit und Soziales* [BMAS]) and included small- and medium-sized as well as large organizations in Germany that employed between 15 and 1,500 workers. To recruit these organizations, the project was advertised on the web and through stakeholders. In all, 19 organizations were selected, which included several industrial sectors, although most were involved in production, information and communication, and social and economic or other services. Employer data were derived from guided interviews and additional web research designed to determine the implementation and regulation of WFH before and during the COVID-19 pandemic, the organizational culture, and the employee structure. Employee data were collected by means of an online survey. All participants were informed about the purpose of the study and about how the data would be used, and they were assured anonymity and were required to actively accept the conditions stipulated and to permit use of their voluntary responses to the survey within the context of the study. In the context of the employer–employee data linkage, employees could be linked to their respective organizations, but no information was obtained that could be used to identify individual employees.

Data were collected between February and May 2021 from a sample of 2,810 employees. Since the present analysis focused on the work–family conflict of employees who worked from home, the sample was then restricted to 1,007 employees who responded to the specific work and family subsection of the questionnaire. Employees for whom the values for independent variables were missing were then excluded (listwise deletion), resulting in a final sample of 885 employees from 18 organizations, which was used for all the analyses presented here. The WFH sample consisted of 52 per cent women and 48 per cent men; 40 per cent had children below the age of 18, and 19 per cent had to care for other relatives. A total of 59 per cent of the respondents worked in jobs that required a university degree (in applied sciences), compared with 41 per cent who worked in jobs that required vocational training or no occupational degree; 27 per cent of the employees had a management position with supervisory responsibilities. The sample included both full-time and part-time workers. The mean total number of working hours was 36.4, with an average of 26.7 hours worked at home at the time of the survey. All respondents were regularly employed, but the sample included 24 trainees and employees who worked marginal part-time (< 20 hours/week), as was evident in their lower gross earnings (< €1,000/month).

3.2. Measurements

Work–family conflict: The dependent variables WFC and FWC were measured using four items of the validated work–family conflict scale (Carlson et al., 2000).

Items were selected based on the highest factor loadings for the strain-based and time-based subscales reported by Carlson et al.: *time-based WFC* ("I have to miss family activities owing to the amount of time I must spend on work responsibilities"); *strain-based WFC* ("I am often so emotionally drained after work that it prevents me from contributing to my family"); *time-based FWC* ("Because of family obligations, I often have problems getting my work done"); and *strain-based FWC* ("Because I am often stressed owing to family responsibilities, I have a hard time concentrating on my work"). Each of these four items was assessed on a 5-point scale ranging from 0 ("Never") to 4 ("Very often"). The two respective scores for WFC and FWC were added up and divided by the number of items, resulting in a range between 0 and 4, with higher values indicating higher levels of conflict. The internal consistency of all dimensions was acceptable, with Cronbach's alpha coefficient of reliability exceeding the conventional level of acceptability (WFC: $\alpha = 0.62$; FWC: $\alpha = 0.63$). WFC and FWC were significantly but moderately correlated (corr = 0.33).

Flexible work: Temporal flexibility, job autonomy, and fixed rules about availability were included to consider the different dimensions of flexibility. All questions were assessed using 5-point scales ranging from 0 ("Does not apply at all") to 4 ("Applies completely"). *Temporal flexibility* was measured by asking whether employees could schedule their work times flexibly, and the existence of *fixed rules about availability* was determined by asking whether these rules were applied when employees worked from home. *Job autonomy* (Breaugh, 1985) was measured using respondents' scores on three items (such as "During my working hours, I have control over the sequencing of my work activities") that were then added up to obtain an index that ranged from 0 to 12, with higher values indicating greater job autonomy (Cronbach's $\alpha = 0.69$).

Relationships with the supervisor and co-workers: Relationships with the direct supervisor and co-workers were assessed in two different ways. First, employees were asked whether their informal and personal relationships (a) with the supervisor and (b) with co-workers suffered as a result of WFH. Both scales were positively reversed so that higher values indicated a *supervisor or co-worker relationship of higher quality*. Second, to assess the *work–family supportiveness* of their supervisors and co-workers, respondents were asked whether their (a) supervisors and (b) co-workers showed an understanding of family requirements and supported the employee during WFH. Relationship quality and work–family supportiveness correlated only minorly, both for supervisors (corr = 0.13) and for co-workers (corr = 0.10), suggesting that these are distinct constructs and should be considered separately. To account for *supervisors/co-workers working from home,* respondents were asked (a) how often their direct supervisor worked from home, differentiating among 0 ("Never"), 1 ("Sometimes"), and 2 ("Often/Regularly") and (b) what proportion of their co-workers worked from home at the time of the survey (0 = "Up to 50%", 1 = "More than 50%, 2 = "All").

Family situation: To account for an employee's family and care situation, the *age of the youngest child* in the household was used (0 = No child/or no child younger than 25 years of age in the household; 1 = age 0 to 6 years, 2 = age 7 to 11 years; 3 = age 12 to 18 years; 4 = age 19 to 25 years). The analyses also considered whether the employee had *other care responsibilities*, such as for an elderly relative (1 = Yes) and whether a *partner was also working from home* in the same household (0 = Partner not WFH; 1 = Partner WFH; 2 = No partner). To take into account gender inequalities in work–family conflict (e.g., Duxbury & Higgins, 1991; Nomaguchi, 2009) and to account for differences in care responsibilities between mothers and fathers (e.g., Bianchi et al., 2000; Gauthier et al., 2004), *gender* was included (1 = Female).

Co-variates: Several co-variates were chosen to account for differences in WFH: *Total working hours* and *share of working hours WFH* during COVID-19, whether employees had worked from home before the crisis (*WFH experiences pre-COVID-19*, 1 = Yes), and whether the *decision to work from home* was made by the employee or was required by the employer (0 = decision by employee, 1 = mandatory with exceptions, 2 = mandatory without exceptions). To consider different jobs and occupational statuses, the analyses included *main job activities* other than standard office activities (production, social services, customer-oriented services, research and development), having a *management position* (1 = Yes), and having the required *educational/occupational degree* (1 = University [of applied sciences]; 0 = Vocational training/none). To account for *company size*, the number of employees was included. Finally, to refer to the employee's life course perspective on work–life integration (Martinengo et al., 2010), *age* (categorized) was included.

3.3. Analytical Strategy

Having multiple employees in the same workplace violates the independence assumption in conventional OLS estimators (Rabe-Hesketh & Skrondal, 2012). Thus, multilevel linear regression models with robust standard errors were used to account for the two-level structure of the employer–employee data. The outcome variables WFC and FWC were used as quasi-metric variables in linear regression.[2] Standardized (mean = 0, standard deviation = 1) versions of all independent metric variables were used for the multivariate analyses. To test *H1a* and *H2*, multilevel linear regressions were conducted stepwise for both outcome variables WFC and FWC. To test for differences depending on (child)care responsibilities (*H1b*), the interaction terms of the flexible working variables with the age of the youngest child/care for other relatives were added. In a second step, the moderation hypothesis (*H3*) was tested by adding interaction terms to the comprehensive model and by interacting all three flexibility measures with all four relationship measures, resulting in a total of 12 possible interactions for WFC and FWC each. For all interactions, contrasts of the predictive margins were also tested to consider possible bias in interpreting the confidence intervals for the interactions (Belia et al., 2005).

3.3.1. Sensitivity Analyses and Further Analyses

Generally, all multivariate models included a set of covariates to adjust for several family, work, and socio-demographic characteristics. In addition, several sensitivity analyses were performed to check for the robustness of the results. The associations between temporal flexibility, job autonomy, fixed rules about availability, the relationship variables and WFC and FWC were tested for possible group differences. No statistically significant differences were found across gender and occupational position. Moreover, the linearity of the main independent variables was tested by re-estimating models with categorical variables. The linear assumptions were supported. Finally, all analyses were re-estimated for the strain-based and time-based subscales of WFC and of FWC, but the findings were very similar to those of the comprehensive measures.

4. RESULTS

4.1. Descriptive Results

Table 2.1 displays means and standard deviations for the unstandardized versions of all study variables. The average level of experienced WFC (1.56) was considerably higher as compared to the average FWC (0.57), which is in line with previous representative studies in Germany (e.g., Reimann et al., 2019). Among the employees who worked from home during the COVID-19 pandemic, 26.7 per cent had been WFH before the crisis, but to a considerably different degree – that is, before the pandemic, employees worked an average of 3.1 hours at home, compared with 26.6 hours during COVID-19. The unique situation during the

Table 2.1. Means and Standard Deviations of Unstandardized Study Variables.

Variables	*Mean*	*SD*	*Min*	*Max*
Work-to-family conflict	**1.56**	**1.02**	**0**	**4**
Family-to-work conflict	**0.57**	**0.73**	**0**	**4**
Temporal flexibility	3.17	0.90	0	4
Autonomy	9.11	1.99	1	12
Fixed rules about availability	2.36	1.06	0	4
Supervisor WFH: Never	0.12	0.33	0	1
Supervisor WFH: Sometimes	0.45	0.50	0	1
Supervisor WFH: Often	0.43	0.50	0	1
Co-workers WFH: Up to 50%	0.23	0.42	0	1
Co-workers WFH: More than 50%	0.53	0.50	0	1
Co-workers WFH: All	0.24	0.43	0	1
Co-worker relationship	1.68	1.26	0	4
Co-workers work–family supportive	3.24	0.97	0	4
Supervisor relationship	2.64	1.25	0	4
Supervisor work–family supportive	3.28	0.80	0	4
Total working hours overall	36.4	9.60	3	70
Share of working hours WFH	0.73	0.29	0.05	1
WFH experience pre-COVID-19	0.27	0.44	0	1
Decision WFH: by employee	0.11	0.31	0	1
Decision WFH: mandatory with exceptions	0.72	0.45	0	1
Decision WFH: mandatory without exceptions	0.17	0.37	0	1
Management position	0.27	0.44	0	1
Job requires university (of applied sciences) degree	0.59	0.49	0	1

Table 2.1. (*Continued*)

Variables	*Mean*	*SD*	*Min*	*Max*
Job (main activity): Production	0.32	0.46	0	1
Job (main activity): Social services	0.56	0.50	0	1
Job (main activity): Customer-oriented services	0.80	0.40	0	1
Female	0.52	0.50	0	1
Age: 16–24	0.04	0.20	0	1
Age: 25–34	0.26	0.44	0	1
Age: 35–44	0.27	0.44	0	1
Age: 45–54	0.24	0.43	0	1
Age: 55+	0.18	.039	0	1
Age of the youngest child in the household: no child/child >25 yrs old	0.54	0.50	0	1
Age of the youngest child in household: <=6 yrs old	0.20	0.40	0	1
Age of the youngest child in household: 7–11 yrs old	0.08	0.27	0	1
Age of the youngest child in household: 12–18 yrs old	0.12	0.32	0	1
Age of the youngest child in household: 19–25 yrs old	0.06	0.24	0	1
Care for other relatives	0.19	0.39	0	1
Partner WFH no	0.36	0.48	0	1
Partner WFH yes	0.41	0.49	0	1
No partner	0.23	0.42	0	1

Note: $N = 885$, WFH = working from home.

crisis becomes apparent when one looks at the decision to work from home: Only 11 per cent of the respondents decided to work from home on a completely voluntary basis, whereas 72 per cent of the employees received mandatory instructions for WFH from their employer, although exceptions were possible through consultation with the employer and/or direct supervisor. Only 17 per cent of employees were obliged to work from home by the employer with no possible exceptions.

4.2. *Multivariate Results*

Tables 2.2 and 2.3 show the results of the stepwise multilevel linear regressions on WFC and FWC. All models included the set of control variables. The first model in Table 2.2 (model 1a) tested *H1a* on the association between different dimensions of flexible work and WFC. The coefficients for all three dimensions of flexibility were statistically significant and negative. In line with *H1a*, the greater the temporal flexibility, the greater the job autonomy, and the more that fixed rules about availability existed, the less employees experienced WFC. However, the coefficient for job autonomy was only significant when based on a 10 per cent significance level. The first model in Table 2.3 (model 2a) indicated that the coefficient for temporal flexibility was not significant in the association with FWC, but higher job autonomy and more fixed rules about availability were related to lower levels of FWC as well. In direct comparison, differences in flexibility and co-variates were slightly better in explaining variation in WFC ($R^2 = 13.2\%$) than in FWC ($R^2 = 11.8\%$).

Table 2.2. Flexible Work, Social Relationships, and WFC.

	Flexibility (Model 1a)		Relationships (Model 1c)	
	Coef.	*SE*	*Coef.*	*SE*
Temporal flexibility	−0.116***	(0.032)	−0.091**	(0.030)
Autonomy	−0.045+	(0.026)	−0.019	(0.029)
Fixed rules about availability	−0.116***	(0.034)	−0.071*	(0.035)
Supervisor WFH (*ref. never*)				
Sometimes			0.014	(0.081)
Often			0.101	(0.119)
Co-workers WFH (*ref. up to 50%*)				
More than 50%			−0.055	(0.073)
All			−0.114	(0.099)
Co-worker relationship			−0.100**	(0.039)
Co-workers work–family supportive			0.024	(0.030)
Supervisor relationship			−0.118***	(0.027)
Supervisor work–family supportive			−0.145***	(0.030)
Controls	yes		yes	
Constant	*0.985****	*(0.229)*	*1.082****	*(0.245)*
R^2 Overall	13.2%		18.2%	

Notes: $N = 885$; Multilevel regression using robust standard errors (SE); + $p < 0.10$, * $p < 0.05$, ** $p < 0.01$, *** $p < 0.001$; WFH = Working from home; Controlled for total working hours overall, total working hours WFH, WFH experience, WFH mandatory, management position, education, job, company size, gender, age, age of youngest child in household, care for other relatives, partner WFH (for detailed results with all control variables see Table A2.1 in the Appendix); "How can working from home succeed?" Survey, own calculations.

Overall, parents with children below the age of 6 had significantly higher WFC and FWC than did other parents or parents without children (models 1a-c, 2a-c). Caring for other relatives was related to greater conflict in both directions as well. However, when compared with other employees, those who were parents with young children in the household or those who cared for other relatives did not benefit more from higher flexibility when WFH (the detailed models including the interaction terms can be found in models 1b and 2b; see Table A2.3 in the Appendix), at least in terms of WFC. When it comes to FWC, however, the impact of greater temporal flexibility when the youngest child in the household was 7 to 11 years of age was slightly stronger than it was for other parents or for individuals with no children in the household. Greater autonomy was more strongly associated with fewer FWC for individuals who cared for other relatives. In short, the assumption that additional flexibility when WFH would be particularly beneficial for those who had high care responsibilities (*H1b*) was only partly supported.

In a second step, variables on co-workers and supervisors WFH as well as on co-worker and supervisor supportiveness were added to the predictions to test *H2* on the relevance of co-worker and supervisor relationships (models 1c and 2c). No statistically significant coefficients were found for the share of co-workers/supervisors who worked from home. Thus, the fact that co-workers/supervisors worked from home in itself did not matter when it came to employees' WFC

Table 2.3. Flexible Work, Social Relationships, and FWC.

	Flexibility (Model 2a)		Relationships (Model 2c)	
	Coef.	*SE*	*Coef.*	*SE*
Temporal flexibility	−0.003	(0.014)	0.000	(0.017)
Fixed rules about availability	−0.085***	(0.016)	−0.071**	(0.022)
Autonomy	−0.072***	(0.017)	−0.047***	(0.014)
Supervisor WFH (*ref. never*)				
Sometimes			−0.052	(0.039)
Often			0.004	(0.051)
Co-workers WFH (*ref. up to 50%*)				
More than 50%			−0.068	(0.066)
All			0.014	(0.084)
Co-worker relationship			−0.083***	(0.018)
Co-workers work–family supportive			−0.062*	(0.029)
Supervisor relationship			−0.085+	(0.048)
Supervisor work–family supportive			−0.006	(0.016)
Controls	yes		yes	
Constant	*0.250****	*(0.184)*	*0.370****	*(0.207)*
R^2 Overall	11.8%		16.7%	

Notes: $N = 885$; Multilevel regression using robust standard errors (SE); + $p < 0.10$, * $p < 0.05$, ** $p < 0.01$, *** $p < 0.001$; WFH = Working from home; Controlled for total working hours overall, total working hours WFH, WFH experience, WFH mandatory, management position, education, job, company size, gender, age, age of youngest child in household, care for other relatives, partner WFH (for detailed results with all control variables see Table A2.2 in the Appendix); "How can working from home succeed?" Survey, own calculations.

or FWC experiences. However, statistically significant and negative coefficients were found for relationships with both co-workers and supervisors (model 1c). In line with *H2*, having good relationships with co-workers and supervisors was associated with experiences of fewer WFC. Work–family support, however, was helpful only in avoiding WFC when such support came from the supervisor. For the association with FWC (model 2c), statistically significant negative effects were observed for good relationships with co-workers and supervisors as well as for work–family support by co-workers but not for support by supervisors. In both regressions on WFC and FWC, the coefficients for the flexibility variables decreased when social relationships were accounted for, and the coefficient for job autonomy on WFC was no longer statistically significant. This provided evidence for the additional relevance of co-worker and supervisor relationships in the associations between flexible work dimensions and work–family conflict. Overall, the comprehensive models explained 18.2 per cent of the variation in WFC, with 16.7 per cent slightly less variation in FWC. An additional model excluding the co-variates revealed that the indicators for flexible work explained the variation in WFC slightly better than they explained the variation in FWC.

Finally, *H3* assumes that the benefits of flexible work with respect to WFC and FWC are fostered by supportive co-worker and supervisor relationships, whereas negative relationships might even counteract the benefits of flexibility. To test the assumptions concerning moderations, interactions between flexibility variables and relationship variables were added to the comprehensive regressions on WFC and FWC. Table 2.4 displays an overview of these interactions; the detailed models can be found in Tables A2.4 to A2.7 in the Appendix. Of the 12 possible interactions for each of the two outcome variables, five showed statistically significant interaction effects for WFC and only one showed an effect for FWC. In sum, the results partially supported *H3*. The negative relationships between temporal flexibility and WFC were more pronounced the better the quality of the relationship with the supervisor and the co-workers, and also the greater the work–family support from the supervisor. For job autonomy and fixed rules about availability, only a good-quality relationship with the supervisor seemed to be important. The results indicated only one statistically significant interaction for FWC. In contrast to *H3*, these findings revealed a reversed relationship: If employees had poor relationships with co-workers, temporal flexibility did not foster or mitigate FWC. However, the higher the quality of the relationships with co-workers, the more pronounced the experiences of FWC when temporal flexibility was available.

Fig. 2.1 illustrates the findings for the interaction between temporal flexibility and the work–family supportiveness of the supervisor. If an employee's supervisor was very supportive, high levels of temporal flexibility were significantly associated with lower levels of WFC. In contrast, if the supervisor was not supportive at all, temporal flexibility was counteracted and was associated with even more experiences of WFC. However, for those employees who received no work–family support from their supervisor, having no temporal flexibility was associated with fewer WFC, as compared with those who received a high level of work–family support.

Table 2.4. Overview of Moderation Analyses.

Flexibility Dimension	Number of Statistically Significant Moderation Effects	Statistically Significant Moderators
Temporal flexibility	3 of 4 (WFC)	Supervisor relationship (-), supervisor work–family supportive (-), co-workers work–family supportive (-)
	1 of 4 (FWC)	Co-worker relationship (+)
Job autonomy	1 of 4 (WFC)	Supervisor relationship (-)
	0 of 4 (FWC)	/
Fixed rules about availability	1 of 4 (WFC)	Supervisor relationship (-)
	0 of 4 (FWC)	/

Notes: Significance of moderation based on multilevel linear regressions with interaction terms and predicted margins; $p < 0.05$; $N = 885$. WFC = work-to-family conflict, FWC = family-to-work conflict; "How can working from home succeed?" Survey, own calculations.

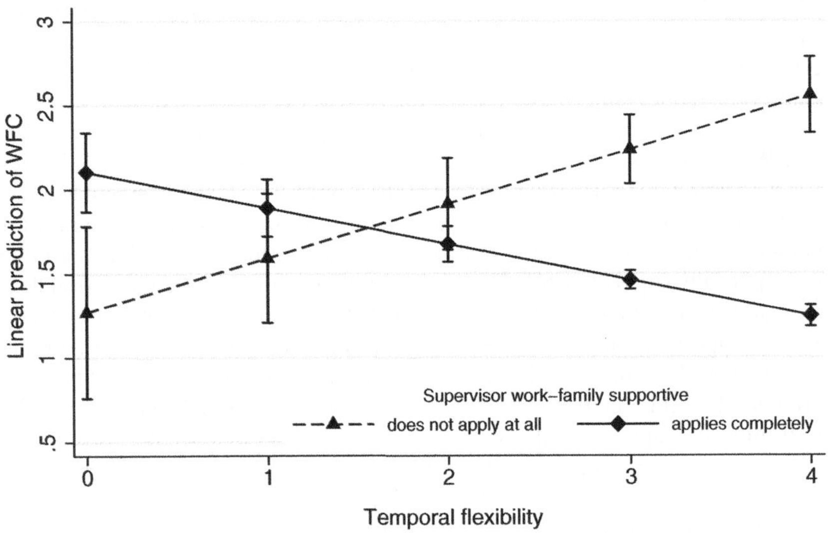

Fig. 2.1. Plotted Interaction of Temporal Flexibility#Supervisor Work–Family Support. *Notes*: Margins plot based on 95% confidence intervals; Only highest and lowest categories of supervisor support were plotted for simplification reasons, but values are based on the full predictions; WFC = Work-to-family conflict; "How can working from home succeed?" Survey, own calculations.

5. DISCUSSION

In the context of work–life research, WFH has been suggested as a form of flexible work to foster work–life integration, but research also points to its risks because of blurred boundaries between these two life domains (Allen et al., 2015; Kossek et al., 2006). During the COVID-19 pandemic, WFH has become the norm in many organizations (Erdsiek, 2021; Felstead & Reuschke, 2020), meaning that the positive and negative implications for work–life integration have become relevant for more employees than ever. Whether WFH during the extreme situation of the pandemic, in combination with parents' need to care for children at home and the lack of social activities and social contacts, is transferable to WFH that takes place under other circumstances is a question that needs to be critically examined. Yet, the situation offers an opportunity to learn about the mechanisms for positive and negative implications of WFH with regard to WFC and FWC. This study aimed to shed further light on the inconsistent findings regarding the relationship between flexible work and work–family conflict (Allen et al., 2013; Hill et al., 2010) by investigating different forms of flexibility (temporal flexibility, job autonomy, fixed rules about availability), as well as the implications of social relationships with co-workers and supervisors among employees who were WFH during the COVID-19 pandemic.

The results of this study, which was based on the linked employer–employee data that were collected in spring 2021, indicate that both WFC and FWC occur among employees who work from home, though the levels of FWC were significantly lower than those of WFC. Therefore, the study adds to the knowledge about the permeability of boundaries between work and family life during the pandemic situation by showing that WFH as a form of location flexibility (flexiplace) poses the risk that work obligations will interfere with employees' family life at home, but also that family responsibilities will impede employees' work life. Flexible work and social relationships with supervisors and co-workers are relevant to work–family conflict in both directions. More precisely, different forms of flexible work when one works from home operate as resources that can mitigate both WFC and FWC. Temporal flexibility is more important for experiencing lower levels of WFC, whereas job autonomy is more predictive when it comes to FWC. Fixed rules about availability as a way to set boundaries between work and family life, however, are important for both WFC and FWC. Parents of young children as well as those individuals who care for other relatives experience greater work–family conflict in both directions, whereas evidence that these employees are able to particularly benefit from additional dimensions of flexibility when they work from home is limited. Thus, the findings add to prior research on the relationship between flexible work and work–family conflict by providing empirical evidence that even when employees who work from home are afforded location flexibility, additional forms of flexibility are needed to foster work–life integration and that this is the case for all individuals and not particularly for those with greater care responsibilities.

Furthermore, supervisors and co-workers are important with respect to employees' experiences of WFC and FWC. It does not matter how often supervisors work from home or how many co-workers work from home; rather, experiences of WFC and FWC depend on whether these relationships are characterized by mutual understanding and support. Positive relationships can also reinforce the benefits of flexibility, whereas in the case of poor relationships, these benefits can be counteracted. In comparison, supervisors seem to be most important in this regard, which supports the idea that, as gatekeepers within organizations, not only do supervisors offer employees the option and the conditions to work from home, but they are also important for the implications for work–family conflict (Bakker et al., 2005; Beauregard, 2011; O'Driscoll et al., 2003).

Overall, the findings of this study represent important assets in the study of flexible work and work–family conflict. A major criticism of existing research on WFH is that the vast majority of the studies have relied on cross-sectional designs (Allen et al., 2015). However, this type of design has important limitations on causality assumptions because individuals with higher levels of WFC or FWC may intentionally choose WFH as a way to better manage their work and family roles. Though the present study cannot provide longitudinal evidence, studying the WFH–conflict relationship within the great experiment of WFH during the COVID-19 pandemic (Felstead & Reuschke, 2021) should help to account for the part played by mere individual decisions regarding WFH and thus to approximate an understanding of the mechanisms in this relationship. Employers based their instructions about WFH on current pandemic laws (with WFH being completely mandatory or it being made clear that employees were expected to work from home during the pandemic situation), thus leaving only marginal leeway for individual choices. Individual preferences, such as those regarding boundary management (Kossek et al., 2006), played only a subordinate role. Nevertheless, because individual preferences regarding role segmentation are very important when it comes to the use of technology in WFH (Piszczek, 2017), it is likely that these preference did not disappear in the context of obligatory WFH during the pandemic. Consequently, employees with strong segmentation preferences in particular might struggle with the challenges of setting boundaries when WFH. Therefore, future research should examine whether those preferences moderate the link between flexible work and work–family conflict among employees who work from home. Moreover, as WFH during COVID-19 has been made possible for many more different jobs and employee groups than was the case before the pandemic, the results of this study should help explain the experiences of work–family conflict among employees who work from home when it comes to the more heterogeneous sectors of the workforce. Therefore, the findings of this study may be more generalizable when compared with previous WFH studies that involved comparably homogeneous groups, despite the limitations attributable to the data used.

Some further limitations regarding the empirical findings of this study need to be considered. First, the data used for the analyses are not representative of all employees in Germany or of all employees who work from home. Therefore, the transferability of the results is limited. The study included data from small-, medium-, and large-sized organizations that employed between 15 and 1,500 workers, and the results regarding the association between flexible work and work–family conflict remained stable across the different company sizes. However, the data did not cover very small organizations that have fewer than 15 employees or self-employed persons who work solo. The situation may have been very different in those types of workplaces (e.g., in terms of the possibilities for WFH, decision making, the availability of social support by co-workers or supervisors), as well as for self-employed persons who have been hit especially hard by the COVID-19 crisis (Wolfe & Patel, 2021; Yue & Cowling, 2021). In these cases, the results are hardly transferable. Thus, further research is needed to look specifically at the situation of very small organizations and of the self-employed. Yet, the use of a heterogeneous sample that includes important socio-demographic characteristics, jobs, and occupations and is drawn from a cross-section of different workplaces, supplemented by various sensitivity analyses, strengthens the validity of the overall findings. Second, the use of cross-sectional data does not allow assumptions about causal relationships; thus, the results need to be re-evaluated using longitudinal data in future research. Finally, this study focused on WFH. However, different dimensions of flexible work, as well as employees' social relationships with supervisors and co-workers, may be similarly important for employees who work on-site at the workplace. Further research is needed to look at the implications for employees' experiences of work–family conflict during the COVID-19 pandemic for those who do not work from home.

From a practical perspective, the findings suggest that the implementation of WFH arrangements alone is not enough to foster work–life integration. Instead, employers need to provide employees who work from home with other forms of flexibility, such as temporal flexibility and job autonomy, and they should set clear rules about availability expectations during WFH for all employees. Also, attention should be paid to social relationships among employees, especially when they work from home. Providing opportunities for informal exchanges to sustain positive relationships despite the limitations of electronic communication and the lack of face-to-face contacts are promising practical approaches for increasing team productivity but also improving work–life integration for individual employee.

NOTES

1. There are many alternative terms for WFH, such as telework, telecommuting, or remote work [for a detailed overview, see Allen et al. (2015)]. Since the focus here is on people who transfer their work to their home setting, the umbrella term "working from home" (WFH) will be used to refer to the specific types.
2. All models were re-estimated with ordered logistic regressions to check for the robustness of results. Results from those analyses did not differ from the linear estimations.

ACKNOWLEDGMENT

This research project was funded by the German Federal Ministry of Labour and Social Affairs within the network for interdisciplinary policy research (grant number MPR.00.00006.20).

REFERENCES

Abendroth, A.-K., & Diewald, M. (2019). Auswirkungen von Teleheimarbeit auf geschlechtsspezifische Einkommensungleichheiten in Arbeitsorganisationen. *KZfSS Kölner Zeitschrift Für Soziologie Und Sozialpsychologie*, *71*(1), 81–109. https://doi.org/10.1007/s11577-019-00614-w

Abendroth, A.-K., & Reimann, M. (2018). Telework and work–family conflict across workplaces: Investigating the implications of work–family-supportive and high-demand workplace cultures. In S. Lee Blair & J. Obradović (Eds.), *Contemporary perspectives in family research: Vol. 13. The work-family interface: Spillover, complications, and challenges* (pp. 323–348). Emerald Publishing Limited. https://doi.org/10.1108/S1530-353520180000013017

Alipour, J.-V., Fadinger, H., & Schymik, J. (2021). My home is my castle – The benefits of working from home during a pandemic crisis. *Journal of Public Economics*, *196*, 104373. https://doi.org/10.1016/j.jpubeco.2021.104373

Alipour, J.-V., Falck, O., & Schüller, S. (2020). Homeoffice während der Pandemie und die Implikationen für eine Zeit nach der Krise (*ifo* Schnelldienst Vol *73, Issue 7*). *ifo Institut - Leibniz-Institut für Wirtschaftsforschung an der Universität München*. http://hdl.handle.net/10419/225150

Allen, T. D., & Finkelstein, L. M. (2014). Work-family conflict among members of full-time dual-earner couples: An examination of family life stage, gender, and age. *Journal of Occupational Health Psychology*, *19*(3), 376–384. https://doi.org/10.1037/a0036941

Allen, T. D., Golden, T. D., & Shockley, K. M. (2015). How effective is telecommuting? Assessing the status of our scientific findings. *Psychological Science in the Public Interest: A Journal of the American Psychological Society*, *16*(2), 40–68. https://doi.org/10.1177/1529100615593273

Allen, T. D., Johnson, R. C., Kiburz, K. M., & Shockley, K. M. (2013). Work-family conflict and flexible work arrangements: Deconstructing flexibility. *Personnel Psychology*, *66*(2), 345–376. https://doi.org/10.1111/peps.12012

Anderson, S. E., Coffey, B. S., & Byerly, R. T. (2002). Formal organizational initiatives and informal workplace practices: Links to work-family conflict and job-related outcomes. *Journal of Management*, *28*(6), 787–810. https://doi.org/10.1177/014920630202800605

Ashforth, B. E., Kreiner, G. E., & Fugate, M. (2000). All in a Day'S Work: Boundaries and micro role transitions. *Academy of Management Review*, *25*(3), 472–491. https://doi.org/10.5465/amr.2000.3363315

Backhaus, N., Wöhrmann, A. M., & Tisch, A. (2019). *BAuA-Arbeitszeitbefragung: Telearbeit in Deutschland*. https://doi.org/10.21934/baua:berichtkompakt20191216

Baillien, E., Cuyper, N. de, & Witte, H. De (2011). Job autonomy and workload as antecedents of workplace bullying: A two-wave test of Karasek's Job Demand Control Model for targets and perpetrators. *Journal of Occupational and Organizational Psychology*, *84*(1), 191–208. https://doi.org/10.1348/096317910X508371

Bakker, A. B., & Demerouti, E. (2007). The job demands-resources model: State of the art. *Journal of Managerial Psychology*, *22*(3), 309–328. https://doi.org/10.1108/02683940710733115

Bakker, A. B., & Demerouti, E. (2017). Job demands-resources theory: Taking stock and looking forward. *Journal of Occupational Health Psychology*, *22*(3), 273–285. https://doi.org/10.1037/ocp0000056

Bakker, A. B., Demerouti, E., & Euwema, M. C. (2005). Job resources buffer the impact of job demands on burnout. *Journal of Occupational Health Psychology*, *10*(2), 170–180. https://doi.org/10.1037/1076-8998.10.2.170

Barry, B., & Crant, J. M. (2000). Dyadic communication relationships in organizations: An attribution/expectancy approach. *Organization Science*, *11*(6), 648–664. https://doi.org/10.1287/orsc.11.6.648.12537

Beauregard, T. A. (2011). Direct and indirect links between organizational work-home culture and employee well-being. *British Journal of Management*, *22*(2), 218–237. https://doi.org/10.1111/j.1467-8551.2010.00723.x

Beauregard, T. A., Basile, K., & Canonico, E. (2013). *Home is where the work is: A new study of homeworking in Acas–and beyond* [Acas research paper 10(13)].

Belia, S., Fidler, F., Williams, J., & Cumming, G. (2005). Researchers misunderstand confidence intervals and standard error bars. *Psychological Methods*, *10*(4), 389–396. https://doi.org/10.1037/1082-989X.10.4.389

Bianchi, S. M., Milkie, M. A., Sayer, L. C., & Robinson, J. P. (2000). Is anyone doing the housework? Trends in the gender division of household labor. *Social Forces*, *79*(1), 191–228. https://doi.org/10.1093/sf/79.1.191

Blau, P. M. (1964). *Exchange and power in social life*. Wiley.

Bosua, R., Gloet, M., Kurnia, S., Mendoza, A., & Yong, J. (2013). Telework, productivity and wellbeing: an Australian perspective. *Telecommunications Journal of Australia*, *63*(1). https://doi.org/10.7790/tja.v63i1.390

Boswell, W. R., & Olson-Buchanan, J. B. (2007). The use of communication technologies after hours: The role of work attitudes and work-life conflict. *Journal of Management*, *33*(4), 592–610. https://doi.org/10.1177/0149206307302552

Breaugh, J. A. (1985). The measurement of work autonomy. *Human Relations*, *38*(6), 551–570. https://doi.org/10.1177/001872678503800604

Bujard, M., den Driesch, E. von, Kerstin, R., Laß, I., Thönnissen, C., Schumann, A., & Schneider, N. (2021). Belastungen von Kindern, Jugendlichen und Eltern in der Corona-Pandemie. *Wiesbaden. Bundesinstitut für Bevölkerungsforschung*. https://doi.org/10.12765/bro-2021-02

Burkart, G. (2005). Die Familie in der Systemtheorie. In G. Runkel & G. Burkart (Eds.), *Funktionssysteme der Gesellschaft* (pp. 101–128). VS Verlag für Sozialwissenschaften. https://doi.org/10.1007/978-3-322-80782-3_6

Buschmeyer, A., Ahrens, R., & Zerle-Elsäßer, C. (2021). Das gute Leben in der Krise – Geschlechterverhältnisse auf dem Prüfstand. GENDER – Zeitschrift Für Geschlecht, *Kultur Und Gesellschaft*, *13*(2-2021), 11–28. https://doi.org/10.3224/gender.v13i2.02

Buthe, T., Messerschmidt, L., & Cheng, C. (2020). Policy responses to the Coronavirus in Germany. *SSRN Electronic Journal*. Advance online publication. https://doi.org/10.2139/ssrn.3614794

Byron, K. (2005). A meta-analytic review of work–family conflict and its antecedents. *Journal of Vocational Behavior*, *67*(2), 169–198. https://doi.org/10.1016/j.jvb.2004.08.009

Carlson, D. S., Kacmar, K. M., & Williams, L. J. (2000). Construction and initial validation of a multidimensional measure of work–family conflict. *Journal of Vocational Behavior*, *56*(2), 249–276. https://doi.org/10.1006/jvbe.1999.1713

Cellini, N., Canale, N., Mioni, G., & Costa, S. (2020). Changes in sleep pattern, sense of time and digital media use during COVID-19 lockdown in Italy. *Journal of Sleep Research*, *29*(4), e13074. https://doi.org/10.1111/jsr.13074

Chiaburu, D. S., & Harrison, D. A. (2008). Do peers make the place? Conceptual synthesis and meta-analysis of coworker effects on perceptions, attitudes, OCBs, and performance. *Journal of Applied Psychology*, *93*(5), 1082–1103. https://doi.org/10.1037/0021-9010.93.5.1082

Chung, H., & van der Horst, M. (2020). Flexible working and unpaid overtime in the UK: The role of gender, parental and occupational status. *Social Indicators Research*, *151*(2), 495–520. https://doi.org/10.1007/s11205-018-2028-7

Clark, S. C. (2000). Work/family border theory: A new theory of work/family balance. *Human Relations*, *53*(6), 747–770. https://doi.org/10.1177/0018726700536001

Cohen, S. G., & Bailey, D. E. (1997). What makes teams work: Group effectiveness research from the shop floor to the executive suite. *Journal of Management*, *23*(3), 239–290. https://doi.org/10.1177/014920639702300303

Collins, A. M., Hislop, D., & Cartwright, S. (2016). Social support in the workplace between teleworkers, office-based colleagues and supervisors. *New Technology, Work and Employment*, *31*(2), 161–175. https://doi.org/10.1111/ntwe.12065

Collins, C., Landivar, L. C., Ruppanner, L., & Scarborough, W. J. (2020). Covid-19 and the gender gap in work hours. *Gender, Work & Organization. Advance online publication*. https://doi.org/10.1111/gwao.12506

Cooper, C. D., & Kurland, N. B. (2002). Telecommuting, professional isolation, and employee development in public and private organizations. *Journal of Organizational Behavior*, *23*(4), 511–532. https://doi.org/10.1002/job.145

Dambrin, C. (2004). How does telework influence the manager-employee relationship? *International Journal of Human Resources Development and Management*, *4*(4), Article 5044, 358. https://doi.org/10.1504/IJHRDM.2004.005044

Diewald, M. (2020). Zukunftsperspektiven von Homeoffice nach Corona. In J. Nachtwei & A. Sureth (Eds.), *HR Consulting Review: Vol. 12. Sonderband Zukunft der Arbeit* (pp. 30–34).

Duxbury, L. E., & Higgins, C. A. (1991). Gender differences in work-family conflict. *Journal of Applied Psychology*, *76*(1), 60–74. https://doi.org/10.1037/0021-9010.76.1.60

Duxbury, L. E., Higgins, C. A., & Lee, C. (1994). Work-family conflict: A comparison by gender, family type, and perceived control. *Journal of Family Issues*, *15*(3), 449–466. https://doi.org/10.1177/019251394015003006

Erdsiek, D. (2021). Working from home during COVID-19 and BEYOND: Survey evidence from employers. *SSRN Electronic Journal*. Advance online publication. https://doi.org/10.2139/ssrn.3875337

Fay, M. J., & Kline, S. L. (2011). Coworker relationships and informal communication in high-intensity telecommuting. *Journal of Applied Communication Research*, *39*(2), 144–163. https://doi.org/10.1080/00909882.2011.556136

Fay, M. J., & Kline, S. L. (2012). The influence of informal communication on organizational identification and commitment in the context of high-intensity telecommuting. *Southern Communication Journal*, *77*(1), 61–76. https://doi.org/10.1080/1041794x.2011.582921

Felstead, A., & Henseke, G. (2017). Assessing the growth of remote working and its consequences for effort, well-being and work-life balance. *New Technology, Work and Employment*, *32*(3), 195–212. https://doi.org/10.1111/ntwe.12097

Felstead, A., & Reuschke, D. (2020). *Homeworking in the UK: Before and During the 2020 Lockdown (WISERD Report)*. Wales Institute of Social and Economic Research. https://wiserd.ac.uk/publications/homeworking-uk-and-during-2020-lockdown

Felstead, A., & Reuschke, D. (2021). A flash in the pan or a permanent change? The growth of homeworking during the pandemic and its effect on employee productivity in the UK. *Information Technology & People*, ahead-of-print. https://doi.org/10.1108/ITP-11-2020-0758

Ferris, G. R., Liden, R. C., Munyon, T. P., Summers, J. K., Basik, K. J., & Buckley, M. R. (2009). Relationships at work: Toward a multidimensional conceptualization of dyadic work relationships. *Journal of Management*, *35*(6), 1379–1403. https://doi.org/10.1177/0149206309344741

Frone, M. R., Russell, M., & Cooper, M. (1992). Prevalence of work-family conflict: Are work and family boundaries asymmetrically permeable? *Journal of Organizational Behavior*, *13*(7), 723–729. http://www.jstor.org/stable/2488392

Gajendran, R. S., & Harrison, D. A. (2007). The good, the bad, and the unknown about telecommuting: Meta-analysis of psychological mediators and individual consequences. *Journal of Applied Psychology*, *92*(6), 1524–1541. https://doi.org/10.1037/0021-9010.92.6.1524

Gallie, D., & Russell, H. (2009). Work-family conflict and working conditions in Western Europe. *Social Indicators Research*, *93*(3), 445–467. https://doi.org/10.1007/s11205-008-9435-0

Gauthier, A. H., Smeeding, T. M., & Furstenberg, F. F. (2004). Are parents investing less time in children? Trends in selected industrialized countries. *Population and Development Review*, *30*(4), 647–672. https://doi.org/10.1111/j.1728-4457.2004.00036.x

Golden, T. D. (2006). The role of relationships in understanding telecommuter satisfaction. *Journal of Organizational Behavior*, *27*(3), 319–340. https://doi.org/10.1002/job.369

Golden, T. D. (2007). Co-workers who telework and the impact on those in the office: Understanding the implications of virtual work for co-worker satisfaction and turnover intentions. *Human Relations; Studies Towards the Integration of the Social Sciences*, *60*(11), 1641–1667. https://doi.org/10.1177/0018726707084303

Golden, T. D., & Fromen, A. (2011). Does it matter where your manager works? Comparing managerial work mode (traditional, telework, virtual) across subordinate work experiences and outcomes. *Human Relations; Studies Towards the Integration of the Social Sciences*, *64*(11), 1451–1475. https://doi.org/10.1177/0018726711418387

Golden, T. D., Veiga, J. F., & Simsek, Z. (2006). Telecommuting's differential impact on work-family conflict: Is there no place like home? *Journal of Applied Psychology*, *91*(6), 1340–1350. https://doi.org/10.1037/0021-9010.91.6.1340

Grant-Vallone, E. J., & Donaldson, S. I. (2001). Consequences of work-family conflict on employee well-being over time. *Work & Stress*, *15*(3), 214–226. https://doi.org/10.1080/02678370110066544

Greenhaus, J. H., & Beutell, N. J. (1985). Sources of conflict between work and family roles. *Academy of Management Review*, *10*(1), 76–88. https://doi.org/10.5465/AMR.1985.4277352

Grunau, P., Ruf, K., Steffes, S., & Wolter, S. (2019). Homeoffice bietet Vorteile, hat aber auch Tücken (IAB-Kurzbericht; no. 11/2019). Nürnberg.

Gutek, B. A., Searle, S., & Klepa, L. (1991). Rational versus gender role explanations for work-family conflict. *Journal of Applied Psychology*, *76*(4), 560–568. https://doi.org/10.1037/0021-9010.76.4.560

Hackman, J., & Oldham, G. R. (1976). Motivation through the design of work: Test of a theory. *Organizational Behavior and Human Performance*, *16*(2), 250–279. https://doi.org/10.1016/0030-5073(76)90016-7

Hammer, L. B., Neal, M. B., Newsom, J. T., Brockwood, K. J., & Colton, C. L. (2005). A longitudinal study of the effects of dual-earner couples' utilization of family-friendly workplace supports on work and family outcomes. *Journal of Applied Psychology*, *90*(4), 799–810. https://doi.org/10.1037/0021-9010.90.4.799

Hill, E. J., Erickson, J. J., Holmes, E. K., & Ferris, M. (2010). Workplace flexibility, work hours, and work-life conflict: Finding an extra day or two. *Journal of Family Psychology*, *24*(3), 349–358. https://doi.org/10.1037/a0019282

Hill, E. J., Grzywacz, J. G., Allen, S., Blanchard, V. L., Matz-Costa, C., Shulkin, S., & Pitt-Catsouphes, M. (2008). Defining and conceptualizing workplace flexibility. *Community, Work & Family*, *11*(2), 149–163. https://doi.org/10.1080/13668800802024678]

Hipp, L., & Bünning, M. (2021). Parenthood as a driver of increased gender inequality during COVID-19? Exploratory evidence from Germany. *European Societies*, *23*(sup1), S658–S673. https://doi.org/10.1080/14616696.2020.1833229

Hoenig, K., & Wenz, S. E. (2021). Education, health behavior, and working conditions during the pandemic: Evidence from a German sample. *European Societies*, *23*(sup1), S275–S288. https://doi.org/10.1080/14616696.2020.1824004

Huebener, M., Waights, S., Spiess, C. K., Siegel, N. A., & Wagner, G. G. (2021). Parental well-being in times of Covid-19 in Germany. *Review of Economics of the Household*, (19), 91–122. https://doi.org/10.1007/s11150-020-09529-4

Innstrand, S. T., Langballe, E. M., Espnes, G. A., Aasland, O. G., & Falkum, E. (2010). Work–home conflict and facilitation across four different family structures in Norway. *Community, Work & Family*, *13*(2), 231–249. https://doi.org/10.1080/13668800903314341

Kahn, R. L., Wolfe, D. M., Quinn, R. P., & Snoek, J. D. (1964). *Organizational stress: Studies in role conflict and ambiguity*. Wiley.

Kelly, E. L., & Kalev, A. (2006). Managing flexible work arrangements in US organizations: Formalized discretion or 'a right to ask'. *Socio-Economic Review*, *4*(3), 379–416. https://doi.org/10.1093/ser/mwl001

Knights, D., & McCabe, D. (2003). Governing through Teamwork: Reconstituting Subjectivity in a *Call Centre Journal of Management Studies*, *40*(7), 1587–1619. https://doi.org/10.1111/1467-6486.00393

Kohlrausch, B., & Zucco, A. (2020). Die Corona-Krise Trifft Frauen Doppelt. Düsseldorf: WSI Policy Brief, pp. 1–14. [WSI Policy Brief No. 40]. Hans-Böckler-Stiftung, Wirtschafts- und Sozialwissenschaftliches Institut (WSI), Düsseldorf.

Konrad, A. M., & Yang, Y. (2012). Is using work-life interface benefits a career-limiting move? An examination of women, men, lone parents, and parents with partners. *Journal of Organizational Behavior*, *33*(8), 1095–1119. https://doi.org/10.1002/job.1782

Kossek, E. E. (2016). Managing work-life boundaries in the digital age. *Organizational Dynamics*, *45*(3), 258–270. https://doi.org/10.1016/j.orgdyn.2016.07.010

Kossek, E. E., Lautsch, B. A., & Eaton, S. C. (2006). Telecommuting, control, and boundary management: Correlates of policy use and practice, job control, and work–family effectiveness. *Journal of Vocational Behavior*, *68*(2), 347–367. https://doi.org/10.1016/j.jvb.2005.07.002

Kurland, N. B., & Cooper, C. D. (2002). Manager control and employee isolation in telecommuting environments. *The Journal of High Technology Management Research*, *13*(1), 107–126. https://doi.org/10.1016/S1047-8310(01)00051-7

Lautsch, B. A., Kossek, E. E., & Eaton, S. C. (2009). Supervisory approaches and paradoxes in managing telecommuting implementation. *Human Relations; Studies Towards the Integration of the Social Sciences*, *62*(6), 795–827. https://doi.org/10.1177/0018726709104543

Lengen, J. C., Kordsmeyer, A.-C., Rohwer, E., Harth, V., & Mache, S. (2020). Soziale Isolation im Homeoffice im Kontext der COVID-19-Pandemie: Hinweise für die Gestaltung von Homeoffice im Hinblick auf soziale Bedürfnisse [Social isolation among teleworkers in the context of the COVID-19 pandemic]. *Zentralblatt für Arbeitsmedizin, Arbeitsschutz und Ergonomie*, (71), 63–68. https://doi.org/10.1007/s40664-020-00410-w

Lesener, T., Gusy, B., & Wolter, C. (2018). The job demands-resources model: A meta-analytic review of longitudinal studies. *Work & Stress*, *5*(6), 1–28. https://doi.org/10.1080/02678373.2018.1529065

Liu, C., Spector, P., & Jex, S. (2005). The relation of job control with job strains: A comparison of multiple data sources. *Journal of Occupational and Organizational Psychology*, *78*(3), 325–336. https://doi.org/10.1348/096317905X26002

Lott, Y., & Abendroth, A.-K. (2020). The non-use of telework in an ideal worker culture: why women perceive more cultural barriers. *Community, Work & Family*, *54*(1), 1–19. https://doi.org/10.1080/13668803.2020.1817726

Martinengo, G., Jacob, J. I., & Hill, E. J. (2010). Gender and the work-family interface: Exploring differences across the family life course. *Journal of Family Issues*, *31*(10), 1363–1390. https://doi.org/10.1177/0192513X10361709

Marx, C. K., Reimann, M., & Diewald, M. (2021). Do work–life measures really matter? The impact of flexible working hours and home-based teleworking in preventing voluntary employee exits. *Social Sciences*, *10*(1), 9. https://doi.org/10.3390/socsci10010009

Mergener, A. (2020). Berufliche Zugänge zum Homeoffice. *KZfSS Kölner Zeitschrift Für Soziologie Und Sozialpsychologie*, *72*(S1), 511–534. https://doi.org/10.1007/s11577-020-00669-0

Mesmer-Magnus, J. R., & Viswesvaran, C. (2006). How family-friendly work environments affect work/family conflict: A meta-analytic examination. *Journal of Labor Research*, *27*(4), 555–574. https://doi.org/10.1007/s12122-006-1020-1

Michel, J. S., Kotrba, L. M., Mitchelson, J. K., Clark, M. A., & Baltes, B. B. (2011). Antecedents of work-family conflict: A meta-analytic review. *Journal of Organizational Behavior*, *32*(5), 689–725. https://doi.org/10.1002/job.695

Moehring, K., Weiland, A., Reifenscheid, M., Naumann, E., Wenz, A., Rettig, T., Krieger, U., Fikel, M., Cornesse, C., & Blom, A. G. (2021). *Inequality in employment trajectories and their socio-economic consequences during the early phase of the COVID-19 pandemic in Germany*. https://doi.org/10.31235/osf.io/m95df

Möhring, K., Naumann, E., Reifenscheid, M., Weiland, A., Blom, A. G., Wenz, A., Rettig, T., Lehrer, R., Krieger, U., Juhl, S., Friedel, S., Fikel, M., & Cornesse, C. (2020). Die Mannheimer Corona-Studie: Schwerpunktbericht zur Nutzung und Akzeptanz von Homeoffice in Deutschland während des Corona-Lockdowns. Mannheim.

Möhring, K., Naumann, E., Reifenscheid, M., Wenz, A., Rettig, T., Krieger, U., Friedel, S., Finkel, M., Cornesse, C., & Blom, A. G. (2021). The COVID-19 pandemic and subjective well-being: Longitudinal evidence on satisfaction with work and family. *European Societies*, *23*(sup1), S601–S617. https://doi.org/10.1080/14616696.2020.1833066

Müller, K.-U., Samtleben, C., Schmieder, J., & Wrohlich, K. (2020). Corona-Krise erschwert Vereinbarkeit von Beruf und Familie vor allem für Mütter – Erwerbstätige Eltern sollten entlastet werden. *Berlin. DIW - Deutsches Institut für Wirtschaftsforschung*. https://doi.org/10.18723/diw_wb:2020-19-1

Netemeyer, R. G., Boles, J. S., & McMurrian, R. (1996). Development and validation of work-family conflict and family-work conflict scales. *Journal of Applied Psychology*, *81*(4), 400–410. https://doi.org/10.1037/0021-9010.81.4.400

Nijp, H. H., Beckers, D. G. J., Geurts, S. A. E., Tucker, P., & Kompier, M. A. J. (2012). Systematic review on the association between employee worktime control and work-non-work balance, health and well-being, and job-related outcomes. *Scandinavian Journal of Work, Environment & Health*, *38*(4), 299–313. https://doi.org/10.5271/sjweh.3307

Nomaguchi, K. M. (2009). Change in work-family conflict among employed parents between 1977 and 1997. *Journal of Marriage and Family*, *71*(1), 15–32. https://doi.org/10.1111/j.1741-3737.2008.00577.x

O'Driscoll, M. P., Poelmans, S., Spector, P. E., Kalliath, T., Allen, T. D., Cooper, C. L., & Sanchez, J. I. (2003). Family-responsive interventions, perceived organizational and supervisor support, work-family conflict, and psychological strain. *International Journal of Stress Management*, *10*(4), 326–344. https://doi.org/10.1037/1072-5245.10.4.326

Olson-Buchanan, J. B., & Boswell, W. R. (2006). Blurring boundaries: Correlates of integration and segmentation between work and nonwork. *Journal of Vocational Behavior*, *68*(3), 432–445. https://doi.org/10.1016/j.jvb.2005.10.006

Parsons, T. (1949). The social structure of the family. In R. N. Anshen (Ed.), *The family: Its function and destiny* (pp. 173–201). Harper.

Piszczek, M. M. (2017). Boundary control and controlled boundaries: Organizational expectations for technology use at the work-family interface. *Journal of Organizational Behavior*, *38*(4), 592–611. https://doi.org/10.1002/job.2153

Rabe-Hesketh, S., & Skrondal, A. (2012). *Multilevel and longitudinal modeling using Stata*. Stata Press.

Reimann, M., Abendroth, A.-K., & Diewald, M. (2020). How digitalized is work in large German workplaces and how is digitalized work perceived by workers? A new employer-employee survey instrument [IAB Forschungsbericht 8/2020].

Reimann, M., Marx, C. K., & Diewald, M. (2019). Work-to-family and family-to-work conflicts among employed single parents in Germany. *Equality, Diversity and Inclusion: An International Journal*, *39*(5), 513–531. https://doi.org/10.1108/EDI-02-2019-0057

Reimann, M., Peters, E., & Diewald, M. (2022). COVID-19 and work–family conflicts in Germany: Risks and chances across gender and parenthood. *Frontiers in Sociology*, *6*, Article 780740. https://doi.org/10.3389/fsoc.2021.780740

Schieman, S., Badawy, P. J., Milkie, M., & Bierman, A. (2021). Work-life conflict during the COVID-19 pandemic. *Socius: Sociological Research for a Dynamic World*, *7*, 237802312098285. https://doi.org/10.1177/2378023120982856

Schieman, S., & Glavin, P. (2008). Trouble at the border? Gender, flexibility at work, and the work-home interface. *Social Problems*, *55*(4), 590–611. https://doi.org/10.1525/sp.2008.55.4.590

Schieman, S., & Young, M. C. (2013). Are communications about work outside regular working hours associated with work-to-family conflict, psychological distress and sleep problems? *Work & Stress*, *27*(3), 244–261. https://doi.org/10.1080/02678373.2013.817090

Shockley, K. M., & Allen, T. D. (2007). When flexibility helps: Another look at the availability of flexible work arrangements and work–family conflict. *Journal of Vocational Behavior*, *71*(3), 479–493. https://doi.org/10.1016/j.jvb.2007.08.006

Solís, M. S. (2016). Telework: Conditions that have a positive and negative impact on the work-family conflict. *Academia Revista Latinoamericana De Administración*, *29*(4), 435–449. https://doi.org/10.1108/ARLA-10-2015-0289

Son, S., & Bauer, J. W. (2010). Employed rural, low-income, single mothers' family and work over time. *Journal of Family and Economic Issues*, *31*(1), 107–120. https://doi.org/10.1007/s10834-009-9173-8

Stavrou, E. T. (2005). Flexible work bundles and organizational competitiveness: A cross-national study of the European work context. *Journal of Organizational Behavior*, *26*(8), 923–947. https://doi.org/10.1002/job.356

Taskin, L., & Bridoux, F. (2010). Telework: A challenge to knowledge transfer in organizations. *The International Journal of Human Resource Management*, *21*(13), 2503–2520. https://doi.org/10.1080/09585192.2010.516600

Taskin, L., & Edwards, P. (2007). The possibilities and limits of telework in a bureaucratic environment: lessons from the public sector. *New Technology, Work and Employment*, *22*(3), 195–207. https://doi.org/10.1111/j.1468-005X.2007.00194.x

Thomas, L. T., & Ganster, D. C. (1995). Impact of family-supportive work variables on work-family conflict and strain: A control perspective. *Journal of Applied Psychology*, *80*(1), 6–15. https://doi.org/10.1037/0021-9010.80.1.6

Van der Lippe, T., & Lippényi, Z. (2020). Co-workers working from home and individual and team performance. *New Technology, Work and Employment*, *35*(1), 60–79. https://doi.org/10.1111/ntwe.12153

van Dyne, L., Kossek, E., & Lobel, S. (2007). Less need to be there: Cross-level effects of work practices that support work-life flexibility and enhance group processes and group-level OCB. *Human Relations; Studies Towards the Integration of the Social Sciences*, *60*(8), 1123–1154. https://doi.org/10.1177/0018726707081657

Voydanoff, P. (2002). Linkages between the work-family interface and work, family, and individual outcomes. *Journal of Family Issues*, *23*(1), 138–164. https://doi.org/10.1177/0192513X02023001007

Voydanoff, P. (2004). The effects of work demands and resources on work-to-family conflict and facilitation. *Journal of Marriage and Family*, *66*(2), 398–412. https://doi.org/10.1111/j.1741-3737.2004.00028.x

Wayne, S. J., Shore, L. M., & Liden, R. C. (1997). Perceived organizational support and leader-member exchange: A social exchange perspective. *Academy of Management Journal*, *40*(1), 82–111. https://doi.org/10.5465/257021

Wiesenfeld, B. M., Raghuram, S., & Garud, R. (2001). Organizational identification among virtual workers: The role of need for affiliation and perceived work-based social support. *Journal of Management*, *27*(2), 213–229. https://doi.org/10.1177/014920630102700205

Winslow, S. (2005). Work-family conflict, gender, and parenthood, 1977–1997. *Journal of Family Issues*, *26*(6), 727–755. https://doi.org/10.1177/0192513X05277522

Wolfe, M. T., & Patel, P. C. (2021). Everybody hurts: Self-employment, financial concerns, mental distress, and well-being during COVID-19. *Journal of Business Venturing Insights*, *15*, e00231. https://doi.org/10.1016/j.jbvi.2021.e00231

Xiao, Y., Becerik-Gerber, B., Lucas, G., & Roll, S. C. (2021). Impacts of working from home during COVID-19 pandemic on physical and mental well-being of office workstation users. *Journal of Occupational and Environmental Medicine*, *63*(3), 181–190. https://doi.org/10.1097/JOM.0000000000002097

Yue, W., & Cowling, M. (2021). The Covid-19 lockdown in the United Kingdom and subjective well-being: Have the self-employed suffered more due to hours and income reductions? *International Small Business Journal: Researching Entrepreneurship*, *39*(2), 93–108. https://doi.org/10.1177/0266242620986763

Zoch, G., Bächmann, A.-C., & Vicari, B. (2021a). *Gender Differences in Reduced Well-being during the COVID-19 Pandemic – The Role of Working Conditions* [IAB-Discussion Paper No. 4/2021]. Institut für Arbeitsmarkt- und Berufsforschung (IAB), Nürnberg.

Zoch, G., Bächmann, A.-C., & Vicari, B. (2021b). Who cares when care closes? Care-arrangements and parental working conditions during the COVID-19 pandemic in Germany. *European Societies*, *23*(sup1), S576–S588. https://doi.org/10.1080/14616696.2020.1832700

APPENDIX

Table A2.1. Flexible Work, Social Relationships, and WFC.

	Flexibility (Model 1a)		Relationships (Model 1b)	
	Coef.	*SE*	*Coef.*	*SE*
Temporal flexibility	−0.116***	(0.032)	−0.091**	(0.030)
Autonomy	−0.045+	(0.026)	−0.019	(0.029)
Fixed rules about availability	−0.116***	(0.034)	−0.071*	(0.035)
Supervisor WFH (*ref. never*)				
Sometimes			0.014	(0.081)
Often			0.101	(0.119)
Co-workers WFH (*ref. up to 50%*)				
More than 50%			−0.055	(0.073)
All			−0.114	(0.099)
Co-worker relationship			−0.100**	(0.039)
Co-workers work–family supportive			0.024	(0.030)
Supervisor relationship			−0.118***	(0.027)
Supervisor work–family supportive			−0.145***	(0.030)
Total working hours overall	0.225***	(0.038)	0.215***	(0.039)
Share of working hours WFH	−0.002	(0.028)	0.040	(0.029)
WFH experience pre-COVID-19	0.051	(0.070)	0.082	(0.056)
Decision WFH (*ref. by employee*)				
Mandatory with exceptions	0.066	(0.109)	0.055	(0.098)
Mandatory without exceptions	0.018	(0.079)	0.018	(0.077)
Management position	0.251**	(0.097)	0.242**	(0.086)
University (of applied sciences) degree (*ref. vocational training/none*)	0.058	(0.095)	0.026	(0.095)
Job (main activity)				
Production	0.060	(0.053)	0.067	(0.052)
Social services	0.090*	(0.039)	0.073*	(0.036)
Customer-oriented services	0.150	(0.105)	0.118	(0.112)
Research and development	0.025	(0.035)	0.042	(0.037)
Company size	0.046	(0.041)	0.007	(0.031)
Female	0.117+	(0.062)	0.132*	(0.060)
Age (*ref. 16-24*)				
25–34	−0.048	(0.212)	−0.061	(0.207)
35–44	−0.061	(0.215)	−0.027	(0.217)
45–54	−0.180	(0.225)	−0.147	(0.230)
55+	−0.186	(0.209)	−0.181	(0.211)
Age of the youngest child in the household (*ref. no child <=25 yrs old*)				
<=6 yrs old	0.330**	(0.110)	0.322**	(0.100)
7–11 yrs old	0.123	(0.180)	0.088	(0.204)
12–18 yrs old	0.050	(0.052)	0.043	(0.051)
19–25 yrs old	0.027	(0.225)	0.045	(0.252)
Care for other relatives	0.168**	(0.055)	0.184***	(0.055)
Partner WFH (*ref. no*)				
Partner WFH	0.040	(0.051)	0.026	(0.053)

Table A2.1. *(Continued)*

	Flexibility (Model 1a)		Relationships (Model 1b)	
	Coef.	*SE*	*Coef.*	*SE*
No partner	0.141+	(0.084)	0.154	(0.095)
Constant	*0.985****	*(0.229)*	*1.082****	*(0.245)*
R^2 Overall	13.2%		18.2%	

Notes: $N = 885$; Multilevel regression using robust standard errors (SE); + $p < 0.10$, * $p < 0.05$, ** $p < 0.01$, *** $p < 0.001$; WFH = Working from home; "How can working from home succeed?" Survey, own calculations.

Table A2.2. Flexible Work, Social Relationships, and FWC.

	Flexibility (Model 2a)		Relationships (Model 2b)	
	Coef.	*SE*	*Coef.*	*SE*
Temporal flexibility	−0.006	(0.013)	0.002	(0.015)
Fixed rules about availability	−0.085***	(0.016)	−0.065**	(0.022)
Autonomy	−0.071***	(0.017)	−0.048***	(0.014)
Supervisor WFH (*ref. never*)				
Sometimes			−0.052	(0.039)
Often			0.004	(0.051)
Co-workers WFH (*ref. up to 50%*)				
More than 50%			−0.068	(0.066)
All			0.014	(0.084)
Co-worker relationship			−0.083***	(0.018)
Co-workers work–family supportive			−0.062*	(0.029)
Supervisor relationship			−0.085+	(0.048)
Supervisor work–family supportive			−0.006	(0.016)
Total working hours overall	−0.067*	(0.031)	−0.069*	(0.029)
Share of working hours WFH	0.010	(0.025)	0.033	(0.024)
WFH experience pre-COVID-19	−0.010	(0.042)	0.014	(0.044)
Decision WFH (*ref. by employee*)				
Mandatory with exceptions	0.163*	(0.075)	0.128	(0.078)
Mandatory without exceptions	0.048	(0.095)	0.011	(0.093)
Management position	0.017	(0.034)	0.004	(0.025)
University (of applied sciences) degree (*ref. vocational training/none*)	−0.045	(0.053)	−0.061	(0.050)
Job (main activity)				
Production	0.088***	(0.026)	0.097**	(0.033)
Social services	0.047	(0.056)	0.043	(0.062)
Customer-oriented services	0.021	(0.047)	0.003	(0.044)
Research and development	0.047	(0.051)	0.055	(0.045)
Company size	−0.009	(0.020)	−0.032+	(0.018)
Female	−0.036	(0.101)	−0.042	(0.091)
Age (*ref. 16-24*)				
25–34	0.037	(0.119)	0.049	(0.117)
35–44	−0.002	(0.124)	0.041	(0.115)
45–54	−0.094	(0.174)	−0.054	(0.173)
55+	−0.140	(0.162)	−0.114	(0.158)
Age of the youngest child in the household (*ref. no child <=25 yrs old*)				
<=6 yrs old	0.328***	(0.062)	0.305***	(0.065)
7–11 yrs old	0.243***	(0.052)	0.218***	(0.062)
12–18 yrs old	0.018	(0.055)	0.009	(0.056)
19–25 yrs old	−0.133	(0.101)	−0.123	(0.117)
Care for other relatives	0.241***	(0.053)	0.240***	(0.053)
Partner WFH (*ref. no*)				
Partner WFH	0.097+	(0.051)	0.096+	(0.053)
No partner	0.127*	(0.064)	0.132*	(0.062)
Constant	*0.250****	*(0.184)*	*0.370****	*(0.207)*
R^2 Overall	11.8%		16.7%	

Notes: $N = 885$; Multilevel regression using robust standard errors (SE); + $p < 0.10$, * $p < 0.05$, ** $p < 0.01$, *** $p < 0.001$; WFH = Working from home; "How can working from home succeed?" Survey, own calculations.

Table A2.3. Care Responsibilities, Flexible Work, and Work-to-Family Conflict (WFC, FWC).

	WFC: Care responsibilities (Model 1b)		FWC: Care responsibilities (Model 2b)	
	Coef.	*SE*	*Coef.*	*SE*
Main effects				
Temporal flexibility	−0.109***	(0.032)	0.010	(0.023)
Autonomy	−0.081**	(0.029)	−0.073**	(0.027)
Fixed rules about availability	−0.097**	(0.037)	−0.057*	(0.029)
Age of the youngest child in the household (*ref. no child <=25 yrs old*)				
<=6 yrs old	0.326**	(0.119)	0.328***	(0.063)
7–11 yrs old	0.098	(0.167)	0.217***	(0.048)
12–18 yrs old	0.055	(0.061)	0.018	(0.057)
19–25 yrs old	−0.019	(0.233)	−0.114	(0.121)
Care for other relatives	0.164*	(0.068)	0.241***	(0.052)
Interaction effects				
Temporal flexibility#Age of youngest child (*ref. no child <=25 in household*)				
<=6 yrs old	−0.033	(0.070)	−0.047	(0.081)
7–11 yrs old	−0.168**	(0.064)	−0.140*	(0.055)
12–18 yrs old	−0.057	(0.074)	−0.067	(0.074)
19–25 yrs old	−0.272***	(0.076)	−0.016	(0.058)
Fixed rules about availability#Age of youngest child (*ref. no child <=25 in household*)				
<=6 yrs old	0.012	(0.055)	-0.084	(0.058)
7–11 yrs old	0.172	(0.152)	0.146	(0.091)
12–18 yrs old	−0.165***	(0.043)	−0.052	(0.088)
19–25 yrs old	−0.116	(0.114)	0.014	(0.048)
Autonomy#Age of youngest child (*ref. no child <=25 in household*)				
<=6 yrs old	0.085	(0.103)	-0.008	(0.075)
7–11 yrs old	0.121	(0.116)	−0.002	(0.165)
12–18 yrs old	0.033	(0.080)	0.031	(0.110)
19–25 yrs old	0.158	(0.140)	0.136***	(0.037)
Temporal flexibility#Care for other relatives	0.235***	(0.071)	0.058	(0.055)
Fixed rules about availability#Care for other relatives	0.011	(0.054)	0.003	(0.053)
Autonomy#Care for other relatives	−0.016	(0.078)	−0.107*	(0.044)
Controls	yes		yes	
Constant	*0.995****	*(0.204)*	*0.239****	*(0.188)*
R^2 Overall	15.1%		13.0%	

Notes: $N = 885$; Multilevel regression using robust standard errors (SE); + $p < 0.10$, * $p < 0.05$, ** $p < 0.01$, *** $p < 0.001$; WFH = Working from home; Controlled for total working hours overall, total working hours WFH, WFH experience, WFH mandatory, management position, education, job, company size, gender, age, partner WFH; 'How can working from home succeed?' Survey, own calculations. "How can working from home succeed?" Survey, own calculations.

Table A2.4. Interactions Flexible Work#Relationships Co-workers on Work-to-Family Conflict (WFC).

	1		2		3		4		5		6	
	Coef.	*SE*	*Coef.*	*SE*	*Coef.*	*SE*	*Coef.*	*SE*	*Coef.*	*SE*	*Coef.*	*SE*
Main effects												
Temporal flexibility	−0.078*	(0.037)	−0.101**	(0.033)	−0.102**	(0.033)	0.007	(0.113)	−0.101**	(0.033)	−0.099**	(0.034)
Fixed rules about availability	−0.009	(0.015)	−0.010	(0.015)	−0.031+	(0.018)	−0.009	(0.015)	−0.010	(0.015)	0.063	(0.086)
Autonomy	−0.067*	(0.033)	−0.076	(0.060)	−0.068*	(0.034)	−0.067*	(0.033)	−0.179+	(0.106)	−0.068*	(0.032)
Co-worker relationship	−0.037	(0.080)	−0.093	(0.058)	−0.189*	(0.092)	−0.081**	(0.031)	−0.080**	(0.031)	−0.080*	(0.031)
Co-workers work–family supportive	0.027	(0.035)	0.027	(0.035)	0.028	(0.035)	0.134	(0.128)	−0.050	(0.063)	0.224	(0.241)
Interaction effects												
Temporal flexibility # Co-worker relationship	−0.014+	(0.023)										
Fixed rules about availability # Co-worker relationship			0.005	(0.031)								
Autonomy # Co-worker relationship					0.012	(0.009)						
Temporal flexibility # Co-workers work–family supportive							−0.034	(0.036)				
Fixed rules about availability # Co-workers work–family supportive									0.034	(0.029)		
Autonomy # Co-workers work–family supportive											-0.023	(0.027)
Controls	yes		yes		yes		yes		yes		yes	
Constant	*1.554****	*(0.345)*	*1.654****	*(0.375)*	*1.821****	*(0.370)*	*1.285**	*(0.506)*	*1.892****	*(0.397)*	*0.970****	*(0.696)*

Notes: $N = 885$; Multilevel regression using robust standard errors (SE); + $p < 0.10$, * $p < 0.05$, ** $p < 0.01$, *** $p < 0.001$; Controlled for total working hours overall, total working hours WFH, WFH experience, WFH mandatory, management position, education, job, company size, gender, age, age of youngest child in household, care for other relatives, partner WFH; "How can working from home succeed?" Survey, own calculations.

Table A2.5. Interactions Flexible Work#Relationships Supervisor on Work-to-Family Conflict (WFC).

	7		8		9		10		11		12	
	Coef.	*SE*	*Coef.*	*SE*	*Coef.*	*SE*	*Coef.*	*SE*	*Coef.*	*SE*	*Coef.*	*SE*
Main effects												
Temporal flexibility	0.086	(0.060)	−0.096**	(0.031)	−0.098**	(0.033)	0.322***	(0.087)	−0.100**	(0.033)	−0.098**	(0.036)
Fixed rules about availability	−0.008	(0.015)	−0.009	(0.015)	0.057**	(0.020)	−0.008	(0.015)	−0.010	(0.015)	0.134	(0.111)
Autonomy	−0.067*	(0.032)	−0.070*	(0.034)	−0.069*	(0.032)	−0.064+	(0.034)	0.018	(0.074)	−0.069*	(0.033)
Supervisor relationship	0.124+	(0.069)	−0.099***	(0.019)	0.126+	(0.074)	−0.082***	(0.020)	−0.094***	(0.022)	−0.089***	(0.019)
Supervisor work–family supportive	−0.172***	(0.039)	−0.183***	(0.038)	−0.176***	(0.039)	0.208*	(0.092)	−0.127**	(0.045)	0.205	(0.308)
Interaction effects												
Temporal flexibility # Supervisor relationship	−0.069**	(0.023)										
Fixed rules about availability # Supervisor relationship			−0.061+	(0.032)								
Autonomy # Co-worker relationship					−0.024**	(0.009)						
Temporal flexibility # Supervisor work–family supportive							−0.134***	(0.026)				
Fixed rules about availability # Supervisor work–family supportive									−0.026	(0.017)		
Autonomy # Supervisor work–family supportive											−0.045	(0.035)
Controls	yes		yes		yes		yes		yes		yes	
Constant	*1.022***	*(0.315)*	*1.636****	*(0.320)*	*1.045****	*(0.297)*	*0.367*	*(0.383)*	*1.434****	*(0.357)*	*0.348****	*(0.860)*

Notes: $N = 885$; Multilevel regression using robust standard errors (SE); + $p < 0.10$, * $p < 0.05$, ** $p < 0.01$, *** $p < 0.001$; Controlled for total working hours overall, total working hours WFH, WFH experience, WFH mandatory, management position, education, job, company size, gender, age, age of youngest child in household, care for other relatives, partner WFH; 'How can working from home succeed?' Survey, own calculations.

Table A2.6. Interactions Flexible Work#Relationships Co-workers on Family-to-Work Conflict (FWC).

	13		14		15		16		17		18	
	Coef.	*SE*	*Coef.*	*SE*	*Coef.*	*SE*	*Coef.*	*SE*	*Coef.*	*SE*	*Coef.*	*SE*
Main effects												
Temporal flexibility	−0.049	(0.032)	0.001	(0.016)	0.002	(0.017)	−0.061	(0.067)	0.002	(0.016)	0.001	(0.017)
Fixed rules about availability	−0.034**	(0.011)	−0.033**	(0.011)	−0.041*	(0.019)	−0.033**	(0.011)	−0.033**	(0.011)	−0.090+	(0.051)
Autonomy	−0.047***	(0.013)	−0.058***	(0.017)	−0.046***	(0.013)	−0.046***	(0.013)	−0.049	(0.095)	−0.045***	(0.013)
Co-worker relationship	−0.162**	(0.052)	−0.085**	(0.032)	−0.107	(0.087)	−0.065***	(0.014)	−0.066***	(0.014)	−0.066***	(0.014)
Co-workers work–family supportive	−0.071*	(0.033)	−0.073*	(0.035)	−0.072*	(0.034)	−0.134	(0.083)	−0.075	(0.066)	−0.226*	(0.096)
Interaction effects												
Temporal flexibility # Co-worker relationship	0.030*	(0.015)										
Fixed rules about availability # Co-worker relationship			0.008	(0.014)								
Autonomy # Co-worker relationship					0.004	(0.010)						
Temporal flexibility # Co-workers work–family supportive							0.020	(0.022)				
Fixed rules about availability # Co-workers work–family supportive									0.001	(0.029)		
Autonomy # Co-workers work–family supportive											0.018	(0.013)
Controls	yes		yes		yes		yes		yes		yes	
Constant	*1.673****	*(0.303)*	*1.538****	*(0.364)*	*1.574****	*(0.379)*	*1.706****	*(0.459)*	*1.512****	*(0.292)*	*2.020****	*(0.319)*

Notes: $N = 885$; Multilevel regression using robust standard errors (SE); + $p < 0.10$, * $p < 0.05$, ** $p < 0.01$, *** $p < 0.001$; Controlled for total working hours overall, total working hours WFH, WFH experience, WFH mandatory, management position, education, job, company size, gender, age, age of youngest child in household, care for other relatives, partner WFH; "How can working from home succeed?" Survey, own calculations.

Table A2.7. Interactions Flexible Work#Relationships Supervisor on Family-to-Work Conflict (FWC).

	19		20		21		22		23		24	
	Coef.	*SE*	*Coef.*	*SE*	*Coef.*	*SE*	*Coef.*	*SE*	*Coef.*	*SE*	*Coef.*	*SE*
Main effects												
Temporal flexibility	0.025	(0.066)	0.005	(0.017)	0.004	(0.016)	0.087	(0.067)	0.004	(0.016)	0.002	(0.016)
Fixed rules about availability	−0.033**	(0.011)	−0.032**	(0.011)	0.007	(0.024)	−0.032**	(0.011)	−0.033**	(0.011)	−0.035	(0.039)
Autonomy	−0.046***	(0.013)	0.018	(0.056)	−0.046***	(0.013)	−0.045***	(0.013)	0.052	(0.064)	−0.046***	(0.013)
Supervisor relationship	−0.041	(0.075)	−0.013	(0.083)	0.065	(0.117)	−0.066+	(0.039)	−0.067+	(0.039)	−0.069+	(0.038)
Supervisor work–family supportive	−0.007	(0.018)	−0.008	(0.020)	−0.004	(0.021)	0.071	(0.070)	0.056	(0.050)	−0.015	(0.095)
Interaction effects												
Temporal flexibility # Supervisor relationship	−0.009	(0.025)										
Fixed rules about availability # Supervisor relationship			−0.025	(0.021)								
Autonomy # Co-worker relationship					−0.015	(0.010)						
Temporal flexibility # Supervisor work–family supportive							−0.027	(0.019)				
Fixed rules about availability # Supervisor work–family supportive									−0.030	(0.019)		
Autonomy # Supervisor work–family supportive											0.001	(0.010)
Controls	yes		yes		yes		yes		yes		yes	
Constant	*1.427****	*(0.269)*	*1.352***	*(0.445)*	*1.148**	*(0.488)*	*1.248***	*(0.440)*	*1.278***	*(0.431)*	*1.526****	*(0.361)*

Notes: $N = 885$; Multilevel regression using robust standard errors (SE); + $p < 0.10$, * $p < 0.05$, ** $p < 0.01$, *** $p < 0.001$; Controlled for total working hours overall, total working hours WFH, WFH experience, WFH mandatory, management position, education, job, company size, gender, age, age of youngest child in household, care for other relatives, partner WFH; "How can working from home succeed?" Survey, own calculations.

CHAPTER 3

WORKING REMOTELY DURING THE COVID 19-PANDEMIC: WORK AND NON-WORK ANTECEDENTS OF WORK–LIFE BALANCE DEVELOPMENT

Liisa Mäkelä, Samu Kemppinen, Heini Pensar and Hilpi Kangas

ABSTRACT

This study investigates work and non-work antecedents for the work–life balance (WLB) development of remote employees during the COVID-19 pandemic. Longitudinal data (N = 1,146, T1; N = 737, T2) was collected in May–June 2020 and December 2020 in one multinational company (MNC) in Finland. In data analysis, structural equation modeling (SEM) with a cross-lagged panel model was utilized. The results revealed that during the pandemic, WLB slightly decreased. The quantitative job demands increased and predicted a decreased WLB at T2. Job autonomy decreased but did not have an effect on WLB development or buffer the negative effect of quantitative job demands on WLB. Time saved from commuting was positively related to WLB development, but the number of children living at home and the age of the youngest child had no statistically significant link to WLB development over time (similar finding for men and women). Although care responsibilities from the gender perspective is not the focus of our study, the additional

Flexible Work and the Family
Contemporary Perspectives in Family Research, Volume 21, 69–97

ISSN: 1530-3535/doi:10.1108/S1530-353520230000021003

analysis show that WLB at T1 was more challenging for women the more children they had, or the younger the youngest child was. For men, children did not make a difference for their WLB at T1. This finding indicates that WLB has been more challenging for mothers compared to fathers already when our first data had been collected, and the continuance of the pandemic did not change the situation in any direction. This research contributes to the knowledge about work and non-work related demands and resources as antecedents for WLB development during the pandemic. As a practical implication during the pandemic, the authors suggest that employers should follow development for employees' WLB as a measure of well-being in remote work. In addition, the workload of remote employees should be followed, and time saved from commuting should be preserved as employees' non-work time and protected from work-related tasks.

Keywords: Work–life balance; autonomy; workload; parenthood; longitudinal study; community

INTRODUCTION

Due to the corona pandemic, expert work has extensively moved from organizational sites to home offices. Remote work, that is, work that would normally be done at the employer's premises but has been agreed to be conducted externally relying on information technology (Bailey & Kurland, 2002; Garrett & Danziger, 2007), has become far more common than ever before. Yet working from home is blurring the boundaries between work and personal life, and has been found to influence remote employees' experiences of their WLB (see Shirmohammadi et al., 2022 for a review), which is defined as an employee's subjective perception of how successful they are in their commitments to their work (e.g., as an employee, supervisor) and non-work roles (e.g., as a partner, parent, friend). Paying attention to the interface of employees' work and personal life spheres (which is close to the concept of WLB) is important, and its negative development during the pandemic has led to negative organizational outcomes, lower employee performance, and a higher intention to quit (Vaziri et al., 2020). Thus, there is a need to increase the knowledge about WLB in modern working life in order to ensure employee well-being, as well as the success of their employing organization. This study focuses on the antecedents and development of remote employees' WLB during the COVID-19 pandemic.

The interface (Bakker et al., 2011) or balance (Jamal et al., 2021; Syrek et al., 2013) between work and non-work life spheres has previously been studied with the help of the Job demands-resources (JD-R) theory. In these studies, work–life interface or WLB has been considered as an indicator of employee well-being. The JD-R model typically focuses only on the characteristics of the psychosocial work environment (Bakker & Demerouti, 2007; Demerouti et al., 2001), and only a few earlier studies take non-work related demands and resources into account (Bakker et al., 2005; Hakanen et al., 2008) as potential antecedents for employee well-being. However, taking into account the demands and resources from both life spheres may be especially important when phenomena involving both life spheres (e.g., WLB) is studied, and also when the main working environment is one's home. Therefore, this study adopts the JD-R model as its theoretical framework, and broadens its scope to also take into account non-work related demands and resources in the remote work context.

In the working life sphere, quantitative workload poses an essential risk for WLB (McCrea et al., 2011; Skinner & Pocock, 2008), and there is also some evidence that workload may increase with remote work (Allen et al., 2015) as seen during the pandemic (Carillo et al., 2021; Wang et al., 2021). Moreover, job autonomy has been found to be an important job resource that improves employees' well-being (Nahrgang et al., 2011), and which has potential to buffer the negative effects of job demands on well-being (see, e.g., Schaufeli & Taris, 2014). Earlier literature about remote work has shown that job autonomy is one essential positive element (Golden & Veiga, 2008; Nakrošien⊠ et al., 2019; Wang et al., 2021). In this study, quantitative workload and job autonomy are relatively considered as "job demand" and "job resource," having the potential to affect the development of remote employees' WLB. Furthermore, during the corona pandemic, the intensive period of remote working from home has increased the importance of issues from the non-work life sphere on employees' WLB. First, family role responsibilities (e.g., those related to parenting) are typical non-work demands linked to well-being also in the context of remote work (Allen et al., 2015; 2021). The corona pandemic caused occasional lockdown of schools and restricted children to attend daycare normally, and it is likely that parents working from home frequently had to take care of their children during work hours Thus, the situation in which remote employees' that have children living at home is approached as a non-work demand, with the potential to decrease their WLB. Although our focus in this chapter is not on gender-related questions, worth for mentioning is that care responsibilities between men and women vary in different countries, women typically being more involved on them than men (Chung & van der Lippe, 2018; Poortman & Van Der Lippe, 2009; Zamarro & Prados, 2021). Remote working from home can contribute to a re-sharing of the responsibilities between parents and reposition the established gender roles at home. However, it is also possible that remote working cause different implications for women and men, and there is some evidence that the increasing home demands related to remote working have added burden specifically on mothers (Kenny & Yang, 2021; Zamarro & Prados, 2021). We do not dig deep on gender-related questions in this chapter but take them account in the additional analysis, as reported in the discussion section. Furthermore, the time available for the non-work life sphere has increased because working from home saves time that was earlier used for commutes between work and home. Therefore, in this chapter, we also study the time saved from commuting as a non-work resource.

THE FINNISH CONTEXT DURING THE COVID-19 PANDEMIC

In Finland, where this study was conducted, a recommendation for remote working was given by the Government during both data collection rounds. It was only after February 28, 2022, that the Government issued a resolution ending the national recommendation on remote work (The Government decree VM/2022/34). The capital region of Finland had among the largest annual increases in the share of employed people usually working from home in 2020, compared to the time before the pandemic. Also, the share of people transiting to remote work was recorded as the highest in the EU (Eurostat, 2021). The willingness to work remotely after the pandemic is also seen to be high in Finland, and as many as 90% of the people working remotely wish to continue working from home after the pandemic at least 25% of the time (Tilastokeskus, 2021).

Restrictions and recommendations concerning, for example, restaurants, hobbies, and social gatherings were also in place during the period of our data collection (Parliament of Finland, 2021). Furthermore, schools were closed and the parents of young children were recommended to keep the children at home from daycare between the 16th of March 2020 and 14th of May 2020 (Government decree A 191/2020). It was also advised to cut down contacts with elderly and people outside of people's own households. In Finland, it is not typical that several generations would live in a same household, and consequently, grandparents were not able to help with child care, and the possibilities to take care of elderly relatives was limited. During the first data collection, schools started to open after having been mainly closed for two months, and during the second data collection, schools were mainly open, although local closures and quarantines due to exposures were typical.

Although our focus in this chapter is not on gender-related questions, worth mentioning is that in the gender division of housework and caring for children, Finland is among one of the most equal countries in EU. In 2016, in the EU, 93% of women aged 25 to 49 (with children under 18) took care of their children on a daily basis, whereas in Finland the figure was 91%. For men, the percentage was 69% in the EU and 79% in Finland. In the ranking of countries on the basis of their equity between women and men in daily childcare, Finland was the fourth most equal, and for housework and cooking, Finland was the fifth most equal (Eurostat, The life of women and men in Europe, 2021).

JD-R THEORY

The JD-R theory is based on the idea that every job has its own characteristics, and that job demands and resources in particular help to explain the processes leading to either employee ill health or well-being (Bakker & Demerouti, 2007; Demerouti et al., 2001). Job demands refer to aspects of the job requiring physical or psychological effort, and are therefore usually related to physiological and psychological costs leading to ill-being (Kinnunen et al., 2011). Job resources may be instrumental in achieving work goals, and in stimulating personal growth and development (Demerouti et al., 2001, 2002). Having adequate job resources leads (via a motivational process) to well-being, and adequate job resources are likely to buffer the negative effects of job demands, thus compensating for the losses in energy that high job demands may cause (Schaufeli & Taris, 2014).

The JD-R theory has been found to be applicable in the context of work and personal life interaction (Bakker et al., 2011). Negative work–home interference has been shown to function as a job demand (Schaufeli & Taris, 2014, p. 64), and also as a negative well-being outcome (Bakker et al., 2011). Additionally, WLB has been studied with the help of the JD-R model (Syrek et al., 2013) in the context of remote work during the COVID-19 pandemic (Jamal et al., 2021).

JD-R theory focuses only on the characteristics of the psychosocial work environment, and ignores those factors that are not related to work. However, some studies (Bakker et al., 2005; Hakanen et al., 2008) have included home demands and resources in the ill health and motivational processes. In those studies, home demands and resources have not been found to play a specific (Hakanen et al., 2008) or less significant role than job demands and resources (Bakker et al., 2005) when work engagement or burnout are studied. However, as this particular study focuses on phenomena related to both work and non-work life spheres (i.e., the development of WLB in the context of working from home), then non-work related demands and resources are worth including, in addition to those related directly to work.

REMOTE WORK AND WLB

WLB refers to an employees' subjective experience of the compatibility between work and non-work activities (including family), in respect of their life priorities (Brough et al., 2014; Kalliath & Brough, 2008). A sense of balance is generated when individuals feel they can spend enough time and successfully respond to demands in roles they value (Brough et al., 2014; Casper et al., 2018; Greenhaus et al., 2003).

Traditionally, remote working has been considered as a means to improve employee WLB, and a way for employees to more efficiently reconcile their work and home commitments (Maruyama & Tietze, 2012). Earlier studies concerning the interface between employees' work and family lives (concepts closely related to WLB, although not exactly same) have shown that remote employees' experience lower levels of work–family conflict than those who work full-time on site (Madsen, 2006), and one meta-analysis showed that high-intensity remote working (more than 2.5 days/week) is related to lower work–family conflict (Gajendran & Harrison, 2007). In addition, it has been found that the more extensive the remote work is, the less work interferes with family life, but the more family interferes with work life (Golden et al., 2006). Therefore, although it seems that a better WLB may be possible due to lowered work-to-family conflict (WFC), increased conflict arising from the family-to-work among remote employees indicates that the situation may not be that simple, and that both life spheres play an important role once the balance between life spheres is considered.

Previous research related to the interface of work and family/non-work (Golden et al., 2006; Lautsch et al., 2009; Madsen, 2006; Maruyama et al., 2009; Russell et al., 2009) has mainly been based on samples where the choice of remote working has been voluntary, or seen primarily as a part-time arrangement. Therefore, the results may not be relevant in the working life situations experienced in the COVID-19 pandemic, during which remote work has been very intensive and based on rules and strong recommendations (i.e., non-voluntary). So far, literature has shown that during the pandemic, WLB has been harder to achieve among parents who continued working outside their home, compared to those who worked from home (Del Boca et al., 2020). It has also been found that WLB remained relatively stable during the pandemic, despite some positive and negative development paths being identified by Vaziri et al. (2020), their sample including both remote and non-remote employees. However, we were unable to find studies utilizing longitudinal data that explored what happens to remote employees' WLB during the pandemic. Therefore, this particular study focuses on the development of WLB in the context of intensive remote work.

Although the empirical evidence concerning remote employees' WLB is not very extensive, earlier literature has identified several factors that may promote or inhibit it. On one hand, remote work has been shown to involve many beneficial factors, such as greater flexibility and autonomy, time saved from commuting, an opportunity to invest more time in non-work activities, and reduced stress levels (Gajendran & Harrison, 2007; Lautsch et al., 2009; Maruyama et al., 2009). On the other hand, it has been argued that remote working increases the tendency for increased workload (Carillo et al., 2021; Wang et al., 2021), and a blurring of the work–family boundary leading to interferences between the work and home domains (Allen et al., 2015; Lapierre et al., 2016; Russell et al., 2009). Given the exceptional situation with the COVID-19 pandemic, the significance of how remote working affects WLB is accentuated (Shirmohammadi et al., 2022). Particularly, periods of intense working from home combined with partial closures of schools and daycare has also increased the importance of the non-working sphere on employees' WLB. However, we were unable to find any research that explores the essential work and non-work related antecedents for WLB development in the context of remote work during the pandemic.

JOB DEMANDS AND RESOURCES AND WLB IN THE REMOTE WORK CONTEXT

Quantitative Workload and WLB

Quantitative workload is an often-studied job demand, and refers to the amount of work expected from an employee in a prescribed time. A high workload influences employees' perceptions that they have too much to do, their work is piling up, and that they might have to overwork (Greenglass et al., 2003; Wännström et al., 2009). When the demands of work exceed employees' capabilities, they are likely to intrude into their non-work life (Skinner & Pocock, 2008). Work overload is an experience of being expected to accomplish more than one can deliver, and can impede an employee's ability to achieve a WLB (Boxall & Macky, 2014). Quantitative workload is a common work attribute related to work–life interference, and generally found to be a stronger predictor of work–life interference compared to other time related demands such as worked hours (McCrea et al., 2011; Skinner & Pocock, 2008). Excessive work pressure (a concept close to workload) has been found to be related to increased work–family conflict (Glavin & Schieman, 2012), and actual working hours, role overload (i.e., too much work to complete in the time available), and job-related time demands have been associated with a greater work–life imbalance (Boxall & Macky, 2014; Pirzadeh & Lingard, 2021).

There is also some evidence that remote employees have perceived that their workload has increased during the pandemic (Carillo et al., 2021; Wang et al., 2021). This is reasoned by the increase of virtual correspondence (online calls, etc.) required in remote working, and also by the additional and urgent work caused by the COVID-19 emergency itself (Wang et al., 2021). It has further been suggested that remote workers adopt a productive working style, and therefore take on more work (Carillo et al., 2021). Overall, quantitative workload seems to be an essential work demand in the context of remote work during pandemic, and therefore is likely to have effect on WLB development.

Although we did not find any earlier empirical studies exploring the link between workload and WLB in remote work contexts, in this study, we follow the JD-R theory assumption that high job demands lead to impaired well-being, and following earlier empirical evidence from contexts other than remote work, we hypothesize:

H1. High quantitative workload decreases remote employees' WLB over time during the pandemic.

Autonomy and WLB

Autonomy has been found to be an important job resource for employees (Nahrgang et al., 2011; Schaufeli & Taris, 2014). Autonomy refers to what extent a person is able to structure when, where and how the job is performed, and also allows freedom, independence and discretion in making decisions related to tasks and how those tasks are completed (Hackman & Oldham, 1976; Morgeson & Humphrey, 2006; Spector, 1986).

In previous studies, job autonomy has been shown to have a positive influence on WLB (Haar & Brougham, 2020; Ronda et al., 2016; Walia, 2014). As autonomy increases the flexibility and possibility to modify the temporal and spatial elements of one's job, it has been seen as adding a flexibility to deal with family matters (Maruyama & Tietze, 2012) and improve possibilities to plan leisure time and allocate home duties (Ten Brummelhuis & Bakker, 2012). Moreover, it has been reported that adding more flexibility in work tasks and schedules (i.e., autonomy) positively affects WLB (Kelliher & Anderson, 2008; Kelly et al., 2011).

Autonomy has been recognized as a positive element of remote work (e.g., Golden & Veiga, 2008; Harpaz, 2002; Nakrošienė et al., 2019). It has been found that high-intensive remote work is linked to higher autonomy related to one's job (see the meta-analysis of Gajendran & Harrison, 2007; Gajendran et al., 2015). However, the transition to intensive remote work due to the pandemic was sudden, and as employees needed to find novel ways of how to organize their work and collaborate with their team, it can be assumed that the level of their work autonomy was high.

Autonomy in remote work has been found to partially mediate the link between remote work and positive outcomes such as job satisfaction and performance (Gajendran et al., 2015; Gajendran & Harrison, 2007). We found three studies (Andrade & Petiz Lousã, 2021; Elfering et al., 2020; Wang et al., 2021) that took autonomy and work–family issues into account in the context of remote work during the COVID-19 pandemic. Especially, the studies have shown that high autonomy is linked to lower WFC (Andrade & Petiz Lousã, 2021; Elfering et al., 2020), although Wang et al. (2021) reported that autonomy was not related to either work-to-family interference or family-to-work interference. However, as stated earlier, there is a stream of research to support the notion that remote working increases job autonomy (e.g., Gajendran & Harrison, 2007; Allen et al., 2015; Anderson & Kelliher, 2020; Lange & Kayser, 2022), and employees with low autonomy have been suffering from higher interference from work to home (Golden et al., 2006). Additionally, the field would benefit from further empirical evidence about autonomy and the positive side of work/non-work issues, for instance, WLB in the remote work context. As resources are especially important for positive well-being outcomes (following the motivation path in JD-R theory), we base our second hypothesis on the JD-R theory and earlier empirical evidence concerning the positive role of autonomy on WLB in work contexts other than remote work:

H2. High job autonomy increases remote employees' WLB over time during the pandemic.

Moreover, JD-R theory states that in addition to job resources' direct positive effects on employees' well-being, job resources have the potential to buffer the negative effects of job demands (Demerouti et al., 2001; 2002). In the remote work context, job autonomy has been found to buffer the negative association of commuting time on commitment and well-being (Emre & De Spiegeleare, 2019), but again, studies that explore the possible buffering effect of job autonomy on the relationship of quantitative job demands and WLB (and especially in the remote work context) were not found. However, we may assume that autonomy plays an especially important role in helping employees to cope with high workload and achieve WLB in the context of pandemic. Even if workload is high, autonomy allows a flexible sharing of time between different life spheres, for instance, with helping children at home school during the day and continue working later in the evening. Therefore, based on JD-R theory and the available empirical evidence of the buffering effect of autonomy on other kinds of demands on WLB, we hypothesize the following:

H3. Job autonomy buffers the negative effect of quantitative workload on WLB over time during the pandemic.

NON-WORK DEMANDS AND RESOURCES

Although earlier studies concerning work well-being (in particular, work engagement and burnout) have found that non-work demands and resources have a minor or non-significant influence (Bakker et al., 2005; Hakanen et al., 2008), their role is likely to be more important when focusing on phenomena involving both life spheres, for instance WLB, and in the specific situation of the pandemic, when different kinds of restrictions in society kept children at home more than normally. Non-work demands and resources may also be especially important when the work place is one's home, and therefore in this study, having children at home has been considered as a non-work demand, and time saved from commuting as considered as a resource.

NUMBER AND AGE OF CHILDREN AT HOME AND WLB

Homeworking employees may have the company of other members of the household while working, and their physical presence at home might trigger greater expectations from others in relation to the employee's participation in home-related responsibilities, regardless of the employee's commitment to working times (Allen et al., 2015).

At times during the pandemic peaks, a majority of children were home-schooled in many parts of the world (see, e.g., ONS, 2020). Consequently, the impact of the non-work demand created by having children at home cannot be neglected. Parents with children at home have been found to be "time-starved" (Perrons, 2003), wanting more time for both work and family. It has further been found that especially small children create a feeling of time pressure, while older children demand less physical care, thereby creating less time constraints (Del Boca et al., 2020; Schieman et al., 2021; van der Lippe, 2007). However, a study examining the balance between work and non-work life spheres found that having children (regardless of their age) was found to lead to impaired WLB (van der Lippe et al., 2006). Also, a more recent study that compared changes in WLB during the COVID-19 emergency between employees with children and those without children, indicated that the presence of children under the age of 18 in the household is an important factor that negatively affects the work–life balance, possibly due to an additional burden of responsibilities related to the presence of children (Lonska et al., 2021). In addition, it has been found that work–life conflict has remained stable during the pandemic for the parents of younger children, and is decreased if employees do not have children or have teenage children living at home (Schieman et al., 2021).

In Finland, the experiences of parents during the first wave of the pandemic (in the spring of 2020) were polarized, and although one third of parents perceived that meaningful family time increased, over half of the interviewees experienced higher stress and a weakened support network (Finnish Institute for Health and Welfare, 2022). In the study of Salanko et al. (2021), although caring for young children at home during the spring of 2020 resulted in a reduced WLB, many respondents felt that this time increased their satisfaction toward family-life.

In the context of remote work, there is some evidence that remote work eases employees' possibilities to manage work and caring responsibilities, especially if they have children (Maruyama & Tietze, 2012). Furthermore, Golden et al. (2006) found that the size of the household (including every person living in the household, i.e., partner, children and other dependents) is related to the interface of work and family in the context of remote work. Here, we assume that the size of the household can be taken to indicate the number of employees' children living at home. In Golden et al.'s study, no direct link between the size of the household and work–family conflict or family-to-work conflict was found, but the size of the household moderated the link between the extent of remote work and family-to-work conflict (Golden et al., 2006). In particular, among those with large households, the more employees did remote work, the stronger their FWC, while for those with small households, the difference in the extent of remote work was not significantly related to FWC.

However, the extent of remote work has been very high during the pandemic, and due to closures of schools and day care, children may have been demanding attention even during work days. By applying the JD-R theory's proposition of the negative effect of demands on well-being, earlier empirical evidence, and taking account of the specific context of the pandemic, we hypothesize:

H4a. A higher number of children living at home decreases remote employees' WLB over time during the pandemic.

H4b. The younger the age of the youngest child living at home, the stronger the decrease in remote employees' WLB over time during the pandemic.

TIME SAVED FROM COMMUTING AND WLB

By working from home, remote employees avoid commuting travel between work and home, and thus save time (Bai et al., 2021; Maruyama & Tietze, 2012). This may be beneficial especially for employees who have lengthy and time-consuming commutes, since the released time may be transformed to a contribution to the non-work life sphere without compromising work (Golden et al., 2006; Hilbrecht et al., 2013). Research findings regarding commute travel and its impact on the reconciliation of employees' work and personal and family life are indecisive. Long commutes have been found to reduce employees' energy, well-being and overall life quality (Emre & De Spiegeleare, 2019). It has also been found to increase employees' work–family conflict (Bai et al., 2021), especially if the freedom of choice of the time and location of working is low (Elfering et al., 2020). Yet, Maruyama et al. (2009) in their study of 1,566 telecom employees found no support for a prediction of employees' WLB by way of commute travel. Nevertheless, they found that remote workers who spent a higher number of working hours at home (90–100%) and thus avoided commuting, were still likely to report a more positive WLB compared to those who worked only 0–40% of their working time from home. They further concluded that extensive remote work provided employees with the possibility to respond to the needs of work and home life, through flexibility and time gain.

The COVID-19 context discouraged people to commute to work during the pandemic by government recommendation, thus reducing their freedom to choose whether to work from the office or from home (Elfering et al., 2020), and limiting the theoretically proposed (Ashforth et al., 2000) benefit of using commuting time as a possibility for boundary management between work and non-work roles. But despite these possible downsides of reduced commuting, the new situation has given people the possibility to experience a no-commute life-style and its benefits (Cornell et al., 2022) and to value the time saved as a new resource. Thereby, we study time commuting as a resource in the home sphere.

Following the core assumption of JD-R theory about the positive role of resources on well-being, and in alignment with earlier empirical findings, we therefore hypothesize:

> *H5*. Time saved from commuting increases remote employees' WLB over time during the pandemic.

As a further consideration, Tremblay (2002) found that for employees with children, remote work can be a preferred option as it allows them to spend more time at home with the family in the mornings and evenings, with a better balance between work and family as an outcome. Reduced commuting saves time (Bai et al., 2021; Maruyama & Tietze, 2012) that can be allocated to cope with non-work demands, for instance, childcare. It is possible that this was especially important in the context of pandemic related restrictions and the increased need to take care of children at home. Aligned with this empirical finding and with the help of JD-R theory suggesting that resources may buffer the negative effects of demands, we pose our last two hypotheses:

> *H6a*. Time saved from commuting buffers the negative effects of the number of children living at home on remote employees' WLB over time during the pandemic.

> *H6b*. Time saved from commuting buffers the negative effects of the age of the youngest child living at home on remote employees' WLB over time during the pandemic.

METHODS

The data used for this study ($N = 1{,}218$, T1; $N = 776$, T2) was collected during the COVID-19 pandemic in May–June 2020 (T1) and December 2020 (T2), from employees in a large multinational corporation in Finland that operates in the field of industrial technology development and manufacturing. As a consequence, the study had an eight-month time lag. The data were collected via an online questionnaire sent to the employees. The questionnaire was originally sent to 2,483 employees in May–June 2020, and 1218 (49% response rate) returned the questionnaire. The same questionnaire was sent again in December 2020 to those who had responded to the previous questionnaire, and 776 (64% response rate) returned the questionnaire.

The employees of the corporation had very little previous experience with remote work. Before the pandemic, most (80%) of the employees used less than 10% of their working time to remote work. Demographically, the sample consisted mostly of men (64%). At T1, the mean age of respondents was 43.9 years (SD = 10.3; range = 20–68), and most participants were in a relationship (70%). Most employees were highly skilled (senior salaried employees).

WLB was measured with four items and had a good reliability at both time points (T1 $\alpha = 0.89$; T2 $\alpha = 0.92$). The scale used was developed and validated by Brough et al. (2014), and participants responded on a five-point scale ranging from 1 (strongly disagree) to 5 (strongly agree). An example item is: "Overall, I believe that my work and non-work life is balanced."

Quantitative workload was measured with four items and had a good reliability at both time points (T1 $\alpha = 0.83$; T2 $\alpha = 0.83$). The scale was based on the QPS-Nordic questionnaire (Wännström et al., 2009), and participants responded on a five-point scale ranging from 1 (strongly disagree) to 5 (strongly agree). An example item is: "Do you have too much to do?"

Job autonomy was measured with six items and had a good reliability at both time points (T1 $\alpha = 0.82$; T2 $\alpha = 0.83$). The Job autonomy scale was based on the Nova-Weba questionnaire (Houtman et al., 1994) and has also been used by Runhaar et al. (2013). An example item is: "I am free to decide how I do my work." Participants responded on a five-point scale ranging from 1 (strongly disagree) to 5 (strongly agree).

Time saved from commuting was measured with a single question: "How long does your one-way commute take in minutes?" The mean value of the time saved from commuting was approximately 28 minutes with a standard deviation of 16. The number of children living at home was measured ranging from 0 (no children) to 10 children living at home. Over half of the respondents (53%) did not have children living at home, 17% had one child, 20% had two children, and 10% had more than two children living at home. The mean for the number of children was approximately 0.83 with a standard deviation of 1.08. The age of the youngest child living at home ranged from 0 (no children) to 18 (children aged one year and under were coded as 1). The mean age of the youngest child was approximately 3.63 with a standard deviation of 5.27.

Quantitative workload, job autonomy and WLB were used as sum scores in descriptive and attrition analysis. Attrition analysis was conducted with logistic regression. After the descriptive analysis and attrition analysis were conducted, SEM was used to investigate the temporal associations between WLB, and work and non-work demands and resources in a remote work context with a cross-lagged panel model. A robust maximum likelihood estimator (MLR) was used due to slightly non-normal distributions, and missing data were handled using a full information maximum likelihood (FIML) method. Quantitative workload, job autonomy and WLB were modeled in the SEM as latent variables with multiple observed indicators. First, tests of longitudinal measurement invariance were conducted to confirm the structural stability of the measured variables in time. Second, the means of the latent variables were compared between time points by constraining the means at T1 to 0 and allowing the means at T2 to be freely estimated. Third, structural paths and covariates were added to the model. Finally, interactions between latent and observed variables were investigated using the LMS-method (Klein & Moosbrugger, 2000). Standard cutoff values (e.g., Hu & Bentler, 1999) were used to determine an adequately fitting model (non-significant χ^2; RMSEA < 0.06; CFI/TLI $\geq 0.95/0.90$; SRMR < 0.08). For longitudinal measurement invariance, the cutoff points suggested by Chen (2007) were used (ΔCFI ≥ -0.01; ΔRMSEA ≥ 0.015; ΔSRMR ≥ 0.03). We investigate the overall development of WLB with latent factor mean comparisons, and the predictors of WLB over time with the cross-lagged panel model.

In the cross-lagged panel model, we adjust for WLB at T1 to adjust for any previous differences in WLB outside the study period. We included control variables that typically have been found to relate to employees' work and non-work issues, such as WLB (Haar et al., 2019; Haar & Brougham, 2020; Park et al., 2022; Thrasher et al., 2022). Therefore, our model controls gender (0 = male, 1 = female), age (in years), and relationship status (0 = single, 1 = in relationship). These variables could influence the direct effects of job autonomy, quantitative workload, age of the youngest child, and number of children on WLB at T2.

In the analysis, those who were not remote working in T1 (n = 72) or T2 (n = 39) were excluded and the sample size used for analysis was 1,146 at T1 and 737 at T2. Gender, age and relationship status were adjusted in the final cross-lagged panel model. Descriptive and attrition analysis were carried out using IBM SPSS version 26, and the cross-lagged panel model was tested with Mplus version 8.6.

RESULTS

The means, standard deviations and correlations between variables are shown in Table 3.1. A descriptive analysis of the means reveals WLB to have been quite high among the employees as the means were 4.04 at T1 and 3.77 at T2, on a scale of 1 to 5. Job autonomy was also high, and quantitative demands were moderate among the employees. Correlations between the variables indicated that the hypothesized associations of quantitative workload, autonomy and time saved from commuting were all significantly related to WLB. Attrition analysis did not reveal any significant predictors of dropout in the demographic or other variables included in the study.

The CFA model with latent variables had acceptable standardized factor loadings, indicating valid latent measures. Standardized factor loadings of WLB at T1 had a range of 0.70 to 0.90, and WLB at T2 had a range of 0.75 to 0.92. Factor loadings of job autonomy at T1 had a range of 0.56 to 0.73, and 0.60 to 0.78 at T2. Quantitative workload at T1 had a range of 0.68 to 0.84, and 0.65 to 0.84 at T2. The model chi-square test ($\chi2 = 873.603$; df $= 321$; $p < 0.001$) indicated a model misfit, but the chi-square test is sensitive to sample size. Thus, the model fit for the measurement model was deemed to be adequate as indicated by RMSEA (0.039), CFI (0.953), TLI (0.945) and SRMR (0.048) values.

The longitudinal measurement invariance of the model was confirmed as the tests of configural, metric, scalar and strict measurement invariance did not show

Table 3.1. Means, Standard Deviations, and Bivariate Correlations of the Study Variables.

Variable	M	SD	1	2	3	4	5	6	7	8	9
1. WLB T1	4.02	0.87	1								
2. WLB T2	3.77	0.97	0.571**	1							
3. Autonomy T1	3.83	0.72	0.320**	0.218**	1						
4. Autonomy T2	3.75	0.73	0.263**	0.326**	0.567**	1					
5. Quantitative workload T1	2.70	0.98	−0.499**	−0.385**	−0.337**	−0.290**	1				
6. Quantitative workload T2	2.99	0.98	−0.355**	−0.520**	−0.245**	−0.375**	0.620**	1			
7. Time saved from commuting	27.7	15.7	0.065*	0.105**	0.056	0.001	−0.03	−0.062	1		
8. Number of children	0.83	1.08	−0.052	0.007	−0.028	0.054	0.066*	0.025	0.061*	1	
9. Age of the youngest child	3.63	5.27	−0.011	0.015	−0.044	−0.010	0.077*	0.024	0.025	0.579**	1

Note: T1 ($N = 1{,}146$), T2 ($N = 737$), * = $p < 0.05$, ** = $p < 0.01$.

Table 3.2. Fit Statistics for Tests of Longitudinal Measurement Invariance.

Model	$\chi 2$	df	p	CFI	TLI	SRMR	RMSEA (90 % CI)	BIC	$\Delta\chi 2$ (p)	ΔCFI	ΔTLI	ΔSRMR	ΔRMSEA	ΔBIC
Configural	873.603	321	< 0.001	0.953	0.945	0.048	0.039 (0.036, 0.042)	64747.037						
Metric	887.011	332	< 0.001	0.953	0.946	0.050	0.038 (0.035, 0.041)	64683.422	12.868 (0.302)	0	0.001	0.002	−0.001	−63.615
Scalar	906.924	343	< 0.001	0.952	0.947	0.050	0.038 (0.035, 0.041)	64624.972	18.974 (0.062)	−0.001	0.001	0	0	−58.450
Strict	914.654	357	< 0.001	0.953	0.950	0.052	0.037 (0.034, 0.040)	64549.266	15.217 (0.364)	0.001	0.003	0.002	−0.001	−75.706

any significant reduction in model fit (see Table 3.2). After strict longitudinal measurement invariance was confirmed, the means of latent variables were compared between time points by constraining the means at T1 to 0 and allowing the means at T2 to be freely estimated. All latent mean differences were significant between WLB, job autonomy and quantitative workload across time. WLB (-0.32, $p < 0.001$) and job autonomy (-0.13, $p < 0.001$) had decreased during the eight-month period and quantitative workload (0.33, $p < 0.001$) had increased.

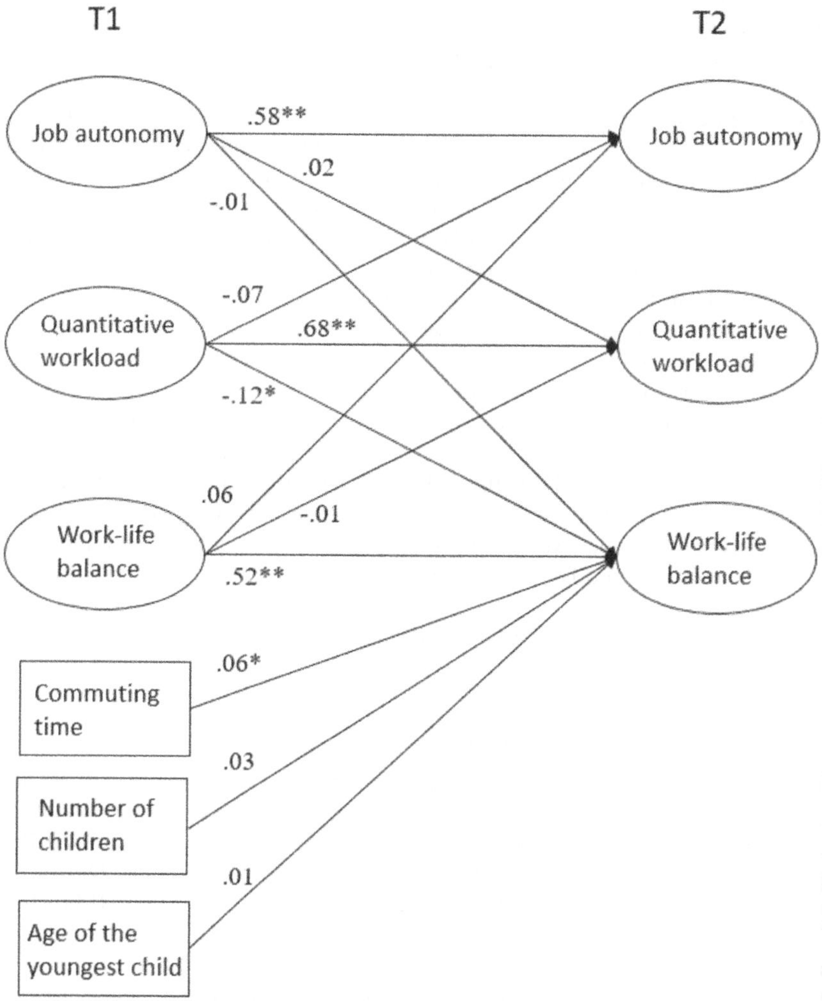

Fig. 3.1. Full Cross-Lagged Panel Model with Standardized Regression Coefficients. *Note:* * = $p < 0.05$, ** = $p < 0.01$. For simplification, indicators, measurement residuals, disturbances, and correlations between variables are not shown in the figure.

After the measurement model was tested, structural paths and covariates were added to the model. The model chi-square test ($\chi 2 = 1174.167$; df = 489; $p < 0.001$) again indicated a model misfit, but the model had an adequate approximate fit with the data indicated by RMSEA (0.035), CFI (0.945), TLI (0.939), and SRMR (0.046) values. The cross-lagged panel model showed that the temporal directions of the studied variables were only one-directional, as the cross-lagged effects from WLB at T1 to quantitative workload and job autonomy at T2 were non-significant, and the cross-lagged effect from quantitative workload at T1 to WLB at T2 was significant (see Fig. 3.1). The autoregressive paths between all three studied measures at T1 and their counterparts at T2 were significant.

The results from the cross-lagged panel model (see Fig. 3.1) indicated that according to our hypothesis (*H1*) based on the JD-R-model, quantitative job demands had a negative cross-lagged effect ($\beta = -0.12$; $p = 0.01$) on WLB while controlling for their autoregressive effects and demographic variables. This indicated that increasing quantitative workload reduced WLB and therefore *H1* was supported. Surprisingly, job autonomy did not have a significant cross-lagged effect ($\beta = -0.01$; $p = 0.92$) on WLB, and therefore *H2* was not supported. The hypothesized buffering effect of job autonomy on the negative effect of quantitative demands on WLB (*H3*) turned out to be non-significant ($\beta = 0.04$; $p = 0.24$). Table of all associations in the final cross-lagged panel model can be found in the Appendix (Table 3.3).

Time saved from commuting was positively related ($\beta = 0.06$; $p = 0.04$) to WLB, but neither the number of children ($\beta = 0.03$; $p = 0.36$) nor the age of the youngest child ($\beta = 0.01$; $p = 0.83$) were related to WLB. More time saved from commuting indicated a better WLB at a later time. Therefore, neither *H4a* nor *H4b* were supported, and *H5* was supported by the data. Both interaction effects between the time saved from commuting and the number of children (*H6a*; $\beta = 0.02$; $p = 0.49$), and between the time saved from commuting and the age of the youngest child (*H6b*; $\beta = 0.03$; $p = 0.28$) were non-significant, and thus neither *H6a* nor *H6b* were supported by the data.

DISCUSSION AND CONCLUSION

The aim of this research was to investigate the temporal associations of work and non-work antecedents for the WLB development of remote employees during the COVID-19 pandemic. This research contributes to the literature of WLB in a situation of intensive remote work caused by the global pandemic. During the pandemic, remote work was strongly recommended by authorities (ILO, 2020; Parliament of Finland, 2021; WHO, 2021) – thus, remote work was involuntary, a main mode of working, and home-based. Earlier research has mainly studied remote work before the pandemic, and treated it typically as a benefit that an employer provided to their employees, or as an opportunity for a company to make cost savings. Unfortunately, we do not yet know how long different kinds of restrictions around the globe will continue due to the pandemic, or if some other global crises will arise in the future which may also lead to involuntary remote work. But it has become clear that working life won't be the same after the pandemic, and it is likely that remote work will be much more common in the future than it was before the pandemic.

Our results revealed that the WLB of remote employees decreased during the pandemic. Earlier literature has found that remote working increases the strain of WFC if the remote work was non-voluntary (Lapierre et al., 2016). However, there are also studies that report the positive effects of remote working on WLB (e.g., Gajendran & Harrison, 2007; Lautsch et al., 2009; Maruyama et al., 2009), and those studies include a variety of remote working arrangements (including part-time and voluntary remote working), and could reflect a preferred choice of the employees and a better matching to their lifestyle. Our results seem to be aligned with these findings to some extent, and WLB decreased the longer that involuntary home-based remote work lasted. On the other hand, the WLB of remote employees seems to be at a relatively high level (with a mean at the first measurement point of 4.04 and 3.77 at the second, with a maximum value of 5), thus indicating that finding a balance between work and non-work in the context of involuntary remote work is very likely. It is also possible that the pandemic actually provided a long-awaited opportunity of remote work, which may have previously been denied by an employer or "presence cultures" in companies, leading to high perceptions of WLB, especially at the beginning. However, studying WLB in the context of the global pandemic may have affected our findings, and for instance, constant restrictions have led to a lack of hobbies, social gatherings, and other important non-work activities in remote employees' lives. With the situation continuing over many months and without any knowledge of how long it might last, may have decreased people's experiences of how satisfied they were with the possibilities to combine their work and non-work life spheres. Therefore, more research is needed regarding the development of WLB during and after the pandemic, and how future work models that combine on-site working and remote work are related to it. In addition, a conceptualization of remote work needs to be developed in order to recognize, for instance, different types of remote work, and taking into account factors such as voluntary versus non-voluntary remote work, the division of working time between remote and on-site, home-office or some other place, etc.

Furthermore, we found that job demand (quantitative workload) and non-work resource (time saved from commuting) predicted remote employees' WLB, whereas job resource (autonomy) and non-work demands (number of children and age of the youngest child living at home) did not. Thus, it seems that non-work related resources and demands should also be taken into account in addition to those related to work, if the focus is to be on phenomena that link to both life spheres of employees, such as WLB. The findings of our study align with earlier findings arrived at during the pandemic (Carillo et al., 2021; Wang et al., 2021), and show that quantitative workload (as an indicator of job demand) grew between the time points, and it is possible that it is because of the challenging work setting posed by remote working (Eddleston & Mulki, 2017) and a decreased access to support (Mann & Holdsworth, 2003; Sardeshmukh et al., 2012), all of which could add to the effort required from remote working employees. However, as we do not have a possibility to compare the development of workload between employees working remotely and them who worked on offices, we are not able to confirm if remote working was the reason to increase of job demands. Moreover, we found that increasing workload had a negative impact on WLB over time. It seems that the remote working situation has been perceived as burdensome, negatively affecting employees' experiences of their overall WLB. Earlier studies have found that work pressure and worked hours (concepts close to quantitative workload) are related to lower WLB and higher work–family conflict (Boxall & Macky, 2014; Glavin & Schieman, 2012), and our results show that it is also the case in a remote work setting in the context of the pandemic. A possible explanation could be drawn from the blurring of boundaries between work and home domains (Allen et al., 2015; Lapierre et al., 2016; Russell et al., 2009), allowing a greater intrusion of work into the non-work sphere (Barber et al., 2019; Suh & Lee, 2017) which may happen easily when demanding work is carried out from home.

The time saved from commute travel that would normally take place between work and home, was in practice almost fully negated in the COVID-19 context. Specifically, it was considered as an indicator of a non-work resource because commuting to work is usually done in the employees' own time. Earlier research has reported that longer commuting time increases the conflict between work and family (Elfering et al., 2020), and in our study, the length of time saved from commuting was found to be a significant factor in the increasing the WLB of remotely working employees. Earlier research has shown that saved commuting time can be spent on family and non-work related activities (Bai et al., 2021; Maruyama et al., 2009), which may also be the case in our study. In addition, it is possible that once employees did not need to commute, it created a less stressful atmosphere for the start and end the working day, avoiding traffic jams or crowded public transportation. However, it is important to note that commute travel itself, and the physical transfer between work and home, has not been seen as entirely harmful in previous literature. Looking at the commuting through a lens of boundary theory, the commuting time could be seen as useful preparation time for workers to psychologically relax and shift into a different role (e.g., from employee to parent/partner or vice versa) (Ashforth et al., 2000), although we were not able to find empirical studies supporting that suggestion. The loss of this routine in remote working during the pandemic, even with the limited possibilities of the freedom to choose whether to work from home or in an office (which is a situation closely related to temporospatial autonomy that has found to decrease the harmful effect of long commutes on WFC: Elfering et al., 2020) did not seem to lead to difficulties for employees in relation to their WLB. Given these considerations, we suggest further research to study the different mechanisms of why and how time saved from commuting promotes remote employees' WLB, how that time is actually spent, and what kinds of benefits employees link to it.

Our study revealed that job autonomy does not have a significant cross-lagged effect on WLB, nor did it buffer the negative effect of quantitative job demands on WLB. This finding did not support our hypothesis in which we expected that autonomy would promote WLB in remote work, based on JD-R theory and earlier findings from other work contexts (Haar & Brougham, 2022; Ronda et al., 2016; Walia, 2014) than remote work. However, our finding was aligned with one study conducted during the COVID-19 pandemic (Wang et al., 2021). In that study, autonomy was not related to either work-to-family interference or family-to-work interference as a negative indicator of work and non-work, and based on our study, it does not have an effect on WLB as a positive indicator. However, two studies have shown that high autonomy and low WFC are related, both before (Elfering et al., 2020) and also in the context of the pandemic (Andrade & Petiz Lousã, 2021). This may mean that although recognized as a typical feature of remote work, autonomy does not always function in a similar way as seen in other work contexts. In fact, it may even be that in order to cope with the high autonomy present in a remote work context, people need to have some additional personal skills (e.g., self-leadership) or traits (e.g., self-discipline) that help them to organize their work in a way that enhances their WLB. Future studies should therefore focus on the role that these kinds of personal resources (which are also acknowledged in JD-R theory: Schaufeli & Taris, 2014) may play in the relationship between job autonomy and different outcomes, for instance WLB. In addition, while this study had an eight-month time lag, more research is needed about the temporal relationships and development of quantitative workload, job autonomy and WLB over longer time periods. Comparison between remote employees and employees working in offices is also needed, especially when hybrid work models are taking place after pandemic restrictions are eased or not existing. In addition, studying only one sector, we acknowledge that some of the changes we have identified may be caused by changes happening in that particular company or sector and more research is needed in other sectors and environments.

As a final area for reflection, our results showed that having children at home was not related to WLB in our study period, despite it having been hypothesized based on earlier research (van der Lippe et al., 2006). Surprisingly, the COVID-19 pandemic meant extraordinary life disruptions such as temporary closures of schools and daycare services, and thus added pressure on parents in way of juggling between home and job demands. At the time of the first data collection, schools and daycare facilities were just opening after being closed for two months in Finland, and this may have had a positive effect on remote employees' thoughts about their WLB. It is therefore possible that their experiences might have been different if the data would have been collected, e.g., two weeks after the restrictions started and families had not yet learned to cope with the situation. Anyhow, it seemed not to have affected their experiences of WLB during pandemic. In fact, being present at home could have contributed to a better reconciliation of home and work duties (Maruyama & Tietze, 2012), and improved the proximity to family simply by being there and being able to spend additional time in the non-work life sphere. It is also possible that the rhythm of life slowed down when parents did not need to take children to their hobbies in the evenings, or they did not need to worry about young children staying at home alone after short school days that are typical in Finland. In this study, we only asked the age and amount of children under 17 years of age living at home, and more detailed information (e.g., if children were at home during the working day) could have led to different results. As we did not find the relationship between time saved from commuting and the number of children living at home to be statistically significant for WLB, we may conclude that time saved from commuting seems to be equally important for employees who had any number of children living in the same household, as it was for those who had none. However, it is likely that the way that the saved time is spent is different for these groups, and this provides an area of examination for future studies.

In addition, existing research has shown that during the pandemic, women (especially mothers) have used more time on childcare and household chores than men (Craig & Churchill, 2021; Giurge et al., 2021), and are more eager to return to work in offices after the pandemic than men (Caligiuri & De Cieri, 2021). Our model was adjusted for gender, and gender was not related to WLB at T1 or T2. We also performed additional multigroup analysis (see Appendix for Table 3.4) to see if the model has different direct effects on WLB at T2 based on gender, and no relationships were found. However, the associations between the age of the youngest child and the number of children and WLB at T1 were different based on gender, which means that WLB at T1 controls their effect on WLB at T2, and therefore, there are no significantly different direct effects on WLB at T2 based on gender. There could be different total effects based on gender through an indirect path from the age of child or number of children to WLB at T2 through WLB at T1, but we were interested in the direct effects observed during the measurement period between T1 and T2 as that period was during the pandemic. Based on the additional multigroup analysis, WLB at T1 was more challenging for women the more children they had, or the younger the youngest child was. For men, children did not make a difference for their WLB at T1. This finding indicates that WLB has been more challenging for mothers compared to fathers already when our first data had been collected, and the continuance of the pandemic did not change the situation in any direction. We studied remote workers' WLB in the Finnish context, a country ranking high in gender equity, which reflects a situation where family responsibilities are typically shared between parents, and men are likely to participate in daily childcare. Despite of that, WLB was more challenging for mothers than father as a starting point (T1). However, the good news is that the development of WLB was not related on gender nor parental status and we can assume that men and women both carried the possible added childcare responsibility related to the COVID-19 precautions in schools and daycare services. However, future studies should utilize longitudinal data with several data points, optimally with at least the first of them collected before the pandemic, in order to explore this phenomenon in more depth. Also, identifying possible confounders and adjusting for them in the analysis would be important to address in future studies.

In studying the topic through a gender specific lens, looking at dual-earner couples in which both partners have a possibility for remote work would be an interesting perspective. For example, research focusing on their experiences of how work and non-work demands and resources are linked to their strategies to combine work and family life with their partner (Shockley et al., 2021), and through that to their WLB, would provide novel knowledge about families in modern working life. However, it is important to acknowledge that gender is a nonbinary spectrum, and still too often, categorizations based on a demographic variable of men and women is applied (Cameron & Stinson, 2019). Thus, the diversity of employees as well as families should be taken into account in future research concerning remote work.

As practical implications drawn from our study findings, we encourage employers to follow development for employee WLB as a measure of their well-being, especially if their work is conducted fully or partly at home. We also recommend the introduction of organizational policies and practices to protect the important time resource gained from reduced commuting (e.g., by not letting worktime flow over into the time previously used for commuting), and for supervisors to maintain regular contact with employees to monitor their general workload.

REFERENCES

Allen, T. D., Golden, T. D., & Shockley, K. M. (2015). How effective is telecommuting? Assessing the status of our scientific findings. *Psychological Science in the Public Interest*, *16*(2), 40–68. https://doi.org/10.1177/1529100615593273

Allen, T. D., Merlo, K., Lawrence, R. C., Slutsky, J., & Gray, C. E. (2021). Boundary management and work-nonwork balance while working from home. *Applied Psychology*, *70*(1), 60–84. https://doi.org/10.1111/apps.12300

Anderson, D., & Kelliher, C. (2020). Enforced remote working and the work-life interface during lockdown. *Gender in Management*, *35* (7), 677–683. https://doi.org/10.1108/GM-07-2020-0224

Andrade, C., & Petiz Lousã, E. (2021). Telework and work–family conflict during COVID-19 lockdown in Portugal: The influence of job-related factors. *Administrative Sciences*, *11*(3), 103. https://doi.org/10.3390/admsci11030103.

Ashforth, B. E., Kreiner, G. E., & Fugate, M. (2000). All in a day's work: Boundaries and micro role transitions. *Academy of Management Review*, *25*(3), 472–491. https://doi.org/10.5465/amr.2000.3363315

Bai, B., Gopalan, N., Beutell, N., & Ren, F. (2021). Impact of absolute and relative commute time on work–family conflict: Work schedule control, child care hours, and life satisfaction. *Journal of Family and Economic Issues*, *42*(4), 586–600. https://doi.org/10.1007/s10834-021-09752-w

Bailey, D. E., & Kurland, N. B. (2002). A review of telework research: Findings, new directions, and lessons for the study of modern work. *Journal of Organizational Behavior*, *23*(4), 383–400. https://doi.org/10.1002/job.144

Bakker, A. B., & Demerouti, E. (2007). The Job Demands-Resources model: State of the art. *Journal of Managerial Psychology*, *22*(3), 309–328. https://doi.org/10.1108/02683940710733115

Bakker, A. B., Demerouti, E., & Schaufeli, W. B. (2005). The crossover of burnout and work engagement among working couples. *Human Relations*, *58*(5), 661–689. https://doi.org/10.1177/0018726705055967

Bakker, A. B., ten Brummelhuis, L. L., Prins, J. T., & der Heijden, F. M. v. (2011). Applying the job demands – resources model to the work – home interface: A study among medical residents and their partners. *Journal of Vocational Behavior*, *79*(1), 170–180. https://doi.org/10.1016/j.jvb.2010.12.004

Barber, L. K., Conlin, A. L., & Santuzzi, A. M. (2019). Workplace telepressure and work–life balance outcomes: The role of work recovery experiences. *Stress and Health*, *35*(3), 350–362. https://doi.org/10.1002/smi.2864

Boxall, P., & Macky, K. (2014). High-involvement work processes, work intensification and employee well-being. *Work, Employment and Society*, *28*(6), 963–984. https://doi.org/10.1177/0950017013512714

Brough, P., Timms, C., O'Driscoll, M. P., Kalliath, T., Siu, O. L., Sit, C., & Lo, D. (2014). Work–life balance: A longitudinal evaluation of a new measure across Australia and New Zealand workers.

International Journal of Human Resource Management, *25*(19), 2724–2744. https://doi.org/10.1080/09585192.2014.899262

Caligiuri, P. M., & De Cieri, H. (2021). Predictors of employees' preference for working from home post-pandemic. *Business and Economic Research*, *11*(2), 1–19. https://doi.org/10.5296/ber.v11i2.18411

Cameron, J. J., & Stinson, D. A. (2019). Gender (mis)measurement: Guidelines for respecting gender diversity in psychological research. *Social and Personality Psychology Compass*, *13*, e12506. https://doi.org/10.1111/spc3.12506

Carillo, K., Cachat-Rosset, G., Marsan, J., Saba, T., & Klarsfeld, A. (2021). Adjusting to epidemic-induced telework: Empirical insights from teleworkers in France. *European Journal of Information Systems*, *30*(1), 69–88. https://doi-org.proxy.uwasa.fi/10.1080/0960085X.2020.1829512

Casper, W. J., Vaziri, H., Wayne, J., DeHauw, S., & Greenhaus, J. (2018). The jingle-jangle of work-nonwork balance: A comprehensive and meta-analytic review of its meaning and measurement. *Journal of Applied Psychology*, *103*(2), 182–214. https://doi.org/10.1037/apl0000259

Chen, F. F. (2007). Sensitivity of goodness of fit indexes to lack of measurement invariance. *Structural Equation Modeling: A Multidisciplinary Journal*, *14*(3), 464–504. https://doi.org/10.1080/10705510701301834

Chung, H., & van der Lippe, T. (2018). Flexible working, work–life balance, and gender equality: introduction. *Social Indicators Research*, *151*(2), 365–381. https://doi.org/10.1007/s11205-018-2025-x

Cornell, S., Nickel, B., Cvejic, E., Bonner, C., McCaffery, K. J., Ayre, J., Copp, T., Batcup, C., Isautier, J., Dakin, T., & Dodd, R. (2022). Positive outcomes associated with the COVID-19 pandemic in Australia. *Health Promotion Journal of Australia*, *33*(2), 311–319. https://doi.org/10.1002/HPJA.494

Craig, L., & Churchill, B. (2021). Dual-earner parent couples' work and care during COVID-19. *Gender Work and Organization*, *28*(S1), 514–527. https://doi org.proxy.uwasa.fi/10.1111/gwao.12497

Del Boca, D., Oggero, N., Profeta, P., & Rossi, M. (2020). Women's and men's work, housework and childcare, before and during COVID-19. *Rev Econ Household 18*, 1001–1017. https://doi-org.proxy.uwasa.fi/10.1007/s11150-020-09502-1

Demerouti, E., Bakker, A., Nachreiner, F., & Ebbinghaus, M. (2002). From mental strain to burn-out. *European Journal of Work and Organizational Psychology*, *11*(4), 423–441. https://doi.org/10.1080/13594320244000274

Demerouti, E., Bakker, A. B., Nachreiner, F., & Schaufeli, W. B. (2001). The job demands-resources model of burnout. *Journal of Applied Psychology*, *86*(3), 499–512. https://doi.org/10.1037/0021-9010.86.3.499

Eddleston, K. A., & Mulki, J. (2017). Toward understanding remote workers' management of work–family boundaries: The complexity of workplace embeddedness. *Group and Organization Management*, *42*(3), 346–387. https://doi.org/10.1177/1059601115619548

Elfering, A., Igic, I., Kritzer, R., & Semmer, N. K. (2020). *Commuting as a work-related demand: Effects on work-to-family conflict, affective commitment, and intention to quit*. https://doi.org/10.1002/pchj.350

Emre, O., & De Spiegeleare, S. (2019). The role of work–life balance and autonomy in the relationship between commuting, employee commitment and well-being. *International Journal of Human Resource Management*, *0*(0), 1–25. https://doi.org/10.1080/09585192.2019

Eurostat, The life of women and men in Europe. (2021). Retrieved August 8, 2022, from https://ec.europa.eu/eurostat/cache/infographs/womenmen/img/pdf/WomenMenEurope-DigitalPublication-2021_en.pdf?lang=en>

Eurostat. (2021). Retrieved August 8, 2022, from https://ec.europa.eu/eurostat/en/web/products-eurostat-news/-/ddn-20210923-1

Finnish Institute for Health and Welfare. (2022). Retrieved August 8, 2022 from https://thl.fi/fi/web/sukupuolten-tasa-arvo/ajankohtaista/korona-ja-sukupuoli

Gajendran, R. S., & Harrison, D. A. (2007). The good, the bad, and the unknown about telecommuting: Meta-analysis of psychological mediators and individual consequences. *Journal of Applied Psychology*, *92*(6), 1524–1541. https://doi.org/10.1037/0021-9010.92.6.1524

Gajendran, R. S., Harrison, D. A., & Delaney-Klinger, K. (2015). Are telecommuters remotely good citizens? Unpacking telecommuting's effects on performance via i-deals and job resources. *Personnel Psychology*, *68*(2), 353–393. https://doi.org/10.1111/peps.12082

Garrett, R. K., & Danziger, J. N. (2007). Which telework? Defining and testing a taxonomy of technology-mediated work at a distance. *Social Science Computer Review*, *25*(1), 27–47. https://doi.org/10.1177/0894439306293819

Giurge, L. M., Whillans, A. V., & Yemiscigil, A. (2021). A multicountry perspective on gender differences intime use during COVID-19. *Proceedings of the National Academy of Sciences of the United States of America*, *118*(12), 1–7. https://doi.org/10.1073/pnas.2018494118

Glavin, P., & Schieman, S. (2012). Work-family role blurring and work-family conflict: The moderating influence of job resources and job demands. *Work and Occupations*, *39*(1), 71–98. https://doi.org/10.1177/0730888411406295

Golden, T. D., & Veiga, J. F. (2008). The impact of superior-subordinate relationships on the commitment, job satisfaction, and performance of virtual workers. *Leadership Quarterly*, *19*(1), 77–88. https://doi.org/10.1016/j.leaqua.2007.12.009

Golden, T. D., Veiga, J. F., & Simsek, Z. (2006). Telecommuting's differential impact on work-family conflict: Is there no place like home? *Journal of Applied Psychology*, *91*(6), 1340–1350. https://doi.org/10.1037/0021-9010.91.6.1340

Government decree on ending the Remote work recommendation to end at the end of February 17.2.2022. Retrived August 26, 2022, from https://stm.fi/-/10623/etatyosuositus-paattyy-helmikuun-lopussa-jonka-jalkeen-tyopaikoilla-siirrytaan-eta-ja-lasnatyon-yhdistamiseen-riskiarvioiden-ja-tautitilanteen-mukaan?languageId=en_US

Government decree on temporary restrictions on the obligation to organize early childhood education 6.4.2020/191. Retrieved August 8, 2022, from https://www.finlex.fi/fi/laki/alkup/2020/20200191

Greenglass, E. R., Burke, R. J., & Moore, K. A. (2003). Reactions to increased workload: Effects on professional efficacy of nurses. *Applied Psychology*, *52*(4), 580–597. https://doi.org/10.1111/1464-0597.00152

Greenhaus, J. H., Collins, K. M., & Shaw, J. D. (2003). The relation between work-family balance and quality of life. *Journal of Vocational Behavior*, *63*(3), 510–531. https://doi.org/10.1016/S0001-8791(02)00042-8

Haar, J., & Brougham, D. (2020). Work antecedents and consequences of work-life balance: A two sample study within New Zealand. *International Journal of Human Resource Management*. *33*(4), 784–807. https://doi.org/10.1080/09585192.2020.1751238

Haar, J. M., Sune, A., Russo, M., Ollier-Malaterre, A., & Russo, M. (2019). A cross-national study on the antecedents of work-life balance from the fit and balance perspective. *Social Indicators Research*, *142*, 261–282. https://doi.org/10.1007/s11205-018-1875-6

Hackman, J. R., & Oldham, G. R. (1976). Motivation through design of work: Test of a Theory. *Organizational Behavior and Human Performance*, *16*(2), 250–279. https://doi.org/10.1016/0030-5073(76)90016-7

Hakanen, J. J., Schaufeli, W. B., & Ahola, K. (2008). The job demands-resources model: A three-year cross-lagged study of burnout, depression, commitment, and work engagement. *Work and Stress*, *22*(3), 224–241. https://doi.org/10.1080/02678370802379432

Harpaz, I. (2002). Advantages and disadvantages of telecommuting for the individual, organization and society. *Work Study*, *51*(2), 74–80. https://doi.org/10.1108/00438020210418791

Hilbrecht, M., Shaw, S. M., Johnson, L. C., & Andrey, J. (2013). Remixing work, family and leisure: Teleworkers' experiences of everyday life. *New Technology, Work and Employment*, *28*(2), 130–144. https://doi.org/10.1111/ntwe.12010

Houtman, I., Bloemhof, A., Dhondt, S., & Terwee, C. (1994). *Weba en Nova-Weba inrelatie tot gezondheid en welbevinden van werknemers [Weba and Nova-Weba in relation to health and well-being of employees]*. TNO.

Hu, L., & Bentler, P. M. (1999). Cutoff criteria for fit indexes in covariance structure analysis: Conventional criteria versus new alternatives. *Structural Equation Modeling: A Multidisciplinary Journal*, *6*(1), 1–55. https://doi.org/10.1080/10705519909540118

International Labour Organization. (2020). Practical Guide on Teleworking during the COVID-19 pandemic and beyond. https://www.ilo.org/travail/info/publications/WCMS_751232/lang--en/index.htm

Jamal, M. T., Anwar, I., Khan, N. A., & Saleem, I. (2021). Work during COVID-19: Assessing the influence of job demands and resources on practical and psychological outcomes for employees.

Asia-Pacific Journal of Business Administration, 13(3), 293–319. https://doi.org/10.1108/APJBA-05-2020-0149

Kalliath, T., & Brough, P. (2008). Work-life balance: A review of the meaning of the balance construct. *Journal of Management and Organization, 14*(3), 323–327. https://doi.org/10.5172/jmo.837.14.3.323

Kelliher, C., & Anderson, D. (2008). For better or for worse? An analysis of how flexible working practices influence employees' perceptions of job quality. *International Journal of Human Resource Management, 19*(3), 419–431. https://doi.org/10.1080/09585190801895502

Kelly, E. L., Moen, P., & Tranby, E. (2011). Changing workplaces to reduce work-family conflict: Schedule control in a white-collar organization. *American Sociological Review, 76*(2), 265–290. https://doi.org/10.1177/0003122411400056

Kenny, C., & Yang, G. (2021). *CGD note the global childcare workload from school and preschool closures during the COVID-19 pandemic*. CGD Notes: Center for Global Development. https://www.cgdev.org/sites/default/files/global-childcare-workload-from-school-closures-covid.pdf

Kinnunen, U., Feldt, T., Siltaloppi, M., & Sonnentag, S. (2011). Job demands–resources model in the context of recovery: Testing recovery experiences as mediators. *European Journal of Work and Organizational Psychology, 20*(6), 805–832. https://doi.org/10.1080/1359432X.2010.524411

Klein, A., & Moosbrugger, H. (2000). Maximum likelihood estimation of latent interaction effect with the LMS method. *Psychometrika, 65*(4), 457–474. https://doi.org/10.1007/BF02296338

Lange, M., & Kayser, I. (2022). The Role of Self-Efficacy, Work-Related Autonomy and Work-Family Conflict on Employee's Stress Level during Home-Based Remote Work in Germany. *International Journal of Environmental Research and Public Health, 19*(9), Article:4955. https://doi.org/10.3390/ijerph19094955

Lapierre, L. M., van Steenbergen, E. F., Peeters, M. C. W., & Kluwer, E. S. (2016). Juggling work and family responsibilities when involuntarily working more from home: A multiwave study of financial sales professionals. *Journal of Organizational Behavior, 37*(6), 804–822. https://doi.org/10.1002/job.2075

Lautsch, B. A., Kossek, E. E., & Eaton, S. C. (2009). Supervisory approaches and paradoxes in managing telecommuting implementation. *Human Relations, 62*(6), 795–827. https://doi.org/10.1177/0018726709104543

Lonska, J., Mietula, I., Litavniece, L., Arbidane, I., Vanadzins, I., Matisane, L. & Paegle, L. (2021). Work–life balance of the employed population during the emergency situation of COVID-19 in Latvia. *Frontiers in Psychology, 12*. https://doi.org/10.3389/fpsyg.2021.682459

Madsen, S. R. (2006). Work and family conflict: Can home-based teleworking make a difference? *International Journal of Organization Theory & Behavior, 9*(3), 307–350. https://doi.org/10.1108/ijotb-09-03-2006-b002

Mann, S., & Holdsworth, L. (2003). The psychological impact of teleworking: Stress, emotions and health. *New Technology, Work and Employment, 18*(3), 196–211. https://doi.org/10.1111/1468-005X.00121

Maruyama, T., Hopkinson, P. G., & James, P. W. (2009). A multivariate analysis of work-life balance outcomes from a large-scale telework programme. *New Technology, Work and Employment, 24*(1), 76–88. https://doi.org/10.1111/j.1468-005X.2008.00219.x

Maruyama, T., & Tietze, S. (2012). From anxiety to assurance: Concerns and outcomes of telework. *Personnel Review, 41*(4), 450–469. https://doi.org/10.1108/00483481211229375

McCrea, R., Boreham, P., & Ferguson, M. (2011). Reducing work-to-life interference in the public service: The importance of participative management as mediated by other work attributes. *Journal of Sociology, 47*(3), 313–332. https://doi.org/10.1177/1440783311407946

Morgeson, F. P., & Humphrey, S. E. (2006). The Work Design Questionnaire (WDQ): Developing and validating a comprehensive measure for assessing job design and the nature of work. *Journal of Applied Psychology, 91*(6), 1321–1339. https://doi.org/10.1037/0021-9010.91.6.1321

Nahrgang, J. D., Morgeson, F. P., & Hofmann, D. A. (2011). Safety at Work: A meta-analytic investigation of the link between job demands, job resources, burnout, engagement, and safety outcomes. *Journal of Applied Psychology, 96*(1), 71–94. https://doi.org/10.1037/a0021484

Nakrošienė, A., Bučiūnienė, I., & Goštautaitė, B. (2019). Working from home: Characteristics and outcomes of telework. *International Journal of Manpower, 40*(1), 87–101. https://doi.org/10.1108/IJM-07-2017-0172

ONS. (2020). Coronavirus and homeschooling in Great Britain – Office for National Statistics. https://www.ons.gov.uk/peoplepopulationandcommunity/educationandchildcare/articles/coronavirusandhomeschoolingingreatbritain/apriltojune2020

Park, Y., MacDonald, G., & Impett, E. A. (2022). Partnership status and satisfaction with work–life balance. *European Journal of Work and Organizational Psychology*, 1–10. https://doi.org/10.1080/1359432X.2022.2104717

Parliament of Finland. (2021). Adoption of the Emergency Powers Act during the COVID-19 pandemic News coverage. https://www.eduskunta.fi/EN/naineduskuntatoimii/kirjasto/aineistot/kotimainen_oikeus/LATI/valmiuslain-kayttoonottaminen-koronavirustilanteessa/Pages/uutisointia.aspx

Perrons, D. (2003). The new economy and the work-life balance: Conceptual explorations and a case study of new media. *Gender, Work and Organization*, *10*(1), 65–93. https://doi.org/10.1111/1468-0432.00004

Pirzadeh, P., & Lingard, H. (2021). Working from home during the COVID-19 pandemic: Health and well-being of project-based construction workers. *Journal of Construction Engineering and Management*, *147*(6), 04021048. https://doi.org/10.1061/(ASCE)CO.1943-7862.0002102

Poortman, A. R., & Van Der Lippe, T. (2009). Attitudes toward housework and child care and the gendered division of labor. *Journal of Marriage and Family*, *71*(3), 526–541. https://doi.org/10.1111/J.1741-3737.2009.00617.X

Ronda, L., Ollo-López, A., & Goñi-Legaz, S. (2016). Family-friendly practices, high-performance work practices and work–family balance: How do job satisfaction and working hours affect this relationship? *Management Research*, *14*(1), 2–23. https://doi.org/10.1108/MRJIAM-02-2016-0633

Runhaar, P., Konermann, J., & Sanders, K. (2013). Teachers' organizational citizenship behaviour: Considering the roles of their work engagement, autonomy and leader-member exchange. *Teaching and Teacher Education*, *30*, 99–108. https://doi.org/10.1016/j.tate.2012.10.008

Russell, H., O'Connell, P. J., & McGinnity, F. (2009). The impact of flexible working arrangements on work-life conflict and work pressure in Ireland. *Gender, Work and Organization*, *16*(1), 73–97. https://doi.org/10.1111/j.1468-0432.2008.00431.x

Salanko,L., Alasuutari, M., & Sulkanen, M. (2021). Varhaiskasvatuspalvelut koronapandemian aikana. JYU Reports: University of Jyväskylä. https://doi.org/10.17011/jyureports/2021/2

Sardeshmukh, S. R., Sharma, D., & Golden, T. D. (2012). Impact of telework on exhaustion and job engagement: A job demands and job resources model. *New Technology, Work and Employment*, *27*(3), 193–208. https://doi.org/10.1111/j.1468-005X.2012.00284.x

Schaufeli, W. B., & Taris, T. W. (2014). A critical review of the job demands-resources model: Implications for improving work and health. In G. F. Bauer & O. Hämmig (Eds.), *Bridging Occupational, organizational and public health: A transdisciplinary approach* (pp. 43–66). Springer Science & Business Media. https://doi.org/10.1007/978-94-007-5640-3

Schieman, S., Badawy, P. J., Milkie, M. A., & Bierman, A. (2021). Work-life conflict during the COVID-19 pandemic. *Socius*, *7*(1), 1–19. https://doi.org/10.1177/2378023120982856

Shirmohammadi, M., Au, W. C., & Beigi, M. (2022). Remote work and work-life balance: Lessons learned from the covid-19 pandemic and suggestions for HRD practitioners, *Human Resource Development International*, *25*(2), 163–181. https://doi.org/10.1080/13678868.2022.2047380

Shockley, K. M., Clark, M. A., Dodd, H., & King, E. B. (2021). Work-family strategies during COVID-19: Examining gender dynamics among dual-earner couples with young children. *Journal of Applied Psychology*, *106*(1), 15–28. https://doi.org/10.1037/apl0000857

Skinner, N., & Pocock, B. (2008). Work-life conflict: Is work time or work overload more important? *Asia Pacific Journal of Human Resources*, *46*(3), 303–315. https://doi.org/10.1177/1038411108095761

Spector, P. E. (1986). Perceived control by employees: A meta-analysis of studies concerning autonomy and participation at work. *Human Relations*, *39*(11), 1005–1016. https://doi.org/10.1177%2F001872678603901104

Suh, A., & Lee, J. (2017). Understanding teleworkers' technostress and its influence on job satisfaction. *Internet Research*, *27*(1), 140–159. https://doi.org/10.1108/IntR-06-2015-0181

Syrek, C. J., Apostel, E., & Antoni, C. H. (2013). Stress in highly demanding IT jobs: Transformational leadership moderates the impact of time pressure on exhaustion and work – life balance. *Journal of Occupational Health Psychology*, *18*(3), 252–261. https://doi.org/10.1037/a0033085

Ten Brummelhuis, L. L., & Bakker, A. B. (2012). A resource perspective on the work-home interface: The work-home resources model. *American Psychologist*, *67*(7), 545–556. https://doi.org/10.1037/a0027974

Thrasher, G. R., Wynne, K., Baltes, B., & Bramble, R. (2022). The intersectional effect of age and gender on the work–life balance of managers. *Journal of Managerial Psychology, ahead-of-print*. https://doi.org/10.1108/JMP-03-2021-0169/FULL/PDF

Tilastokeskus. (2021). Retrieved of August 8, 2022, from https://www.stat.fi/tietotrendit/blogit/2021/uusi-normaali-kutsuu-vanhaan-ei-ole-paluuta-jos-tyontekijoilta-kysytaan/>

Tremblay, D. G. (2002). Balancing work and family with telework? Organizational issues and challenges for women and managers. *Women in Management Review*, *17*(3), 157–170. https://doi.org/10.1108/09649420210425309

van der Lippe, T. (2007). Dutch workers and time pressure: Household and workplace characteristics. *Work, Employment and Society*, *21*(4), 693–711. https://doi.org/10.1177/0950017007082877

van der Lippe, T., Jager, A., & Kops, Y. (2006). Combination pressure: The paid work-family balance of men and women in European countries. *Acta Sociologica*, *49*(3), 303–319. https://doi.org/10.1177/0001699306067711

Vaziri, H., Casper, W. J., Wayne, J. H., & Matthews, R. A. (2020). Changes to the work–family interface during the COVID-19 pandemic: Examining predictors and implications using latent transition analysis. *Journal of Applied Psychology*, *105*(10), 1073–1087. https://doi.org/10.1037/apl0000819

Walia, P. (2014). Work-life balance in relation to task variety and task autonomy: A study of bank employees. *Journal of Strategic Human Resource Management*, *3*(1), 15.

Wang, B., Liu, Y., Qian, J., & Parker, S. K. (2021). Achieving effective remote working during the COVID-19 pandemic: A work design perspective. *Applied Psychology*, *70*(1), 16–59. https://doi.org/10.1111/apps.12290

Wännström, I., Peterson, U., Åsberg, M., Nygren, Å., & Gustavsson, J. P. (2009). Psychometric properties of scales in the General Nordic Questionnaire for Psychological and Social Factors at Work (QPSNordic): Confirmatory factor analysis and prediction of certified long-term sickness absence: Personality and Social Sciences. *Scandinavian Journal of Psychology*, *50*(3), 231–244. https://doi.org/10.1111/j.1467-9450.2008.00697

World Health Organization. (2021). Preventing and mitigating COVID-19 at work. *Policy Brief*. https://www.who.int/publications/i/item/WHO-2019-nCoV-workplace-actions-policy-brief-2021-1

Zamarro, G., & Prados, M. J. (2021). Gender differences in couples' division of childcare, work and mental health during COVID-19. *Review of Economics of the Household*, *19*(1), 11–40. https://doi.org/10.1007/S11150-020-09534-7/TABLES/10

APPENDIX

Table A3.1. All Structural Paths and Correlations Between the Variables of Interest in the Final Cross-Lagged Panel Model.

Association	*β*	*R*
WLB T1 → WLB T2	0.52**	–
WLB T1 → Autonomy T2	0.06	–
WLB T1 → Quantitative workload T2	−0.01	–
WLB T1 ←→ Quantitative workload T1	–	−0.54**
WLB T1 ←→ Autonomy T1	–	0.36**
Autonomy T1 ←→ Quantitative workload T1	–	−0.39**
Autonomy T1 → Autonomy T2	0.58**	–
Autonomy T1 → WLB T2	−0.01	–
Autonomy T1 → Quantitative workload T2	0.02	–
Quantitative workload T1 → Quantitative workload T2	0.68**	–
Quantitative workload T1 → WLB T2	−0.12*	–
Quantitative workload T1 → Autonomy T2	−0.07	–
WLB T2 ←→ Quantitative workload T2	–	−0.46**
WLB T2 ←→ Autonomy T2	–	0.27**
Autonomy T2 ←→ Quantitative workload T2	–	−0.40**
Time saved from commuting → WLB T1	0.07*	–
Time saved from commuting → WLB T2	0.06*	–
Time saved from commuting → Quantitative workload T1	−0.05	–
Time saved from commuting → Quantitative workload T2	−0.04	–
Time saved from commuting → Autonomy T1	0.06*	–
Time saved from commuting → Autonomy T2	−0.03	–
Time saved from commuting ←→ Number of children	–	0.06
Time saved from commuting ←→ Age of the youngest child	–	0.02
Number of children → WLB T1	−0.06	–
Number of children → WLB T2	0.03	–
Number of children → Quantitative workload T1	0.06	–
Number of children → Quantitative workload T2	−0.01	–
Number of children → Autonomy T1	−0.01	–
Number of children → Autonomy T2	0.11**	–
Number of children ←→ Age of the youngest child	–	0.58**
Age of the youngest child → WLB T1	0.03	–
Age of the youngest child → WLB T2	0.01	–
Age of the youngest child → Quantitative workload T1	0.03	–
Age of the youngest child → Quantitative workload T2	−0.03	–
Age of the youngest child → Autonomy T1	−0.04	–
Age of the youngest child → Autonomy T2	−0.03	–

Note. * = $p < 0.05$, ** = $p < 0.01$. Correlations (R) are represented as (←→) and regressions (β) as (→).

Table A3.2. Post-Hoc Multigroup Analysis of All Structural Paths and Correlations Between the Variables of Interest in the Final Cross-Lagged Panel Model.

Association	β_M	R_M	β_W	R_W
WLB T1 → WLB T2	0.50**	–	0.59**	–
WLB T1 → Autonomy T2	0.01	–	0.25**	–
WLB T1 → Quantitative workload T2	0.01	–	−0.08	–
WLB T1 ←→ Quantitative workload T1	–	−0.54**	–	−0.50**
WLB T1 ←→ Autonomy T1	–	0.36**	–	0.33**
Autonomy T1 ←→ Quantitative workload T1	–	−0.39**	–	−0.39**
Autonomy T1 → Autonomy T2	0.59**	–	0.57**	–
Autonomy T1 → WLB T2	−0.02	–	0.02	–
Autonomy T1 → Quantitative workload T2	0.05	–	−0.01	–
Quantitative workload T1 → Quantitative workload T2	0.73**	–	0.59**	–
Quantitative workload T1 → WLB T2	−0.16**	–	−0.03	–
Quantitative workload T1 → Autonomy T2	−0.10	–	0.03	–
WLB T2 ←→ Quantitative workload T2	–	−0.44**	–	−0.49**
WLB T2 ←→ Autonomy T2	–	0.25**	–	0.34**
Autonomy T2 ←→ Quantitative workload T2	–	−0.38**	–	−0.47**
Time saved from commuting → WLB T1	0.08*	–	0.04	–
Time saved from commuting → WLB T2	0.10**	–	−0.09	–
Time saved from commuting → Quantitative workload T1	−0.04	–	−0.07	–
Time saved from commuting → Quantitative workload T2	0.01	–	−0.05	–
Time saved from commuting → Autonomy T1	0.08*	–	−0.01	–
Time saved from commuting → Autonomy T2	−0.03	–	−0.07	–
Time saved from commuting ←→ Number of children	–	0.06	–	0.07
Time saved from commuting ←→ Age of the youngest child	–	0.01	–	0.10
Number of children → WLB T1	0.01	–	−0.26**	–
Number of children → WLB T2	0.02	–	0.05	–
Number of children → Quantitative workload T1	0.02	–	0.23**	–
Number of children → Quantitative workload T2	0.01	–	−0.01	–

Table A3.2. *(Continued)*

Association	β_M	R_M	β_W	R_W
Number of children → Autonomy T1	0.06	–	−0.26**	–
Number of children → Autonomy T2	0.09*	–	0.16	–
Number of children ←→ Age of the youngest child	–	0.56**	–	0.68**
Age of the youngest child → WLB T1	−0.01	–	0.23**	–
Age of the youngest child → WLB T2	−0.03	–	0.06	–
Age of the youngest child → Quantitative workload T1	0.02	–	−0.06	–
Age of the youngest child → Quantitative workload T2	0.01	–	−0.11	–
Age of the youngest child → Autonomy T1	−0.07	–	0.15*	–
Age of the youngest child → Autonomy T2	−0.04	–	0.01	–

Note: * = $p < 0.05$, ** = $p < 0.01$. Correlations (R) are represented as (←→) and regressions (β) as (→). Subscript M represents men ($n = 845$) and W represents women ($n = 262$).

SECTION 2

GENDER, PARENTHOOD, AND STATUS-SPECIFIC PATTERNS OF FLEXIBLE WORK AND THE FAMILY

CHAPTER 4

DOES TELEWORK MEDIATE THE IMPACT OF OCCUPATIONAL STATUS ON WORK-TO-FAMILY CONFLICTS? AN INVESTIGATION OF CONDITIONAL EFFECTS OF GENDER AND THE COVID-19 PANDEMIC

Antje Schwarz, Ayhan Adams and Katrin Golsch

ABSTRACT

This study analyzes the effects of gender and occupational status differences on parents' work-to-family conflicts, comparing COVID-19 pandemic and pre-pandemic periods. It is examined whether this association is mediated by parents' telework. Theoretically, we use the work/family border theory and flexible resource versus greedy role perspectives to shed light on the gender- and status-related use of telework and illustrate the influence of flexible working practices on parents' work-to-family conflicts. Using moderated mediation analysis combined with bootstrapping, we analyze data from two waves of the German Family Panel (pairfam), covering pre-pandemic (2017/18, 2019/2020) and pandemic periods (2020) (N = 3,315). Our results show higher work-to-family conflicts for parents with higher occupational status as well as teleworking parents. Furthermore, we find supporting evidence for the mediation from occupational status to work-to-family conflicts via telework, with a slightly

Flexible Work and the Family
Contemporary Perspectives in Family Research, Volume 21, 101–127

ISSN: 1530-3535/doi:10.1108/S1530-353520230000021004

stronger relationship among mothers than fathers. Under the consideration of the pandemic, the mediating effect was only provable for mothers but not for fathers. However, the mediating effect of telework does not strengthen under the pandemic conditions. Our findings support the greedy role perspective, in particular for employees with higher-status occupations, and the assumption of a negative influence of work–family integration through telework for work-to-family conflicts.

Keywords: work-to-family conflicts; WFC; occupational status; gender; telework; COVID-19 pandemic

INTRODUCTION

With the beginning of the global COVID-19 crisis, social life has changed fundamentally. In Germany, the first explored cases were identified at the end of January 2020 (Federal Ministry of Health, 2021). From the mid of March 2020, the reduction of physical contact in nearly every aspect of social life was handled as the priority issue in public and private life.

For households, especially those caring for children, the lockdown measures to contain the pandemic have initiated demanding situations by interfering with the daily schedules (Eurofound, 2020; Hipp & Bünning, 2020; Kohlrausch & Zucco, 2020; Schieman et al., 2021). Established institutions of education and childcare, such as schools and kindergartens, stopped their regular business or reduced their service temporarily to a minimum (Müller et al., 2020). Often last-minute announcements were made to communicate school and day-care closures. This has led to significant challenges in the organization of work and family life for parents. Moreover, companies and enterprises were assigned to expand flexible working conditions to avoid contact with colleagues in their workforce and disrupt the chains of infection (Fadinger & Schymik, 2020). Therefore, the use of digital working tools has reached a new climax during the pandemic crisis. This is particularly visible in the spread of telework (Abendroth et al., 2022), understood as paid work done outside the regular workplace, usually from home (Allen et al., 2015).

These fundamental changes of work and family imply a need to examine changes in the work–family interface of men and women. According to the work/family border theory (Clark, 2000), it is assumed that the level of integration of work and family life has increased for many families during the pandemic. However, research that examines whether and how this differs according to gender and occupational status is still scarce.

For this reason, we address the complex relationships: The first aim of our study is to gain insight into how gender and occupational status interact to create work-to-family conflicts among employed parents in Germany. First, one rationale behind this is that paid and unpaid work in Europe are still distributed unequally via gender (Ferrant et al., 2014; OECD, 2017; Stier & Lewin-Epstein, 2007; Sullivan, 2000; Winqvist, 2004). Despite the rise of women's employment (Beck-Gernsheim, 1983), women carry the majority of unpaid care work on an average – and experience a "second shift" (Hochschild, 1990) – especially after the birth of a child (Baxter et al., 2008; Dechant & Blossfeld, 2015; Schober, 2013). In Germany, the majority of employed women are working part-time to harmonize the duties of housework, childcare, and paid work (Destatis, 2018). However, there is evidence of a buffering effect on mothers' involvement in care work through higher absolute wages (Schober, 2013). Therefore, we assume variation in the dynamics according to occupational status.

Second, we aim to fill the gap in knowledge on how this relationship has changed during the first lockdown of the COVID-19 pandemic. With the pandemic, some scholars assume that processes of retraditionalism could occur in couples and the gendered distribution of work could be strengthened (Allmendinger, 2020; Kohlrausch & Zucco, 2020), while others provide evidence for strong heterogeneity between families, also varying by factors of the occupational status, as income or level of education (Hank & Steinbach, 2020; Kreyenfeld & Zinn, 2021; Möhring et al., 2020). On the current state of the debate, the effects of the pandemic on the perception of work-to-family conflicts remain unclear.

Considering location-independent telework, indeed, variation in access to telework varies with occupational status. Before the COVID-19 crisis, access to telework was more often provided for high-skilled workers (Felstead et al., 2002; Golden, 2008) and executives (Grunau et al., 2019). This relationship has strengthened under pandemic conditions in Germany (Abendroth et al., 2022; Schröder et al., 2020). The trend potentially leads to systematic disadvantages for persons in low-status occupations, not only in terms of financial insecurities and health-related risks (Holst et al., 2021), but also according to their ability to make work compatible with family life. So far, it is unclear if the perception of work-to-family conflicts has changed differently depending on occupational status in the course of the pandemic via working conditions.

To understand how gender, occupational status, and telework matter for work-to-family conflicts, this study uses data from two waves of the German Family Panel (pairfam), covering pre-pandemic (2017/18, 2019/2020) and pandemic periods (2020). We address three research questions: First, is there a relationship between occupational status and work-to-family conflicts among parents which is mediated by the use of telework? Second, to what extent does gender moderate this association between occupational status and work-to-family conflicts? And finally, to what extent has the COVID-19 pandemic changed this pattern?

Focusing on employed fathers and mothers in three birth cohorts (1971–1973, 1981–1983, and 1991–1993), this study makes a significant contribution to understanding experiences of work-to-family conflicts in pre-pandemic and pandemic periods among parents. In addition, our intersectional approach will contribute to the demand for research on linked social inequalities of gender and class in the field of study (Chung & van der Lippe, 2018).

Beginning with the next section, we develop a framework for understanding the relationship between occupational status, gender, telework, and work-to-family conflicts, and discuss the current state of research on the access to and use of telework as well as the relationship between telework and work-to-family conflicts. Next, we identify possible mechanisms for change and potential outcomes during the pandemic. We then describe the data and methods used and present the results of the empirical analysis. Finally, we will conclude with a discussion.

STATE OF RESEARCH: WORK-TO-FAMILY CONFLICTS AND TELEWORK AMONG PARENTS

Work–family conflicts were defined by Greenhaus and Beutell (1985) as "a form of interrole conflict in which the role pressures from the work and family domains are mutually incompatible in some respect" (p. 77). From this theoretical perspective, spheres are interconnected, and thus behavior in one sphere can affect conflicts in other spheres. With regard to the reconciliation of family and work, Greenhaus and Beutell (1985) distinguished between time-based, strain-based, and behavior-based conflicts that occur in bidirectional ways. Therefore, demands of work can impinge conflicts in personal life (work-to-family conflicts), and demands of personal life can lead to conflicts at work (family-to-work conflicts) (Carlson et al., 2000; Gutek et al., 1991), resulting in serious work-related, non-work-related, and stress-related consequences (Allen et al., 2000). Nevertheless, previous studies describe a stronger impact of work-related conditions on work-to-family conflicts than family-to-work conflicts (Byron, 2005). Therefore, this study focuses on work-to-family conflict (WFC) only.

Both spheres – private and professional – are juxtaposed in the work/family border theory by Clark (2000) with the overriding aim of "satisfaction and good functioning at work and at home, with a minimum of role conflict" (p. 751). From this perspective, central attention is paid to the borders between the spheres, which can exist physically, temporally, and psychologically, and are created and organized by the border crossers. The relationship between the two spheres can be located on a continuum from integration (i.e., dissolution of boundaries and strong intermixing of the spheres of life) to segmentation (i.e., strong separation of the spheres) (Clark, 2000; Nippert-Eng, 1996).

However, the individual practice of integration or segmentation does not determine the emergence of conflicts per se, and there is a need for strategies to reconcile family duties with work demands. In particular, parents caring for children are dependent on possibilities to adjust their daily life (Winslow, 2005), especially if having more than one child or children are younger (Byron, 2005). For example, telework can increase the permeability between work and family life, and it has the potential to enable work fulfillment and supervisory responsibilities from the distance, by decoupling work from physical presence. Moreover, telework can facilitate short-term reactions to different demands in the spheres, and therefore ease compatibility (Chung & van der Horst, 2018; Hill et al., 2010). On the other hand, current research describes the ambivalent character of flexible working arrangements. Telework contains the risk of lacking control on the organization of spheres, for instance through blending (Pfeiffer, 2012) or continuous switching between the areas of life (Schieman & Young, 2010). Thus, telework must not only be considered in its social context. The structural conditions of telework must also be taken into account.

AVAILABILITY AND USE OF TELEWORK IN GERMANY

With the emergence of information and communication technologies (Messenger et al., 2017) and larger shifts toward flexibilization of work (Sennett, 1999; Voß, 1998), new working arrangements have developed. Allen et al. (2015) describe telework as a flexible work practice in which employees work some working hours independently of a central workplace – usually from home. In Germany in the mid of the 2010s, only 12% of a sample representing the German working population worked predominantly or partly from home, albeit 40% of the sample were working in home office-compatible occupations (Brenke, 2016). The number of people using telework in Germany thus remained below the European average in 2019 (Sostero et al., 2020).

These findings illustrate that the distinction between availability and use of telework is crucial (Allen et al., 2013). First, access and use are related in a unidirectional relation: If the availability of telework is not given, for instance, if the job is not compatible with telework, there is no way to use the flexible practice. Second, if telework is available for employees different barriers may hinder its use. Even though telework can be considered as a strategy to please both – employers through lowering the cost of the working infrastructure or the facilitated possibility to work anywhere at any time (Lott, 2019), and employees through enabling better compatibility of family- and work-related duties (Chung & van der Horst, 2018; Hill et al., 2010) – there is skepticism on both sides (Brenke, 2016; Grunau et al., 2019; Messenger et al., 2017; Mokhtarian et al., 1998). Moreover, perceptions of flexible working vary by occupational status as well as gender (Mokhtarian et al., 1998).

The Importance of Occupational Status

Current research proposes that access to telework varies according to occupational status. It is more often provided for high-skilled workers (Felstead et al., 2002; Golden, 2008) and executives (Grunau et al., 2019). Whether jobs are compatible with teleworking arrangements depends on the tasks and activities that have to be done. For example, working on machines, or clients, at special places, or with sensitive data cannot be easily substituted by telework (Grunau et al., 2019). Likewise, the access does depend on the cognitive complexity of the work assignments. The possibility to work from home increases with the number of cognitive activities at work, while manual activities decrease this chance (Mergener, 2020).

With possible access to telework in a special occupation, barriers to its use come into account, regardless of the technical possibility to spatial flexibility. Superiors can refuse telework, because of a strong culture of attendance in line with ideal worker norms (Acker, 1990; Williams et al., 2013), or a feared loss of control over employees by not seeing them at work (Grunau et al., 2019; Messenger et al., 2017). Similarly, a reduction in productivity can occur because of limited interactions with colleagues (van der Lippe & Lippényi, 2019). Such experiences may raise employers' concerns about telework.

At the same time employees can be skeptical about working partly or exclusively from home. For parents, lack of visibility to management and household distractions are reasons for not working from home (Mokhtarian et al., 1998). The attempt to maintain the appearance of being a "zero drag" (Hochschild, 1997, p. XVII) employee, and to uphold the ideal worker norm (Acker, 1990; Williams et al., 2013), can lead to non-use of telework, even if the flexible work practice is offered (Hochschild, 1997).

Mokhtarian et al. (1998) show, that reasons for being critical vary by occupational status: Clerical workers mentioned misunderstanding or perceived reduced social interaction – besides supervisor unwillingness and job unsuitability – while professional workers also referred to displeasure because of household distractions, the need for discipline, lack of visibility to management, and perceived reduced professional and social interaction. In contrast, managerial workers, as the group with the highest status, mentioned first and foremost, less professional interaction and household distractions as problems.

Gender Differences

Current research on varying samples in Europe yield mixed results on gender differences in the use of telework (Eurostat, 2021). In Germany, Zhang et al. (2020) and Lott and Abendroth (2019) claimed that men are more likely to telework. In contrast, Brenke (2016) did not find any gender-specific patterns in the availability and use of telework. Compared to childless persons, the likelihood of being able to telework is lower for parents (Brenke, 2016; Zhang et al., 2020), albeit a higher probability of telework was observed for mothers (Zhang et al., 2020).

While men experience more often technical barriers to telework, women are more likely to face cultural barriers (Lott & Abendroth, 2019). Following vertical and horizontal gender segregation, men are more likely to work under flexible working conditions because they hold a greater range of jobs and higher hierarchical positions (Williams et al., 2013). In addition, Lott and Abendroth (2019) show that cultural barriers faced by women cannot be explained through occupational gender segregation. Therefore, other reasons have to be considered. For example, the use of flexible work opportunities could be prevented through the "flexibility stigma" (Williams et al., 2013, p. 211) which describes a negative interpretation of flexible working practices through a perceived lesser work devotion (Blair-Loy, 2003). For men, in contrast, flexible work practices due to child care – named the "fatherhood bonus" (Munsch, 2016, p. 1571) – could lead to opposed perceptions and fewer barriers to telework.

OCCUPATIONAL STATUS AND WORK-TO-FAMILY CONFLICTS AMONG PARENTS: MEDIATION AND MODERATION EFFECTS

Considering parents' opportunities to harmonize work and family life, telework is expected to play a large role (Chung & van der Horst, 2018; Hill et al., 2010). From the "flexible-resource perspective" (Glavin & Schieman, 2012, p. 76), telework increases role blurring, which facilitates parents' coping with competing role demands. Working at home may reduce time-based conflicts due to reduced commuting times as well as strain-based conflicts because of the absence of social control by colleagues and superiors, and a gain in autonomy, flexibility, or job control.

From the opposing "greedy-role perspective" (Glavin & Schieman, 2012, p. 76), role-blurring due to telework may increase the likelihood of WFC. It is assumed that work demands will expand and require attention, time, and energy in the private sphere, for example by work intensification (Kelliher & Anderson, 2010; Kossek et al., 2006). In this context, telework may be seen as a privilege provided by employers to reward committed employees (Kelly & Kalev, 2006). Following exchange theory (Blau, 1964), this privilege, in turn, goes along with the expectation of hard work, commitment, and work dedication through effort and time in return to flexibility and trust. Additionally, Schieman and Young (2010) describe that the share of professional and family obligations pursued simultaneously, named "work-family multitasking" (p. 1392), increases and acts as a mediator for WFC because of a higher border permeability. As a result, WFC can arise, especially if the behavior in the sphere is important for a person's self-concept, or if not fulfilling demands in one sphere is negatively related to sanctions (Greenhaus & Beutell, 1985).

Hence, it is questionable whether telework is a resource or a demand (Bakker & Demerouti, 2007) which leads to a decrease or increase of WFC among working parents. In line with Glavin and Schieman (2012), we assume differential influences on the perception of WFC depending on two important characteristics of (tele)workers: occupational status and gender.

The Mediating Role of Telework

In line with work/family border theory, the role of parents as border crossers between the spheres has to be considered (Clark, 2000). For roles that are linked to central positions in the spheres, fewer conflicts between the spheres are assumed, because the shape of borders can then be determined and controlled to a greater extent (Clark, 2000). For example, a high occupational status opens up new possibilities to control border permeability, and reconcile family life and gainful employment. The availability of additional socio-economic resources provides not only more general advantages to avoid the emergence of reconciliation conflicts (Conger et al., 2010), for example through supplemental childcare. Also, the use of telework can be seen as a resource to reduce WFC.

From the greedy role perspective, teleworking in higher occupational positions may negatively influence WFC, through increased role blurring. In line with this argument, Schieman et al. (2009) introduced the "stress of higher status hypothesis" (p. 969) proposing that employees in high-status jobs (that are mostly perceived as providing greater work resources) will have to meet new work and family demands due to an increase in border permeability. For a sample of adults in the United States, Schieman et al. (2009) found a moderating effect of schedule control according to working hours per week. Participants with less than 50 working hours per week reported a stable level of work–nonwork interference, regardless of whether they had the possibility to structure their work schedule on their own or not. Otherwise, employees working more than 50 hours per week showed increasing measures of work–nonwork interference with the extent of schedule control. Similar effects were observed for increased overtime work for employees in flexible working arrangements as telework or flexitime (Lott, 2015, 2019), especially for men. With these two perspectives on telework in mind, we propose the following hypothesis with occupational status as the independent variable:

> *H1.* Telework mediates the relationship between occupational status and work-to-family conflicts among parents.

The Moderating Role of Gender

Besides the structural distribution of telework, gender-specific role expectations and behavior in the use of telework may lead to different levels of perceived WFC. Previous research has indicated that teleworking mothers are more likely to expand their time spend on childcare (Lott, 2019). For fathers, in contrast, the use of telework is related to a stable lower number of hours in childcare, and a greater expansion of overtime hours. In detail, Lott (2019) reported an increase of two overtime hours per week on average for fathers in addition to a generally higher number of overtime hours. Teleworking mothers expanded their lower levels of overtime hours only by one additional hour.

The difference in extending working hours can be explained by gender-specific asymmetrical permeable boundaries between work and family (Pleck, 1977). From this theoretical perspective, traditional gender roles cause a prioritization of family needs for women, while men give priority to their job duties. Moreover, expanding effort and time in the work or family sphere can be a practice to conform to gender role expectations, following the doing gender approach (West & Zimmerman, 1987). In line with the approach of specific asymmetrical permeable boundaries, men experience more extension of work to family but are less devoted to prevent demands from border-crossing to the family sphere than women. Even though role blurring from work to family life may be less intensive among women, we assume that female teleworkers tend to put more effort into the protection of the family sphere, and hence experience more WFC. We assume that this association has not reversed despite the fact that others point to egalitarian trends through changing gender roles, for example with men filling the role of involved fathers (Gerson, 2010; McGill, 2014).

For a broad understanding of gender-specific differences in WFC, a joint examination of gender and occupational status is important (Acker, 2000;

Williams et al., 2013). With the increase of women's employment rate in the second half of the twentieth century, work and family role expectations of women have risen (Beck-Gernsheim, 1983), and women are likely to seek flexibility at work in order to reconcile competing work and family demands. For mothers especially, the reconciliation of employment with raising young children may be problematic, particularly for those in higher status positions (Hochschild, 1990).

Female teleworkers in high-status positions are particularly likely to experience time-based WFC. Both spheres demand a special amount of time from mothers, while telework is indirectly fostering a time expansion in both spheres (Lott, 2019). Moreover, mothers working in high-status jobs may feel a stronger burden of reconciliation than male counterparts working in similar occupations because of gender-specific expectations on parenting.

Even though processes of retraditionalization of the distribution of labor are buffered by higher absolute wages of mothers after the birth of the first child (Schober, 2013), mothers often do the greater share of care work (Baxter et al., 2008; Dechant & Blossfeld, 2015). On the other hand, employed mothers who work in low-status occupations are faced with lower work commitment expectations. Working part-time is known as a common strategy to reconcile work–family demands in Germany, but is not yet common for higher-status occupations (Kleinert, 2007). The expectations on mothers in high-status occupations may lead to more strain-based WFC because of a higher expected commitment to work (Hochschild, 1990). Similarly, specific aspects of higher-status occupations such as a higher decision-making-latitude, job authority, and excessive work pressure increase role blurring which is a predictor for WFC (Glavin & Schieman, 2012). We test the following hypothesis:

> *H2*. Gender will moderate the relationship between occupational status and work-to-family conflicts, mediated by telework. The relationship will be stronger among mothers than among fathers.

The Moderating Role of the COVID-19 Pandemic

With the COVID-19 pandemic, different dynamics supporting a wider spread of telework became relevant. Often parents were obligated to work from home to reduce the spread of the virus and simultaneously had to provide child care because of closed school and child care facilities. In addition, care by older relatives, such as grandparents, could no longer be provided due to the risk of infection (Müller et al., 2020). Only in exceptional cases when child care could not be provided by the parents, care was offered in emergency care facilities. Previously, in the pre-pandemic period organizations had begun to integrate telework as a flexible work practice, albeit it remained a specialty mostly in occupations with home office-compatible assignments for rather highly qualified and committed employees (Brenke, 2016; Grunau et al., 2019). In the pandemic, parents who had never worked from home, or had never been trained to telework, faced a sudden need to work from home and improvised change in the way they work.

In the very dynamic situation of the pandemic, occupational status and gender may have more predictive power as predictors of WFC. Compared to the pre-pandemic period we assume a further differentiation of unequal effects of occupational status and gender on WFC with the opportunity to and frequency of telework. Various COVID-19 studies show an increase in telework in favor of employees with higher occupational status in Germany in the pandemic (Abendroth et al., 2022; Schröder et al., 2020). Employees with higher formal education and higher income were more likely to be able to continue pre-pandemic work in telework at home because these employees often used telework already before the pandemic (Schröder et al., 2020). Unlike high-qualified employees, low-qualified workers have experienced negative effects such as a greater implementation of short-time work ("Kurzarbeit") by employers (Schröder et al., 2020). Following our previous considerations on telework-compatible occupations in the pre-pandemic period, we assume that occupations carried out by low-status workers were mostly not transformed to telework because of a lack of compatibility. As a result, employees were able to continue their occupation at a central workplace with extended safety requirements or stopped working, for instance, due to job loss or short-time work.

For ongoing work at central workplaces, new safety requirements could increase the perceived strain of the employees, and job loss or short-time work may highly affect parents' concerns about the economic situation in their families due to financial insecurity. Notwithstanding, the scenarios do not indicate a substantial increase of role-blurring or integration of the family and work spheres which may contribute to increasing WFC. Simultaneously, parents with a higher occupational status needed to cope with increasing role blurring due to increased border permeability through telework, while having to meet requirements of child care or homeschooling. Following the explanations of increased heterogeneity by occupational status in the pandemic, we assume that:

H3. The pandemic will moderate the relationship between occupational status and work-to-family conflicts, mediated by telework. The occupational status will be more strongly associated with work-to-family conflicts in the pandemic period through increased telework among parents.

Equivalent to the interactions of gender and occupational status before the beginning of the COVID-19 pandemic, different effects could arise for men and women under the new circumstances. Approximately half of the women have provided the majority of care work in couples during the pandemic (Kohlrausch & Zucco, 2020; Möhring et al., 2020). Estimations for fathers who are predominantly caring for children vary from nearly 25% (Möhring et al., 2020) to 12% (Kohlrausch & Zucco, 2020). Taking gender-specific effects into account, Kohlrausch and Zucco (2020) examined a decreasing amount of egalitarian distribution of child care in couples, to the disadvantage of women. On the contrary, Hipp and Bünning (2020) described only slight changes in the division of child care and housework and a stable gendered division among parents throughout the pandemic. Therefore, appraisals in the current debate on a gendered distribution of labor vary from increasing unequal distribution to no significant change or further diversification (Boll & Schüller, 2020; Hipp & Bünning, 2020). In the light of the previously stated approach of asymmetrical permeable boundaries between work and family (Pleck, 1977), we assume increasing WFC among parents, and mothers in particular, who had to perform paid work and child care simultaneously in their homes.

Focusing on the interplay of status and gender, Kohlrausch and Zucco (2020) showed that women, besides employees with rather low incomes, have reduced their working time more than men because of child care. Hence, women with low incomes were most likely to reduce their working time. This could result from women's (self-)perception as primary caregivers in families, on a normative as well as a structural basis. From this perspective, a reduction in working time could also be seen as a strategy to prevent WFC. Conversely, we expect that mothers who have more time-intensive jobs will continue to be predominantly responsible for child care during the pandemic, leading to increased WFC. To examine interacting relations between gender and occupational status in the pre-pandemic period compared with the pandemic, we suggest:

> *H4.* For mothers, the effect of the occupational status on work-to-family conflicts via telework is stronger in the pandemic period than in the pre-pandemic period.

In summary, Fig. 4.1 describes the hypothesized relationships between occupational status and work-to-family conflicts as well as the hypothesized mediating/moderating roles of telework, gender, and the pandemic period.

DATA AND METHOD

Hereinafter, we give further insight into the survey data of the German Family Panel (pairfam), the preparation as well as the applied strategies of the hypotheses-driven analyses.

DATA AND SAMPLE RESTRICTION

Empirical analyses are based on data provided by the pairfam study (Brüderl et al., 2019, 2021). Yearly follow-up interviews are conducted with respondents

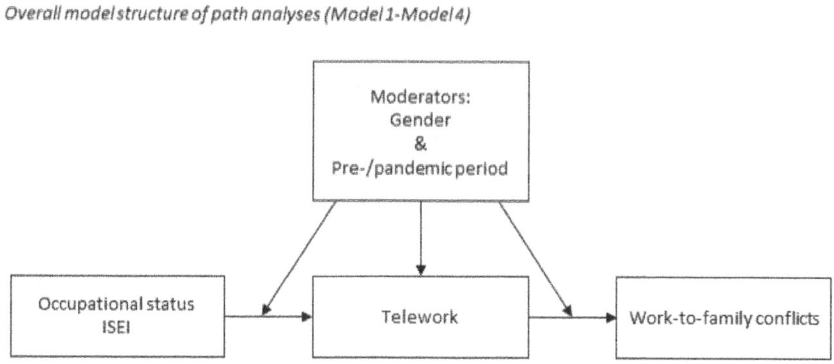

Fig. 4.1. Overall Model Structure of Path Analyses (Models 1–4).

(anchor persons) who were exclusively drawn from the birth cohorts 1971–1973, 1981–1983, and 1991–1993. The partners of the anchor persons are also interviewed via separate questionnaires. The pairfam study provides, amongst others, information on employment characteristics and WFC. For a detailed description of the study, see Huinink et al. (2011). In the present study, three analytic samples are included: pre-pandemic sample in wave 10 (fielding period October 2017 – May 2018), pre-pandemic sample (fielding period November 2019 – March 2020), and pandemic sample (fielding period May 2020 – July 2020) in wave 12. The analytic samples are restricted to employed mothers and fathers working a minimum of 20 hours per week without commuting from a second place of residence. Also, we limited the data to parents in heterosexual couples living with at least one child younger than 18 years of age. The final analytical sample consists of $N = 2{,}203$ parents ($n = 1{,}090$ women and $n = 1{,}113$ men) and 3,315 person-years.

MEASURES

The exogenous variable of the present study is perceived work-to-family conflict. We use four items that are commonly used to measure WFC (Carlson et al., 2000; Thönnissen et al., 2020). Participants were asked to what extent the following four statements apply to them: *"Because of my workload in my job, vocational training, or university education, my personal life suffers."*, *"My work prevents me from doing things with my friends, partner, and family more than I'd like."*, *"Even when I am doing something with my friends, partner, or family, I must often think about work."*, and *"After the stress of work, I find it difficult to relax at home and/ or to enjoy my free time with others."* The first two statements indicate time-based WFC, the latter two statements strain-based WFC. Response choices using a five-point Likert scale range from "not at all" (= 1) to "absolutely" (= 5). The intermediate values represent partial agreement/disagreement to the statements. Based on available data, we created a single measure by taking the mean value of the respondents' answers to all four items, which keeps the same scale as the initial items. High values, therefore, indicate strong perceptions of WFC.

Occupational status is represented by the International Socio-Economic Index of occupational status (ISEI) (Ganzeboom et al., 1992). ISEI is covering status through education and income based on the ISCO-08 classification schema (e.g., kitchen helpers = 10, specialist medical practitioners = 89) (Ganzeboom, 2010b, 2010a). Gender is provided as a binary variable restricted to men (= 0) and women (= 1).

As recommended by Allen et al. (2015), the frequency of telework is measured as a continuous variable. Employed interviewees who mentioned having the possibility to work from home beside an unchanging work location, were asked how often they work from home. Parents who mentioned not having the possibility to work from home or having constantly changing workplaces, e.g., truck drivers, traveling salespersons, or people away on a job for installation/repairs, were not covered in this question but were coded manually as less often/never. Likewise, persons working exclusively from home were excluded by the filter and coded to daily.

The original item asked the respondents who do not exclusively work from home "How often do you work from home?" and provided the response choices "Daily" (= 1), "Several times per week" (= 2), "Once per week" (= 3), "1-3 times per month" (= 4), and "Less often" (= 5). Because of the varying time frame within the survey question, we applied percentages of working time per month to standardize the response categories. Based on the operationalization by van der Lippe and Lippényi (2020), we measure the proportion of monthly telework from total work (Daily/exclusively from home = 1, Several times per week = 0.55, Once per week = 0.18, 1–3 times per month = 0.09, Less often/never = 0.02). The sample restriction on working hours enables the assumption of a working week consisting of five days, even though teleworking is not mutually exclusive with same-day work at a central workplace.

To measure different outcomes under the conditions of the pandemic period, the data from 2017 to 2018 (t_1) and from 2019 to 2020 (t_2) were joint to represent the pre-pandemic period, while survey data from 2020 (t_3) exhibits the pandemic period.

Given the conceptual framework and design of the pairfam, the birth cohort was separated into three variables: 1991–1993, 1981–1983, and 1971–1973. Moreover, we cover average weekly working hours including overtime hours by anchor person and their partner. The number of children and the age of the youngest child living in a household with the anchor person are measured in metric variables.

Additionally, educational status (no degree, lower secondary education = lower 1; upper secondary education vocational, upper secondary education general, post-secondary non-tertiary education general = intermediate 2; first and second stage of tertiary education = higher 3) based on ISCED-97, monthly personal net income, and household net income were reported in the description (Table 4.1, Appendix 4.1), even though they were not included in the analysis due to multicollinearity. We also present a dummy indicating whether the respondent lives in East Germany or not.

METHOD

The analysis is performed gradually, starting with the computation of cross-sectional path analysis over all three time points (Fig. 4.1). We use moderated mediation with maximum likelihood estimation, following Hayes (2013). We begin with the initial model of mediation analysis between occupational status and WFC via telework (Model 1). In the second place, gender is included as a moderator variable (Model 2). To examine changes in the course of the pandemic, the time point of the COVID-19 pandemic is integrated as a binary moderator variable to the initial model (Model 3). To test gender-specific effects, the previous model, including the time-varying factor as a moderator, is calculated for women and men separately (Model 4). The bootstrap re-sampling technique with 5,000 resamples was executed (Preacher & Hayes, 2008) to avoid biased results in the mediation of cross-sectional data (Maxwell et al., 2011; Shrout, 2011). Moreover,

Table 4.1. Descriptive Statistics for Mothers and Fathers.

Variable	Mothers		Fathers	
	M	*SD*	*M*	*SD*
Work-to-family conflicts	2.30	0.91	2.44***	0.86
ISEI	52.86	19.39	50.90*	21.65
Telework				
Daily	8.43	–	6.38*	–
Two – four times per week	7.50	–	5.73	–
Once per week	2.97	–	4.37*	–
One – three times per month	2.79	–	5.97***	–
Less often / Never	78.31	–	77.55	–
Telework (continuous)	0.11	0.27	0.09	0.24
Weekly working hours [a]	32.77	9.10	43.12***	8.17
Partners weekly working hours [a]	40.92	12.37	21.06***	15.65
Personal net income last month	1669.32	915.42	2819.50***	1362.93
Monthly net household income	4418.75	2297.23	4542.77	3518.26
Number of children in household	1.81	0.74	1.84	0.80
Age of youngest child in household	9.55	5.56	7.06***	5.50
ISCED				
Lower	3.52	–	4.36	–
Intermediate	52.56	–	47.70*	–
Higher	43.92	–	47.94	–
East	37.37	–	31.92*	–
Birth cohort				
1971–1973	47.07	–	47.41	–
1981–1983	47.99	–	47.17	–
1991–1993	4.94	–	5.42	–

Source: pairfam, waves 10 and 12.
Notes: $N = 3{,}315$; Female sample ($n = 1{,}619$); Male sample ($n = 1{,}696$). We present means for continuous variables and percentages for categorical variables over all time points analyzed. Asterisks symbolize significant differences between mothers and fathers examined by *t*-tests (two-tailed) across continuous variables and logistic regression for all binary variables with cluster-adjusted standard errors.
[a] Average working hours including overtime hours estimated by anchor person.
$^{*}p < 0.05$. $^{**}p < 0.01$. $^{***}p < 0.001$.

we applied robust standard errors clustered at the individual level to take into account double representation of respondents in data of wave 10 and 12.

RESULTS

Descriptive and Bivariate Analysis

We begin this section with descriptive statistics separately for mothers and fathers (Table 4.1) and observation periods (Table A4.1). We present means for continuous variables and percentages for categorical variables. To test for statistically significant differences, we perform *t*-tests (two-tailed) across continuous variables and logistic regression for all binary variables with cluster-adjusted standard errors.

Fathers report on average significantly higher WFC than mothers (Table 4.1). Unlike previous assumptions, women in our study sample work on average in jobs with slightly higher occupational status than men. Even though the vast majority of the sample does telework less than once a month or never, mothers are working more often from home on a daily basis than fathers. Conversely, fathers are more likely to telework less often. However, using a continuous variable for telework, no significant difference in the average telework frequency between mothers and fathers is found.

The further information on working hours shows structures of men as breadwinners and women as supplemental earners. Means for weekly working hours for male anchor persons and partners are similar to full-time employment, whereas women's weekly working hours remain on a lower average level. Moreover, men report higher incomes than women, but the monthly net household income does not differ significantly. Furthermore, differences in means are found on average age of youngest child in the household, and slightly more mothers live in eastern parts of Germany.

Considering the three time points, no change is seen in our focal variable WFC, pointing out that not every parent experienced greater WFC during the pandemic (Table A4.1). We find an increase over time in telework frequency which can be mainly attributed to pandemic containment measures. Other differences can be traced back to changes across the life course. Educational level and occupational status increase over the career, particularly in the youngest cohort. Likewise, men and women from the youngest cohort are most likely to become parents at the end of the observation period, thus lowering the mean for the age of the youngest child.

However, the distribution of birth cohorts is not without problems. While the youngest cohort (1991–1993) is underrepresented during the pre-pandemic period, it consists of nearly one-fifth of the sample during the pandemic. These cohort differences are less of a problem in the analysis without pandemic effects, but they may become problematic in the analysis of changes through the pandemic. Moreover, the relatively small sample size of the pandemic sample in wave 12, due to the interference of the pandemic in March 2020 in the process of survey conduction, may lead to an underscoring of the influence of the pandemic. Although some variables show significant differences between both pre-pandemic time points, we will only distinguish between the pre-pandemic ($t_1 + t_2$) and pandemic time points (t_3) to test our theoretical assumptions on the pandemic influence.

Moderated Mediation Analysis

All presented models converge. The use of clustered standard errors avoids the computation of standard measures of model fit. We, therefore, run the initial model without clustered standard errors which shows sufficient values of the RMSEA, CFI, and TLI (Acock, 2013), see Table A4.2. On this basis, we assume that also the models with clustered standard errors fit well to the data.

Effects of Occupational Status, Telework and Gender on WFC

We start with Model 1 in which we include only telework and occupational status. The direct, indirect, and total effects are shown in Table 4.2. The direct effects

Table 4.2. Direct, Indirect and Total Effects Predicting Parents' WFC (Model 1).

Variable	Direct Effect			Indirect Effect			Total Effect		
	b	*SE*	*p*	*b*	*SE*	*p*	*b*	*SE*	*p*
Telework	0.303	0.067	<0.001	–	–	–	0.303	0.067	<0.001
ISEI	0.003	0.001	<0.001	0.001	0.000	<0.001	0.005	0.001	<0.001

Source: pairfam, waves 10 and 12.
Notes: Unstandardized coefficients and bootstrapped SEs (5,000 repetitions); $N = 3{,}315$. Further controlled for age of the youngest child, the number of children, weekly working hours, partner's weekly working hours, and birth cohort.

of telework ($b = 0.303$, $p < 0.001$) as well as occupational status ($b = 0.003$, $p < 0.001$) have significant positive effects on WFC. Accordingly, the higher frequency of telework and the higher the occupational status, the higher the perceived levels of WFC. Hypothesis *H1* can be confirmed through the significant indirect ($b = 0.001$, $p < 0.001$) and total effect ($b = 0.005$, $p < 0.001$) of occupational status. Consistent with our expectations in *H1*, telework mediates the relationship between occupational status and WFC.

In Model 2, hypothesis *H2* is tested (Table 4.3a). As discussed above, we assume that gender moderates the relationship between occupational status and telework and the relationship between telework and WFC. The direct effect for telework decreases in strength and significance ($b = 0.177$, $p < 0.10$), but the relationship remains positive. The indirect effect of occupational status becomes less significant too ($b = 0.001$, $p < 0.10$), but its effects reach at least the 90% level of significance. Again, this result lends support to the hypothesis that the relationship between occupational status and WFC is mediated by parents' telework frequency. Overall, mothers report higher levels of WFC ($b = 0.239$, $p < 0.05$). This finding contrasts the previously stated higher mean of WFC for fathers in the description (Table 4.1) but can be explained through our choice of control variables, in particular weekly working hours. Telework is associated with higher levels of WFC for mothers in reference to fathers ($b = 0.224$, $p < 0.10$). Above that, Model 2 shows an insignificant direct effect ($b = 0.001$, $p > 0.10$) and an insignificant indirect effect ($b = 0.000$, $p > 0.10$) for the interaction between gender and occupational status.

Table 4.3a. Direct, Indirect and Total Effects Predicting Parents' WFC (Model 2).

Variable	Direct Effect			Indirect Effect			Total Effect		
	b	*SE*	*p*	*b*	*SE*	*p*	*b*	*SE*	*p*
Telework	0.177	0.096	0.063	–	–	–	0.177	0.096	0.063
ISEI	0.003	0.001	0.006	0.001	0.000	0.069	0.004	0.001	0.001
Female	0.239	0.100	0.017	−0.006	0.006	0.274	0.232	0.101	0.021
Female X ISEI	0.001	0.002	0.652	0.000	0.000	0.137	0.001	0.002	0.561
Female X Telework	0.224	0.131	0.086	–	–	–	0.224	0.131	0.086

Source: pairfam, waves 10 and 12.
Notes: Unstandardized coefficients and bootstrapped SEs (5,000 repetitions); $N = 3{,}315$. Further controlled for age of the youngest child, the number of children, weekly working hours, partner's weekly working hours, and birth cohort.

The analysis of whether the mediation of the occupational status on WFC via telework is conditional on gender shows a significant impact for both men and women (Table 4.3b). Regarding hypothesis *H2*, we find slight differences in the gender-specific effect strength and levels of significance (fathers $b = 0.001, p < 0.05$; mothers $b = 0.002, p < 0.001$). Further computation confirms gendered differences at the 99% level of significance (Wald-Test: $p < 0.01$). Therefore, hypothesis *H2* can be accepted. Occupational status is associated with WFC, but this link is not only mediated via telework. This mediation is also moderated by gender and perceived WFC is slightly more influenced by occupational status among mothers than among fathers.

Effects of Occupational Status, Telework and COVID-19 Pandemic on WFC

The mediation results and moderation test predicted in hypothesis *H3* are provided in Table 4.4a. The analysis shows stable direct effects for telework and occupational status when distinguishing between pre-pandemic and pandemic periods. Contrary to our expectation, the direct ($b = -0.239, p > 0.10$) and the indirect effect ($b = -0.016, p > 0.10$) of the pandemic are negative and do not reach statistical significance. Although the direct effect of the interaction between the pandemic and the occupational status is insignificant ($b = 0.004, p > 0.10$), there is a significant indirect effect for the interaction ($b = 0.001, p < 0.05$). However, the interacting effect between the pandemic period and telework frequency fails to reach an acceptable significance level ($b = -0.145, p > 0.10$).

Next, we investigate whether the indirect effect is moderated by the pandemic (Table 4.4b). Our findings suggest that occupational status is not more strongly

Table 4.3b. Bootstrap Test of Moderating Mediation Effects Predicting Parents' WFC (Model 2).

Moderator		Effect	*SE*	*p*
Gender				
	Men	0.001	0.000	0.047
	Women	0.002	0.000	<0.001

Source: pairfam, waves 10 and 12.

Table 4.4a. Direct, Indirect and Total Effects Predicting Parents' WFC (Model 3).

Variable	Direct effect			Indirect effect			Total effect		
	b	*SE*	*p*	*b*	*SE*	*p*	*B*	*SE*	*p*
Telework	0.325	0.076	<0.001	–	–	–	0.325	0.076	<0.001
ISEI	0.003	0.001	0.001	0.001	0.000	<0.001	0.004	0.001	<0.001
Pandemic	−0.239	0.157	0.128	−0.016	0.017	0.346	−0.255	0.158	0.106
Pandemic X ISEI	0.004	0.003	0.215	0.001	0.000	0.012	0.005	0.003	0.115
Pandemic X Telework	−0.145	0.151	0.339	–	–	–	−0.145	0.151	0.339

Source: pairfam, waves 10 and 12.
Notes: Unstandardized coefficients and bootstrapped SEs (5,000 repetitions); $N = 3{,}315$. Further controlled for age of the youngest child, the number of children, weekly working hours, partner's weekly working hours, and birth cohort.

Table 4.4b. Bootstrap Test of Moderating Mediation Effects Predicting Parents' WFC (Model 3).

Moderator		Effect	*SE*	*p*
Period				
	Pre-pandemic	0.001	0.000	<0.001
	Pandemic	0.001	0.001	0.199

Source: pairfam, waves 10 and 12.

associated with higher WFC in the pandemic period via increased telework ($b = 0.001$, $p > 0.10$). Evidence for the presumed relation between occupational status and WFC via telework is only significant in the pre-pandemic period ($b = 0.001$, $p < 0.001$). Hence, we do not find support for our hypothesis *H3*.

The final Model 4 enables a comparison of the results of Model 3 for mothers and fathers through separate analyses (Table 4.5a). Telework and occupational status both increase mothers' and fathers' WFC. Overall, the effects of telework and occupational status are larger and statistically more significant for mothers. Fathers report significantly lower levels of WFC in the period of COVID-19 ($b = -0.520$, $p < 0.05$). Only in the interplay with occupational status, fathers report significantly higher WFC in the pandemic period ($b = 0.010$, $p < 0.05$). For mothers, in contrast, no significant effect of the observation period is found, neither exclusively, nor in interplay with occupational status or telework.

Table 4.5a. Direct, Indirect and Total Effects Predicting Mothers' and Fathers' WFC (Model 4).

Group	Variable	Direct Effect			Indirect Effect			Total effect		
		b	*SE*	*p*	*b*	*SE*	*p*	*b*	*SE*	*p*
Fathers										
	Telework	0.204	0.111	0.066	–	–	–	0.204	0.111	0.066
	ISEI	0.002	0.001	0.050	0.001	0.000	0.074	0.003	0.001	0.013
	Pandemic	–0.520	0.222	0.019	–0.019	0.015	0.210	–0.539	0.222	0.015
	Pandemic X ISEI	0.010	0.004	0.017	0.001	0.001	0.107	0.011	0.004	0.010
	Pandemic X Telework	–0.318	0.237	0.179	–	–	–	–0.318	0.237	0.179
Mothers										
	Telework	0.416	0.102	<0.001	–	–	–	0.416	0.102	<0.001
	ISEI	0.005	0.002	0.002	0.002	0.000	<0.001	0.007	0.001	<0.001
	Pandemic	0.074	0.216	0.731	0.007	0.035	0.846	0.081	0.221	0.714
	Pandemic X ISEI	–0.003	0.004	0.446	0.001	0.001	0.295	–0.002	0.004	0.587
	Pandemic X Telework	–0.010	0.196	0.957	–	–	–	–0.010	0.196	0.957

Source: pairfam, waves 10 and 12.
Notes: Unstandardized coefficients and bootstrapped SEs (5,000 repetitions); $N = 3{,}315$ ($n = 1{,}696$ fathers and $n = 1{,}619$ mothers). Further controlled for age of the youngest child, the number of children, weekly working hours, partner's weekly working hours, and birth cohort.

The results of the moderated mediation indicate that the impact from the occupational status on WFC via telework is significant for fathers only in the pre-pandemic period ($b = 0.001$, $p < 0.05$) but not in the pandemic ($b = -0.001$, $p > 0.10$) (Table 4.5b). Hence, the occupational status loses its association with WFC for fathers during the pandemic period through increased telework.

For mothers, the moderation in the pre-pandemic period ($b = 0.002$, $p < 0.001$) is significant as well as in the pandemic, but on a lower significance level ($b = 0.002$, $p < 0.10$), whereas the effect strengths are similar (Table 4.5b). Further control by Wald-test results in no significant differences between the effects ($p > 0.10$). Therefore, hypothesis *H4* cannot be accepted. For mothers, the effect of the occupational status on work-to-family conflicts via telework is not stronger in the pandemic period than in the pre-pandemic period.

SUMMARY AND DISCUSSION

As previously stated, different status-related and gendered factors that ease or complicate the use of flexible telework endure from the pre-pandemic period (Felstead et al., 2002; Golden, 2008; Grunau et al., 2019) to the pandemic time (Abendroth et al., 2022; Schröder et al., 2020). Working from home has not been feasible for all employed mothers and fathers in Germany, and the limited access to telework, indeed, leads to different perceptions of work-to-family conflicts.

Our analysis shows an increase in work-to-family conflicts for parents with higher occupational status and parents working more often in telework. In respect to hypothesis *H1*, there is also a mediating effect of telework for parents with a higher occupational status. These findings do not only support the stress of the higher status hypothesis (Schieman & Young, 2010) through the direct effect of occupational status on the perception of work-to-family conflicts. Integration of work and family spheres (Clark, 2000) through telework is related to higher work-to-family conflicts as well. In addition to the factors already reviewed, role-blurring may increase the difficulty of reconciliation. Otherwise, work intensification could be facilitated through the possibility of working from home in the free time. Surprisingly, the greedy role perspective (Glavin & Schieman, 2012) sheds light on unequal social patterns on work-to-family conflicts to the advantage of parents with lower occupational status, who are less often (or never) working from home. Even if the flexibility causes new opportunities in other

Table 4.5b. Bootstrap Test of Moderating Mediation Effects Predicting Mothers' and Fathers' WFC (Model 4).

Moderator		Men			Women		
		Effect	*SE*	*p*	Effect	*SE*	*p*
Period							
	Pre-pandemic	0.001	0.000	0.045	0.002	0.000	<0.001
	Pandemic	–.001	0.001	0.586	0.002	0.001	0.059

Source: pairfam, waves 10 and 12.

cases, these employees do not have to manage their role boundaries and cope with role-blurring in the same way and to the same extent as teleworkers with higher occupational status.

However, non-telework segregating family and work spheres may only be one solution out of many to prevent work-to-family conflicts, while other strategies may arise from work and family responsibilities within couples, such as adjustments in the division of labor or scaling back on working hours (Adams & Golsch, 2022). This leads to the gender-specific analysis of the research questions. Holding the control variables fixed, women do not only show higher perceived conflicts than men, they significantly do so in the interaction with telework. These gender differences could arise from asymmetric permeability of the boundaries and the burden of fulfilling caregiving demands simultaneously to work. Schieman and Young (2010) provide further evidence for increasing conflicts as a consequence of work–family-multitasking. On the contrary, no gender-specific effects are found for occupational status. Gender roles may not be as decisive to occupational status as to flexible working.

Nevertheless, we tested a moderation effect by gender on the interplay of occupational status, telework, and work-to-family conflicts as hypothesized in *H2*. We find supporting results for the moderation for men and women. Mothers with higher occupational status perceive slightly higher work-to-family conflicts than fathers, mediated by a higher frequency of telework. While fathers perceive slightly lower work-to-family conflicts when working from home as high occupational employees, mothers often have to cope with the double burden of caring and doing high-quality work. This can result in feelings of conflict from work to family because work demands are breaking through the gender-specific extra border in the family sphere (Pleck, 1977). In addition, cultural beliefs as the flexibility stigma (Williams et al., 2013) and fatherhood bonus (Munsch, 2016) may produce further pressure on mothers to fulfill job requirements.

With the pandemic, the situations in the work and family spheres changed a lot for many families. In particular, parents with younger children perceived higher conflicts between private and professional spheres (Schieman et al., 2021) Therefore, we compared effects from the pre-pandemic period to the pandemic. We found a strong increase in teleworking in the data over the three time points, while the perception of work-to-family conflicts remained on a stable level. Similar to the first expression in the description, we found no significant systematics in parents' perception of work-to-family conflicts by occupational status mediated by telework in the pandemic, see *H3*. Even though our results give further insight into the systematics of the emergence of work-to-family conflicts in the pandemic. With an indirect significant effect, the analysis shows more conflicts for parents with higher occupational status under the pandemic conditions. Support for this result can be provided by findings of higher work–life conflicts for individuals with higher educational attainment and work weeks of 50 hours or more in the pandemic period (Schieman et al., 2021).The increase may arise from a stronger responsibility of managing the changing situation at work. Against our assumptions, perception of work-to-family conflicts by telework did not change between pre-pandemic and pandemic periods, even though preliminary findings from qualitative studies focusing on the pandemic support the presumption of increased role blurring as a disadvantage (Adisa et al., 2020). Moreover, work intensification in the family sphere during telework, for example due to supporting children in their school routine, was reported (Adisa et al., 2020).

However, the separated examination via gender also revealed effects that were previously overlooked. Fathers show significantly less work-to-family conflicts in the pandemic, but the effect of occupational status does strengthen conflicts under the conditions of the pandemic. The first effect could be interpreted as an indicator of reduced work commitment, for example through less importance of ideal worker norms (Williams et al., 2013) and attendance culture in the exceptional situation of the pandemic. Men could have used the increased opportunity to participate in family life (Adisa et al., 2020; Chung et al., 2020). Only higher occupational status changed this relation. Possible reasons may be a higher work commitment or an increasing responsibility at work in the pandemic. Following the results of the moderation test, the impact of occupational status on work-to-family conflicts does not indicate a stable effect in the pandemic for men. The absence of the mediating effect in the pandemic for fathers may result from the described reduction in work pressure or increased flexibility in scheduling work and family activities, such as breaks or meals.

Again, this significant evidence was found for mothers. The adverse effect of occupational status on work-to-family conflicts mediated by telework was also found in the pandemic, but the effect strength does not vary from the pre-pandemic to the pandemic period. Therefore, hypothesis *H4*, stating an increase of the effect in the pandemic in particular for women, cannot be supported. This finding could result from further differentiation in the distribution of work in couples in the course of the pandemic.

The presented results could be limited through the cross-sectional analysis with the time points only as moderating variables. The highly minimized sample in the pandemic period as well as only two waves of data including the focal variables restricted the appliance of a longitudinal perspective to our regret. Considering limitations in the structure of the variables, we see more potential in the differentiation of ability to and use of telework. Unfortunately, information on the compatibility of occupations to telework was not available in the analyzed data. In the pandemic, especially differences due to a decrease in the possibility of not working from home in own favor may have led to varying outcomes. Furthermore, the effects of role blurring or demanding work were not examined, and only theoretically applied. For a better understanding of the underlying mechanisms, future research should follow on from this to explain the inherent social processes of social inequalities in more detail.

Finally, the analysis underlines the importance of the joint examination of gender and status (Chung & van der Lippe, 2018). Positional advantages and disadvantages mingle with gender norms and form different outcomes on the work–family interface which should not be overlooked. It has to be considered that a higher occupational status and flexibility of telework does not lead to lower levels of work-to-family conflicts. Therefore, further research should be conducted on the interplay of class and gender, and their influence on flexible working practices and boundary management to measure the future dynamics that emerge and remain through the pandemic.

Table A4.1. Descriptive Statistics for Pre-pandemic and Pandemic Period (t_1–t_3).

Variable	*Pre-pandemic period*				*Pandemic period*	
	t_1 2017/2018		t_2 2019/2020		t_3 2020	
	M	*SD*	*M*	*SD*	*M*	*SD*
Work-to-family conflicts	2.36	0.88	2.39	0.90	2.34	0.89
ISEI	50.75***	20.67	52.55	20.59	54.14	19.91
Telework						
Daily	6.03	–	6.52	–	18.06***	–
Two – four times per week	4.72***	–	7.54	–	11.29*	–
Once per week	3.15	–	4.01	–	4.84	–
One – three times per month	3.61*	–	5.37	–	3.87	–
Less often / Never	82.49***	–	76.56	–	61.94***	–
Telework (continuous)	0.08**	0.24	0.10	0.25	0.22***	0.36
Mothers	48.69	–	48.41	–	51.60	–
Weekly working hours [a]	38.38	10.12	38.00	9.91	36.86	10.48
Partners weekly working hours [a]	30.73	17.64	31.00	16.80	29.22	17.77
Personal net income last month	2141.67***	1217.30	2364.20	1376.50	2365.02	1289.16
Monthly net household income	4290.89***	3116.08	4684.27	3108.40	4500.73	1541.57
Number of children in household	1.81	0.77	1.84	0.77	1.88	0.77
Age of youngest child in household	8.45	5.56	8.44	5.83	6.70***	5.20
East	37.30***	–	33.38	–	26.92*	–
ISCED						
Lower	4.12	–	3.86	–	3.53	–
Intermediate	52.16**	–	48.27	–	48.40	–
Higher	43.72***	–	47.86	–	48.08	–
Birthcohort						
1971–1973	56.15***	–	43.53		12.18***	
1981–1983	40.90***	–	50.44	–	66.67***	–
1991–1993	2.95***	–	6.03	–	21.15***	–

Source: pairfam, waves 10 and 12.
Notes: $N = 3{,}315$; t_1 sample ($n = 1{,}528$); t_2 sample ($n = 1{,}475$); t_3 sample ($n = 312$). We present means for continuous variables and percentages for categorical variables. Asterisks symbolize significant differences between t_2 and t_1, and t_2 and t_3 examined by OLS regression for continuous variables and logistic regression for all binary variables with cluster-adjusted standard errors.
[a] Average working hours including overtime hours estimated by anchor person.
$^*p < 0.05$. $^{**}p < 0.01$. $^{***}p < 0.001$.

Table A4.2. Model fit of Model 1.

	Measures
Chi²	1301.663 ($p < 0.001$)
RMSEA	0.000
[90% CI]	[0.000; 0.000]
CFI	1.000
TLI	1.000

Source: pairfam, waves 10 and 12.

REFERENCES

Abendroth, A.-K., Lott, Y., Hipp, L., Müller, D., & Carstensen, T. (2022). Has the COVID-19 pandemic changed gender- and parental-status-specific differences in working from home? Panel evidence from Germany. Gender, *Work & Organization*. Advance online publication. https://doi.org/10.1111/gwao.12836

Acker, J. (1990). Hierachies, jobs, bodies: A theory of gendered organizations. *Gender & Society*, *4*(2), 139–158. https://doi.org/10.1177/089124390004002002

Acker, J. (2000). Revisiting class: Thinking from gender, race, and organizations. *Social Politics*, *7*(2), 192–214. https://doi.org/10.1093/sp/7.2.192

Acock, A. C. (2013). *Discovering structural equation modeling using Stata*. Stata Press.

Adams, A., & Golsch, K. (2022). Employed parents' reactions to work-family conflicts: Adaptive strategies of scaling back in *Germany. Journal of Family Research*, *34*(4), 1101–1125. https://doi.org/10.20377/jfr-712

Adisa, T. A., Aiyenitaju, O., & Adekoya, O. D. (2020). The work–family balance of British working women during the COVID-19 pandemic. *Journal of Work-Applied Management*, *13*(2), 241–260. https://doi.org/10.1108/JWAM-07-2020-0036

Allen, T. D., Golden, T. D., & Shockley, K. M. (2015). How effective is telecommuting? Assessing the status of our scientific findings. *Psychological Science in the Public Interest*, *16*(2), 40–68. https://doi.org/10.1177/1529100615593273

Allen, T. D., Herst, D. E. L., Bruck, C. S., & Sutton, M. (2000). Consequences associated with work-to-family conflict: A review and agenda for future research. *Journal of Occupational Health Psychology*, *5*(2), 278–308. https://doi.org/10.1037/1076-8998.5.2.278

Allen, T. D., Johnson, R. C., Kiburz, K. M., & Shockley, K. M. (2013). Work-family conflict and flexible work arrangements: Deconstructing flexibility. *Personnel Psychology*, *66*(2), 345–376. https://doi.org/10.1111/peps.12012

Allmendinger, J. (2020). Zurück in alte Rollen: Corona bedroht die Geschlechtergerechtigkeit [Back to old roles: Corona threatens equality]. *WZB Mitteilungen*, *168*, 45–47.

Bakker, A. B., & Demerouti, E. (2007). The job demands-resources model: State of the art. *Journal of Managerial Psychology*, *22*(3), 309–328. https://doi.org/10.1108/02683940710733115

Baxter, J., Hewitt, B., & Haynes, M. (2008). Life course transitions and housework: Marriage, parenthood, and time on housework. *Journal of Marriage and the Family*, *70*(2), 259–272. https://doi.org/10.1111/j.1741-3737.2008.00479.x

Beck-Gernsheim, E. (1983). Vom ‚Dasein für Andere' zum Anspruch auf ein Stück ‚eigenes Leben': Individualisierungsprozesse im weiblichen Lebenszusammenhang [Individualization processes in the female life context]. *Soziale Welt*, *34*(3), 307–340.

Blair-Loy, M. (2003). *Competing devotions: Career and family among women executives*. Harvard University Press.

Blau, P. (1964). *Exchange and power in social life*. Wiley.

Boll, C., & Schüller, S. (2020). *Die Lage ist ernst, aber nicht hoffnungslos: Empirisch gestützte Überlegungen zur elterlichen Aufteilung der Kinderbetreuung vor, während und nach dem COVID-19 Lockdown* [Empirically supported considerations of parental sharing of child care before, during, and after the COVID-19 lockdown]. SOEP Papers No. 1089. https://www.diw.de/documents/publikationen/73/diw_01.c.792058.de/diw_sp1089.pdf

Brenke, K. (2016). Home Office: Möglichkeiten werden bei weitem nicht ausgeschöpft [Telework: Opportunities are far from being fully exploited]. *DIW Wochenbericht*, *5*, 95–106.

Brüderl, J., Drobnič, S., Hank, K., Nauck, B., Neyer, F. J., Walper, S., Alt, P., Bozoyan, C., Buhr, P., Finn, C., Garrett, M., Greischel, H., Gröpler, N., Hajek, K., Herzig, M., Huyer-May, B., Lenke, R., Minkus, L., Müller, B., … Wilhelm, B. (2019). *The German Family Panel (pairfam): ZA5678 Data file Version 10.0.0*. GESIS Data Archive. https://doi.org/10.4232/pairfam.5678.10.0.0

Brüderl, J., Drobnič, S., Hank, K., Neyer, F. J, Walper, S., Alt, P., Borschel, E., Bozoyan, C., Garrett, M., Geissler, S., Gonzalez Avilés, T., Gröpler, N., Hajek, K., Herzig, M., Huyer-May, B., Lenke, R., Lorenz, R., Lutz, K., Minkus, L., … Wetzel, M. (2021). *The German Family Panel (pairfam): ZA5678 Datenfile Version 12.0.0*. GESIS Data Archive. https://doi.org/10.4232/PAIRFAM.5678.12.0.0

Byron, K. (2005). A meta-analytic review of work–family conflict and its antecedents. *Journal of Vocational Behavior*, *67*(2), 169–198. https://doi.org/10.1016/j.jvb.2004.08.009

Carlson, D. S., Kacmar, K., & Williams, L. J. (2000). Construction and initial validation of a multidimensional measure of work–family conflict. *Journal of Vocational Behavior*, *56*(2), 249–276. https://doi.org/10.1006/jvbe.1999.1713

Chung, H., & van der Horst, M. (2018). Women's employment patterns after childbirth and the perceived access to and use of flexitime and teleworking. *Human Relations*, *71*(1), 47–72. https://doi.org/10.1177/0018726717713828

Chung, H., & van der Lippe, T. (2018). Flexible working, work-life balance, and gender equality: Introduction. *Social Indicators Research*, *151*, 365–381. https://doi.org/10.1007/s11205-018-2025-x

Chung, H., Seo, H., Forbes, S. & Birkett, H. (2020). *Working from home during COVID-19 lockdown: Changing preferences and the future of work*. Kent. https://www.birmingham.ac.uk/Documents/college-social-sciences/business/research/wirc/epp-working-from-home-COVID-19-lockdown.pdf

Clark, S. C. (2000). Work/family border theory: A new theory of work/family balance. *Human Relations*, *53*(6), 747–770. https://doi.org/10.1177/0018726700536001

Conger, R. D., Conger, K. J., & Martin, M. J. (2010). Socioeconomic status, family processes, and individual development. *Journal of Marriage and the Family*, *72*(3), 685–704. https://doi.org/10.1111/j.1741-3737.2010.00725.x

Dechant, A., & Blossfeld, H.-P. (2015). Changes in the division of labor within highly educated German couples when the first child is born. *Journal of Family Research*, *27*(3), 373–396. https://doi.org/10.3224/zff.v27i3.21279

Destatis. (2018). *Datenreport 2018: Ein Sozialbericht für die Bundesrepublik Deutschland* [Data report 2018: A social report for the Federal Republic of Germany]. Bundeszentrale für politische Bildung. https://www.wzb.eu/system/files/docs/sv/iuk/dr2018_bf_pdf_ganzes_buch.pdf

Eurofound. (2020). *Living, working and COVID-19*. Dublin. https://www.eurofound.europa.eu/data/covid-19; https://doi.org/10.2806/467608

Eurostat. (2021). *Employed persons working from home as a percentage of the total employment, by sex, age and professional status (%)*. Luxembourg. https://data.europa.eu/data/datasets/orjjzgdf3cnximvsokdfxw?locale=en

Fadinger, H., & Schymik, J. (2020). The costs and benefits of home office during the COVID-19 pandemic: Evidence from infections and an input-output model for Germany. *Covid Economics*, *9*, 107–134.

Felstead, A., Jewson, N., Phizacklea, A., & Walters, S. (2002). The option to work at home: Another privilege for the favoured few? *New Technology, Work and Employment*, *17*(3), 204–223. https://doi.org/10.1111/1468-005X.00105

Ferrant, G., Pesando, L. M., & Nowacka, K. (2014). *Unpaid care work: The missing link in the analysis of gender gaps in labour outcomes*. https://www.oecd.org/dev/development-gender/Unpaid_care_work.pdf

Ganzeboom, H. B. (2010a). *International standard classification of occupations ISCO-08: With ISEI-08 scores*. http://www.harryganzeboom.nl/ISCO08/isco08_with_isei.pdf

Ganzeboom, H. B. (2010b). *A new international socio-economic index [ISEI] of occupational status for international standard classification of occupation 2008 [ISCO-08] constructed with data from the ISSP 2002-2007*. http://www.harryganzeboom.nl/Pdf/2010%20-%20Ganzeboom-ISEI08-ISSP-Lisbon-(paper).pdf

Ganzeboom, H. B., de Graaf, P. M., & Treiman, D. J. (1992). A standard international socio-economic index of occupational status. *Social Science Research*, *21*(1), 1–56. https://doi.org/10.1016/0049-089X(92)90017-B

Gerson, K. (2010). *The unfinished revolution: How a new generation is reshaping family, work, and gender in America*. Oxford University Press.

Glavin, P., & Schieman, S. (2012). Work–family role blurring and work–family conflict. *Work and Occupations*, *39*(1), 71–98. https://doi.org/10.1177/0730888411406295

Golden, L. (2008). Limited access: Disparities in flexible work schedules and work-at-home. *Journal of Family and Economic Issues*, *29*(1), 86–109. https://doi.org/10.1007/s10834-007-9090-7

Greenhaus, J. H., & Beutell, N. J. (1985). Sources of conflict between work and family roles. *The Academy of Management Review*, *10*(1), 76–88. https://doi.org/10.2307/258214

Grunau, P., Ruf, K., Steffes, S., & Wolter, S. (2019). *Homeoffice bietet Vorteile, hat aber auch Tücken* [Home office offers advantages, but also has pitfalls]. IAB-Kurzbericht No. 11. http://doku.iab.de/kurzber/2019/kb1119.pdf

Gutek, B., Searle, S., & Klepa, L. (1991). Rational versus gender role explanations for work-family conflict. *Journal of Applied Psychology*, *76*(4), 560–568.

Hank, K., & Steinbach, A. (2020). The virus changed everything, didn't it? Couples' division of housework and childcare before and during the corona crisis. *Journal of Family Research*, *33*(1), 99–114. https://doi.org/10.20377/jfr-488

Hayes, A. F. (2013). *Introduction to mediation, moderation, and conditional process analysis: A regression-based approach*. The Guilford Press.

Hill, E. J., Erickson, J. J., Holmes, E. K., & Ferris, M. (2010). Workplace flexibility, work hours, and work-life conflict: Finding an extra day or two. *Journal of Family Psychology*, *24*(3), 349–358. https://doi.org/10.1037/a0019282

Hipp, L., & Bünning, M. (2020). Parenthood as a driver of increased gender inequality during COVID-19? Exploratory evidence from Germany. *European Societies*, 1–16. https://doi.org/10.1080/14616696.2020.1833229

Hochschild, A. R. (1990). *The second shift: Working parents and the revolution at home*. Piatkus.

Hochschild, A. R. (1997). *The time bind: When work becomes home and home becomes work*. Metropolitan Books.

Holst, H., Fessler, A., & Niehoff, S. (2021). Covid-19, social class and work experience in Germany: Inequalities in work-related health and economic risks [Special issue]. *European Societies*, *23*(1), 495–512. https://doi.org/10.1080/14616696.2020.1828979

Huinink, J., Brüderl, J., Nauck, B., Walper, S., Castiglioni, L., & Feldhaus, M. (2011). Panel analysis of intimate relationships and family dynamics (pairfam): Conceptual framework and design. *Journal of Family Research*, *23*(1), 77–101.

Kelliher, C., & Anderson, D. (2010). Doing more with less? Flexible working practices and the intensification of work. *Human Relations*, *63*(1), 83–106. https://doi.org/10.1177/0018726709349199

Kelly, E. L., & Kalev, A. (2006). Managing flexible work arrangements in US organizations: Formalized discretion or 'a right to ask'. *Socio-Economic Review*, *4*(3), 379–416. https://doi.org/10.1093/ser/mwl001

Kleinert, C. (2007). *Frauen an der Spitze: Arbeitsbedingungen und Lebenslagen weiblicher Führungskräfte* [Women at the top: Working conditions and life situations of female executives]. Campus.

Kohlrausch, B., & Zucco, A. (2020). *Die Corona-Krise trifft Frauen doppelt: Weniger Erwerbseinkommen und mehr Sorgearbeit* [Corona crisis hits women twice: Less earned income and more care work]. Policy Brief WSI No. 40. https://www.wsi.de/de/faust-detail.htm?sync_id=HBS-007676

Kossek, E. E., Lautsch, B. A., & Eaton, S. C. (2006). Telecommuting, control, and boundary management: Correlates of policy use and practice, job control, and work–family effectiveness. *Journal of Vocational Behavior*, *68*(2), 347–367. https://doi.org/10.1016/j.jvb.2005.07.002

Kreyenfeld, M., & Zinn, S. (2021). Coronavirus and care: How the coronavirus crisis affected fathers' involvement in Germany. *Demographic Research*, *44*(4), 99–124. https://doi.org/10.4054/DemRes.2021.44.4

Lott, Y. (2015). Working-time flexibility and autonomy: A European perspective on time adequacy. *European Journal of Industrial Relations*, *21*(3), 259–274. https://doi.org/10.1177/0959680114543604

Lott, Y. (2019). *Weniger Arbeit, mehr Freizeit? Wofür Mütter und Väter flexible Arbeitsarrangements nutzen [Less work, more free time? Why mothers and fathers use flexible working arrangements]*. WSI Report 47, pp. 1–16.

Lott, Y., & Abendroth, A. (2019). *Reasons for not working from home in an ideal worker culture: Why women perceive more cultural barriers*. WSI Working Paper No. 211. https://www.boeckler.de/en/faust-detail.htm?sync_id=HBS-007527

Maxwell, S. E., Cole, D. A., & Mitchell, M. A. (2011). Bias in cross-sectional analyses of longitudinal mediation: Partial and complete mediation under an autoregressive model. *Multivariate Behavioral Research*, *46*(5), 816–841. https://doi.org/10.1080/00273171.2011.606716

McGill, B. S. (2014). Navigating new norms of involved fatherhood. *Journal of Family Issues*, *35*(8), 1089–1106. https://doi.org/10.1177/0192513X14522247

Mergener, A. (2020). Berufliche Zugänge zum Homeoffice: Ein tätigkeitsbasierter Ansatz zur Erklärung von Chancenungleichheit beim Homeofficezugang [Professional access to the home office: An activity-based approach to explaining inequality of opportunity in home office access.]. *Kölner Zeitschrift für Soziologie und Sozialpsychologie*, *72*, 511–534. https://doi.org/10.1007/s11577-020-00669-0

Messenger, J., Vargas Llave, O., Gschwind, L., Boehmer, S., Vermeylen, G., & Wilkens, M. (2017). *Working anytime, anywhere: The effects on the world of work*. Eurofound. https://www.eurofound.europa.eu/sites/default/files/ef_publication/field_ef_document/ef1658en.pdf

Möhring, K., Naumann, E., Reifenscheid, M., Blom, A. G., Wenz, A., Rettig, T., Lehrer, R., Krieger, U., Juhl, S., Friedel, S., Fikel, M., & Cornesse, C. (2020). *Die Mannheimer Corona-Studie: Schwerpunktbericht zu Erwerbstätigkeit und Kinderbetreuung* [The Mannheim corona study: Focus report on employment and child care]. https://madoc.bib.uni-mannheim.de/55139/1/2020-04-05_Schwerpunktbericht_Erwerbstaetigkeit_und_Kinderbetreuung.pdf

Mokhtarian, P. L., Bagley, M. N., & Salomon, I. (1998). The impact of gender, occupation, and presence of children on telecommuting motivations and constraints. *Journal of the American Society for Information Science*, *49*(12), 1115–1134.

Müller, K.-U., Samtleben, C., Schmieder, J., & Wrohlich, K. (2020). Corona-Krise erschwert Vereinbarkeit von Beruf und Familie vor allem für Mütter: Erwerbstätige Eltern sollten entlastet werden. [Corona crisis makes work-life balance more difficult, especially for mothers: Working parents should be relieved]. *DIW Wochenbericht*, *19*, 331–340. https://doi.org/10.18723/diw_wb:2020-19-1

Munsch, C. L. (2016). Flexible work, flexible penalties: The effect of gender, childcare, and type of request on the flexibility bias. *Social Forces*, *94*(4), 1567–1591. https://doi.org/10.1093/sf/sov122

Nippert-Eng, C. E. (1996). *Home and work: Negotiating boundaries through everyday life*. University of Chicago Press.

OECD. (2017). *Dare to Share: Deutschlands Weg zur Partnerschaftlichkeit in Familie und Beruf* [Dare to share: Germany's path to partnership in family and work]. OECD. http://dx.doi.org/10.1787/9789264263420-de

Pfeiffer, S. (2012). Technologische Grundlagen der Entgrenzung: Chancen und Risiken [Technological foundations of the dissolution of boundaries: Opportunities and risks]. In B. Badura, A. Ducki, H. Schröder, J. Klose, & M. Meyer (Eds.), *Fehlzeitenreport 2012: Gesundheit in der flexiblen Arbeitswelt* (pp. 15–21). Springer.

Pleck, J. H. (1977). The work-family role system. *Social Problems*, *24*(4), 417–427. https://doi.org/10.1525/sp.1977.24.4.03a00040

Preacher, K. J., & Hayes, A. F. (2008). Asymptotic and resampling strategies for assessing and comparing indirect effects in multiple mediator models. *Behavior Research Methods*, *40*(3), 879–891. https://doi.org/10.3758/BRM.40.3.879

Schieman, S., & Young, M. (2010). Is there a downside to schedule control for the work-family interface? *Journal of Family Issues*, *31*(10), 1391–1414. https://doi.org/10.1177/0192513X10361866

Schieman, S., Badawy, P. J., A. Milkie, M., & Bierman, A. (2021). Work-life conflict during the COVID-19 pandemic. *Socius*, *7*, 1–19. https://doi.org/10.1177%2F2378023120982856

Schieman, S., Glavin, P., & Milkie, M. A. (2009). When work interferes with life: Work-nonwork interference and the influence of work-related demands and resources. *American Sociological Review*, *74*(6), 966–988. https://doi.org/10.1177/000312240907400606

Schober, P. S. (2013). The parenthood effect on gender inequality: Explaining the change in paid and domestic work when British couples become parents. *European Sociological Review*, *29*(1), 74–85. https://doi.org/10.1093/esr/jcr041

Schröder, C., Entringer, T., Göbel, J., Grabka, M., Graeber, D., Kröger, H., Kroh, M., Kühne, S., Liebig, S., Schupp, J., Seebauer, J., & Zinn, S. (2020). *Vor dem Covid-19-Virus sind nicht alle Erwerbstätigen gleich* [Not all workers are equally affected by Covid 19 virus]. DIW aktuell No. 41. https://www.econstor.eu/bitstream/10419/222872/1/1702045633.pdf

Sennett, R. (1999). *The corrosion of character: The personal consequences of work in the new capitalism*. Norton.

Shrout, P. E. (2011). Commentary: Mediation analysis, causal process, and cross-sectional data. *Multivariate Behavioral Research*, *46*(5), 852–860. https://doi.org/10.1080/00273171.2011.606718

Sostero, M., Milasi, S., Hurley, J., Fernandez Macias, E., & Bisello, M. (2020). *Teleworkability and the COVID-19 Crisis: A new digital divide?* European Commission. https://ec.europa.eu/jrc/en/publication/eur-scientific-and-technical-research-reports/teleworkability-and-covid-19-crisis-new-digital-divide

Stier, H., & Lewin-Epstein, N. (2007). Policy effects on the division of housework. *Journal of Comparative Policy Analysis*, *9*(3), 235–259. https://doi.org/10.1080/13876980701494657

Sullivan, O. (2000). The division of domestic labour: Twenty years of change? *Sociology*, *34*(3), 437–456. https://doi.org/10.1177/S0038038500000286

Thönnissen, C., Wilhelm, B., Alt, P., Reim, J., & Walper, S. (2020). *Pairfam: Scales and Instruments Manual A5678 Data file Version 11.0.0*. GESIS Datenarchiv. https://doi.org/10.4232/pairfam.5678.11.0.0

van der Lippe, T., & Lippényi, Z. (2019). Co-workers working from home and individual and team performance. *New Technology, Work and Employment*, *35*(1), 60–79. https://doi.org/10.1111/ntwe.12153

van der Lippe, T., & Lippényi, Z. (2020). Beyond formal access: Organizational context, working from home, and work-family conflict of men and women in European workplaces. *Social Indicators Research*, *151*(2), 383–402. https://doi.org/10.1007/s11205-018-1993-1

Voß, G. (1998). Die Entgrenzung von Arbeit und Arbeitskraft: Eine subjektorientierte Interpretation des Wandels der Arbeit [The dissolution of boundaries between work and labor: A subject-oriented interpretation of the transformation of work]. *Mitteilungen aus der Arbeitsmarkt- und Berufsforschung*, *31*(3), 473–487.

West, C., & Zimmerman, D. H. (1987). Doing gender. *Gender & Society*, *1*(2), 125–151. https://doi.org/10.1177/0891243287001002002

Williams, J. C., Blair-Loy, M., & Berdahl, J. L. (2013). Cultural schemas, social class, and the flexibility stigma. *Journal of Social Issues*, *69*(2), 209–234. https://doi.org/10.1111/josi.12012

Winqvist, K. (2004). *How europeans spend their time: Everyday life of women and men*. European Commission. https://ec.europa.eu/eurostat/documents/3930297/5953614/KS-58-04-998-EN.PDF

Winslow, S. (2005). Work-family conflict, gender, and parenthood, 1977–1997. *Journal of Family Issues*, *26*(6), 727–755. https://doi.org/10.1177/0192513X05277522

Zhang, S., Moeckel, R., Moreno, A. T., Shuai, B., & Gao, J. (2020). A work-life conflict perspective on telework. *Transportation Research*, *141*, 51–68. https://doi.org/10.1016/j.tra.2020.09.007

CHAPTER 5

DOES WORKING FROM HOME IMPROVE THE TEMPORAL ALIGNMENT OF WORK AND PRIVATE LIFE? DIFFERENCES BETWEEN TELEWORK AND INFORMAL OVERTIME AT HOME BY GENDER AND FAMILY RESPONSIBILITIES

Alexandra Mergener, Ines Entgelmeier and Timothy Rinke

ABSTRACT

This chapter examines the extent to which Working from Home (WfH) affects the temporal alignment of work and private life, i.e., the consideration of personal and family interests in work scheduling, for male and female employees with and without children. A distinction is made between telework that is formally recognized home working time by the employer, and informal overtime at home that is not recorded. It is argued that while the first represents a job resource, by increasing flexibility in work scheduling, the latter constitutes a job demand, which hinders the consideration of personal and family responsibilities in work time planning. Due to differences in status beliefs, identification and the distribution of childcare, gender gaps as well as differences according

Flexible Work and the Family
Contemporary Perspectives in Family Research, Volume 21, 129–157

ISSN: 1530-3535/doi:10.1108/S1530-353520230000021005

to family responsibilities are predicted in these associations. Using data from the German BIBB/BAuA Employment Survey 2018, the temporal alignment of work and private life is found to be positively associated with telework, particularly so for men, and negatively associated with informal overtime at home, particularly so for women. While mothers do not benefit from telework during regular working hours in particular, they have the worst temporal alignment of work and private life when they work informal overtime at home.

Keywords: Working from Home (WfH); telework; informal overtime; gender; flexibility in work scheduling; family responsibilities

INTRODUCTION

The consideration of family and personal requirements into working life presents a challenge for most employees today and has been further exacerbated by the COVID-19-related shutdowns. Particularly working women with young children, who tend to perform more housework and childcare than men (Hobler et al., 2020) are confronted with coordinating these competing demands.

As one opportunity for employees to overcome these challenges and achieve a better balance and fewer conflicts between private and occupational demands, WfH is frequently discussed as a job resource both in research and public debate (Ojala et al., 2014). More specifically, it is argued that WfH can increase employees' autonomy in organizing their working time so that they can better consider personal and family requirements (e.g., Gajendran & Harrison, 2007). Moreover, employees who spend at least some of their regular working days at home can use time they would otherwise have spent on commuting to meet private needs. This time flexibility and time savings can be a resource, especially for employees with family responsibilities, who can use this for providing childcare in addition to their gainful employment and, thus, reduce time-based work–family conflicts (Greenhaus & Beutell, 1985).

However, empirical studies have so far produced ambivalent results regarding WfH and its impact on the interrelation between work and private life (for an overview, see Allen et al., 2015). One reason for the inconclusive findings could be that WfH is considered in a relatively undifferentiated way. Many previous studies refer only to a rough consideration of work in private spaces, i.e., whether or not people worked from home (e.g., Kurowska, 2018; Peters et al., 2009; Sarbu, 2018; Sullivan & Smithson, 2007) but could not take further WfH conditions into account (mainly due to not having more detailed information available in the data). We know, however, that WfH is qualitatively very heterogeneous, with home working hours that are not always completely recognized by contract, but supplement and continue work already performed at home or at the employer's workplace, e.g., in the evenings and weekends (Fenner & Renn, 2010; Kim et al., 2020; Mergener, 2020b; Mergener & Fank, 2021; Ojala, 2011; Ojala et al., 2014; Song, 2009).

If these differences in WfH remain unconsidered, the effects due to flexibility gains or time savings cannot be separated from the effects of overtime, which is more of a job demand and may even increase with WfH (Abendroth & Reimann, 2018; Chung & van der Lippe, 2020; Lott, 2020a; Sarbu, 2018). Our study therefore examines whether, and under what conditions, WfH constitutes a resource that helps or a demand that impedes the temporal alignment of work and private life. By explicitly examining the time dimension of the alignment of work and private life, i.e., the extent to which employees can consider private and family interests when planning their working hours, we focus on a specific and widely discussed aspect affecting work–family balance or conflicts, rather than the broad and more general concepts. In doing so, we ask the two research questions: To what extent does the heterogeneity of WfH affects the temporal alignment of private life and work requirements differently? And how does this differ according to gender and family responsibilities?

To answer these questions, our study explicitly distinguishes WfH into *telework* that is formally recognized home working time and *informal overtime at home* when analyzing the temporal alignment of work and private life. Following Allen et al. (2015), we define telework as a work practice that enables employees to perform work for the company from home (at least temporarily), substituting for regular working time that they would typically spend at the employer's premises.[1] Thus, in the case of telework, the employee's working time at home is completely recognized by the employer. In contrast, we define informal overtime at home as additional work performed at home that is not recognized by the employer, e.g., in the evening hours or on weekends. Here, informal overtime at home occurs in two forms. First, employees who telework but extend their working hours into additional informal work from home (partly informal overtime at home). Second, employees who work from home only before or after a working day at the employer's premises or on weekends, completely in addition to their scheduled hours (completely informal overtime at home).

Accounting for this WfH heterogeneity is particularly relevant with regard to gender and family-specific differences in the consideration of private matters into working life. Since working women are still more involved in housework and childcare and, thus, have much more strained time resources than their male counterparts, we assume that women are likely to be especially affected by the temporal effects of both telework and informal overtime at home, with the former facilitating the temporal alignment of work and private life and the latter making it more difficult, and even more so if children are living in the household.

For this purpose, we use high-quality data from the probability based German Employment Survey 2018, carried out by the Federal Institute for Vocational Education and Training (BIBB) and the Federal Institute for Occupational Safety and Health (BAuA). The BIBB/BAuA Employment Survey 2018 (Hall et al., 2020) offers unique potential for addressing our research question, as it is the only large-scale survey that captures the indicator of the temporal alignment of work and private life and allows for an explicit distinction of WfH into telework and informal overtime at home.

The focus of our study is on Germany, which is representative in that the share of employees using WfH has so far roughly corresponded to the European average, but increased substantially during the COVID-19 pandemic and has even greater potential to increase (Mergener & Winnige, 2021). Furthermore, considering Germany as a case is also relevant, as the gender-specific division of gainful employment and care work is particularly persistent here (Esping-Anderson, 1993; Hobler et al., 2020; Pfau-Effinger, 1998).

Our study contributes to the previous literature in several ways. First, it offers a more precise definition and consideration of recognized working time when telework and informal overtime at home. Second, our analysis highlights the relevance of the recognition of working time when WfH when considering the temporal alignment of work and private life, while at the same time identifying relevant gender gaps. Third, the study considers the extent to which family responsibility entails different risks and opportunities for the temporal alignment of work and private life when using different forms of WfH.

THEORETICAL CONSIDERATIONS AND PREVIOUS RESEARCH

WfH builds a special form of a temporal and spatial delimitation of work. In this process, previously strict boundaries between occupational and private life increasingly dissolve, which enables working demands to enter private life as well as private requirements to enter working life (Pongratz & Voß, 2004; Voß, 1998). With reference to the Job-Demand-Resources Model (Demerouti et al., 2001), telework without doing extra work at home can be described as a job resource, more precisely as a boundary-spanning resource (Voydanoff, 2005), by providing more temporal and spatial flexibility in the organization of work and personal life compared to a fixed workplace at the employer's premises (Ashforth et al., 2000; Pongratz & Voß, 2004). In contrast, overtime at home may be a job demand, respectively a boundary-spanning demand (Voydanoff, 2005), since extra work takes valuable time to attend to private matters. Boundary-spanning demands or resources are characterized by the fact that they originate in one area of life, e.g., the work domain, but have an impact on the interaction with another area of life, e.g., the family domain (Voydanoff, 2005).

TELEWORK AS AN ENABLER OF BETTER TEMPORAL ALIGNMENT OF WORK AND PRIVATE LIFE: DIFFERENT EFFECTS FOR WOMEN AND MEN WITH AND WITHOUT FAMILY RESPONSIBILITIES?

Telework allows timesaving by reducing the need for commuting, more autonomous work organization and greater flexibility in terms of working time and space. Thus, employees might be better able to take family and personal matters into account when planning their working hours compared to people who do not have telework opportunities. However, whether telework is perceived as a job resource or a job demand with regard to the coordination of working and private tasks may differ for women and men.

Due to cultural and social structures, women and men are confronted with different expectations regarding the shaping of their working and private domain (Ashforth et al., 2000). As a result, women and men (have to) use flexible working arrangements differently and are faced with different outcomes (Chung & van der Lippe, 2020). While employed women are still more responsible for additional private requirements, as house and care work, men are more often exclusively responsible for gainful employment (Hobler et al., 2020).

Therefore, integrating multiple tasks into their daily lives may be more challenging for women than for men, and therefore women perceive flexibility and autonomy in the organization of working time more as a job resource regarding their temporal alignment of work and private life (Chung & van der Lippe, 2020; Lott, 2020a). Men, on the contrary, may perceive telework less as a resource in terms of their temporal alignment of work and private life compared to working in the office because there is less need for this flexibility.

This circumstance may not be understood exclusively as a personal choice of women and men, but is conditioned by social norms and expectations (Lott, 2020a). According to Ashforth et al. (2000), boundary creation between the private and working spheres may be affected by gender-specific role identification and expectations. Boundaries that are more flexible will be formed around that role, which is more important to a person's identity and greater efforts will be made to integrate that role into others. Thus, women may create more flexible boundaries around their family role and extend it to their working sphere (Ammons & Markham, 2004), while men form more permeable boundaries around their working role and extend it to their private sphere to express their gender identity.

In addition to these expectations regarding performance in private life, there are also gender-specific expectations regarding performance in working life. Thus, the ideal worker norm (Acker, 1990), which implies a comprehensive and constant availability for gainful employment and a subordination of private matters to professional concerns, still primarily affects men who do and are mainly expect to take on the role of the breadwinner, particularly after childbirth (Trappe et al., 2015). In contrast, women are still left to and are expected to assign greater responsibility for care work (Steinbach & Schulz, 2022). Thus, according to the ideal worker norm, men are expected to use telework to intensify their work, and this has already been demonstrated in empirical studies (Chung & van der Lippe, 2020; Lott, 2019).

This different use of flexibility is also accompanied by different effects. Lott (2014) shows that men with autonomous working hours have a worse work–life balance than women. This can be explained not only by an extension, but also mainly by an intensification of their work. For men, more working time autonomy, as also associated with telework, does not coincide with the feeling of having more space for considering private demands due to their focusing on gainful employment. Furthermore, with a stronger commitment to domestic and family work, men would go against the ideal worker norm and be more likely to face career penalties. In contrast, women are expected to use flexible working, like telework to meet additional private requirements (Williams et al., 2013). Thus, Carlson et al. (2010) and Hofäcker and König (2013) came to the result that women, in general, benefit more from schedule flexibility regarding work family conflicts than men. However, for women, but not for men, the conflicts increase when work is done at times that are usually reserved for social life, such as weekends (Hofäcker & König, 2013). In addition, a recent study by Kim et al. (2020) found that women's work family conflicts increased when they were able to change the beginning and ending of working time or when WfH, while men showed less conflicts when having this work time autonomy.

Several empirical studies point to these gender-specific assumptions regarding telework or not telework (e.g., Lott, 2019; Lott & Abendroth, 2020; Powell & Craig, 2015; Samtleben et al., 2020). Powell and Craig (2015) showed that women who telework spend more time on domestic work and childcare than men, but also than women who do not telework. In the study by Samtleben et al. (2020), telework also led to an increase in the time spent on care work for men, but the increase was stronger for women. This implies that telework may be a job resource for employed women to better fulfill their ascribed gender role expectations of care work and thus to better deal with the "double burden" (Becker-Schmidt, 1987) of meeting working and private demands. However, these better opportunities for the temporal alignment of work and private life do not necessarily imply better reconciliation (Carstensen, 2019). The coordination and organization required to integrate different spheres of life can be an enormous effort that telework opportunities enable or reinforce in the first place.

In addition to gender differences, the relation of telework and the temporal alignment of work and private life may differ by children living in the household. Maternity and paternity are status characteristics, which are linked to expectations of performance and competence at work (Ridgeway & Correll, 2004) and can lead to an ideal mother and ideal father norm (Lott & Klenner, 2018; Williams et al., 2013). While fathers still tend to increase their gainful employment in order assume the role of breadwinner (e.g., Bielby & Bielby, 1992; Jürges, 2006), German mothers do and are still mainly expected to reduce their gainful employment in order to take up their caring role (Geyer & Steiner, 2007). That is why employers and colleagues assume that mothers use flexible working hours for family work, while they expect fathers to intensify their working efforts. In this context, Sullivan and Lewis (2001) show that women consider telework as flexibility and autonomy to meet the time demands of children, while men do not see this as the main reason for telework, but only as a way to "help" with childcare. According to this, especially for mothers, telework with recognized home working time may be a job resource with regard to the temporal alignment of work and family life because they are more able to act according to what is already expected of them and, thus, use this flexibility for considering family requirements into their working day. These explanations lead to the following hypotheses:

H1. Telework with recognized home working time is associated with a better temporal alignment of work and private life.

H1a. This positive effect is stronger for women than for men.

H1b. This positive effect is strongest for women with children.

Here, it must be emphasized that better opportunities for the temporal alignment of work and private life are not to be understood as an unlimited advantage for women. Through a better consideration of personal and family interests in work scheduling, women may be able to fulfill their ascribed responsibilities better. However, the coordination and organization of various demands will still require effort.

INFORMAL OVERTIME AT HOME AS AN IMPEDIMENT: CAN IT IMPAIR THE TEMPORAL ALIGNMENT OF WORK AND PRIVATE LIFE MORE FOR MOTHERS THAN FATHERS?

Abendroth and Reimann (2018) provide evidence that the negative associations of telework and time- and strain-based work–family conflict can be partly attributed to the overtime work associated with telework. Our study complements these findings with a focus on informal overtime at home. WfH does not occur only during the employees' working hours or recognized overtime, but often means informal overtime that is performed during free time or weekend in addition to telework or in addition to work already done at the employer's spaces (Fenner & Renn, 2010; Mergener, 2020b; Mergener & Fank, 2021; Noonan & Glass, 2012; Ojala, 2011; Ojala et al., 2014; Song, 2009). Informal overtime could represent a job demand (Demerouti et al., 2001), because extending working time reduces the time that can be spent on recreation, leisure, or domestic work (Voydanoff, 2004). Analyses with US American data have already shown differences in the reasons for WfH and work family conflict (Kim et al., 2020). In this study, both WfH during regular working hours and WfH to catch up on additional work increased the work family conflict for employees. However, the latter form increased more. Research indicated that informal overtime at home occurs mainly among highly motivated and committed employees who hold management positions, have a high workload, or receive performance-based wages (Fenner & Renn, 2010; Ojala, 2011; Song, 2009). Thus, it is more an instrument to enhance performance and less as a way to better consider private demands in work scheduling (Lott, 2020b; Noonan & Glass, 2012).

Due to the varying degrees of its consequences for the temporal alignment of work and private life, we would also like to address the notion that informal overtime at home can be further differentiated. Employees can do informal overtime at home in addition to their formal recognized home working time when telework (partly informal overtime at home) or they can work from home only in addition to their scheduled hours at the employer's premises without having formal WfH regulations (completely informal overtime at home). While the first offers at least partially benefits of recognized home working, e.g., saving commuting times or working time autonomy, the latter does not. Thus, the motivation of employees doing informal overtime at home differs. Employees who have telework opportunities tend to work unpaid overtime at home to express their appreciation for this flexibility (Chung & van der Lippe, 2020). They could also use the flexibility they have gained in the sense of an "enabled intensification," e.g., because they are enabled to work their most productive hours or because they now use saved commuting time as additional working time (Chung & van der Horst, 2020). Employees who only work at home outside of their recognized working hours are more likely to have excessive workloads and work pressures, which prevent them from getting their work done in the time available at employer's location.

The consequences may also vary by gender. Lott and Chung (2016) show that, even if the amount of overtime when using schedule control does not differ between men and women when working full-time, the remuneration does. This may reflect differences between men and women, besides possible stigmatization or discrimination by the employer. According to Lott and Chung (2016), it could be that men use schedule control more as a high performance strategy, while women use it as a means to combine different life domains. These results suggest that existing norms lead to women being more likely than men to create more flexible boundaries around their family role and extend it to their working lives (Ashforth et al., 2000). Expanding work hours through informal overtime at home are therefore more likely a job demand for women because overtime conflict with the norm directed at them and thus could impede them to a greater extent than men. Accordingly, the above-mentioned study by Kim et al. (2020) shows that women suffer more from working at home to catch up on work regarding work–family conflict compared to men.

This relationship is probably even stronger when children need to be cared for. Williams et al. (2013) argue that fathers can extend their working time, in compliance with the so-called "work devotion schema" and still, in their traditional role as the family breadwinner, correspond to the norm of a good father. Mothers, in contrast, find themselves in a kind of dilemma because if they extend their working time and comply with the work devotion schema, they contradict the norm of a good mother. Empirical evidence is, however, currently inconclusive in this regard. On the one hand, Kim et al. (2020) conclude from their study for the United States that there are no differences between mothers who take work home to catch up (i.e., not WfH as a regular part of their job) and fathers or men and women without children regarding their work family conflict. On the other hand, a study by Young and Schieman (2018) shows for Canada that mothers with young children are more likely to reduce their work demands and seek more schedule control compared to fathers with young children in work–family conflicts. Support for this finding can also be observed for German employees using WfH, as fathers extend their working hours to a greater extent than mothers, who invest more time in childcare (Lott, 2019). This indicated double burden (Becker-Schmidt, 1987) of mothers compared to fathers may mean that mothers who work informal overtime at home have greater difficulty in considering family interests in work scheduling. These theoretical and empirical considerations lead us to the following hypotheses:

> *H2*. Informal overtime at home is associated with a poorer temporal alignment of work and private life.
>
> *H2a*. This negative effect is stronger for women than for men.
>
> *H2b*. This negative effect is strongest for women with children.

DATA AND METHODS

Data

The analysis used data from the German BIBB/BAuA Employment Survey 2018 (doi 10.7803/501.18.1.1.10). This representative survey of more than 20,000 persons in active employment with a minimum of 10 working hours per week includes rich and detailed information on workplace characteristics, occupations, education, employment history and personal characteristics. Moreover, it allows the differentiation between telework and informal overtime at home and contains information on employees' success in aligning work and private life. Given our focus on employer recognition of home-based working time, we restricted the sample to employees, i.e., excluded freelancers and self-employed individuals who lack formal employers. Our analyses based on 16,244 employees, aged 18 to 65 years.

Measures

The *dependent variable*, the temporal alignment of work and private life, follows a subjective approach. Employees indicated how often they are successful in planning their working time in such a way that their family and personal interests are considered. The responses include never (0), rarely (1), sometimes (2) and frequently (3).

The *predictor variables* are WfH, gender and children living in the household. A distinction was made between telework as completely recognized home working time, partly informal overtime at home, and completely informal overtime at home, while comparing it with no WfH. Employees were first asked whether they work for the employer from home, at least temporarily. WfH users additionally indicated to what extent the hours they work from home are credited as working time by the employer with the categories completely, partly, or not at all.

To consider the gender-children constellation, a differentiation was made between men and women with and without children under the age of 12 living in the household. Twelve years was deemed an appropriate age at which to draw this distinction, as children under 12 require a higher level of parental care, whereas older children tend to be more self-sufficient.

The analysis includes several *control variables* that account for the different employment patterns of men and women, which can influence both the temporal alignment of work and private life and the use of WfH. Previous research showed that WfH was more likely to be available for employees with academic degree, a relatively high level of pay and who were expected to work long hours and overtime (e.g., Glass, 2004; Kelliher & Anderson, 2010; Lott & Chung, 2016; Mergener & Winnige, 2021; Swanberg et al., 2005). Moreover, Abendroth and Reimann (2018) found that employees using WfH in a high demanding workplace culture, i.e., where employers have high expectations of extended working hours and constant availability, can increase the risk of conflicts between private and work life. Thus, the employees' level of education, age, management position, wage, and total weekly working hours were taken into consideration. To account for the potentially confounding effect of employees' unpaid extra hours at all, we disentangle the effects of informal overtime at home from unpaid overtime in the employer's premises by additionally controlling for overtime in the company, distinguishing between no overtime, recognized overtime, and unpaid overtime in the company.[2] Moreover, whether the employee's partner is active in the labor market was included, as this might influence the requirement for flexible worktime and the household demands, as well as potentially being unevenly distributed between men and women. In order to reflect flexibility stigmas, the employees' performance pressure and their career aspirations were considered.[3] Since occupational tasks are crucial in explaining WfH (Mergener, 2020a) and the ability to consider private matters into work scheduling, controls were included for employees' occupations (at the two-digit level of the German Classification of Occupations 2010, KldB 2010). The company size is also included in the analyses, as it can influence the opportunity to WfH and possibilities to combine private life and work (Jurado-Guerrero et al., 2018). Years of work experience in the company were considered, as employees who are satisfied, also with the temporal alignment of work and private life typically remain in the company and employers may be more willing to offer WfH option to workers with large company experience based on mutual trust. Due to different labor market structures and gender ideologies in East and West Germany (Ebner et al., 2020), dummies were included for the company's regional location.

Table A5.1 in the Appendix presents distributions of all variables used for the analyses, overall and differentiated by the four WfH categories, to provide descriptive information about individual and job characteristics across WfH.

Methods

The dependent variable the temporal alignment of work and private life was considered as a quasi-metric variable and OLS regression models were applied, which are regarded as a robust method for variables with rating scales (Allerbeck, 1978; Jaccard & Wan, 1996). The preferred use of OLS regression when analyzing rating variables is widespread, especially among researchers of life satisfaction (e.g., Sacks et al., 2012; Stone et al., 2010) as it provides intuitive interpretation of estimated coefficients and interaction effects. The estimates provided by nonlinear models are very similar to those provided by OLS regression (Studer & Winkelmann, 2011).[4] To test *H1a* and *H2a*, the models were expanded to include interactions between WfH and gender. To test *H1b* and *H2b*, interactions between

WfH and men and women with and without children in the household were included. The interaction effects are illustrated using margins plots. All models were controlled for the above-mentioned confounders affecting the use of WfH and the temporal alignment of work and private life.

RESULTS

Descriptive Analyses

On average, the employees were quite successful in considering their private lives into their working time planning (see Table 5.1). Employees who telework within their completely recognized working hours correlated positively with the temporal alignment of work and private life. One fifth of the employees teleworked within their completely recognized working hours, 2% did informal overtime at home in addition to their formal recognized teleworking hours, and 6% worked only informal overtime at home in addition to work at the employer's premises. Employees with children under 12 living in the household tended to use telework more often compared to employees without children.

Focusing on the different groups of men and women with and without children, women with children show, compared to all other groups, a better ability to consider personal and family interests in work scheduling (see Table 5.2). They are also more frequently represented in the group of telework users, than women without children. The same applies to fathers compared to men without children. No differences were found between men with and without children concerning their capacity to temporally align work and private life.

Regarding the distribution of successful temporal alignment of work and private life among the categories regarding use of WfH, gender and children (see Fig. 5.1), the difference between telework and no WfH is largest for men with and without children. Women with and without children also benefit from telework, but the difference in the mean value for non-WfH users is much smaller. Informal

Table 5.1. Minimum, Maximum and Mean Score, Standard Deviation and Bivariate Correlations Between the Variables.

	Min	Max	Mean	SD	1	2	3
1 Temporal alignment of work and private life	0	3	2.42	0.84	1		
2 Women	0	1	0.46	0.50	0.06***	1	
3 Children < 12 years in household	0	1	0.22	0.42	0.04***	0.00	1
No WfH	0	1	0.72	0.45	−0.06***	0.01	−0.06***
Telework	0	1	0.20	0.40	0.10***	−0.01	0.06***
Partly informal overtime	0	1	0.02	0.15	−0.02**	0.01	0.01
Completely informal overtime	0	1	0.06	0.24	−0.04***	−0.01	0.00

Source: BIBB/BAuA Employment Survey 2018, weighted data. Sample includes employees (i.e., no freelancers, assisting family members, self-employed) aged 18–65. Authors' own calculations.
Notes: * $p < 0.05$, ** $p < 0.01$, *** $p < 0.001$.

Table 5.2. Descriptives of the Temporal Alignment of Work and Private Life and WfH by Men and Women With and Without Children Under 12 Years in Household.

	Men	Men Without Child. u12	Men with Child. u12	Women	Women Without Child. u12	Women With Child. u12
	Mean (SD)	Mean (SD)	Mean (SD)	Mean (SD)	Mean (SD)	Mean (SD)
Temporal alignment of work and private life	2.37 (0.87)	2.37 (0.87)	2.38 (0.86)	2.47 (0.80)	2.44 (0.82)	2.58 (0.73)
No WfH	0.72 (0.45)	0.74 (0.44)	0.66 (0.47)	0.72 (0.45)	0.73 (0.44)	0.69 (0.46)
Telework	0.20 (0.40)	0.19 (0.39)	0.24 (0.43)	0.19 (0.40)	0.18 (0.39)	0.23 (0.42)
Partly informal overtime	0.02 (0.15)	0.02 (0.14)	0.02 (0.14)	0.02 (0.15)	0.02 (0.15)	0.03 (0.18)
Completely informal overtime	0.06 (0.24)	0.06 (0.23)	0.07 (0.26)	0.06 (0.23)	0.06 (0.24)	0.05 (0.21)
	N = *7,979*	*N* = *6,219*	*N* = *1,760*	*N* = *8,265*	*N* = *6,589*	*N* = *1,676*

Source: BIBB/BAuA Employment Survey 2018, weighted data. Sample includes employees (i.e., no freelancers, assisting family members, self-employed) aged 18–65. Authors' own calculations.

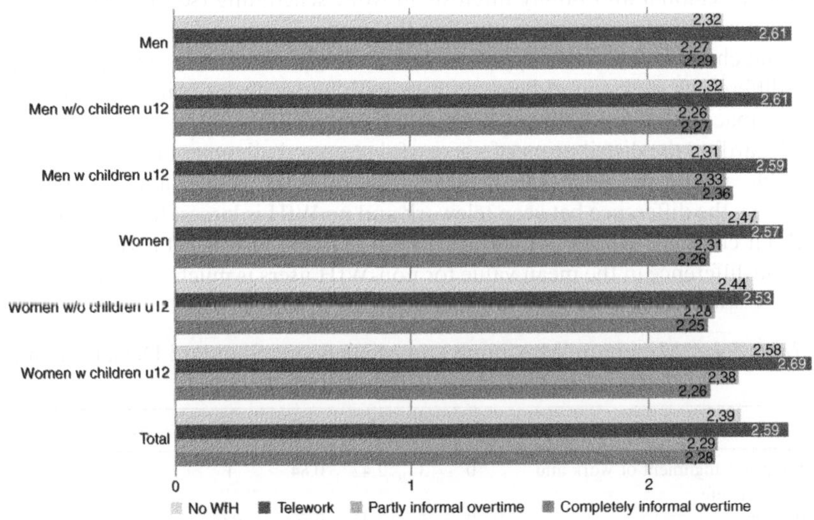

Fig. 5.1. Mean Score of the Temporal Alignment of Work and Private Life of Men and Women With and Without Children Under 12 years in Household by WfH Use. *Source*: BIBB/BAuA Employment Survey 2018. Sample includes employees aged 18–65. Authors' own calculations.

overtime at home reduces the capacities to consider private requirements into work scheduling for women with and without children and men with children. Men with children seem to temporally align work and private life slightly better when WfH outside the recognized working hours than when not using WfH. In contrast, women with children seem to be much less successful in the temporal alignment of work and private life if they work informal overtime at home.

The descriptive distributions give the impression that especially parents of children use telework. Moreover, mothers are on average more likely to be able to consider private matters into work scheduling than women without children. This could mean that they already have adapted their working lives to their private requirements and, for example, have chosen occupations with a high level of cognitive and a low level of manual tasks that allow more time and spatial flexibility (Mergener, 2020b). It is also possible that they have adapted their career aspirations in accordance with their private requirements. The multivariate analysis in the next section takes the possibility of these confounding effects into account.

MULTIVARIATE ANALYSES

The OLS regressions estimate the impact of WfH on the temporal alignment of work and private life (see Table 5.3). Model 1a presents the main effects of WfH and men and women, Model 2a distinguishes between men and women with and without children.

Compared to non-WfH users, employees with telework report better temporal alignment of work and private life – even when the control variables are included. The opposite is true if home working time is not recognized. Employees then show a significantly worse temporal alignment of work and private life with the strongest negative effect of completely informal overtime at home. These results support the theory that fully recognize teleworking presents a job resource. Employees gain time and spatial flexibility by substituting working hours at the company with working hours spent at home, which facilitates the reconciliation of family and personal life with work. Otherwise, if home working time is not recognized, it constitutes an increase in the informal work time and thus extends to the employee's free time. This is considered as a job demand and makes it harder to combine private matters with work, slightly more so in the case of completely informal overtime than in the case of partly informal overtime. Thus, *H1* and *H2* are supported by these results. Models 1a and 2a additionally show that, when accounting for all control variables, women (with and without children) have significantly more difficulties in the temporal alignment of work and private life than men (with children).

To test *H1a* and *H2a*, an interaction between gender and WfH was included alongside all control variables (Model 1b). In the group of non-WfH users, no gender-specific differences in the temporal alignment of work and private life were found, but the use of WfH shows different effects for women and men (see Fig. 5.2).

Men and women who telework within their completely recognized working time have better temporal alignment of work and private life, but contrary the expectations outlined in *H1a*, the positive correlation is stronger for men than for women. There are various theoretical explanations as to why, in this case, telework is less of a job resource for women to consider private needs. First, it

Table 5.3. OLS Regression Models of the Temporal Alignment of Work and Private Life by Gender, Children and the Use of WfH.

	M1a		M1b		M2a		M2b	
No WfH	*Reference*		*Reference*		*Reference*		*Reference*	
Telework	0.121***	(0.016)	0.182***	(0.022)	0.120***	(0.016)	0.188***	(0.041)
Partly informal overtime	−0.069*	(0.037)	−0.064	(0.054)	−0.069*	(0.037)	−0.086	(0.113)
Completely informal overtime	−0.089***	(0.024)	0.018	(0.033)	−0.090***	(0.024)	0.113*	(0.063)
Men	*Reference*		*Reference*					
Women	−0.051***	(0.015)	0.001	(0.018)				
Interactions								
Telework # Women			−0.116***	(0.028)				
Partly informal overtime # Women			−0.008	(0.073)				
Completely informal overtime # Women			−0.221***	(0.047)				
Men, children u12								
Men, w/o children u12					−0.034	(0.021)	−0.013	(0.028)
Women, w/o children u12					−0.081***	(0.023)	−0.014	(0.029)
Women, w children u12					−0.066**	(0.028)	0.008	(0.036)
Interactions								
Telework# Men, w/o child. u12							−0.009	(0.045)
Telework# Women, w/o child. u12							−0.120***	(0.046)
Telework# Women, child. u12							−0.129**	(0.057)
Partly informal overtime # Men, w/o child. u12							0.029	(0.128)
Partly informal overtime # Women, w/o child. u12							−0.002	(0.127)
Partly informal overtime # Women, child. u12							0.055	(0.147)
Completely informal overtime # Men, w/o child. u12							−0.129*	(0.072)
Completely informal overtime # Women, w/o child. u12							−0.305***	(0.073)
Completely informal overtime # Women, w child. u12							−0.361***	(0.099)
Controls								
Education								
No vocational degree	*Reference*		*Reference*		*Reference*		*Reference*	
Vocational education	0.110***	(0.028)	0.111***	(0.028)	0.108***	(0.028)	0.110***	(0.028)
Further vocational training	0.165***	(0.034)	0.168***	(0.034)	0.163***	(0.034)	0.167***	(0.034)
Academic degree	0.200***	(0.030)	0.201***	(0.030)	0.197***	(0.030)	0.199***	(0.030)
Age	−0.003***	(0.001)	−0.003***	(0.001)	−0.002***	(0.001)	−0.003***	(0.001)

	M1a		M1b		M2a		M2b	
Management position								
No	*Reference*		*Reference*		*Reference*		*Reference*	
Lower	0.002	(0.021)	0.006	(0.021)	0.002	(0.021)	0.006	(0.021)
Middle	0.021	(0.017)	0.019	(0.017)	0.020	(0.017)	0.018	(0.017)
Upper	0.018	(0.029)	0.014	(0.029)	0.017	(0.029)	0.011	(0.029)
Wage	0.000***	(0.000)	0.000***	(0.000)	0.000***	(0.000)	0.000***	(0.000)
Total working time (hours/week)	−0.016***	(0.001)	−0.016***	(0.001)	−0.016***	(0.001)	−0.016***	(0.001)
Overtime in the company								
No overtime in the company	*Reference*		*Reference*		*Reference*		*Reference*	
Recognized overtime	−0.001	(0.013)	−0.001	(0.013)	−0.001	(0.013)	−0.001	(0.013)
Non-recognized overtime	−0.170***	(0.023)	−0.175***	(0.023)	−0.170***	(0.023)	−0.176***	(0.023)
Overtime, but no info about recogn. of overtime hours	−0.108	(0.081)	−0.107	(0.081)	−0.106	(0.081)	−0.107	(0.081)
Partner employed	0.058***	(0.012)	0.056***	(0.012)	0.054***	(0.012)	0.052***	(0.012)
Pressure to perform								
No	*Reference*		*Reference*		*Reference*		*Reference*	
Rarely	0.049	(0.037)	0.049	(0.037)	0.049	(0.037)	0.050	(0.037)
Sometimes	0.007	(0.034)	0.006	(0.034)	0.007	(0.034)	0.007	(0.034)
Often	−0.277***	(0.034)	−0.278***	(0.034)	−0.278***	(0.034)	−0.278***	(0.034)
Carrier aspirations	0.007	(0.014)	0.007	(0.014)	0.007	(0.014)	0.008	(0.014)
Work experience (years)	0.002***	(0.001)	0.002***	(0.001)	0.002***	(0.001)	0.002***	(0.001)
Company size								
1–9 employees	*Reference*		*Reference*		*Reference*		*Reference*	
10–49 employees	0.021	(0.022)	0.023	(0.022)	0.021	(0.022)	0.023	(0.022)
50–249 employees	0.020	(0.022)	0.020	(0.022)	0.019	(0.022)	0.020	(0.022)
250+ employees	0.057***	(0.022)	0.057**	(0.022)	0.056**	(0.022)	0.056**	(0.022)
Company in West-Germany	−0.025*	(0.015)	−0.025*	(0.015)	−0.025*	(0.015)	−0.025*	(0.015)
Occupational groups[a]								
Constant	2.853***	(0.114)	2.839***	(0.114)	2.869***	(0.115)	2.836***	(0.116)
Observations	16,244		16,244		16,244		16,244	
Adj. R^2	0.135		0.137		0.135		0.137	

Source: **BIBB/BAuA** Employment Survey 2018. Sample includes employees aged 18–65. Authors' own calculations. Standard errors in parentheses.
Notes: * $p < 0.1$, ** $p < 0.05$, *** $p < 0.01$.
[a] Controls for employees' occupations with 36 dummies for occupational groups (at the two-digit level of the German Classification of Occupations 2010, KldB 2010) are included but not displayed. The results are available upon request.

could be that, because of the demands and expectations on women in terms of performing care work, they have already adapted their paid work to allow for a (relatively) good reconciliation. However, the regression analysis already accounts for working time, overtime in the company, occupation, and career aspiration of the employees and thus controls for important variables in this context. Second, working in an employer's premises comes with more planning security in terms of time and space, which could make it easier for women to consider private matters when planning working hours. Third, telework may increase the expectation for women to take on even more private tasks than when they work in the office. Study results show that women who work at home regularly spend more time on domestic and care work than men but also than women who work from home less often or not at all (Powell & Craig, 2015). Even more tasks that women have to integrate into their working life when telework could explain why their perception of a good temporal alignment of work and private life increases only to a small extent. Fourth, it is conceivable that women will also have to prove that they deserve telework. Studies indicate that women who use flexible work options are more likely to be devalued due to gender stereotypes and are therefore forced to compensate for this with particularly good performance (Williams et al., 2013). In this case, telework is not reflected in an extension of informal overtime, but possibly in an intensification of work and an increase in women's commitment to work and postponement of private demands, which will make the temporal alignment of work and private life more difficult.

In contrast, the negative correlation between informal overtime at home and success in temporal alignment of work and private life is only evident for women. While for men, it makes no statistically significant difference whether they do not work from home or home working time is partly or completely unrecognized, for women there is a substantial negative effect of informal overtime at home on the consideration of private demands into work scheduling. This meets the expectation, outlined in *H1b*, that men and women are confronted with different norms that have a different impact on the temporal alignment of work and private life. Women are more likely than men to be assigned much of the responsibility for caregiving and informal work in addition to their paid work. Considering this double burden, informal overtime at home, which extends into private time, builds a job demand for women because it makes it more difficult to combine both spheres. Especially in Germany, where gender relations with regard to the division of gainful employment and care work are still very traditional.

Particularly regarding this double burden for women, we expect in *H1b* and *H2b* that children additionally strengthen the effects of WfH. However, regarding those who telework within their completely recognized working time, there are no statistically significant differences between fathers and men without children or mothers and women without children (see Fig. 5.2). The assumption of *H1b* that the positive correlation between telework and the temporal alignment of work and private life is strongest for mothers can thus not be confirmed. Mothers do not even report better temporal alignment of work and private life when telework than when not WfH. Here again, the theoretical explanations regarding *H1a* can be referred to.

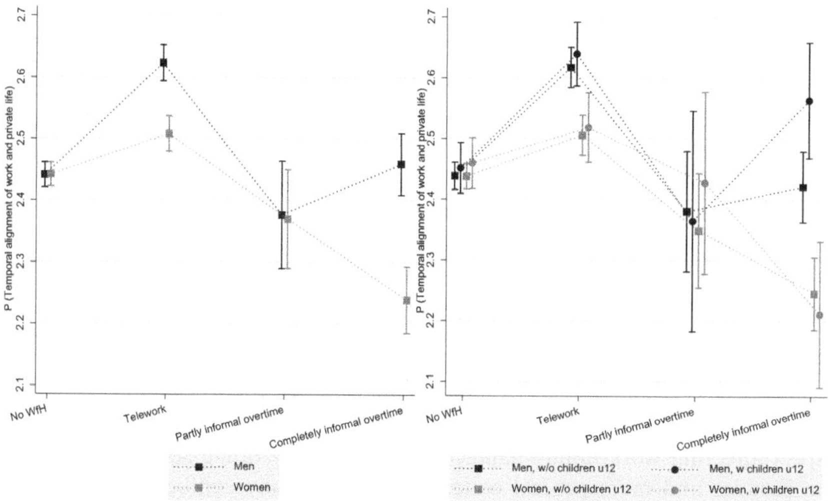

Fig. 5.2. Probability of the Temporal Alignment of Work and Private Life. Estimates of M1b (Interaction Between Gender and WfH, Left Side) and M2b (Interaction Between Gender-Children-Combination and WfH, Right Side). *Source:* BIBB/BAuA Employment Survey 2018. Sample includes employees aged 18–65. Authors' own calculations.
Notes: 90% confidence intervals. Control for employees' overtime hours in the company, age, qualification, working time, wage, leading position, career aspiration, pressure to perform, work experience in company (years) and occupation (KldB 2010, two-digit), employment of partner, company size and region are included but not displayed.

In contrast, mothers doing informal overtime at home have the worst temporal alignment of work and private life, which confirms our *H2b*. However, there is no statistically significant difference in the effect sizes between women with and without children.

Interestingly, our analyses suggest that fathers who only work informal overtime when WfH have a statistically significant better temporal alignment of work and private life than fathers who do not work from home at all (see Table 5.3, Fig. 5.2). It indicates that this informal flexibility allows fathers to participate in family life, even though they also work overtime in their role as breadwinner and ideal worker. Similar results are shown by Ojala et al. (2014), who found that only informal overtime at home slightly improves parental ability to cope with children.

CONCLUSIONS AND DISCUSSION

The increasing prevalence of WfH makes it necessary to take a more differentiated look at the working time recognition and its effects. To shed light on the possible resources and demands of WfH, this chapter distinguishes between telework that is formally recognized home working time and informal overtime at home. Furthermore, resources and demands associated with these different forms of WfH can affect employees differently depending on their gender and family responsibilities. Women, especially mothers, are still more responsible for care work in addition to their gainful employment due to their stronger social identification and attribution. WfH within regular working hours could therefore be particularly beneficial for mothers, as it can increase temporal flexibility and free up time resources that can relax the fulfillment of responsibilities in both spheres of life. WfH outside regular working hours, in contrast, could lead to special burdens, as it overlaps time resources that mothers could use for family matters with gainful employment. Therefore, this chapter has examined different ways in which WfH impact the temporal alignment of work and private life of women and men, both with and without children.

With the focus on the temporal alignment of work and private life, we explicitly address the specific time dimension that is widely discussed as an important aspect affecting work-family balance or conflicts. By doing so, we differ from the broader and more general concept of work–family conflict (Greenhaus & Beutell, 1985) or work-life enrichment (Greenhaus & Powell, 2006) and, thus, cannot exactly interpret positive or negative outcomes for a better or worse work–life reconciliation. While a successful temporal alignment of work and private life might be helpful for organizing everyday life, it does not necessarily mean that meeting demands of work and private life is less challenging. Concepts of work–life conflict or enrichment base on the idea of reconciliation and, thus, hide organizational efforts and can mask burdens for women in particular, who continue to be more responsible for the consideration of private and professional demands (Carstensen, 2019; Jürges, 2006).

Our results indicated that the temporal alignment of work and private life is positively associated with telework. It can be assumed that telework then functions as a job resource that allows boundaries to be crossed (Voydanoff, 2004) and allows employees to use the flexibility gained to consider private matters when planning working time (Ashforth et al., 2000). This association is reversed as soon as home working is informal overtime. The temporal alignment of work and private life seems to become more difficult, which may be a result of an intensification and extension of working time at home. Telework then seems more like a job demand that can reduce the time available leisure, domestic work or family responsibilities.

Our results also reveal that the effects of the different forms of WfH considered are gender-specific, but within gender, family responsibilities do not appear to make a difference. Contrary to the hypotheses outlined in this article, telework seems to be more of a resource for men in terms of considering private demands into work scheduling. This may be explained by the fact that telework for women means that they take on even more private tasks. Study results show that women who work at home regularly spend more time on domestic and care work than men but also than women who work from home less often or not at all (Powell & Craig, 2015). Men are confronted with fewer demands from the private sphere than women, which is why they have better temporal alignment of work and private life, resulting from the flexibility gained through telework. Beyond this explanation, it may also be that women who use telework arrangements are under particular pressure to perform, since according to traditional gender status beliefs (Ridgeway & Correll, 2004; Williams et al., 2013) they are more devalued than men when using flexible work arrangements. This could lead to women being faced with increased expectations regarding their performance and commitment, reducing their ability to accommodate private concerns.

The hypothesis that women with informal overtime at home would report more difficulty with the temporal alignment of work and private life than their male counterparts was supported by the analysis. This also indicates that the double burden (Becker-Schmidt, 1987) for women still exists and supports the theory that, due to traditional gender-role models, the extension of informal working time has different effects on women and men. While men do not seem to have any greater problems with an extension of informal home working time, it leads to greater difficulties in combining work with personal and family matters for women, who continue to have higher demands in the area of care work. This explanation may be particularly applicable to the German case examined in this chapter, where traditional gender arrangements are still widespread. In countries with more egalitarian gender arrangements, such as Scandinavia, where the allocation to gainful employment and care work is less gender-specific, the differences between women and men regarding their temporal alignment of work and private life when WfH may be less pronounced.

Furthermore, we could not find any confirmation that mothers benefit particularly in terms of their temporal alignment of work and private life when they work from home within regular working hours. However, it could be shown that they are more burdened when they do informal overwork than fathers. WfH is therefore not in itself an unrestricted support for working women to better combine family and work. The arrangement of WfH is important.

Despite the usefulness of this study in furthering the research on WfH in relation to the temporal alignment of work and private life, there are some limitations to consider. Even if our study considered the qualitative heterogeneity of WfH, we know that WfH in Germany is also quantitatively very heterogeneous with most employees working only sometimes or rarely from home – at least in pre-pandemic times (e.g., Alipour et al., 2020; Mergener, 2020b; Mergener & Fank, 2021). Future research should therefore additionally consider the associations between WfH intensity and employees' consideration of personal and family demands into work scheduling. In this context, it is also worth mentioning that experiences with WfH during the compulsory phases of WfH of the COVID-19 pandemic and periods of closed schools and child care facilities, are not transferable to our research results. Apart from the additional burden of home schooling or childcare in home office, many employees have also had good experiences and want to continue WfH at least partially in the future (Frodermann et al., 2021). As a consequence, it is to be expected that telework will no longer remain the privilege of a few and especially highly qualified employees, as it was before the pandemic in Germany. In order to check whether this will also change the relation between telework and the temporal alignment of work and private life, our pre-pandemic study should be replicated in the post-pandemic period. Furthermore, our data set contains only employed persons, meaning those (presumably especially mothers) unable to work due to higher difficulty in accounting for private matters while working, or more demanding personal and family lives, are not present in the data set. It can therefore be assumed that the results presented here, e.g., on the gender gap in reconciliation problems, tend to be underestimated. Moreover, it would be beneficial to be able to control for the specific personal and family demands with which the employees are confronted but on which we had no data available. Finally, it would be desirable to conduct comparative analyses with panel data in order to control for potentially unobserved heterogeneity by eliminating all time-constant unobserved characteristics. Nevertheless, we rely in our study on the most appropriate data, which are the only ones that allow for the highly differentiated consideration of recognized working time when telework and informal overtime at home.

In doing so, the results show that telework can be a job resource for increasing challenges in the temporal alignment of work and private life for employees. However, it does not apply to all employees to the same extent, but varies dependent on gender and family responsibility. Furthermore, even if employees are successful in the temporal alignment of work and private life when working from home, this may involve a great deal of effort and may not lead to a better work–life balance automatically. This again might be more relevant for women who are still more often confronted with family and working demands at the same time, especially in Germany (Carstensen, 2019; Jürgens, 2019). Furthermore, while women perceive home-based work as a helpful way to consider demands from both spheres of life, it may reinforce the gendered division of work and family life (Sullivan & Lewis, 2001). In addition, the results support the idea that flexibility also needs regulation, which cannot be the sole responsibility of the employees due to differences in how it is used. The law on the recording of working time, which was recently confirmed by the European Court of Justice, must also apply to employees working outside the office to be a beneficial instrument for employees. Otherwise, WfH, through a greater mix of private and occupational activities but also the stereotypical assumptions of employers regarding the work performance of their employees at home, carries the risk of leading to an increase in informal working time, which, even with more flexibility, will not contribute to an improvement in the organization of occupational and personal and family life.

NOTES

1. Here, we would like to emphasize that telework is not understood as a company-agreed form of WfH within the meaning of the German Workplace Ordinance (vgl. ArbStättV § 2 Abs. 7).

2. In our sample, 517 employees did not indicate whether or not overtime in the company was recognized by the employer. They are included in our analysis as "no information on recognition of overtime."

3. The survey question for career aspiration reads: "How strongly do you pursue the goal of a professional career? Very strongly, strongly, not much or not at all." To measure performance pressure, the employees were asked: "How often does your job require you to work under strong deadline or performance pressure? Often, sometimes, rarely or never."

4. In order to test the robustness of our results, we also compared the OLS estimates with those based on ordered logit regressions (see Table 5A.2). Similar results were produced in terms of the direction and significance of the coefficients, further supporting the conclusions made on the basis of the OLS results. This additionally supports the findings of Studer and Winkelmann (2011) regarding the comparison of estimations of ordered logit with OLS regressions and encourages with the use of linear models.

REFERENCES

Abendroth, A.-K., & Reimann, M. (2018). Telework and work–family conflict across workplaces: investigating the implications of work–family-supportive and high-demand workplace cultures. In S. L. Blair & J. Obradović (Eds.), *Contemporary perspectives in family research: Vol. 13. The work-family interface: Spillover, complications, and challenges* (pp. 323–348). Emerald Publishing Limited. https://doi.org/10.1108/S1530-353520180000013017

Acker, J. (1990). Hierarchies, jobs, bodies: A theory of gendered organizations. *Gender & Society, 4*(2), 139–158. https://doi.org/10.1177/089124390004002002

Alipour, J.-V., Falck, O., Mergener, A., & Schüller, S. (2020). Wiring the labor market revisited: Working from home in the Digital Age. *CESifo Forum, 21*(3), 10–14.

Allen, T. D., Golden, T. D., & Shockley, K. M. (2015). How effective is telecommuting? Assessing the status of our scientific findings. *Psychological Science in the Public Interest, 16*(2), 40–68. https://doi.org/10.1177/1529100615593273

Allerbeck, K. R. (1978). Meßniveau und Analyseverfahren - Das Problem „strittiger "Intervallskalen. *Zeitschrift Für Soziologie, 3*, 199–214. https://doi.org/10.1515/zfsoz-1978-0301

Ammons, S. K., & Markham, W. T. (2004). Working at home: Experiences of skilled white collar workers. *Sociological Spectrum: Mid-South Sociological Association, 24*(2), 191–238. https://doi.org/10.1080/02732170490271744

ArbStättV. http://www.gesetze-im-internet.de/arbst_ttv_2004

Ashforth, B., Kreiner, G., & Fugate, M. (2000). All in a day's work: Boundaries and micro role transitions. *Academy of Management Review, 25*, 472–491. https://doi.org/10.5465/AMR.2000.3363315

Becker-Schmidt, R. (1987). Die doppelte Vergesellschaftung – die doppelte Unterdrückung: Besonderheiten der Frauenforschung in den Sozialwissenschaften. In L. Unterkirchen & I. Wagner (Eds.), *Die andere Hälfte der Gesellschaft* (pp. 10–25). Österreichischer Soziologentag 1985.

Bielby, W. T., & Bielby, D. D. (1992). I will follow him: Family ties, gender-role beliefs, and reluctance to relocate for a better job. *American Journal of Sociology, 97*(5), 1241–1267. https://doi.org/10.1086/229901

Carlson, D. S., Grzywacz, J. G., & Michele Kacmar, K. (2010). The relationship of schedule flexibility and outcomes via the work-family interface. *Journal of Managerial Psychology, 25*(4), 330–355. https://doi.org/10.1108/02683941011035278

Carstensen, T. (2019). Verunsichtbarung von Geschlechterungleichheiten? Digitalisierte Arbeit zwischen Rhetoriken neuer Möglichkeiten und der Reorganisation alter Muster. In B. Kohlrausch, C. Schildman, & D. Voss (Eds.), *Neue Arbeit- neue Ungleichheiten? Folgen der Digitalisierung* (pp. 69–87). Beltz Juventa Weinheim.

Chung, H., & van der Horst, M. (2020). Flexible working and unpaid overtime in the UK: The role of gender, parental and occupational status. *Social Indicators Research, 151*, 495–520. https://doi.org/10.1007/s11205-018-2028-7

Chung, H., & van der Lippe, T. (2020). Flexible working, work–life balance, and gender equality: Introduction. *Social Indicators Research, 151*, 1–17. https://doi.org/10.1007/s11205-018-2025-x

Demerouti, E., Bakker, A. B., Nachreiner, F., & Schaufeli, W. B. (2001). The job demands-resources model of burnout. *Journal of Applied Psychology, 86*(3), 499–512.

Ebner, C., Kühhirt, M., & Lersch, P. (2020). Cohort Changes in the level and dispersion of gender ideology after German Reunification: Results from a natural experiment. *European Sociological Review*. Advance online publication. https://doi.org/10.1093/esr/jcaa015

Esping-Anderson, G. (1993). *The three worlds of Welfare Capitalism*. Princeton University Press.

Fenner, G. H., & Renn, R. W. (2010). Technology-assisted supplemental work and work-to-family conflict: The role of instrumentality beliefs, organizational expectations and time management. *Human Relations*, *63*(1), 63–82. https://doi.org/10.1177/0018726709351064

Frodermann, C., Grunau, P., Haas, G.-C., & Müller, D. (2021). *Homeoffice in Zeiten von Corona: Nutzung, Hindernisse und Zukunftswünsche* (IAB-Kurzbericht).

Gajendran, R. S., & Harrison, D. A. (2007). The good, the bad, and the unknown about telecommuting: Meta-analysis of psychological mediators and individual consequences. *Journal of Applied Psychology*, *92*(6), 1524–1541.

Geyer, J., & Steiner, V. (2007). Short-run and long-term effects of childbirth on mothers' employment and working hours across institutional regimes. An empirical analysis based on the European Community Household Panel. IZA Discussion Paper No. 2693. http://dx.doi.org/10.2139/ssrn.981166

Glass, J. (2004). Blessing or curse? Work–family policies and mother's wage growth over time. *Work and Occupations*, *31*(3), 367–394. https://doi.org/10.1177/0730888404266364

Greenhaus, J. H., & Beutell, N. J. (1985). Sources of conflict between work and family roles. *Academy of Management Review*, *10*(1), 76–88. https://doi.org/10.5465/amr.1985.4277352

Greenhaus, J. H., & Powell, G. N. (2006). When work and family are allies: A theory of work-family enrichment. *Academy of Management Review*, *31*(1), 72–92. https://doi.org/10.5465/amr.2006.19379625

Hall, A., Hünefeld, L., & Rohrbach-Schmidt, D. (2020). *BIBB/BAuA Employment Survey of the Working Population on Qualification and Working Conditions in Germany* 2018. Federal Institute for Vocational Education and Training. https://doi.org/10.7803/501.18.1.1.10

Hobler, D., Lott, Y., Pfahl, S., & Schulze Buschoff, K. (2020). *Stand der Gleichstellung von Frauen und Männern in Deutschland* [WSI Report].

Hofäcker, D., & König, S. (2013). Flexibility and work-life conflict in times of crisis: a gender perspective. *International Journal of Sociology and Social Policy*, *33*(9/10), 613–635. https://doi.org/10.1108/IJSSP-04-2013-0042

Jaccard, J., & Wan, C. K. (1996). *LISREL approaches to interaction effects in multiple regression*.

Jurado-Guerrero, T., Monferrer, J. M., Botía-Morillas, C., & Abril, F. (2018). Formal and informal workplace support for New Fathers in Spain. In Musumeci, R., Santero, A. (Ed.), *Contemporary perspectives in family research: Vol. 12. Fathers, childcare and work: Cultures, practices and policies* (pp. 131–153). Emerald Publishing Limited. https://doi.org/10.1108/S1530-353520180000012006

Jürges, H. (2006). Gender ideology, division of housework, and the geographic mobility of families. *Review of Economics of the Household*, *4*(4), 299–323. https://doi.org/10.1007/s11150-006-0015-2

Jürgens, K. (2019). Das "smart" Leben. Ein Versprechen der Digitalisierung auf dem Prüfstand, in: Kohlrausch, B. Schildmann, Voss, D. (Hrsg.), Neue Arbeit - neue Ungleichheiten? Folgen der Digitalisierung, Weinheim Basel Beltz Juventa, pp. 53–68.

Kelliher, C., & Anderson, D. (2010). Doing more with less? Flexible working practices and the intensification of work. *Human Relations*, *63*(1), 83–106. https://doi.org/10.1177/0018726709349199

Kim, J., Henly, J. R., Golden, L. M., & Lambert, S. J. (2020). Workplace flexibility and worker well-being by gender. *Journal of Marriage and Family*, *82*(3), 892–910. https://doi.org/10.1111/jomf.12633

Kurowska, A. (2018). Gendered effects of home-based work on parents' capability to balance work with non-work: Two countries with different models of division of labour compared. *Social Indicators Research*, 1–21. https://doi.org/10.1007/s11205-018-2034-9

Lott, Y. (2014). *Flexibilität und Autonomie in der Arbeitszeit: Gut für die Work-Life Balance? Analysen zum Zusammenhang von Arbeitszeitarrangements und Work-Life Balance in Europa* [WSI Report].

Lott, Y. (2019). *Weniger Arbeit, mehr Freizeit? Wofür Mütter und Väter flexible Arbeitsrarrangements nutzen* [WSI Report].

Lott, Y. (2020a). Does flexibility help employees switch off from work? Flexible working-time arrangements and cognitive work-to-home spillover for women and men in Germany. *Social Indicators Research*, *151*(2), 471–494. https://doi.org/10.1007/s11205-018-2031-z

Lott, Y. (2020b). *Work-Life Balance im Homeoffice: Was kann der Betrieb tun? Welche betrieblichen Bedingungen sind für eine gute Work-Life Balance im Homeoffice notwendig?* [WSI Report No. 54].

Lott, Y., & Abendroth, A.-K. (2020). The non-use of telework in an ideal worker culture: Why women perceive more cultural barriers. *Community, Work & Family*, 1–19. https://doi.org/10.1080/13668803.2020.1817726

Lott, Y., & Chung, H. (2016). Gender discrepancies in the outcomes of schedule control on overtime hours and income in Germany. *European Sociological Review*, *32*(6), 752–765. https://doi.org/10.1093/esr/jcw032

Lott, Y., & Klenner, C. (2018). Are the ideal worker and ideal parent norms about to change? The acceptance of part-time and parental leave at German workplaces. *Community, Work & Family*, *21*(5), 564–580. https://doi.org/10.1080/13668803.2018.1526775

Mergener, A. (2020a). Berufliche Zugänge zum Homeoffice. Ein tätigkeitsbasierter Ansatz zur Erklärung von Chancenungleichheit beim Homeofficezugang. *Kölner Zeitschrift Für Soziologie Und Sozialpsychologie*, (72), 511–534. https://doi.org/10.1007/s11577-020-00669-0

Mergener, A. (2020b). *Homeoffice in Deutschland – Zugang, Nutzung und Regelung. Ergebnisse aus der BIBB/BAuA-Erwerbstätigenbefragung 2018*. Bonn.

Mergener, A., & Fank, J. (2021). *Arbeiten von zuhause aus: anerkannte Arbeitszeiten im Homeoffice oder unbezahlte Mehrarbeit? Unterschiede in Anerkennung und Ausmaß der von zuhause geleisteten Arbeitszeit nach ausgewählten Beschäftigtenmerkmalen*. Bonn.

Mergener, A., & Winnige, S. (2021). The surge in Working from Home in the wake of the COVID-19 pandemic: What are the long-term potentials for academically and vocationally qualified people? *Berufsbildung in Wissenschaft Und Praxis*, *50*(2), 27–31.

Noonan, M. C., & Glass, J. L. (2012). The hard truth about telecommuting. *Monthly Labor Review*, *135*(6), 38–45.

Ojala, S. (2011). Supplemental work at home among Finnish Wage Earners: Involuntary overtime or taking the advantage of flexibility? *Nordic Journal of Working Life Studies*, *1*(2), 77–97. https://doi.org/10.19154/njwls.v1i2.2346

Ojala, S., Nätti, J., & Anttila, T. (2014). Informal overtime at home instead of telework: Increase in negative work-family interface. *International Journal of Sociology and Social Policy*, *34*(1), 69–87. https://doi.org/10.1108/IJSSP-03-2013-0037

Peters, P., Dulk, L. den, & van der Lippe, T. (2009). The effects of time-spatial flexibility and new working conditions on employees' work–life balance: The Dutch case. *Community, Work & Family*, *12*(3), 279–297. https://doi.org/10.1080/13668800902968907

Pfau-Effinger, B. (1998). Gender cultures and the gender arrangement: A theoretical framework for cross-national gender research. *Innovation: The European Journal of Social Science Research*, *11*(2), 147–166. https://doi.org/10.1080/13511610.1998.9968559

Pongratz, H. J., & Voß, G. G. (2004). Arbeitskraft und Subjektivität. Einleitung und Stellungnahme aus Sicht der Arbeitskraftunternehmer. In H. J. Pongratz & G. G. Voß (Eds.), *Typisch Arbeitskraftunternehmer? Befunde der empirischen Arbeitsforschung* (pp. 7–31). edition sigma.

Powell, A., & Craig, L. (2015). Gender differences in working at home and time use patterns: Evidence from Australia. *Work, Employment and Society*, *29*(4), 571–589. https://doi.org/10.1177/0950017014568140

Ridgeway, C. L., & Correll, S. J. (2004). Motherhood as a status characteristic. *Journal of Social Issues*, *60*(4), 683–700. https://doi.org/10.1111/j.0022-4537.2004.00380.x

Sacks, D. W., Stevenson, B., & Wolfers, J. (2012). The new stylized facts about income and subjective well-being. *Emotion*, *12*(6), 1181. https://doi.org/10.1037/a0029873

Samtleben, C., Lott, Y., & Müller, K.-U. (2020). *Auswirkungen der Ort-Zeit-Flexibilisierung von Erwerbsarbeit auf informelle Sorgearbeit im Zuge der Digitalisierung: Expertise für den Dritten Gleichstellungsbericht der Bundesregierung ((Keine Angabe))*. Berlin.

Sarbu, M. (2018). The role of telecommuting for work-family conflict among German employees. *Research in Transportation Economics*, (70), 37–51. https://doi.org/10.1016/j.retrec.2018.07.009

Song, Y. (2009). Unpaid work at home. *Industrial Relations*, *48*(4), 578–588. https://doi.org/10.1111/j.1468-232X.2009.00576.x

Steinbach, A., & Schulz, F. (2021). Stability and Change in German Parents' Childcare Patterns Across Two Decades. Social Politics. *International Studies in Gender, State & Society*, *29*(2), 428–445. https://doi.org/10.1093/sp/jxab017

Stone, A. A., Schwartz, J. E., Broderick, J. E., & Deaton, A. (2010). A snapshot of the age distribution of psychological well-being in the United States. *Proceedings of the National Academy of Sciences*, *107*, 9985–9990. https://doi.org/10.1073/pnas.1003744107

Studer, R., & Winkelmann, R. (2011). Specification and Estimation of Rating Scale Models - with an Application to the Determinants of Life Satisfaction [University of Zurich Working Paper Series]. https://doi.org/10.2139/ssrn.1815067

Sullivan, C., & Lewis, S. (2001). Home-based telework, gender, and the synchronization of work and family: Perspectives of teleworkers and their co-residents. *Gender, Work and Organization*, *8*(2), 123–145. https://doi.org/10.1111/1468-0432.00125]

Sullivan, C., & Smithson, J. (2007). Perspectives of homeworkers and their partners on working flexibility and gender equity. *International Journal of Human Resource Management*, *18*(3), 448–461. https://doi.org/10.1080/09585190601167797

Swanberg, J. E., Pitt-Catsouphes, M., & Drescher-Burke, K. (2005). A question of justice: Disparities in employees' access to flexible schedule arrangements. *Journal of Family Issues*, *26*(6), 866–895. https://doi.org/10.1177/0192513X05277554

Trappe, H., Pollmann-Schult, M., & Schmitt, C. (2015). The Rise and Decline of the Male Breadwinner Model: Institutional Underpinnings and Future Expectations. *European Sociological Review*, *31*, 230–242. https://doi.org/10.1093/esr/jcv015

Voß, G. G. (1998). Die Entgrenzung von Arbeit und Arbeitskraft. *Mitteilungen Aus Der Arbeitsmarkt-Und Berufsforschung*, *31*(3), 473–487.

Voydanoff, P. (2004). The effects of work demands and resources on work-to-family conflict and facilitation. *Journal of Marriage and Family*, *66*(2), 398–412. https://doi.org/10.1111/j.1741-3737.2004.00028.x

Voydanoff, P. (2005). Toward a conceptualization of perceived work-family fit and balance: A demands and resources approach. *Journal of Marriage and Family*, *67*(4), 822–836. https://doi.org/10.1111/j.1741-3737.2005.00178.x

Williams, J. C., Blair-Loy, M., & Berdahl, J. L. (2013). Cultural schemas, social class, and the flexibility stigma. *Journal of Social Issues*, *69*(2), 209–234. https://doi.org/10.1111/josi.12012

Young, M., & Schieman, S. (2018). Scaling back and finding flexibility: Gender differences in parents' strategies to manage work–family conflict. *Journal of Marriage and Family*, *80*(1), 99–118. https://doi.org/10.1111/jomf.12435

APPENDIX

Table A5.1. Distribution of Considered Variables, Overall and by WfH Categories.

	No WfH ($n = 11{,}468$)	Telework ($n = 4{,}675$)	Partly Informal Overtime ($n = 444$)	Completely Informal Overtime ($n = 1{,}180$)	Total ($n = 16{,}244$)
Women	46.6	46.0	50.7	44.7	46.5
Children < 12 years	20.8	27.0	26.1	22.8	22.2
Education					
No vocational degree	10.3	3.5	3.4	2.8	8.4
Vocational education	67.8	29.8	33.1	39.6	57.9
Further vocational training	6.8	8.8	8.6	11.0	7.5
Academic degree	15.1	58.0	54.9	46.6	26.2
Age	43.4 (11.9)	43.1 (11.0)	42.7 (11.7)	43.5 (11.3)	43.4 (11.7)
Management position					
No	75.7	68.3	57.2	54.3	72.5
Lower	9.2	9.1	11.7	9.6	9.3
Middle	12.6	15.5	23.4	24.9	14.2
Upper	2.5	7.1	7.7	11.2	4.0
Wage	2,639.8 (1,757.1)	4,182.6 (3,662.7)	3,682.5 (2,640.7)	3,999.5 (4,345.9)	3,046.6 (2,563.3)
Total working time (hours/week)	37.4 (10.7)	39.2 (10.6)	40.4 (10.8)	41.7 (11.0)	38.0 (10.7)
Overtime in the company					
No overtime in the company	52.5	40.9	33.9	46.1	49.4
Recognized overtime	43.1	42.8	47.2	32.0	42.5
Non-recognized overtime	4.0	15.5	18.6	21.6	7.6
Overtime, but no info about recognition of overtime hours	0.5	0.7	0.3	0.2	0.5
Partner employed	55.2	65.8	64.0	61.2	57.8
Pressure to perform					
No	5.8	1.7	34.6	45.8	4.6
Rarely	13.8	9.4	35.7	53.2	12.3

(Continued)

Table A5.1. *(Continued)*

	No WfH ($n = 11{,}468$)	Telework ($n = 4{,}675$)	Partly Informal Overtime ($n = 444$)	Completely Informal Overtime ($n = 1{,}180$)	Total ($n = 16{,}244$)
Sometimes	34.6	7.6	34.2	57.9	34.6
Often	45.8	5.4	30.9	62.6	48.5
Carrier aspirations	33.9	42.4	45.7	46.1	36.5
Work experience (years)	12.0 (11.3)	11.6 (10.3)	11.8 (10.7)	12.1 (10.8)	11.9 (11.0)
Company size					
1–9 employees	12.7	11.4	11.6	10.5	12.3
10–49 employees	28.1	22.9	28.0	25.9	27.0
50–249 employees	26.5	26.4	34.7	29.8	26.8
250+ employees	32.7	39.3	25.7	33.9	33.9
Company in West-Germany	80.5	83.6	80.4	81.2	81.1
Occupational group					
Armed forces personnel	0.7	0.2	0.0	0.2	0.5
Agriculture, forestry, farming	0.7	0.4	0.2	0.1	0.6
Gardening and floristry	1.2	0.2	1.7	0.3	1.0
Production and processing of raw materials, glass-,ceramic	0.4	0.1	0.0	0.2	0.3
Plastic-making, wood-working, -processing	2.0	0.3	0.1	0.3	1.5
Paper-making, printing, technical media design	0.9	0.4	1.2	0.5	0.8
Metal-making, -working, -construction	5.0	0.3	0.7	1.1	3.8
Technical occupations in machine-building and automotive industry	6.8	2.7	3.1	3.6	5.8
Mechatronics, energy electronics and electrical engineering	3.5	3.7	2.6	2.9	3.5
Technical research, develop., construction, production, planning and scheduling	3.0	3.4	1.8	4.8	3.2
Textile-, leather-making, and -processing	0.4	0.2	0.1	0.0	0.3
Food-production, -processing	3.3	0.8	0.0	3.2	2.7
Construction scheduling, architecture and surveying	0.7	1.3	1.5	0.6	0.8
Building construction above and below ground	1.5	0.2	0.5	0.5	1.2
Interior construction	1.7	0.3	1.0	0.2	1.3
Building services engineering, technical building services	2.8	1.0	0.2	2.1	2.3

Mathematics, biology, chemistry, and physics	1.8	1.1	0.9	2.4	1.7
Geology, geography and environmental protection	0.1	0.2	0.0	0.7	0.2
Computer science, ICT	1.2	12.9	5.5	1.8	3.6
Traffic and logistics (without vehicle driving)	6.5	1.8	2.4	3.6	5.3
Drivers, operators of vehicles and transport equipment	5.0	0.5	1.9	0.7	3.8
Safety and health protection, security and surveillance	2.2	0.9	2.8	1.6	1.9
Cleaning services	2.1	0.5	0.9	0.6	1.7
Purchasing, sales and trading	1.7	6.0	2.6	4.9	2.8
Retail sales	6.9	1.3	2.2	5.0	5.6
Tourism, hotels, restaurants	2.2	1.0	0.7	2.9	2.0
Business management and organization	7.0	15.5	8.9	10.4	8.9
Financial services, accounting, and tax consultancy	4.0	6.0	6.1	3.9	4.5
Law and public administration	4.9	5.1	2.2	4.3	4.8
Medical and healthcare	8.4	2.8	5.4	5.8	7.0
Non-medical healthcare, body care, wellness, and medical technicians	3.1	0.8	1.3	2.3	2.6
Education and social work, housekeeping, and theology	5.4	5.5	12.0	10.1	5.8
Teaching and training	1.1	16.8	25.2	13.3	5.5
Philology, literature, humanities, social sciences, economics	0.2	1.3	2.4	0.8	0.5
Advertising, marketing, commercial, editorial media design	1.4	4.1	1.2	3.3	2.0
Product design, artisan craftwork, fine arts, making of musical instruments	0.1	0.1	0.0	0.5	0.1
Performing arts and entertainment	0.3	0.8	0.8	0.8	0.4

Source: BIBB/BAuA Employment Survey 2018. Authors' calculations.

Notes: Weighted percentages. Categorical variables in percent. Continuous variables with mean and standard deviations in parentheses. Total sample includes employees aged 18 to 65 years.

Table A5.2. Ordered Logit Regression Models of the Temporal Alignment of Work and Private Life by Gender and Children and the Use of WfH.

	M1a		M1b		M2a		M2b	
No WfH	*Reference*		*Reference*		*Reference*		*Reference*	
Telework	1.403***	(0.068)	1.620***	(0.103)	1.399***	(0.068)	1.664***	(0.198)
Partly informal overtime	0.794**	(0.078)	0.791*	(0.110)	0.792**	(0.078)	0.714	(0.200)
Completely informal overtime	0.805***	(0.052)	1.067	(0.095)	0.803***	(0.052)	1.412**	(0.245)
Men	*Reference*		*Reference*					
Women	0.880***	(0.036)	1.002	(0.051)				
Interactions								
Telework # Women			0.758***	(0.063)				
Partly informal overtime # Women			1.008	(0.191)				
Completely informal overtime # Women			0.565***	(0.069)				
Men, children u12								
Men, w/o children u12					0.901*	(0.053)	0.958	(0.074)
Women, w/o children u12					0.799***	(0.051)	0.949	(0.078)
Women, w children u12					0.869*	(0.071)	1.071	(0.113)
Interactions								
Telework# Men, w/o child. u12							0.964	(0.126)
Telework# Women, w/o child. u12							0.737**	(0.098)
Telework# Women, child. u12							0.732*	(0.128)
Partly informal overtime # Men, w/o child. u12							1.145	(0.366)
Partly informal overtime # Women, w/o child. u12							1.134	(0.359)
Partly informal overtime # Women, child. u12							1.041	(0.396)
Completely informal overtime # Men, w/o child. u12							0.685*	(0.134)
Completely informal overtime # Women, w/o child. u12							0.448***	(0.088)
Completely informal overtime # Women, w child. u12							0.346***	(0.091)
Controls								
Education								
No vocational degree	*Reference*		*Reference*		*Reference*		*Reference*	
Vocational education	1.325***	(0.104)	1.334***	(0.105)	1.320***	(0.104)	1.331***	(0.105)
Further vocational training	1.554***	(0.151)	1.568***	(0.152)	1.546***	(0.150)	1.564***	(0.152)

Academic degree	1.666***	(0.143)	1.674***	(0.143)	1.656***	(0.142)	1.668***	(0.143)
Age	0.994***	(0.002)	0.994***	(0.002)	0.995**	(0.002)	0.995***	(0.002)
Management position								
No	*Reference*		*Reference*		*Reference*		*Reference*	
Lower	1.013	(0.060)	1.022	(0.060)	1.012	(0.060)	1.023	(0.061)
Middle	1.034	(0.049)	1.030	(0.049)	1.030	(0.049)	1.024	(0.049)
Upper	1.048	(0.082)	1.034	(0.081)	1.040	(0.081)	1.022	(0.080)
Wage	1.000***	(0.000)	1.000**	(0.000)	1.000***	(0.000)	1.000**	(0.000)
Total working time (hours/week)	0.953***	(0.002)	0.954***	(0.002)	0.954***	(0.002)	0.954***	(0.002)
Overtime in the company								
No overtime in the company	*Reference*		*Reference*		*Reference*		*Reference*	
Recognized overtime	0.967	(0.037)	0.967	(0.037)	0.966	(0.037)	0.967	(0.037)
Non-recognized overtime	0.653***	(0.040)	0.644***	(0.039)	0.651***	(0.040)	0.641***	(0.039)
Overtime, but no info about recog. of overtime hours	0.787	(0.177)	0.791	(0.178)	0.790	(0.178)	0.787	(0.177)
Partner employed	1.175***	(0.040)	1.169***	(0.040)	1.158***	(0.040)	1.154***	(0.040)
Pressure to perform								
No	*Reference*		*Reference*		*Reference*		*Reference*	
Rarely	1.099	(0.134)	1.098	(0.134)	1.097	(0.134)	1.102	(0.135)
Sometimes	0.835	(0.093)	0.836	(0.093)	0.837	(0.093)	0.839	(0.093)
Often	0.382***	(0.042)	0.381***	(0.042)	0.381***	(0.042)	0.381***	(0.042)
Carrier aspirations	0.998	(0.039)	1.001	(0.039)	1.001	(0.039)	1.004	(0.040)
Work experience (years)	1.003*	(0.002)	1.003*	(0.002)	1.003*	(0.002)	1.004*	(0.002)
Company size								
1–9 employees	*Reference*		*Reference*		*Reference*		*Reference*	
10–49 employees	1.062	(0.067)	1.064	(0.067)	1.061	(0.067)	1.064	(0.067)
50–249 employees	1.037	(0.065)	1.036	(0.065)	1.034	(0.065)	1.035	(0.065)
250+ employees	1.136**	(0.072)	1.133**	(0.072)	1.134**	(0.072)	1.132*	(0.072)
Company in West-Germany	0.952	(0.040)	0.951	(0.040)	0.953	(0.040)	0.952	(0.040)
Occupational groups[a]								
Observations	16,244		16,244		16,244		16,244	
Pseudo R^2	0.077		0.078		0.077		0.078	

Notes: Odds ratios are displayed.

[a] Controls for employees' occupations with 36 dummies for occupational groups (at the two-digit level of the German Classification of Occupations 2010, KldB 2010) are included but not displayed. The results are available upon request.

SECTION 3

LINKED-LIVES PERSPECTIVE ON FLEXIBLE WORK AND THE FAMILY

CHAPTER 6

INDIVIDUAL AND CROSS-PARTNER TRANSITIONS TO FLEXITIME AND TELEWORKING AND COGNITIVE SUBJECTIVE WELL-BEING

Aneesa F. Qadri

ABSTRACT

Previous theoretical and empirical literature has advocated growth in the access and use of flexible working arrangements by establishing their link with individual and especially parental subjective well-being. Given this, the current research investigates impact that their own or their partners' transition to flexitime and teleworking has on parental subjective well-being. The cross-partner dimension has not been explored yet by prior studies. Measures for cognitive, subjective well-being include satisfaction with life overall, satisfaction with the amount of leisure time, and satisfaction with health. Ordered logit longitudinal models are estimated using Understanding Society data from 2009 to 2019. Corroborating prior studies, the current analysis finds that mothers' transition to flexitime and teleworking has a positive impact on their leisure time and health satisfaction. For fathers, switching to telework improves satisfaction with their amount of leisure time, while adopting flexitime can take a toll on self-reported health satisfaction. However, contrary to expectations, mothers' move to teleworking can be injurious for fathers' life satisfaction levels, yet fathers' adoption of flexitime fosters mothers' satisfaction with their leisure time amount.

Keywords: Flexible working; work–life balance; Division of Domestic Labour; gender inequality; family dynamics; life satisfaction

Flexible Work and the Family
Contemporary Perspectives in Family Research, Volume 21, 161–200

Published under exclusive licence by Emerald Publishing Limited
ISSN: 1530-3535/doi:10.1108/S1530-353520230000021006

INTRODUCTION

In the past decade, subjective well-being, relating to one's feelings and evaluations about their life (Diener et al., 2013), has become a key indicator of individual and societal welfare[1] and thus an integral component of British governmental policy agenda (House of Commons, 2018). A critical factor in undermining general and domain-specific subjective well-being is the work–life conflict resulting from individuals' inability to balance work and non-work domains. Given childcare responsibilities, parents, especially mothers, are most likely to experience the conflict (Schober, 2013). Recognizing these patterns, scholars and the British government have proposed adopting flexible working arrangements, which may grant work–life balance through facilitating individuals in simultaneously fulfilling work and non-work commitments (House of Commons, 2018). The current chapter examines whether the transition to flexible working drives an impact on the general and domain-specific subjective well-being of parents. It focuses on flexitime, which refers to an individual's ability to alter the timing of paid work, and teleworking, which encompasses working outside of the regular work premises, usually from home (Wheatley, 2017). These two arrangements mostly remain unexplored by prior research on the impact of flexible working on individuals' life trajectories. Moreover, the current study adds to the existing literature by evaluating whether, in heterosexual families, one partner's subjective well-being undergoes changes following the other's adoption of flexitime and teleworking.

Theoretical literature presents conflicting arguments about parents' transitions to flexitime and teleworking and their subjective well-being. On the one hand, the autonomy that workplace and work hour flexibility grant their users are linked with the ability to undertake time inflexible domestic tasks, experience low levels of commuting related stress, and partake in leisure activities, all of which positively influence subjective well-being (Song & Gao, 2019). In contrast, the use of these flexible working arrangements may reinforce women's caregiving role within the family and lead to an increase in their domestic burden. Furthermore, users of flexibility are also likely to experience discriminatory attitudes from employers, manifested in lower career advancement opportunities and pay rises (Chung, 2018).

Some prior studies show that flexibly working mothers are more likely to experience workplace discrimination than fathers, given assumed differences in the purpose behind men and women's uptake of flexible working arrangements (Lott & Chung, 2016). Women usually use flexitime and teleworking to engage with childcare, while career advancement goals typically drive men's use (Chung & van der Horst, 2018). Thus, employers may view flexibly working women negatively while flexibly working men positively when measuring work commitment. However, an opposing perspective holds that their ability to conform to gender-role expectations and finish domestic tasks whilst sustaining employment through working flexibly improves mothers' self-perception of well-being. On the contrary, the work intensification which flexibly working fathers may experience can increase their stress levels, reduce their leisure time, and thus negatively impact their subjective well-being (Chandola et al., 2019). Overall, empirical findings on the gendered impact of flexitime and teleworking on cognitive well-being are mixed, creating the need for further exploration, which this chapter aims to fulfill.

In terms of cross-partner effects, previous studies ranging from over two decades have established that a husband's/male partner's employment patterns can impact his wife's/female partner's life trajectory and vice versa (Bredtmann et al., 2017; Greenhaus et al., 1989; Hodges & Budig, 2010; Killewald, 2013; Killewald & Garcia-Manglano, 2016; Lundberg & Rose, 2000; Lyonette & Crompton, 2014; Parasuraman et al., 1992; Westman & Etzion, 1995). To date, only one study engages with the cross-partner dimension of flexible work to analyze couples' wages in Germany (Langner, 2017). By acknowledging existing gaps, my research will study the outcome of one partner's move to flexitime and teleworking on the other partner's self-reported well-being.

Moreover, previous quantitative research on the association between flexitime and teleworking and subjective well-being has used cross-sectional analyses, which has allowed selection and omitted variable biases to impact findings. The current study aims to remove these biases by taking a longitudinal approach.

In this chapter, making mothers and fathers my unit of analysis, I aim to address all above-mentioned empirical and methodological gaps surrounding transitions to flexitime and teleworking and their influence on subjective well-being. I will exploit British household data from Understanding Society to answer the following questions:

(1) Does mothers' and fathers' transition to flexitime or teleworking impact their subjective well-being levels?
(2) Does one partner's transition to flexitime or teleworking impact the subject well-being levels of the other partner? Does this impact differ by gender?

I will, firstly, engage with the definitions of flexitime and teleworking, as well as the concept of subjective well-being and its underpinnings. Secondly, previous theoretical and empirical research lending insight about the relation between working flexibly and subjective well-being will be discussed and then considered for the empirical design of the current study. Taking a longitudinal approach, this study will utilize fixed-effects ordered logit models to answer the above research questions, thus accounting for selection bias to some extent.

FLEXITIME AND TELEWORKING: DEFINITIONS AND GROWTH WITHIN THE BRITISH LABOR MARKET

The umbrella term, flexible working arrangements, is used to describe work arrangements "which suit an employee's needs" (U.K. Government Equalities Office, 2019). Broad definitions of workplace flexibility may encompass leave options (e.g., maternity/paternity) and flexibility in work contracts. Nevertheless, my paper restricts this definition to having the ability to alter the time, place and duration of paid work to fit individual needs. Thus, flexible working arrangements include part-time working, working term-time only, job sharing, flexitime, working a compressed week, working annualized and remote working (Wooden et al., 2009).

In the past, most research has engaged with the outcomes that part-time produce on women's/mothers' lives and careers because most British working women are likely to transition to part-time work at some point in their lives, especially following childbirth (Lyonette, 2015). While acknowledging the significance and the use of part-time work within the British labor market, this article diverges from previous studies by exploring two emerging flexible working arrangements, flexitime and teleworking. Flexitime is strictly defined as having the ability to change work timing (that is, to alternate the starting and ending times) and to fluctuate the number of hours worked per day or week (Chung & van der Horst, 2018). In a broader sense, flexitime can also include the following: annualized hours, where "working hours" is not defined per day or week but calculated throughout the year; and compressed hours, where workers maintain their working hours, usually full-time, but work fewer days. This article will conform to the strict definition of flexitime. Teleworking typically entails working outside of regular work premises, typically from home (Wheatley, 2017).

In recognition of their countless benefits to individual and societal welfare, the access and use of flexible working arrangements have grown in the British labor market over the last decades. Accounting for these changes are legislative measures taken from 2002 when employees with young or disabled children were granted the right to request flexible working arrangements from their employers. In 2007, this right was extended to carers of dependent adults and, in 2009, to parents of older children. The most recent flexibility legislation, in 2014, enabled all employees with 26 weeks or more of service to request flexible working arrangements (The Flexible Working Regulations, 2014). Employers are required to handle these requests in a reasonable manner. Further developments have also surfaced with the introduction of a bill in the British parliament in 2019, which propositions that flexible working should be made the default position for all employees. This bill is currently under review.

Following these governmental endeavors to extend access to flexible working arrangements to a broad population in the UK, employers and organizations within the British labor market have also promoted workplace flexibility. The Eurobarometer survey from 2018 shows that 80% of respondents in the UK had access to flexible working arrangements, compared with the EU average of 67% (Eurobarometer, 2018). However, further measures need to be taken to increase access to flexibility, create friendly work environments for flexible workers, and encourage the use of all flexible working arrangements, especially flexitime and teleworking, among a broader population, especially parents.

Current usage of flexitime and teleworking may be filtered through many factors, including gender, occupational status, income, work sector and work status. While workplace support offered to parents is gender-neutral in its design, fathers' usage rates of flexible working arrangements generally tend to be different from those of mothers in the UK (Moran & Koslowski, 2018). Accounting for this pattern is the prevalence of gender norms in British society, where fathers continue to resume the role of "instrumental economic providers" while mothers are classified as expressive parents with childcare responsibilities (Gatrell et al., 2014). Within this context, work–life balance is a more significant concern for mothers (Hampson, 2018), and thus, they may be more likely to take flexitime and teleworking. However, opposing perspectives suggest that fathers' use of flexitime and teleworking is likely to match mothers' use as the latter use these arrangements to increase their work hours and earn wage premiums (Grawitch et al., 2010).

Another determinant of parents' use of flexitime and teleworking is their access to these arrangements, often contingent upon occupational status (Wheatley, 2017). Higher status jobs are more likely to offer employees autonomy over their work routines because employers want to evade the risk of losing managerial and professional workers who want to combine work and family demands (Langner, 2017). Thus, the users of flexitime and teleworking are mostly working higher or middle-tier jobs than lower-tier jobs.

Furthermore, the use of flexitime and teleworking is also mediated by the work sector. The public sector in the UK is generally more motivated by ideals such as work–life balance and employee well-being. Thus, flexibility provisions within this sector are high, and attitudes toward flexible workers tend to be less discriminatory than those exhibited by private sectors. Thus, parents working in public sector organizations are more likely to adopt flexitime and teleworking.

SUBJECTIVE WELL-BEING: CONCEPT AND MEASUREMENT

Subjective well-being refers to people's cognitive and affective appraisals and evaluations of their lives (Diener et al., 2013). It grew in significance through scholarly acknowledgement that measures of economic resources were insufficient indicators of individual and societal welfare (Stiglitz et al., 2009). Self-reported well-being had to be taken into account (Steptoe et al., 2014), and thus, two elements of subjective well-being developed that captured different aspects of life; cognitive and affective components (Bücker et al., 2018). The cognitive components consist of life satisfaction and satisfaction with other life domains like job, health, marriage, and leisure time (Diener et al., 2013).

On the other hand, the affective component comprises two sub-components, positive effect, which relates to positive emotions like happiness and pride, and negative effect, which relates to negative emotions like anger, sorrow, and worry. Responses from the affective component are primarily derived from the emotional state in the past week or month. Usually, these measures utilize a response scale either ranging from "completely dissatisfied" to "completely satisfied" (bipolar) or from "not at all satisfied" to "completely satisfied." Using 11-point (0 to 10) response scales has become common, but some studies use shorter scales.

From a policy perspective, it is argued that the cognitive component is a better measure of subjective well-being as it is more stable over time (Diener et al., 2013). The current research focuses on the cognitive component; it engages with overall satisfaction with life and domain-specific satisfaction relating to health and given amount of leisure time.

FLEXIBLE WORKING ARRANGEMENTS AND SUBJECTIVE WELL-BEING AMONG PARENTS

Individual Transitions

Theoretical models outlining the relationship between the use of flexitime and teleworking and subjective well-being are rooted in the phenomenon of autonomy; in this case, autonomy translates to employees' discretion over the schedule and location of their work (Glavin & Schieman, 2012). The demand-control-support (DCS) model introduced by Karasek and Theorell (1992), acknowledging that individuals' time, attention, and energy are finite resources for which their work and non-work engagements compete, suggests that the autonomy extended by flexitime and teleworking enables work–life balance, which is integral to well-being (Laurijssen & Glorieux, 2013). For parents, these dynamics are even more applicable given their childrearing responsibilities (Hokke et al., 2020).

The flexibility enactment theory (Kossek et al., 2005) and work–family border theory (Clark, 2000) further entrench the implications of the DCS model by establishing that the autonomy over temporal and physical boundaries between their work and home is a key device for individuals to determine the best possible way to allocate resources to both domains (Lin et al., 2015). In countries and regions with a lack of affordable childcare provisions, like in Britain, employees' ability to tailor paid work according to their needs is vital (Grönlund, 2007).

However, more recent theoretical literature draws attention to a critical mediating factor in the association between flexitime and teleworking and subjective well-being levels, gender (Gregory et al., 2013). Due to the prevalence of traditional gender roles in most parts of the world, including Britain, fathers exhibit a more outstanding commitment to paid work while mothers shoulder the lion's share of housework and childcare (Minnotte et al., 2016). Given this, the intent behind mothers' and fathers' use of flexible working arrangements may be different. For mothers, the use could be driven by their need to manage domestic responsibilities alongside paid work (Grönlund & Öun, 2018) while for fathers, arrangements like flexitime and teleworking may be seen as an opportunity to work overtime in the hopes of career advancement and income premiums (Glass & Noonan, 2016). As a result, for mothers, work autonomy could achieve an optimal work–life balance, permitting both full-time labor market engagement alongside domestic roles, while for fathers, the former may lead to high-stress levels, an inability to participate in the household, and burnout (Lott & Chung, 2016).

Opposing perspectives draw attention to the stigma attached to flexibly working women; they are likely to experience workplace discrimination and low career mobility prospects for not appearing to be committed workers to colleagues and employers. As a result, these women experience dissatisfaction across work and life domains (Hampson, 2018). Scholars also discuss how arrangements like flexitime and teleworking may entrench a traditional gendered division of labor within dual-earner households, which may negatively impact women's well-being. In contrast, flexibly working men might not experience such stigma due to a general perception that their use of flexitime or teleworking may not be motivated by domestic commitments (Kelliher & Anderson, 2009).

When studying the implications of flexibility on parents' lives, it is important to account for the differences between flexitime and teleworking. As mentioned in prior sections, flexitime may allow mothers to adjust schedules and undertake time inflexible tasks including meal times, school pick-ups and so on (Grönlund, 2018). While the conventional "9 to 5" working day would leave mothers stressed and considering shifting jobs or decreasing their role in the labor market, arrangements like flexitime lend hope for a tailored work–life balance and sustained employment (van der Lippe et al., 2011). While some prior literature, as mentioned above, has dealt with the repercussions of the stigma attached with women who use flexitime or drawn attention to how the possibility of adjustments to work schedules nurtures traditional gender roles, most scholars have argued in favor of flexitime.

In contrast, fathers' use of flexitime is mostly associated negatively with their cognitive well-being. Beckmann et al.'s (2017) modified moral-hazard model suggests that arrangements like flexitime encourage employees to increase their effort in paid work. Men are likely to work intensively in the hopes of furthering their careers and receiving income premiums (Glass & Noonan, 2016). While the additional work may be monetarily rewarded it can exacerbate stress and anxiety levels by creating work–life conflict and limiting time for leisure activities (Lott & Chung, 2016). In an alternative scenario, where fathers may adjust work timings for domestic responsibilities, they may encounter very discriminatory attitudes from employers and colleagues, due to gender expectations, which can produce deleterious outcomes for their well-being (Davies & Frink, 2014).

Empirical studies investigating the impact of the use of flexitime discover that its overall use is positively associated with life satisfaction and domain-specific well-being, for example, leisure time satisfaction and job satisfaction (Wheatley, 2017). These findings corroborate the conclusions drawn by Allen et al.'s (2013) meta-analysis. In terms of gendered impact, findings are inconsistent. Both Carlson et al.'s (2010) and Hofäcker and König's (2013) studies conclude that flexitime reduces work-to-family conflict among female workers, thus improving their cognitive wellbeing. Yet, when exploring the mediating role of gender, Wheatley (2017) finds that flexitime is associated with lower life satisfaction among women but higher life, leisure time, and job satisfaction among men. Kim et al. (2019) arrive at similar conclusions using data from the General Social Survey in the United States; they find that when given the ability to change start and end times, women experience high work–family conflict and fatigue, whereas men do not. On the other hand, Hokke et al (2020) discover that both Australian mothers and fathers who use flexitime experience lower fatigue and less burnout, and thus higher satisfaction with health. Given these mixed findings and the lack of analyses regarding the use of flexitime among parents, the current project intends to fill empirical gaps and study multiple dimensions of parental well-being including general and domain-specific. Based on theoretical models and empirical guidance the following hypotheses are drawn:

H1a. Mothers' transition to flexitime can improve their overall and domain-specific well-being levels.

H1b. Fathers' transition to flexitime can be injurious to their overall and domain-specific well-being levels

By working from home, mothers can attend to domestic responsibilities like childcare alongside paid work. While some scholars view these attributes as advantageous for leisure time allowance and a reduction in commuting related stress, others draw attention to a blurring of boundaries between paid and non-work domains, which can be deleterious for women's work–life balance, and in turn, their well-being (Tietze & Musson, 2002). Moreover, previous literature also implies that women's ability to work from home may create or exacerbate the unequal domestic labor division in heterosexual dual-earner households; aware of their female partners' improved ability to attend to household responsibilities, male partners may to some extent withdraw their involvement (Lorenz, 2018).

In the case of fathers, similar to the case of flexitime, their use of teleworking could lead to overtime work and burnout. However, most prior scholarship does not support a negative association (Glass & Noonan, 2016). As fathers are not expected to take up a large share of housework, they are less likely to experience spillover from non-work to work domains when working from home (Wheatley, 2017). Moreover, fathers can invest the time saved from not commuting to work on leisure activities, which would not benefit both their general and domain-specific well-being (Sullivan & Lewis, 2001).

Hilbrecht et al.'s (2014) study using the 2010 Canadian General Social Survey finds that lengthier commuting time is associated with lower overall life satisfaction. Similar conclusions are made by Clark et al. (2019), who use Understanding Society data from 2009 to 2014; they also add that use of teleworking is most strongly associated with leisure time satisfaction compared with other cognitive, subjective well-being components. Taking gender into account, Binder's (2016) study using British household data from Understanding Society attests to the above-mentioned insights, finding a positive association between working from home and job satisfaction only for men. Similarly, Giménez-Nadal et al.'s (2021) study, which uses the American Time Use Survey from 2003 to 2015 also arrives at similar conclusions, finding that only male teleworkers experience higher well-being levels than commuters. Yet, as with the case of flexitime, literature on teleworking and parental well-being is scarce. Thus, the current study explores this topic based on the following hypotheses:

H2a. Mothers' transition to teleworking can be injurious to their overall and domain-specific well-being levels

H2b. Fathers' transition to teleworking can improve their overall and domain-specific well-being levels.

CROSS-PARTNER TRANSITIONS

Within heterosexual, dual-earner households, partners' work patterns can influence each other's lives (Bredtmann et al., 2017; Greenhaus et al., 1989; Hodges & Budig, 2010, Killewald, 2013; Killewald & Garcia-Manglano, 2015; Lundberg &

Rose, 2000; Lyonette & Crompton, 2014; Parasuraman et al., 1992; Westman & Etzion, 1995). Despite these conclusions, prior studies have not investigated if husbands' work flexibility creates an impact on wives' well-being self-perfections and vice versa. Thus, I aspire to explicate the effect of cross-partner use of flexitime and teleworking.

Insight from the previous sections of this chapter, which established the mediating role of gender in the relationship between individuals' use of flexitime and teleworking and their well-being outcomes, holds in the cross-partner context as well. As female partners' flexibility may allow them to comply with gender role expectations and bear most of the household responsibilities, male partners may see this as an opportunity to decrease their participation in the latter. Thus, men may experience a reduction in their levels and more time for leisure activities, which may reflect on their general and domain-specific well-being levels (Killewald, 2013). Furthermore, men can also increase the time they spend in paid employment, for which they are through career mobility opportunities and wage premiums. As a result, fathers may secure a greater bargaining power within the household, delegating more time to themselves to distress (Maume, 2015).

Contrarily, as discussed before, in dual-earner households, fathers' uptake of flexible working arrangements can be driven by advancing career goals through working more intensely, in which case, they are likely to decrease their role in domestic responsibilities, increasing mothers' burden. In some cases, mothers might even need to decrease the time they spend in paid employment to make time for household tasks. Unfairness in the domestic division of labor can espouse negative feelings like stress and frustration among female partners, affecting their subjective well-being (Schieman et al., 2018). Furthermore, changes in housework dynamics may be detrimental to mothers' careers and their leisure time availability (Cha, 2010).

Cross-partner effects of flexibility can also differ across flexitime and teleworking. For instance, in households where fathers use flexitime, they can delegate time-inflexible domestic tasks to themselves, thus lending support to mothers (Langner, 2017). In such a case, division of labor can be more egalitarian, from which mothers' careers and well-being can benefit. On the contrary, most previous research has implied that fathers' use of teleworking can be detrimental to mothers; despite being within the home premises, fathers are unlikely to increase their involvement in domestic activities due to gender role expectations, which leaves mothers frustrated and stressed out. Extending from the previous point, fathers may use the time saved from not commuting to work on leisure activities instead of utilizing it toward dividing household responsibilities equally (Langner, 2017).

Variations in fathers' well-being outcomes across mothers' use of flexitime and teleworking may be less pronounced; overall, previous research implies that mothers' use of both arrangements can positively impact fathers' well-being (Maume, 2015). Due to mothers' improved ability to take on and complete domestic tasks, whether housework or childcare, fathers are likely to decrease their involvement within the household, and invest time either in leisure activities or toward paid work. In both cases, fathers are likely to benefit, which would reflect on their self-reported general or domain-specific well-being (Clark et al., 2019). Thus, the current study engages with the following hypotheses:

H3a. Mothers' transition to flexitime can improve fathers' overall and domain-specific well-being.

H3b. Fathers' transition to flexitime can improve mothers' overall and domain-specific well-being.

H4a. Mothers' transition to teleworking can improve fathers' overall and domain-specific well-being.

H4b. Fathers' transition to teleworking can be injurious for mothers' overall and domain-specific well-being.

DATA AND METHOD

Data and Sample

This chapter uses data from Understanding Society, an ongoing panel study, started in 2009, which interviews around 40,000 British households annually to explore economic and social changes in Britain at societal, household, and individual levels. The study is representative of the UK population as it covers people of all ages and socio-economic backgrounds and contains information on the employment patterns of individuals and married/cohabitating partners, which is necessary for my analysis. Data on individuals' availability and use of flexible working arrangements are present in alternate waves (2, 4, 6, 8, 10) of Understanding Society. The longitudinal nature of the study allows researchers to explore within-individual changes over the life course which lies at the center of my empirical framework. Lastly, the study's individual and household level demographic attributes serve as key control variables for the empirical analyses in this chapter.

My analytical sample comprises parents who stay in paid employment throughout the observation period; those who took parental leave are not included. Moreover, only those respondents who work for more than one hour a week are included, while self-employed individuals are omitted. Respondents' age is restricted to 18–55, which is working age in the UK. A sub-sample is drawn for cross-partner analyses, which comprises only heterosexual married/cohabitating mothers and fathers whose partners' data is also present in the data set. Furthermore, the sub-sample is restricted to only those respondents whose partners also stay in paid employment throughout the observation period.

Dependent Variables

In the Understanding Society data set, variables measure overall and domain-specific cognitive well-being. To strengthen my findings, my analysis engages with both types of variables. Overall cognitive well-being is measured by the following question about life satisfaction: "*How dissatisfied or satisfied are you with your life overall?*". Similarly, domain-specific dimensions are measured by the following questions: "*How dissatisfied or satisfied are you with your health?*" and "*How dissatisfied or satisfied are you with your amount of leisure time?*". Response categories for all three questions range from 1 to 7, with 1 denoting "Completely dissatisfied,"

2 "Mostly dissatisfied," 3 "Somewhat dissatisfied," 4 "Neither satisfied nor dissatisfied," 5 "Somewhat satisfied," 6 "Mostly satisfied" and 7 "Completely satisfied."

As very few respondents were present in the first two response categories, I merged categories 1 and 2 and 6 and 7, creating a five-category variable to denote life satisfaction. The new response categories were: 1 "Very dissatisfied," 2 "Somewhat dissatisfied," 3 "Neither satisfied nor dissatisfied," 4 "Somewhat satisfied," 5 "Very satisfied."

Independent Variables

The two main independent variables in this study are flexitime and teleworking. As mentioned above, flexitime encompasses three flexible working arrangements, flexitime, working a compressed week, and working annualized hours. In the Understanding Society data set, individual binary variables represent the three arrangements. Using these variables, I create a new dummy variable called "flexitime" which takes the value "1" when individuals use one, two or all three of the arrangements above, and the value "0" if they do not use any of them. Chung & van der Horst's (2017) study inspired this operationalization approach, which used cross-sectional methods to explore the relationship between flexitime and women's likelihood to stay in the labor market post-childbirth.

The second independent variable in this chapter, teleworking, is operationalized in the Understanding Society data set by a binary variable that takes the value "1" if the respondent uses teleworking and "0" if they do not. I retain this operationalization in my models.

Control Variables

To strengthen the validity of my analysis, I also include a set of control variables. Use of other flexible working arrangements, like part-time work and term-time work, are included as a binary variable in my model, taking the value "1" in case the respondent does avail them and the value "0" otherwise. Other binary control variables include a change in current employment, which takes the value "1" if the respondent has changed their employer since the last wave and "0" if they have not. I also control for long-term illness status with a variable which equals "0" if the respondent has no long-term illness and "1" if they do. Similarly, whether an individual works for the private or the public sector is also controlled for. The categorical control variables in my analysis are the number of children, marital status, number of children in the household across different age groups, and sector of employment. As my unit of analysis are parents, the reference category for the variable "number of children" is "having one child" with the other two categories being "having two children" and "having three or more children." The categories for marital status are "never married/single" (reference category: denoted by 0), "married/cohabitating" (denoted by 1), and "divorced/widowed/separated" (denoted by 2). The variable sector of employment has three categories: "routine" as the reference category, "intermediate" denoted by "1," and "managerial or professional" denoted by 2. Lastly, my models also control for two continuous variables, age, household income, and the number of work hours.

In the cross-partner models, I also control for some spousal/partner characteristics, including spousal use of other flexible working arrangements, and spousal employment sector and health status. Furthermore, marital status is not controlled for in the cross-partner model as the sample selected only contains heterosexual married/cohabitating couples.

Adding the variables mentioned above to my analyses will improve the robustness of my findings by controlling for confounding factors in the relationship between the use of flexitime and teleworking and life satisfaction (Allen et al., 2013).

ANALYTICAL STRATEGY

Using a balanced panel, my empirical analysis applies fixed-effects ordered logit models to estimate the impact that their own or their spouse's/partner's transition to flexitime or teleworking has on mothers' and fathers' well-being (Berge & Houle, 2016). Each individual serves as their own control and thus confounding effects arising from unobserved time-constant variables relating to both the independent and dependent variables, such as religiosity, lifestyle preferences and family values, are removed (Zhou & Kan, 2019). Using this approach lowers the vulnerability of my models to omitted-variable bias and selection bias, creating great confidence in the robustness of my conclusions (Zhou & Kan, 2010)

In the first part of my analysis, I evaluate the odds of reporting higher subjective well-being levels among mothers and fathers following their transition to using flexitime and teleworking, whilst the second part engages with the cross-partner effects of these transitions. In both cases, relevant time-varying variables are controlled for, including income, use of other flexible working arrangements, changes in employment, and the number of children. Additionally, in cross-partner models, the spouse's/partner's characteristics are also controlled for. The following equation defines both models:

$$\log\left(\frac{Y_{ijt}}{1-Y_{ijt}}\right) = \mu_{it} + \beta Flexwork_{it} + \gamma Z_{it} + \theta\vartheta_i + \varepsilon_i$$

where Y_{ijt} is the cumulative probability of being in a cognitive, subjective well-being category j or higher for individual i at time t. $Flexwork_{it}$ is the vector of my time-varying predictor, which in this case is either the individual's or their spouse's/partner's uptake of flexitime/teleworking. Z_{it} is the vector of time-varying control variables. ϑ_i is a vector of time-invariant predictors. ϵ_i is the combined effects of all time-constant unobservable factors, with a fixed value for each respondent.

ADDITIONAL ANALYSES

I engage with cross-sectional models to test the correlation between individual and cross-partner use of flexitime and teleworking and cognitive, subjective well-being. They give me some preliminary insight into the magnitude and directionality of the association between flexible working and well-being. Results are in the Appendix (Tables A6.3 and A6.4)

Furthermore, to check for the robustness of my findings, I also run linear fixed-effects models (see Appendix Tables A6.5 and A6.6). Estimates from these models can confirm the main empirical models in this chapter.

DESCRIPTIVE STATISTICS

Table 6.1 presents the weighted summary statistics for key variables in the present study. My total sample in Wave 2 (2010–2011) is 4,225, reducing to 2,474 in Wave 10 (2018–2019). Overall usage of flexitime is seen to slightly increase between Waves 4 and 6. However, the proportion of women who use flexitime remains relatively stable across the waves while men's usage increases between waves 8 and 10. The overall usage of teleworking also grows across the waves (from 9% in Wave 2 to 10% in Wave 10). Similar patterns are seen across the sample for men, for which proportion of usage increase from 14% to 19% across waves, and the sample for women, for which the proportion of usage grows from 6% to 12%. These developments are likely to be driven by a growth in access to flexible working arrangements and encouraging work environments which promote and sustain flexibility (Wheatley, 2017).

Table 6.1 also shows that women's usage of other flexible working arrangements like part-time work stays consistently high across all waves in the Understanding Society data set, while men's usage of these arrangements remains consistently low. These findings corroborate previous empirical evidence, which shows that among flexible working arrangements, women are most likely to avail the option of working part-time (Wheatley, 2017), often due to structural and normative expectations.

For life satisfaction levels, the highest proportion of individuals are concentrated in the "very satisfied" category, as seen in Table 6.2. Nevertheless, there is a slight decline in the proportion over the waves, from 59% to 56%. A similar decline is also seen across the "very dissatisfied" category, which shifts from 5% to 3% between waves 2 and 10. Overall, the proportion of individuals across all life satisfaction categories stays stable over time. Comparably, for the categories of satisfaction with the amount of leisure time and health, stability in the proportion of individuals also holds across all fives waves in the data set. In the "very dissatisfied" category for satisfaction with amount of leisure time, there is a meager decline from 13% to 11% between 2010–2011 and 2018–2019. On the other hand, during this time frame, the proportion of people in the "very satisfied" category grows from 24% to 26%. For satisfaction with health, the most noticeable changes are seen for the category "very satisfied" in which the proportion of individuals declines from 58% in 2010–2011 to 54% in 2018–2019. Generally, the proportion of individuals in all categories of cognitive, subjective well-being measures in my data set is stable over time, experiencing only minor variations.

Table 6.1. Weighted Descriptive Statistics for Categorical Variables Across Waves 2 – 10.

Variables	2010–2011			2012–2013			2014–2015			2016–2017			2018–2019		
	All	Men	Women	All	Men	Women	All	Men	Women	All	Men	Women	All	Men	Women
Flexitime															
Practiced	19%	23%	17%	19%	22%	17%	21%	23%	19%	19%	23%	17%	20%	25%	17%
Not Practiced	81%	77%	83%	81%	78%	83%	79%	77%	81%	81%	77%	83%	80%	75%	83%
Teleworking															
Practiced	9%	14%	6%	11%	15%	7%	12%	16%	8%	12%	16%	9%	15%	19%	12%
Not Practiced	91%	86%	94%	89%	85%	93%	88%	84%	92%	88%	84%	91%	85%	18%	88%
Other Flexible Working Arrangements															
Practiced	50%	16%	70%	46%	17%	68%	47%	20%	68%	46%	15%	68%	47%	18%	68%
Not Practiced	50%	84%	30%	54%	83%	32%	53%	80%	32%	54%	85%	32%	53%	82%	32%
Satisfaction with Life Overall															
Very dissatisfied	5%	4%	5%	6%	5%	7%	5%	4%	5%	4%	4%	5%	3%	4%	4%
Somewhat dissatisfied	8%	6%	9%	9%	7%	9%	6%	7%	6%	8%	6%	8%	8%	7%	8%
Neither satisfied or dissatisfied	8%	8%	8%	9%	9%	8%	8%	8%	8%	7%	8%	7%	11%	10%	11%
Somewhat satisfied	20%	22%	19%	20%	20%	19%	19%	20%	18%	20%	20%	21%	22%	22%	21%
Very satisfied	59%	60%	59%	56%	59%	57%	62%	61%	63%	61%	63%	59%	56%	57%	56%
Satisfaction with Leisure Time															
Very dissatisfied	13%	13%	13%	15%	13%	15%	12%	12%	12%	11%	12%	11%	11%	12%	10%
Somewhat dissatisfied	25%	25%	25%	24%	26%	22%	23%	24%	22%	22%	23%	21%	23%	23%	24%
Neither satisfied or dissatisfied	13%	16%	12%	14%	14%	14%	12%	12%	14%	14%	14%	14%	13%	12%	13%
Somewhat satisfied	25%	25%	25%	24%	24%	24%	28%	28%	27%	27%	26%	27%	27%	28%	27%
Very satisfied	24%	22%	25%	23%	23%	25%	25%	24%	25%	26%	26%	27%	26%	25%	26%
Satisfaction with Health															
Very dissatisfied	7%	5%	7%	17%	15%	18%	11%	10%	12%	6%	6%	6%	6%	7%	6%
Somewhat dissatisfied	14%	15%	14%	12%	13%	12%	13%	13%	12%	13%	14%	12%	15%	14%	15%
Neither satisfied or dissatisfied	7%	8%	7%	7%	7%	8%	7%	7%	7%	8%	7%	8%	8%	8%	8%
Somewhat satisfied	14%	14%	14%	13%	13%	13%	13%	14%	13%	17%	16%	17%	17%	18%	17%
Very satisfied	58%	58%	58%	51%	52%	49%	56%	56%	56%	56%	56%	57%	54%	53%	54%
Number of observations	4,225	1,513	2712	4,354	1,642	2,712	3,567	1,391	2,176	3,171	1,206	1,965	2,474	973	1,501

Note: For a more detailed descriptive statistics table, refer to Appendix Tables A6.1 and A6.2.

RESULTS

Individual Effects

Table 6.2 summarizes the results from my fixed effects ordered logit models which studied the impact of parents' transition to flexitime or teleworking on their well-being levels. Model 1 shows that their take up of flexitime or teleworking does impact parents' life satisfaction levels. However, some domain-specific satisfaction levels are likely to benefit from the switch to flexitime; parents' odds of reporting high levels of satisfaction with leisure time increase by approximately 19%. Moreover, the take up of teleworking can lead to an increase in the odds of high levels of health satisfaction by a factor of 1.25 approximately.

For the subsample of fathers, transitioning to flexitime or teleworking has no impact on life satisfaction. However, in the case of teleworking, fathers' odds of reporting satisfaction with their leisure time increase by approximately 32%. On the contrary, the switch to flexitime can decreases levels of health satisfaction a factor of 0.81. So far, results lend some support to *H1b*, which states that fathers' transition to flexitime can be injurious to their overall and domain-specific well-being levels, and *H2b*, which states that fathers' transition to using teleworking can improve their overall and domain-specific well-being levels. However, findings have revealed clear differences in effects on general and domain-specific well-being outcomes; the adoption of flexibility is likely to impact the latter than the former. These differences will be discussed later.

For mothers, Model 3 (Table 6.2) shows that the transition to flexitime can increase their odds of reporting greater satisfaction with their amount of leisure time by a factor of 1.22 (or 22% higher). Similarly, switching to using teleworking is advantageous to mothers' health satisfaction; their odds of reporting high levels of satisfaction with their health increase by almost 38%. While these findings lend support to *H1a* which establishes a positive effect of adopting flexitime on mothers' well-being outcomes, they do not support *H2a* which assumes a negative effect of mothers' switch to teleworking on the latter. Thus, in the case of *H2a*, there is not enough evidence to reject the null hypothesis. However, as with the case of the subsample of fathers, findings from the subsample of mothers also reveal differences in effects across general and domain-specific well-being outcomes.

Cross-Partner Effects

Table 6.3 summarizes the results from my fixed effects ordered logit models which studied the impact that one partner's transition to flexitime or teleworking has on the other partner's subjective well-being within heterosexual dual-earner households. Model 1 reveals that mothers' adoption of teleworking can decrease the odds of fathers reporting high levels of life satisfaction by approximately 47%. All other domains of fathers' subjective well-being are unaffected by mothers' switch to flexitime or teleworking. Overall findings do not lend support to affiliated hypotheses, *H3a* and *H4a*, which assume the mothers' switch to flexibility as leading to improved well-being outcomes for fathers.

Most findings relevant to fathers' uptake of flexitime or teleworking and its impact on mothers' subjective well-being (Model 2 from Table 6.3) are also

Table 6.2. Parental Transition to Flexitime and Teleworking and Their Subjective Well-Being Levels.

Variables	All			Fathers			Mothers		
	Model 1			Model 2			Model 3		
	Satisfaction with Life	Satisfaction with Leisure Time	Satisfaction with Health	Satisfaction with Life	Satisfaction with Leisure Time	Satisfaction with Health	Satisfaction with Life	Satisfaction with Leisure Time	Satisfaction with Health
Flexitime	1.066	1.188*	0.927	0.950	1.145	0.809+	1.160	1.217+	1.008
	(0.117)	(0.108)	(0.093)	(0.171)	(0.174)	(0.129)	(0.160)	(0.137)	(0.130)
Teleworking	1.080	1.419	1.247+	0.962	1.319+	1.133	1.201	0.901	1.381*
	(0.143)	(0.117)	(0.156)	(0.193)	(0.213)	(0.209)	(0.216)	(0.132)	(0.239)
Other Flexible Working Arrangements	0.928	1.072	0.956	0.963	0.992	0.955	0.908	1.112	0.951
	(0.064)	(0.062)	(0.064)	(0.123)	(0.105)	(0.116)	(0.076)	(0.077)	(0.067)
Marital Status (reference category: single/never married									
Married/Cohabitating	1.448	1.287	0.956	8.759*	2.296	0.585	1.361	1.277	0.985
	(0.317)	(0.229)	(0.192)	(9.562)	(1.839)	(0.285)	(0.301)	(0.233)	(0.209
Divorced/Separated/ Widowed	1.092	1.083	1.064	3.497	3.785	1.183	1.057	1.018	1.029
	(0.265)	(0.225)	(0.248)	(4.419)	(3.794)	(0.971)	(0.261)	(0.216)	(0.249
Number of Children (reference category: one child)									
Two	1.454*	0.966	1.127	1.563	1.094	0.863	1.368	0.883	1.333
	(0.225)	(0.120)	(0.161)	(0.382)	(0.206)	(0.187)	(0.275)	(0.146)	(0.255)
More than two	1.794	0.861	1.046	1.632	0.773	0.535	1.823	0.893	1.608
	(0.540)	(0.211)	(0.290)	(0.767)	(0.282)	(0.222)	(0.714)	(0.292)	(0.595)
Number of children aged 0–2 in household (reference category: none)									
One	0.778	0.705**	1.014	0.884	0.660*	1.250	0.711	0.752	0.879
	(0.120)	(0.085)	(0.139)	(0.204)	(0.119)	(0.259)	(0.147)	(0.123)	(0.162)
More than one	0.687	0.482**	1.252	0.694	0.533	2.017	0.708	0.455*	0.916
	(0.216)	(0.125)	(0.357)	(0.332)	(0.199)	(0.860)	(0.299)	(0.165)	(0.350)
Number of children aged 3–4 in household (reference category: none)									
One	0.667**	0.735**	0.931	0.748	0.781	1.268	0.617*	0.713*	0.761
	(0.098)	(0.085)	(0.125)	(0.166)	(0.134)	(0.253)	(0.121)	(0.112)	(0.139)
More than one	0.481*	0.565	0.966	0.606	0.733	1.622	0.396	0.497	0.693
	(0.162)	(0.165)	(0.309)	(0.288)	(0.330)	(0.744)	(0.189)	(0.193)	(0.313)

Table 6.2. *(Continued)*

Number of children aged 5–11 in household (reference category: none)									
One	0.714*	0.876	1.114	0.685	0.845	1.327	0.741	0.905	0.970
	(0.105)	(0.102)	(0.150)	(0.158)	(0.150)	(0.270)	(0.141)	(0.141)	(0.175)
More than one	0.558*	0.885	1.020	0.532	0.930	1.548	0.587	0.872	0.756
	(0.159)	(0.199)	(0.268)	(0.234)	(0.311)	(0.610)	(0.220)	(0.265)	(0.266)
Number of children aged 12–15 in household (reference category: none)									
One	0.770	1.004	1.012	0.699	0.951	1.200	0.816	1.052	0.885
	(0.115)	(0.120)	(0.141)	(0.165)	(0.177)	(0.260)	(0.159)	(0.166)	(0.163)
More than one	0.667	1.058	1.047	0.550	1.033	1.473	0.759	1.109	0.794
	(0.188)	(0.240)	(0.277)	(0.246)	(0.353)	(0.581)	(0.279)	(0.336)	(0.284)
Employment Sector (reference category: semi routine or routine)									
Intermediate	1.084	0.970	1.216	1.610	0.925	2.087**	0.943	0.990	1.032
	(0.174)	(0.124)	(0.176)	(0.524)	(0.234)	(0.567)	(0.176)	(0.145)	(0.177)
Management & Professional	1.016	0.879	0.999	1.279	0.884	2.032**	0.928	0.878	0.761
	(0.148)	(0.103)	(0.132)	(0.353)	(0.188)	(0.482)	(0.161)	(0.124)	(0.124)
Private Sector	0.914	0.916	0.918	0.898	0.824	0.797	0.936	0.946	0.979
	(0.092)	(0.079)	(0.085)	(0.168)	(0.135)	(0.137)	(0.111)	(0.096)	(0.107)
Long standing illness	0.767***	0.804***	0.529***	0.891	0.893	0.599***	0.711***	0.761***	0.497***
	(0.056)	(0.051)	(0.036)	(0.108)	(0.098)	(0.070)	(0.065)	(0.059)	(0.041)
Job Change	1.187*	1.143*	1.233**	1.357*	1.247*	1.270	1.092	1.096	1.211*
	(0.099)	(0.077)	(0.095)	(0.193)	(0.133)	(0.161)	(0.113)	(0.095)	(0.118)
Age	0.943***	1.009	1.001	0.954*	1.011	1.011	0.937***	1.007	0.997
	(0.012)	(0.011)	(0.012)	(0.022)	(0.019)	(0.020)	(0.015)	(0.013)	(0.014)
Hours spent in paid work	1.004	0.982***	1.008+	1.008	0.975**	1.003	1.001	0.985**	1.010*
	(0.005)	(0.004)	(0.005)	(0.010)	(0.007)	(0.009)	(0.006)	(0.005)	(0.006)
Log Household Income	1.182	1.018	0.931	1.170	1.130	0.976	1.197	0.979	0.904
	(0.116)	(0.082)	(0.081)	(0.251)	(0.189)	(0.182)	(0.133)	(0.090)	(0.090)
Log Likelihood	−7499.806	−10288.244	−10129.88	−2583.557	−3540.688	−3506.308	−4893.106	−6721.356	−6590.734
Observations	20,604	20,604	20,604	7,145	9,807	9,692	13,459	18,296	18,222

Notes: The table reports odd ratios. The standard error value for each estimate is mentioned in the parentheses. + $p < 0.1$ * $p < 0.05$ ** $p < 0.01$ *** $p < 0.001$.

Table 6.3. Spousal Transition to Flexitime/Teleworking and Parents' Subjective Well-Being Levels.

Variables	Fathers			Mothers		
	Model 1			Model 2		
	Satisfaction with Life	Satisfaction with Leisure Time	Satisfaction with Health	Satisfaction with Life	Satisfaction with Leisure Time	Satisfaction with Health
Spousal/Partner Characteristics						
Flexitime	0.980	1.161	0.814	1.090	1.484+	0.815
	(0.470)	(0.357)	(0.302)	(0.384)	(0.404)	(0.265)
Teleworking	0.467+	0.626	1.621	0.837	0.646	0.922
	(0.238)	(0.267)	(0.751)	(0.369)	(0.220)	(0.346)
Other Flexible Working Arrangements	0.856	1.198	0.837	0.840	0.647*	0.980
	(0.223)	(0.234)	(0.198)	(0.232)	(0.137)	(0.235)
Age	0.966	0.935	0.832	1.371	0.981	0.931
	(0.159)	(0.120)	(0.151)	(0.373)	(0.199)	(0.223)
Employment Sector (reference category: semi routine or routine)						
Intermediate	0.608	1.313	0.718	1.143	0.600	1.251
	(0.328)	(0.628)	(0.353)	(0.559)	(0.367)	(0.810)
Management & Professional	0.394*	1.004	0.944	1.312	0.824	1.356
	(0.180)	(0.410)	(0.393)	(0.585)	(0.406)	(0.687)
Private Sector	0.911	0.676	1.210	1.027	0.767	1.840
	(0.400)	(0.198)	(0.470)	(0.379)	(0.203)	(0.647)
Long standing illness	1.323	0.953	1.189	0.926	0.917	1.207
	(0.356)	(0.226)	(0.294)	(0.241)	(0.200)	(0.252)
Job Change	0.807	0.826	0.862	1.359	1.072	1.137
	(0.253)	(0.199)	(0.271)	(0.432)	(0.284)	(0.322)
Hours Spent in Paid Work	1.033+	1.014	1.017	1.021	0.978+	0.988
	(0.020)	(0.014)	(0.017)	(0.019)	(0.015)	(0.018)
Individual Characteristics						
Employment Sector (reference category: semi routine or routine)						
Intermediate	1.625	1.008	2.732	1.649	1.718	1.560
	(1.218)	(0.551)	(1.469)	(0.831)	(0.707)	(0.719)
Management & Professional	0.742	0.594	2.435*	1.078	1.145	0.594
	(0.457)	(0.256)	(1.070)	(0.463)	(0.431)	(0.261)
Private Sector	0.642	0.908	0.477*	1.056	0.999	0.943
	(0.258)	(0.325)	(0.167)	(0.374)	(0.293)	(0.293)
Long standing illness	1.194	0.704	0.642	0.649	0.535**	0.457***
	(0.303)	(0.165)	(0.165)	(0.171)	(0.111)	(0.102)
Job Change	1.620	1.002	1.057	1.109	0.950	1.037
	(0.515)	(0.245)	(0.340)	(0.376)	(0.229)	(0.287)
Age	1.043	1.173	1.296	0.697	1.049	1.054
	(0.172)	(0.150)	(0.234)	(0.190)	(0.217)	(0.255)
Number of Children (reference category: one child)						
Two	1.437	1.392	0.612	1.676	0.399*	1.083
	(0.738)	(0.639)	(0.346)	(0.945)	(0.178)	(0.537)
More than two	3.738	1.084	0.368	1.540	0.166*	0.600
	(3.597)	(1.012)	(0.403)	(1.704)	(0.134)	(0.570)

Table 6.3. (*Continued*)

Number of children aged 0–2 in household (reference category: none)						
One	0.746	0.657	1.354	0.400	1.167	0.633
	(0.384)	(0.298)	(0.730)	(0.222)	(0.486)	(0.291)
More than one	1.109	0.557	1.616	0.631	1.067	1.155
	(1.114)	(0.501)	(6.848)	(0.665)	(0.872)	(1.087)
Number of children aged 3–4 in household (reference category: none)						
One	0.894	0.942	1.464	0.480	1.253	0.825
	(0.433)	(0.410)	(0.807)	(0.241)	(0.511)	(0.388)
More than one	0.233	0.304	1.500	0.501	1.648	2.552
	(0.245)	(0.304)	(1.427)	(0.668)	(1.494)	(3.078)
Number of children aged 5–11 in household (reference category: none)						
One	0.563	0.695	1.252	0.501	1.727	1.462
	(0.264)	(0.307)	(0.667)	(0.266)	(0.711)	(0.683)
More than one	0.270	0.642	1.090	0.400	4.331	1.282
	(0.238)	(0.548)	(1.158)	(0.408)	(3.441)	(1.184)
Number of children aged 12–15 in household (reference category: none)						
One	0.438	0.556	0.811	0.702	2.515*	1.184
	(0.203)	(0.254)	(0.454)	(0.386)	(1.042)	(0.577)
More than one	0.225	0.349	0.639	0.920	5.542*	1.233
	(0.201)	(0.313)	(0.707)	(0.964)	(4.384)	(1.157)
Log household income	1.048	0.954	0.795	0.332*	1.023	0.570
	(0.651)	(0.443)	(0.367)	(0.182)	(0.451)	(0.267)
Hours Spent in Paid Work	1.023	0.973+	0.992	0.999	0.992	1.018
	(0.020)	(0.015)	(0.017)	(0.017)	(0.011)	(0.014)
Log Likelihood	−564.668	−809.732	−739.965	−603.446	−922.935	−905.781
Observations	1648	2331	2174	1754	2675	2634

Notes: The table reports odd ratios. The standard error value for each estimate is mentioned in the parentheses. + $p < 0.1$ * $p < 0.05$ ** $p < 0.01$ *** $p < 0.001$.

non-significant. Yet, it is interesting to note that fathers' adoption of flexitime can increase the odds of mothers reporting satisfaction with their amount of leisure time by 48%, which offers support to *H3b*. This finding may point toward positive mechanisms that the use of flexitime may introduce into the lives of dual-earner partners within households. However, findings from Table 6.3 also point to differences in effects of flexibility on general and domain-specific subjective well-being.

Findings from cross-sectional models testing the association between flexibility measures and subjective well-being mostly differ from the conclusions drawn from the longitudinal models above. A key reason for such differences can be omitted variable bias, which may translate into more inflated values in the cross-sectional models. Yet, estimates from robustness checks conducted using fixed effect linear models largely corroborate the findings of my main models adding to their validity.

DISCUSSION AND CONCLUSION

The current study offered novel insight into the impact of transitions to using flexitime and teleworking on cognitive, subjective well-being. Previous literature established gender differences in wellbeing outcomes following parents' transitions to both flexitime and teleworking. Mothers' transition to flexitime was found to be advantageous for their subjective well-being levels, while their transition to teleworking was disadvantageous to the latter (Grönlund, 2018). On the contrary, fathers' adoption of flexitime was deemed injurious for their well-being, while their ability to work from home benefitted the latter (Glass & Noonan, 2016).

Empirical results firstly reveal that mothers' transition to flexitime increases their levels of satisfaction with their amount of leisure time. The current finding negates Kim et al.'s (2019) conclusion from the General Social Survey in the United States, and reflects on how the autonomy granted by flexitime may enable mothers to adjust their schedule and make time for leisure when required (Wheatley, 2017). My estimates also show that following their adoption of teleworking, mothers are likely to be more satisfied with their health. Commuting to work can be stressful, especially for mothers with young children who feel socially obligated to invest the most time in childcare (Song & Gao, 2019). Working from home can act as a buffer against commuting related stress, enabling higher health satisfaction.

Statistical estimates from the subsample of fathers, on the contrary, establish that the adoption of flexitime can be injurious to their satisfaction with their health and hence do not corroborate previous findings on the subject (see Hokke et al., 2020). These conclusions are put into perspective by studies that reveal that scheduling flexibility can lead to an increase in work intensity (Kelliher & Anderson, 2009). In the case of fathers, flexitime can lend itself as an opportunity to obtain monetary rewards and upward career mobility by investing more time and energy in work. Yet, it comes at a cost; high levels of stress, anxiety, and burn-out, resulting in low levels of satisfaction with health (Glass & Noonan, 2016). On the other hand, fathers' move to working from home can allow them to invest the time saved from not commuting on leisure activities. Thus, empirical results from the current study show that fathers' transition to teleworking increases their likelihood of reporting higher levels of satisfaction with their amount of leisure time.

My study also introduced a cross-partner dimension of flexible working by analyzing the impact one parent's transition to flexitime or teleworking has on the other parent's well-being outcomes in heterosexual households. There is a dearth of previous literature which looks into the subject, although there is consensus across prior studies that partners' work patterns can influence each other's life patterns (Bredtmann et al., 2017; Killewald & Garcia-Manglano, 2015; Lyonette & Crompton, 2014). When theories about the individual use of flexitime and teleworking are applied to the cross-partner scenario, it is assumed that mothers' switch to flexibility can benefit fathers' well-being outcomes (Killewald, 2013; Maume, 2015). On the other hand, fathers' move to flexitime may benefit mothers' well-being while their move to teleworking can have deleterious consequences on the latter (Schieman et al., 2018).

Results from my empirical models show that generally cross-partner effects of transitions to working flexibly on well-being outcomes are insignificant. However, the significant estimates reveal that when mothers adopt teleworking, fathers' life satisfaction can suffer. Seeing an increase in mothers' ability to complete domestic tasks due to working from home, fathers may increase their engagement in the labor market which can increase work-related stress, disengagement with other life domains, and thus low life satisfaction levels (Kelliher & Andersen, 2009). Yet, fathers' switch to flexitime appeared to benefit mothers' satisfaction with their amount of leisure time. Placing this observation within the context of prior literature, one can assume that as flexitime allows fathers to take up more domestic tasks, especially time inflexible ones (Langner, 2017), it takes some weight of household responsibilities off of mothers' shoulders, allowing them more time to rest or engage in self-care or recreational activities.

Another key finding is that life satisfaction levels mostly remain unaffected by changes in work patterns brought by flexible working arrangements. Prior literature on subjective well-being states that life satisfaction levels are an amalgamation of satisfaction in many domains of life (Cummins, 1996, 1998, 2003; Headey & Wearing, 1992; Headey et al., 1985; Meadow et al., 1992; Rampichini & D'Andrea, 1998; Salvatore & Munõz Sastre, 2001; Saris & Ferligoj, 1996; Sirgy et al., 1995; Veenhoven, 1996). It could be the case that a switch to work flexibility may not induce changes in many life domains like consumption, ownership of commodities and property, national political climate, and relationships with friends, due to which life satisfaction levels may not display changes (Rojas, 2006). Another theoretical dimension relevant to explaining the stability of life satisfaction despite flexibility changes is offered by the set-point theory (Kuhn, 1962). Its central position is that adult individuals have stable life satisfaction levels all their life. Major life events, such as the death of a loved one and warfare in one's country of residence, might drive some temporary changes, but people often return to their set-points (Headey, 2010). Switching to flexible working itself may not be a major life event. Therefore, my results do not show a change in people's life satisfaction.

In their totality, my results offer mixed conclusions about the efficacy of flexible working arrangements in benefitting well-being outcomes. I reinforce the significance of gender when considering the impact of flexitime and teleworking; mothers generally appear to benefit from flexibility more than fathers. As discussed in previous sections, for fathers, flexibility can have different purposes and implications than for mothers. The use of flexitime can enforce a self-exploitative dynamic in fathers' lives where they see work autonomy as an opportunity to enhance their competitive edge and market chances (Putnam et al., 2013). In other cases, the flexibility stigma attached to fathers who adjust schedules for domestic responsibilities may come into play, resulting in flexitime using or teleworking fathers reporting lower levels of well-being (Kelliher & Anderson, 2009).

Yet, results showing mothers' apparent benefit from flexibility must be taken with a grain of salt. Firstly, flexibility provisions may result in mothers' free labor at home being exploited even more. Furthermore, women might unconsciously be working for longer hours due to arrangements like flexitime, which may impact other life domains. Lastly, mothers are also most likely to experience the flexibility stigma overtly and covertly, which could translate into fewer career mobility opportunities for them and lower levels of job satisfaction (Williams et al., 2013).

From a cross-partner perspective, my study lends hope to those who advocate for the growth in the availability and use of flexible working arrangements. Fathers' use of flexitime may be a step in the path of an egalitarian domestic division of labor that could benefit all members of a household (Langner, 2017). For mothers, it could mean not just the availability of more leisure time, but also an increased ability to invest time in the labor market and take up roles and responsibilities that match their educational level and skill set.

However, my study is subject to some limitations. Firstly, as discussed in prior sections of this study, responses for my outcomes variables, satisfaction with life, satisfaction with leisure time, and satisfaction with health, are mostly constant over time and experience only minor variations across time. Therefore, my sample sizes are not ideal, especially for cross-partner analyses. Furthermore, pre-flexible working well-being figures may not be a valid indicator for well-being levels among those individuals who have experienced key life events just before the observation period of my study (Headey, 2010). Moreover, the current research does not explore if the impact of transitioning to flexitime or teleworking on well-being levels changes or sustains itself in the years to follow. My results may also be subject to omitted variable bias as respondents' home address and church attendances levels were not a part of my empirical models. Both general and domain-specific subjective well-being is measured through single items in the Understanding Society survey data, which limits the analytical dimensions of my models. Lastly, my study only engages with three measures of cognitive, subjective well-being, which is partly due to data availability. In the future, it would be insightful to explore more dimensions of well-being and their link with flexible working arrangements.

Despite these limitations, my study contributes to the existing literature by exploring parental transitions to flexitime and teleworking and their impact on cognitive, subjective well-being. The cross-partner dimensions of my research offer novel insight into the influence of partners' work patterns upon each other's lives and self-perceptions. Generally, flexitime and teleworking can impact cognitive well-being outcomes, particularly those with direct and indirect ties with time availability (Lorenz, 2018). The magnitude and directions of these impacts are contingent upon a variety of factors, including the purpose for the use, workplace environment, and underlying gender roles and norms. British policymakers who believe that flexibility is the way forward for safeguarding individuals' autonomy, agency, and mental health, and creating an egalitarian division of labor in the household, should work toward normalizing the use of flexible working arrangements within the British labor market. Legislative measures that offer some protection to flexible workers against discrimination and unpaid overtime should be put in place. Furthermore, family policies should target the increase fathers' role in the household.

Future research must investigate the cross-partner dimension of flexible working in more detail and examine it over the period of the life course as family size may increase. Upcoming studies could also analyze the use of flexible working arrangements during the COVID-19 period and changes in mental health or subjective well-being across the period of national lockdowns. It would be interesting to see if the results of the current study hold for larger sample sizes in the UK and the extent to which they differ cross-nationally.

NOTE

1. According to the World Happiness Report 2015 of the United Nations, happier and more satisfied people are generally more likely to be healthy, productive and interactive, which benefits the society as a whole, i.e., higher economic productivity, stronger social insurance, greater social resilience to natural calamities, and greater mutual care (Helliwell et al., 2015).

REFERENCES

Allen, T. D., Johnson, R. C., Kiburz, K. M., & Shockley, K. M. (2013). Work-Family Conflict and Flexible Work Arrangements: Deconstructing Flexibility. *Personnel Psychology*, *66*(2), 345–376.

Beckmann, M., Cornelissen, T., & Kräkel, M. (2017). Self-managed working time and employee effort: Theory and evidence. *Journal of Economic Behavior & Organization*, *133*, 285–302.

Berger, L. M., & Houle, J. N. (2016). Parental debt and children's socioemotional well-being. *Pediatrics (Evanston)*, *137*(2), E20153059.

Binder, M. (2016). "…Do it with joy!" - Subjective well-being outcomes of working in non-profit organizations. *Journal of Economic Psychology*, *54*, 64–84.

Booth, A. L., & van Ours, J. C. (2008). Job satisfaction and family happiness: The part-time work puzzle. *The Economic Journal*, *118*(526), F77–F99.

Bredtmann, J., Otten, S., & Rulff, C. (2017). Husband's unemployment and wife's labor supply: The added worker effect across Europe. *ILR Review*, *71*(5), 1201–1231.

Bryan, M. L., & Sevilla, A. (2017). Flexible working in the UK and its impact on couples' time coordination. *Review of Economics of the Household*, *15*(4), 1415–1437.

Bücker, S., Nuraydin, S., Simonsmeier, B. A., Schneider, M., & Luhmann, M. (2018). Subjective well-being and academic achievement: A meta-analysis. *Journal of Research in Personality*, *74*, 83–94.

Budig, M. J., Misra, J., & Boeckmann, I. (2016). Work–family policy trade-offs for mothers? Unpacking the cross-national variation in motherhood earnings penalties. *Work and Occupations*, *43*(2), 119–177.

Carlson, D. S., Grzywacz, J. G., & Michele Kacmar, K. (2010). The relationship of schedule flexibility and outcomes via the work-family interface. *Journal of Managerial Psychology*, *25*(4), 330–355.

Cha, Y. (2010). Reinforcing separate spheres. *American Sociological Review*, *75*(2), 303–329.

Chandola, T., Booker, C. L., Kumari, M., & Benzeval, M. (2019). Are flexible work arrangements associated with lower levels of chronic stress-related biomarkers? A study of 6025 employees in the UK Household Longitudinal Study. *Sociology*, *53*(4), 779–799.

Chung, H. (2018). Gender, flexibility stigma and the perceived negative consequences of flexible working in the UK. *Social Indicators Research*, *151*(2), 521–545.

Chung, H., & van der Horst, M. (2018). Flexible working and unpaid overtime in the UK: The role of gender, parental and occupational status. *Social Indicators Research*, *151*(2), 495–520.

Clark, B., Chatterjee, K., Martin, A., & Davis, A. (2019). How commuting affects subjective well-being. *Transportation*, *47*(6), 2777–2805.

Clark, S. C. (2000). Work/Family Border Theory: A New Theory of Work/Family Balance. *Human Relations (New York)*, *53*(6), 747–770.

Davies, A. R., & Frink, B. D. (2014). The origins of the ideal worker: The separation of work and home in the United States from the market revolution to 1950. *Work and Occupations*, *41*(1), 18–39.

Desrochers, S., Sargent, L. D., & Hostetler, A. J. (2012). Boundary-spanning demands, personal mastery, and family satisfaction: Individual and crossover effects among dual-earner parents. *Marriage & Family Review*, *48*(5), 443–464.

Diener, E., Inglehart, R., & Tay, L. (2013). Theory and validity of life satisfaction scales. *Social Indicators Research*, *112*(3), 497–527.

Fein, E. C., & Skinner, N. (2015). Clarifying the effect of work hours on health through work-life conflict. *Asia Pacific Journal of Human Resources*, *53*(4), 448–470.

García-Manglano, J. (2015). Opting Out and Leaning In: The Life Course Employment Profiles of Early Baby Boom Women in the United States. *Demography*, *52*(6), 1961–1993.

Gatrell, C. J., Burnett, S. B., Cooper, C. L., & Sparrow, P. (2014). Parents, Perceptions and Belonging: Exploring Flexible Working among UK Fathers and Mothers. *British Journal of Management*, *25*(3), 473–487.

Giménez, J., Molina Chueca, J., & Sevilla, A. (2021). Temporal flexibility, breaks at work, and the motherhood wage gap. *SSRN Electronic Journal*.

Giménez-Nadal, J. I., Molina, J. A., & Velilla, J. (2021). Two-way commuting: Asymmetries from time use surveys. *Journal of Transport Geography*, *95*, 103146.

Glass, J. L., & Noonan, M. C. (2016). Telecommuting and earnings trajectories among American women and men 1989–2008. *Social Forces*, *95*(1), 217–250.

Glavin, P., & Schieman, S. (2012). Work–Family Role Blurring and Work–Family Conflict. *Work and Occupations*, *39*(1), 71–98.

Gracia, P., & Esping-Andersen, G. (2015). Fathers' child care time and mothers' paid work: A cross-national study of Denmark, Spain, and the United Kingdom. *Family Science*, *6*(1), 270–281.

Grawitch, M. J., Barber, L. K., & Justice, L. (2010). Rethinking the work-life interface: It's not about balance, it's about resource allocation. *Applied Psychology: Health and Well-Being*. Published.

Greenhaus, J. H., Parasuraman, S., Granrose, C. S., Rabinowitz, S., & Beutell, N. J. (1989). Sources of work-family conflict among two-career couples. *Journal of Vocational Behavior*, *34*(2), 133–153.

Gregory, A., Milner, S., & Windebank, J. (2013). Work-life balance in times of economic crisis and austerity. *International Journal of Sociology and Social Policy*, *33*(9/10), 528–541.

Grönlund, A., & Öun, I. (2018). In search of family-friendly careers? Professional strategies, work conditions and gender differences in work-family conflict. *Community, Work & Family*, *21*(1), 87–105.

Gronlund, A. (2007). More Control, Less Conflict? Job Demand-Control, Gender and Work-Family Conflict. *Gender, Work, and Organization*, *14*(5), 476–497.

Hampson. (2018). Mothers do not make good workers: The role of work/life balance policies in reinforcing gendered stereotypes. *Global Discourse*, *8*(3), 510–531.

Headey, B. (2010). The set point theory of well-being has serious flaws: On the eve of a scientific revolution? *Social Indicators Research*, *97*(1), 7–21.

Headey, B., Holmstrom, E., & Wearing, A. (1985). Models of Well-Being and Ill-Being. *Social Indicators Research*, *17*(3), 211–234.

Headey, B., & Wearing, A. (1992). *Understanding happiness: A theory of subjective well-being*. Melbourne: Longman Cheshire.

Hilbrecht, M., Smale, B., & Mock, S.E. (2014). Highway to health? Commute time and well-being among Canadian adults. *World Leisure Journal*, *56*(2), 151–163.

Hodges, M. J., & Budig, M. J. (2010). WHO GETS THE DADDY BONUS? Organizational Hegemonic Masculinity and the Impact of Fatherhood on Earnings. *Gender & Society*, *24*(6), 717–745.

Hofäcker, D., & König, S. (2013). Flexibility and work-life conflict in times of crisis: A gender perspective. *International Journal of Sociology and Social Policy*, *33*(9/10), 613–635.

Hokke, S., Bennetts, S., Crawford, S., Leach, L., Hackworth, N., & Strazdins, L., Nguyen, C., Nicholson, J. M., & Cooklin, A. R. (2020). Does flexible work 'work' in Australia? A survey of employed mothers' and fathers' work, family and health. *Community, Work & Family*, *24*(4), 488–506.

Karasek, R., & Theorell, T. (1990). *Healthy work: Stress, productivity, and the reconstruction of working life*. New York: Basic Books.

Kelliher, C., & Anderson, D. (2009). Doing more with less? Flexible working practices and the intensification of work. *Human Relations*, *63*(1), 83–106.

Killewald, A. (2013). A reconsideration of the fatherhood premium. *American Sociological Review*, *78*(1), 96–116.

Killewald, A., & García-Manglano, J. (2016). Tethered lives: A couple-based perspective on the consequences of parenthood for time use, occupation, and wages. *Social Science Research*, *60*, 266–282.

Kim, S., Kim, Y, Lim, S. -S., Ryoo, J. -H., & Yoon, J. -H. (2019). Long Commute Time and Sleep Problems with Gender Difference in Work–Life Balance: A Cross-sectional Study of More than 25,000 Workers. *Safety and Health at Work*, *10*(4), 470–475.

Kossek, E., Lautsch, B., & Eaton, S. (2005). Flexibility enactment theory: relationships between type, boundaries, control and work-family effectiveness. In E. E. Kossek & S. Lambert (Eds). *Work And Life Integration: Organizational, Cultural and Psychological Perspectives*. Mahwah, N.J.: Lawrence Erlbaum Associates (LEA) Press.

Kuhn, T. (1962). *The structure of scientific revolutions* (International encyclopaedia of unified science. (Vol. 2, no. 2). Chicago, London: University of Chicago Press.

Langner, L. A. (2017). Flexible men and successful women: The effects of flexible working hours on German Couples' Wages. *Work, Employment and Society*, *32*(4), 687–706.

Laurijssen, I., & Glorieux, I. (2013). Balancing work and family: A panel analysis of the impact of part-time work on the experience of time pressure. *Social Indicators Research*, *112*(1), 1–17.

Lin, Jo-Hui, Wong, Jehn-Yih, & Ho, Ching-Hua. (2015). The role of work-to-leisure conflict in promoting frontline employees' leisure satisfaction: Examining the job demand-control-support model. *International Journal of Contemporary Hospitality Management*, *27*(7), 1539–1555.

Lorenz, O. (2018). Does commuting matter to subjective well-being? *Journal of Transport Geography*, *66*, 180–199.

Lott, Y., & Chung, H. (2016). Gender discrepancies in the outcomes of schedule control on overtime hours and income in Germany. *European Sociological Review*, *32*(6), 752–765.

Lundberg, S., & Rose, E. (2000). Parenthood and the earnings of married men and women. *Labour Economics*, *7*(6), 689–710.

Lyonette, C. (2015). Part-time work, work–life balance and gender equality. *Journal of Social Welfare and Family Law*, *37*(3), 321–333.

Lyonette, C., & Crompton, R. (2014). Sharing the load? Partners' relative earnings and the division of domestic labour. *Work, Employment and Society*, *29*(1), 23–40.

Maume, D. J. (2015). Can men make time for family? Paid work, care work, work-family reconciliation policies, and gender equality. *Social Currents*, *3*(1), 43–63.

Meadow, H. L., Mentzer, J. T., Rahtz, D. R., & Sirgy, M. J. (1992). A Life Satisfaction Measure Based on Judgment Theory. *Social Indicators Research*, *26*(1), 23–59.

Minnotte, K. L., Minnotte, M. C., & Thompson, K. (2016). The life satisfaction of dual-earner mothers and fathers: Does flexible scheduling matter? *Journal of Happiness Studies*, *17*(6), 2365–2388.

Moran, J., & Koslowski, A. (2018). Making use of work–family balance entitlements: how to support fathers with combining employment and caregiving. *Community, Work & Family*, *22*(1), 111–128.

Pagnan, C. E., Lero, D. S., & MacDermid Wadsworth, S. M. (2011). It doesn't always add up: examining dual-earner couples' decision to off-shift. *Community, Work & Family*, *14*(3), 297–316.

Parasuraman, S., Greenhaus, J. H., & Granrose, C. S. (1992). Role stressors, social support, and well-being among two-career couples. *Journal of Organizational Behavior*, *13*(4), 339–356.

Piszczek, M. M., & Berg, P. (2014). Expanding the boundaries of boundary theory: Regulative institutions and work–family role management. *Human Relations*, *67*(12), 1491–1512.

Platt, L., & Polavieja, J. (2016). Saying and doing gender: Intergenerational Transmission of Attitudes towards the Sexual Division of Labour. *European Sociological Review*, *32*(6), 820–834.

Pollmann-Schult, M. (2014). Parenthood and life satisfaction: Why don't children make people happy? *Journal of Marriage and Family*, *76*(2), 319–336.

Putnam, L., Myers, K., & Gailliard, B. (2013). Examining the tensions in workplace flexibility and exploring options for new directions. *Human Relations*, *67*(4), 413–440.

Rampichini, C., & D'Andrea, S. S. (1998). A Hierarchical Ordinal Probit Model for the Analysis of Life Satisfaction in Italy. *Social Indicators Research*, *44*(1), 41–69.

Rojas, M. (2006). Life satisfaction and satisfaction in domains of life: Is it a simple relationship? *Journal of Happiness Studies*, *7*(4), 467–497.

Salvatore, N., & Sastre, M. T. M. (2001). Appraisal of lifecolon: "area" versus "dimension" conceptualizations. *Social Indicators Research*, *53*(3), 229–255.

Saris, W. E., & Ferligoj A. (1996). Life satisfaction and domain satisfaction in 10 european countries: Correlation at the individual level. In W. E. Saris, et al (Eds.), *A Comparative Study of Satisfaction with Life in Europe* (pp. 275–280). Hungary: Eötvös University Press.

Schieman, S., Glavin, P., & Milkie, M. A. (2009). When work interferes with life: Work-nonwork interference and the influence of work-related demands and resources. *American Sociological Review*, *74*(6), 966–988.

Schieman, S., Ruppanner, L., & Milkie, M. A. (2018). Who helps with homework? Parenting inequality and relationship quality among employed mothers and fathers. *Journal of Family and Economic Issues*, *39*(1), 49–65.

Schober, P. S. (2013). The parenthood effect on gender inequality: Explaining the change in paid and domestic work when British couples become parents. *European Sociological Review*, *29*(1), 74–85.

Sirgy, M. J., Cole, D., Kosenko, R., Meadow, H. L., Rahtz, D., Cicic, M., Jin, G. X., Yarsuvat, D., Blenkhorn, D. L., & Nagpal, N. (1995). A Life Satisfaction Measure: Additional Validational Data for the Congruity Life Satisfaction Measure. *Social Indicators Research*, *34*(2), 237–259. Web.

Song, Y., & Gao, J. (2019). Does telework stress employees out? A study on working at home and subjective well-being for wage/salary workers. *Journal of Happiness Studies*, *21*(7), 2649–2668.

Steptoe, A., Deaton, A., & Stone, A. A. (2015). Subjective wellbeing, health, and ageing. *The Lancet (British Edition)*, *385*(9968), 640–648.

Stiglitz, J. E., Sen, A., & Jean-Paul, A. F. (2009). The measurement of economic performance and social progress revisited. *IDEAS Working Paper Series from RePEc*, IDEAS Working Paper Series from RePEc, 2009.

Sullivan, C., & Lewis, S. (2001). Home-based Telework, Gender, and the Synchronization of Work and Family: Perspectives of Teleworkers and their Co-residents. *Gender, Work, and Organization*, *8*(2), 123–145.

Tietze, S. (2002). When 'Work' Comes 'Home': Coping Strategies of Teleworkers and their Families. *Journal of Business Ethics*, *41*, 385–397.

Van der Lippe, T., de Ruijter, J., de Ruijter, E., & Raub, W. (2011). Persistent inequalities in time use between men and women. *European Sociological Review*, *27*(2), 164–179.

Veenhoven, R. (1996). Developments in Satisfaction-Research. *Social Indicators Research*, *37*(1), 1–46.

Verbakel, E., & de Graaf, P. M. (2009). Partner effects on labour market participation and job level: Opposing mechanisms. *Work, Employment and Society*, *23*(4), 635–654.

Westman, M., & Etzion, D. (1995). Crossover of stress, strain and resources from one spouse to another. *Journal of Organizational Behavior*, *16*(2), 169–181.

Wheatley, D. (2017). Employee satisfaction and use of flexible working arrangements. *Work, Employment and Society*, *31*(4), 567–585.

Wickrama, K. A. S., Klopack, E. T., & O'Neal, C. W. (2020). How midlife chronic stress combines with stressful life events to influence later life mental and physical health for husbands and wives in enduring marriages. *Journal of Aging and Health*, *33*(1–2), 14–26.

Williams, J., Blair-Loy, M., & Berdahl, J. (2013). Cultural schemas, social class, and the flexibility stigma. *Journal of Social Issues*, *69*(2), 209–234.

Wooden, M., Warren, D., & Drago, R. (2009). Working time mismatch and subjective well-being. *British Journal of Industrial Relations*, *47*(1), 147–179.

Zhou, M., & Kan, M. Y. (2019). A new family equilibrium? Changing dynamics between the gender division of labor and fertility in Great Britain, 1991–2017. *Demographic Research*, *40*, 1455–1500.

APPENDIX

Table A6.1. Sample Descriptive Statistics for Categorical Variables from Understanding Society Waves 2 – 10.

Variables	2010–11			2012–13			2014–15			2016–17			2018–19		
	All	Men	Women	All	Men	Women	All	Men	Women	All	Men	Women	All	Men	Women
Flexitime															
Practiced	19%	23%	17%	19%	22%	17%	21%	23%	19%	19%	23%	17%	20%	25%	17%
Not Practiced	81%	77%	83%	81%	78%	83%	79%	77%	81%	81%	77%	83%	80%	75%	83%
Teleworking															
Practiced	9%	14%	6%	11%	15%	7%	12%	16%	8%	12%	16%	9%	15%	19%	12%
Not Practiced	91%	86%	94%	89%	85%	93%	88%	84%	92%	88%	84%	91%	85%	18%	88%
Other Flexible Working Arrangements															
Practiced	50%	16%	70%	46%	17%	68%	47%	20%	68%	46%	15%	68%	47%	18%	68%
Not Practiced	50%	84%	30%	54%	83%	32%	53%	80%	32%	54%	85%	32%	53%	82%	32%
Marital Status															
Single	5%	0.20%	8%	6%	1%	10%	6%	0.4%	10%	7%	1%	11%	6%	1%	10%
Married/Cohabitating	88%	99%	82%	89%	98%	81%	90%	99%	83%	89%	98%	83%	90%	98%	84%
Divorced/Widowed/Separated	7%	0.80%	10%	5%	1%	9%	4%	0.60%	7%	4%	1%	6%	4%	1%	6%
Number of Children															
One	46%	41%	49%	45%	41%	49%	43%	38%	46%	43%	41%	45%	44%	41%	46%
Two	42%	45%	41%	42%	44%	40%	46%	47%	44%	46%	46%	45%	46%	48%	45%
More than two	12%	14%	11%	12%	15%	11%	11%	15%	10%	11%	13%	10%	10%	11%	9%
Number of Children aged 0–2 in household															
None	74%	66%	79%	73%	67%	79%	74%	69%	78%	78%	74%	80%	79%	78%	80%
One	23%	30%	19%	24%	30%	20%	25%	30%	21%	21%	24%	18%	20%	21%	19%
More than one	3%	4%	2%	3%	3%	1%	1%	1%	1%	1%	2%	2%	1%	1%	1%
Number of Children aged 3–4 in household															
None	80%	76%	83%	80%	76%	83%	78%	75%	80%	79%	76%	81%	81%	79%	83%
One	19%	23%	17%	19%	23%	16%	21%	24%	19%	20%	23%	18%	18%	20%	16%
More than one	1%	1%	1%	1%	1%	1%	1%	1%	1%	1%	1%	1%	1%	1%	1%
Number of Children aged 5–11 in household															
None	46%	47%	46%	44%	43%	44%	42%	42%	42%	39%	40%	39%	40%	39%	42%
One	36%	35%	36%	38%	37%	38%	38%	35%	40%	41%	33%	43%	40%	41%	38%
More than one	18%	18%	18%	18%	19%	18%	20%	23%	18%	20%	23%	18%	20%	20%	20%
Number of Children aged 12–15 in household															

(*Continued*)

Table A6.1. *(Continued)*

Variables	2010–11			2012–13			2014–15			2016–17			2018–19		
	All	Men	Women	All	Men	Women	All	Men	Women	All	Men	Women	All	Men	Women
None	61%	66%	58%	63%	67%	59%	65%	68%	62%	63%	66%	61%	61%	64%	59%
One	32%	27%	35%	31%	27%	35%	29%	25%	32%	31%	28%	34%	31%	28%	34%
More than one	7%	7%	7%	6%	6%	6%	6%	6%	6%	6%	6%	5%	8%	8%	7%
Employment sector															
Routine	30%	26%	32%	31%	27%	33%	29%	26%	31%	29%	24%	32%	26%	20%	31%
Intermediate	18%	12%	22%	16%	11%	20%	16%	11%	19%	16%	11%	18%	16%	14%	18%
Management & professional	52%	62%	47%	53%	62%	47%	55%	63%	50%	55%	65%	50%	58%	66%	51%
Private Sector															
Yes	54%	65%	48%	58%	67%	51%	59%	70%	51%	59%	70%	51%	61%	72%	53%
No	46%	35%	52%	42%	33%	49%	41%	30%	49%	41%	30%	49%	39%	28%	47%
Long standing illness															
Affected	21%	20%	21%	20%	18%	21%	19%	18%	20%	21%	19%	22%	22%	21%	23%
Not Affected	79%	80%	79%	80%	82%	79%	81%	82%	80%	79%	81%	78%	78%	79%	77%
Job Change															
Yes	5%	6%	5%	10%	11%	9%	12%	12%	11%	14%	12%	15%	13%	12%	14%
No	95%	94%	95%	90%	89%	91%	88%	88%	89%	86%	88%	85%	87%	88%	86%
Satisfaction with Life Overall															
Very dissatisfied	5%	4%	5%	6%	5%	7%	5%	4%	5%	4%	4%	5%	3%	4%	4%
Somewhat dissatisfied	8%	6%	9%	9%	7%	9%	6%	7%	6%	8%	6%	8%	8%	7%	8%
Neither satisfied or dissatisfied	8%	8%	8%	9%	9%	8%	8%	8%	8%	7%	8%	7%	11%	10%	11%
Somewhat satisfied	20%	22%	19%	20%	20%	19%	19%	20%	18%	20%	20%	21%	22%	22%	21%
Very satisfied	59%	60%	59%	56%	59%	57%	62%	61%	63%	61%	63%	59%	56%	57%	56%
Satisfaction with Leisure Time															
Very dissatisfied	13%	13%	13%	15%	13%	15%	12%	12%	12%	11%	12%	11%	11%	12%	10%
Somewhat dissatisfied	25%	25%	25%	24%	26%	22%	23%	24%	22%	22%	23%	21%	23%	23%	24%
Neither satisfied or dissatisfied	13%	16%	12%	14%	14%	14%	12%	12%	14%	14%	14%	14%	13%	12%	13%
Somewhat satisfied	25%	25%	25%	24%	24%	24%	28%	28%	27%	27%	26%	27%	27%	28%	27%
Very satisfied	24%	22%	25%	23%	23%	25%	25%	24%	25%	26%	26%	27%	26%	25%	26%
Satisfaction with Health															
Very dissatisfied	7%	5%	7%	17%	15%	18%	11%	10%	12%	6%	6%	6%	6%	7%	6%
Somewhat dissatisfied	14%	15%	14%	12%	13%	12%	13%	13%	12%	13%	14%	12%	15%	14%	15%
Neither satisfied or dissatisfied	7%	8%	7%	7%	7%	8%	7%	7%	7%	8%	7%	8%	8%	8%	8%
Somewhat satisfied	14%	14%	14%	13%	13%	13%	13%	14%	13%	17%	16%	17%	17%	18%	17%
Very satisfied	58%	58%	58%	51%	52%	49%	56%	56%	56%	56%	56%	57%	54%	53%	54%
Number of observations	4,225	1,513	2712	4,354	1,642	2,712	3,567	1,391	2,176	3,171	1,206	1,965	2,474	973	1,501

Table A6.2. Sample Descriptive Statistics for Continuous Variables from Understanding Society Waves 2 – 10.

Outcome variables	2010–11			2012–13			2014–15			2016–17			2018–19		
	All	Men	Women	All	Men	Women	All	Men	Women	All	Men	Women	All	Men	Women
Household Income	3475 (1870)	3654 (1904)	3369 (1840)	3588 (1980)	3716 (1847)	3489 (2073)	4083 (8570)	4074 (4986)	4089 (10486)	4073 (2359)	4255 (2103)	3943 (2519)	4289 (2769)	4479 (2243)	4154 (3081)
Age	39 (6.98)	40 (7.01)	39 (6.94)	39 (6.98)	40 (6.94)	39 (6.98)	39 (7.08)	40 (6.82)	39 (7.22)	40 (7.03)	41 (6.94)	39 (7.04)	41 (7.0)	42 (6.91)	40 (7)
Number of observations	4,225	1,513	2712	4,354	1,642	2,712	3,567	1,391	2,176	3,171	1,206	1,965	2,474	973	1,501

Table A6.3. Cross-Sectional Models for Individual Use of Flexitime/Teleworking and Subjective Well-Being.

Variables	All			Fathers			Mothers		
	Model 1			Model 2			Model 3		
	Satisfaction with Life	Satisfaction with Leisure Time	Satisfaction with Health	Satisfaction with Life	Satisfaction with Leisure Time	Satisfaction with Health	Satisfaction with Life	Satisfaction with Leisure Time	Satisfaction with Health
Flexitime	0.949	1.038	0.952	0.949	0.985	0.900	0.965	1.101+	1.013
	(0.045)	(0.044)	(0. 044)	(0.071)	(0.064)	(0.064)	(0.059)	(0.062)	(0.060)
Teleworking	1.151*	1.079	0.993	1.196*	1.115	1.013	1.083	1.018	0.942
	(0.075)	(0.061)	(0. 060)	(0.107)	(0.089)	(0.087)	(0.103)	(0.080)	(0.078)
Other Flexible Working Arrangements	1.075+	1.263***	0.997	0.916	1.033	0.956	1.134*	1.377***	1.000
	(0.047)	(0.050)	(0. 041)	(0.072)	(0.080)	(0.071)	(0.0579)	(0.063)	(0.049)
Female	1.009	0.964	1.084+	–	–	–	–	–	–
	(0.050)	(0.047)	(0. 052)						
Marital Status (reference category: single/never married									
Continued on next page									
Married/Cohabitating	1.525***	1.267***	1.201**	1.203	0.939	0.908	1.759***	1.518***	1.402***
	(0.090)	(0.069)	(0.065)	(0.129)	(0.094)	(0.094)	(0.125)	(0.097)	(0.088)
Divorced/Separated/Widowed	1.113	1.043	0.988	1.302	1.201	0.895	1.161	1.121	1.065
	(0.094)	(0.079)	(0.078)	(0.313)	(0.218)	(0.177)	(0.105)	(0.095)	(0.092)
Number of Children (reference category: one child)									
Two	1.111	0.973	1.151+	0.909	0.953	0.992	1.312*	0.993	1.274*
	(0.105)	(0.095)	(0.095)	(0.131)	(0.136)	(0.125)	(0.161)	(0.134)	(0.140)
More than two	1.084	0.836	1.216	0.871	0.888	1.021	1.331	0.805	1.384
	(0.200)	(0.161)	(0.196)	(0.245)	(0.254)	(0.246)	(0.312)	(0.209)	(0.294)
Number of children aged 0–2 in household (reference category: none)									
One	1.100	0.761**	0.983	1.206	0.764	1.034	1.015	0.746*	0.940
	(0.105)	(0.074)	(0.080)	(0.175)	(0.110)	(0.123)	(0.125)	(0.098)	(0.103)
More than one	1.167	0.588*	1.203	1.515	0.741	1.461	0.937	0.458*	1.038
	(0.251)	(0.133)	(0. 232)	(0.505)	(0.229)	(0.419)	(0.251)	(0.150)	(0.265)

Table A6.3. (*Continued*)

Number of children aged 3–4 in household (reference category: none)									
One	0.902	0.801*	0.950	1.011	0.849	1.016	0.821	0.752*	0.914
	(0.084)	(0.077)	(0.076)	(0.141)	(0.117)	(0.118)	(0.100)	(0.100)	(0.101)
More than one	0.599*	0.639*	0.736	0.809	0.785	0.971	0.434*	0.495*	0.567
	(0.147)	(0.141)	(0.159)	(0.262)	(0.228)	(0.290)	(0.154)	(0.158)	(0.169)
Number of children aged 5–11 in household (reference category: none)									
One	0.884	0.951	0.953	0.988	0.972	1.024	0.791*	0.903	0.903
	(0.081)	(0.091)	(0.077)	(0.139)	(0.137)	(0.126)	(0.093)	(0.119)	(0.096)
More than one	0.779	0.884	0.843	0.931	0.897	0.904	0.641	0.830	0.794
	(0.139)	(0.165)	(0.128)	(0.250)	(0.239)	(0.202)	(0.146)	(0.215)	(0.161)
Number of children aged 12–15 in household (reference category: none)									
One	0.870+	1.091	0.900	1.000	1.152	0.910	0.765*	1.034	0.884
	(0.080)	(0.104)	(0.073)	(0.142)	(0.161)	(0.114)	(0.090)	(0.135)	(0.092)
More than one	0.811	1.091	0.875	1.067	1.126	1.019	0.619*	1.036	0.776
	(0.142)	(0.200)	(0.131)	(0.282)	(0.296)	(0.221)	(0.141)	(0.263)	(0.158)
Employment Sector (reference category: semi routine or routine)									
Intermediate	1.198**	1.036	1.077	1.225	0.909	1.060	1.178*	1.075	1.074
	(0.073)	(0.060)	(0.061)	(0.140)	(0.092)	(0.117)	(0.085)	(0.075)	(0.073)
Management & Professional	1.255***	0.923+	1.135**	1.352***	0.961	1.168	1.195**	0.898	1.112
	(0.064)	(0.043)	(0.055)	(0.113)	(0.073)	(0.095)	(0.076)	(0.053)	(0.067)
Private Sector	0.959	1.000	0.894**	1.033	0.930	0.898	0.905	1.018	0.879**
	(0.324)	(0.040)	(0.037)	(0.075)	(0.066)	(0.067)	(0.047)	(0.049)	(0.043)
Long standing illness	0.590***	0.652***	0.341***	0.583***	0.703***	0.378***	0.596***	0.620***	0.316***
	(0.026)	(0.028)	(0.014)	(0.045)	(0.050)	(0.026)	(0.033)	(0.033)	(0.016)
Job Change	1.000	0.969	1.110+	1.049	1.088	1.258*	0.978	0.888	1.013
	(0.060)	(0.052)	(0.064)	(0.104)	(0.095)	(0.116)	(0.074)	(0.061)	(0.074)
Age	0.983***	0.990**	1.001	0.985*	0.997	1.006	0.982***	0.984***	0.998
	(0.004)	(0.004)	(0.004)	(0.006)	(0.006)	(0.006)	(0.005)	(0.005)	(0.005)

(*Continued*)

Table A6.3. (*Continued*)

Variables	All			Fathers			Mothers		
	Model 1			Model 2			Model 3		
	Satisfaction with Life	Satisfaction with Leisure Time	Satisfaction with Health	Satisfaction with Life	Satisfaction with Leisure Time	Satisfaction with Health	Satisfaction with Life	Satisfaction with Leisure Time	Satisfaction with Health
Wave (reference category : wave 2)									
Wave 4	0.882**	0.932+	0.643***	0.897	0.973	0.680***	0.879*	0.915	0.623***
	(0.390)	(0.036)	(0.029)	(0.067)	(0.062)	(0.051)	(0.048)	(0.045)	(0.034)
Wave 6	1.069	1.080+	0.842***	1.027	1.082	0.872	1.125	1.113*	0.832**
	(0.052)	(0.046)	(0.040)	(0.083)	(0.074)	(0.066)	(0.068)	(0.060)	(0.050)
Wave 8	1.007	1.143**	0.956	1.052	1.122	0.876	0.984	1.185**	1.030
	(0.052)	(0.052)	(0.046)	(0.090)	(0.085)	(0.070)	(0.063)	(0.067)	(0.061)
Wave 10	0.842**	1.127*	0.853**	0.815*	1.103	0.798**	0.868*	1.183**	0.906
	(0.046)	(0.057)	(0.045)	(0.074)	(0.091)	(0.068)	(0.060)	(0.075)	(0.060)
Log Household Income	1.652***	1.139**	1.284***	1.859***	1.225*	1.459***	1.484***	1.066	1.153*
	(0.087)	(0.053)	(0.063)	(0.170)	(0.101)	(0.133)	(0.095)	(0.059)	(0.065)
Log Likelihood	−20595.591	−27682.[illegible]29	−22474.536	−7616.448	−10498.603	−8552.318	−12957.903	−17117.988	−13871.815
Observations	17,836	17,836	17,836	6,742	6,742	6,742	11,094	11,094	11,094

Notes: A pooled sample from Understanding Society (Wave 2–10) has been used to draw above-mentioned estimates. The standard error value for each estimate can be found in the parentheses. + $p < 0.1$ * $p < 0.05$ ** $p < 0.01$ *** $p < 0.001$.

Table A6.4. Cross-Sectional Models for Spousal/Partners' Use of Flexitime/Teleworking and Parental Subjective Well-Being.

Variables	Fathers			Mothers		
	Model 1			Model 2		
	Satisfaction with Life	Satisfaction with Leisure Time	Satisfaction with Health	Satisfaction with Life	Satisfaction with Leisure Time	Satisfaction with Health
Spousal/Partner Characteristics						
Flexitime	0.909	1.115	0.835	1.378+	1.087	1.061
	(0.140)	(0.144)	(0.119)	(0.323)	(0.179)	(0.222)
Teleworking	0.867	0.657*	0.777	1.920*	1.179	1.404+
	(0.177)	(0.114)	(0.158)	(0.612)	(0.335)	(0.349)
Other Flexible Working Arrangements	0.902	1.006	1.036	1.266	1.039	0.964
	(0.113)	(0.108)	(0.128)	(0.322)	(0.219)	(0.208)
Age	1.009	0.990	1.008	0.959*	0.976	1.020
	(0.017)	(0.014)	(0.015)	(0.020)	(0.021)	(0.022)
Employment Sector (reference category: semi routine or routine)						
Intermediate	1.083	0.699*	0.879	1.230	0.607*	0.917
	(0.175)	(0.099)	(0.148)	(0.406)	(0.152)	(0.251)
Management & Professional	1.116	0.980	1.022	1.211	1.069	1.048
	(0.170)	(0.130)	(0.156)	(0.245)	(0.212)	(0.210)
Private Sector	1.127	1.029	0.910	0.975	0.937	0.864
	(0.140)	(0.118)	(0.108)	(0.193)	(0.160)	(0.165)
Long standing illness	0.841	0.792	0.969	0.769	0.774	1.103
	(0.116)	(0.100)	(0.121)	(0.167)	(0.147)	(0.260)
Job Change	0.976	1.138	1.155	1.378	1.139	0.986
	(0.170)	(0.185)	(0.198)	(0.553)	(0.316)	(0.291)
Individual Characteristics						
Employment Sector (reference category: semi routine or routine)						
Continued on next page						
Intermediate	1.512	1.098	1.039	0.808	1.206	0.844
	(0.331)	(0.177)	(0.200)	(0.217)	(0.296)	(0.208)

(Continued)

Table A6.4. *(Continued)*

Variables	Fathers			Mothers		
	Model 1			Model 2		
	Satisfaction with Life	Satisfaction with Leisure Time	Satisfaction with Health	Satisfaction with Life	Satisfaction with Leisure Time	Satisfaction with Health
Management & Professional	1.198	0.956	1.164	0.830	1.212	1.195
	(0.166)	(0.121)	(0.165)	(0.195)	(0.248)	(0.274)
Private Sector	0.820	0.868	0.806	0.882	1.266	0.885
	(0.111)	(0.109)	(0.108)	(0.170)	(0.204)	(0.168)
Long standing illness	0.630***	0.692**	0.360***	0.658+	0.672	0.299***
	(0.082)	(0.095)	(0.046)	(0.151)	(0.137)	(0.058)
Job Change	1.537*	1.303	1.572**	0.928	0.780	1.034
	(0.302)	(0.192)	(0.274)	(0.230)	(0.165)	(0.287)
Age	0.973	1.000	1.006	1.034+	1.003	0.974
	(0.014)	(0.013)	(0.014)	(0.022)	(0.022)	(0.021)
Number of Children (reference category: one child)						
Two	0.756	0.756	0.836	1.629	3.945*	1.307
	(0.247)	(0.304)	(0.248)	(0.988)	(2.326)	(0.667)
More than two	0.671	0.412	0.793	1.453	8.588	1.284
	(0.422)	(0.327)	(0.459)	(1.667)	(10.039)	(1.196)
Number of children aged 0–2 in household (reference category: none)						
One	1.289	1.154	0.994	0.902	0.202**	0.607
	(0.427)	(0.458)	(0.290)	(0.525)	(0.113)	(0.281
More than one	3.030	1.155	2.010	2.875	0.0838*	0.987
	(2.105)	(0.956)	(1.255)	(4.453)	(0.098)	(1.146)
Number of children aged 3–4 in household (reference category: none)						
One	1.314	1.474	1.239	0.736	0.364	0.795
	(0.424)	(0.591)	(0.367)	(0.463)	(0.219)	(0.388)
More than one	1.797	2.440	2.173	0.0722	0.0562	1.091
	(1.248)	(2.046)	(1.854)	(0.138)	(0.107)	(1.335)

Table A6.4. *(Continued)*

Number of children aged 5–11 in household (reference category: none)						
One	1.251	1.395	1.036	0.563	0.271*	0.707
	(0.406)	(0.556)	(0.302)	(0.330)	(0.158)	(0.350)
More than one	1.290	1.773	1.001	0.428	0.0867*	0.532
	(0.808)	(1.395)	(0.558)	(0.504)	(0.098)	(0.491)
Number of children aged 12–15 in household (reference category: none)						
One	1.246	1.834	0.960	0.469	0.385	0.530
	(0.395)	(0.715)	(0.283)	(0.283)	(0.221)	(0.248)
More than one	1.951	2.226	1.160	0.354	0.0973*	0.338
	(1.260)	(1.741)	(0.649)	(0.407)	(0.114)	(0.324)
Log household income	1.823**	1.270	1.326	1.605	0.667	0.682
	(0.370)	(0.226)	(0.257)	(0.533)	(0.174)	(0.218)
Wave (reference category : wave 2)						
Wave 4	1.001	0.994	0.767	0.756	0.770	0.687
	(0.147)	(0.135)	(0.113)	(0.182)	(0.180)	(0.173)
Wave 6	1.045	0.964	0.878	1.554+	1.322	1.316
	(0.167)	(0.135)	(0.133)	(0.433)	(0.305)	(0.357)
Wave 8	1.131	1.179	0.946	1.270	1.433	1.874*
	(0.188)	(0.173)	(0.146)	(0.340)	(0.339)	(0.494)
Wave 10	0.777	1.069	0.927	1.002	1.444	1.164
	(0.140)	(0.179)	(0.163)	(0.314)	(0.366)	(0.309)
Log Likelihood	−2038.545	−2931.825	−2341.042	−812.713	−1167.153	−884.700
Observations	1,892	1,892	1,892	765	765	765

Notes: A pooled sample from Understanding Society (Wave 2–10) has been used to draw above-mentioned estimates. The standard error value for each estimate can be found in the parentheses. $+ p < 0.1$ $* p < 0.05$ $** p < 0.01$ $*** p < 0.001$.

Table A6.5. Fixed Effects Linear Models for the Impact of Parents' Transition to Flexitime/Teleworking on Their Subjective Well-Being.

Variables	All			Fathers			Mothers		
	(1)			(4)			(7)		
	Satisfaction with Life	Satisfaction with Leisure Time	Satisfaction with Health	Satisfaction with Life	Satisfaction with Leisure Time	Satisfaction with Health	Satisfaction with Life	Satisfaction with Leisure Time	Satisfaction with Health
Flexitime	0.0271	0.0909*	−0.0324	−0.0241	0.0706	−0.0998	0.0645	0.106+	0.00611
	(0.042)	(0.048)	(0.053)	(0.066)	(0.076)	(0.084)	(0.055)	(0.062)	(0.068)
Teleworking	0.0311	0.0463	0.113+	−0.0117	0.155*	0.0593	0.0767	−0.0529	0.165*
	(0.049)	(0.057)	(0.064)	(0.070)	(0.080)	(0.091)	(0.068)	(0.082)	(0.090)
Other Flexible Working Arrangements	−0.0335	0.0373	−0.0378	−0.0184	−0.0116	−0.00431	−0.0346	0.0612	−0.0544
	(0.028)	(0.033)	(0.034)	(0.050)	(0.059)	(0.061)	(0.033)	(0.040)	(0.040)
Log household income	0.0672	0.00656	−0.0391	0.0601	0.0703	−0.00829	0.0762	−0.0169	−0.0545
	(0.041)	(0.044)	(0.047)	(0.077)	(0.083)	(0.092)	(0.049)	(0.052)	(0.055)
Number of Children (reference category: one child)									
Two	0.148*	−0.0263	0.0521	0.158	0.0382	−0.0726	0.132	−0.0699	0.138
	(0.057)	(0.067)	(0.072)	(0.083)	(0.097)	(0.107)	(0.080)	(0.094)	(0.097)
More than two	0.228*	−0.105	0.00131	0.159	−0.161	−0.330	0.258	−0.0723	0.229
	(0.114)	(0.134)	(0.142)	(0.164)	(0.185)	(0.208)	(0.157)	(0.189)	(0.192)
Marital Status (reference category: single/never married									
Married/Cohabitating	0.178	0.146	−0.0281	0.802*	0.377	−0.337	0.137	0.142	−0.0134
	(0.103)	(0.107)	(0.108)	(0.313)	(0.374)	(0.315)	(0.107)	(0.111)	(0.113)
Divorced/Separated/Widowed	0.0100	0.0499	0.0287	0.281	0.710	0.103	−0.000129	0.0147	0.0124
	(0.118)	(0.123)	(0.132)	(0.453)	(0.535)	(0.537)	(0.121)	(0.126)	(0.135)
Age	−0.0232***	0.00432	−0.000902	−0.0171*	0.00456	0.00425	−0.0268***	0.00303	−0.00290
	(0.005)	(0.006)	(0.006)	(0.008)	(0.010)	(0.010)	(0.006)	(0.007)	(0.008)
Number of children aged 0–2 in household (reference category: none)									
One	−0.0934	−0.188**	0.0137	−0.0323	−0.217*	0.100	−0.139	−0.163	−0.0563
	(0.057)	(0.066)	(0.070)	(0.080)	(0.094)	(0.102)	(0.080)	(0.093)	(0.096)

Table A6.5. *(Continued)*

More than one	−0.154	−0.389**	0.125	−0.119	−0.309	0.333	−0.165	−0.459*	−0.0148
	(0.115)	(0.140)	(0.145)	(0.160)	(0.189)	(0.214)	(0.163)	(0.204)	(0.197)
Number of children aged 3–4 in household (reference category: none)									
One	−0.147**	−0.159*	−0.0306	−0.0890	−0.118	0.115	−0.186*	−0.189*	−0.138
	(0.053)	(0.062)	(0.067)	(0.076)	(0.086)	(0.099)	(0.075)	(0.089)	(0.092)
More than one	−0.305*	−0.309*	−0.0272	−0.182	−0.128	0.234	−0.402	−0.435	−0.212
	(0.144)	(0.154)	(0.169)	(0.191)	(0.204)	(0.226)	(0.211)	(0.228)	(0.250)
Number of children aged 5–11 in household (reference category: none)									
One	−0.125*	−0.0639	0.0689	−0.128	−0.0779	0.144	−0.121	−0.0556	0.00108
	(0.055)	(0.063)	(0.068)	(0.081)	(0.091)	(0.101)	(0.076)	(0.088)	(0.093)
More than one	−0.212*	−0.0515	0.0309	−0.205	−0.0202	0.210	−0.212	−0.0744	−0.120
	(0.106)	(0.122)	(0.131)	(0.154)	(0.172)	(0.196)	(0.147)	(0.172)	(0.177)
Number of children aged 12–15 in household (reference category: none)									
One	−0.0936	0.00972	0.0124	−0.119	−0.0230	0.0836	−0.0785	0.0311	−0.0557
	(0.057)	(0.065)	(0.070)	(0.085)	(0.094)	(0.108)	(0.078)	(0.090)	(0.094)
More than one	−0.142	0.0408	0.0450	−0.195	0.0271	0.196	−0.106	0.0544	−0.0925
	(0.106)	(0.123)	(0.132)	(0.155)	(0.174)	(0.194)	(0.147)	(0.173)	(0.180)
Job change	0.0653*	0.0741	0.111**	0.113*	0.122*	0.126	0.0363	0.0500	0.104
	(0.032)	(0.038)	(0.042)	(0.052)	(0.060)	(0.065)	(0.040)	(0.049)	(0.054)
Employment Sector (reference category: semi routine or routine)									
Intermediate	0.0239	−0.0208	0.0991	0.176	−0.0308	0.396**	−0.0305	−0.0124	−0.00189
	(0.066)	(0.074)	(0.080)	(0.125)	(0.146)	(0.146)	(0.078)	(0.085)	(0.094)
Managerial & Professional	0.00263	−0.0722	0.00220	0.0939	−0.0543	0.375**	−0.0359	−0.0774	−0.155
	(0.062)	(0.068)	(0.073)	(0.113)	(0.127)	(0.120)	(0.074)	(0.082)	(0.090)
Private sector	−0.0309	−0.0468	−0.0477	−0.0354	−0.109	−0.113	−0.0257	−0.0280	−0.0157
	(0.042)	(0.048)	(0.051)	(0.081)	(0.091)	(0.097)	(0.048)	(0.057)	(0.060)
illness	−0.125***	−0.122***	−0.385***	−0.0544	−0.0589	−0.295***	−0.165***	-0.157***	−0.435***
	(0.033)	(0.035)	(0.040)	(0.052)	(0.057)	(0.066)	(0.043)	(0.045)	(0.051)
Number of observations	20984	20984	20984	7912	7912	7912	13072	13072	13072

Notes: The standard error value for each estimate is mentioned in the brackets. + $p < 0.1$ * $p < 0.05$ ** $p < 0.01$ *** $p < 0.001$.

Table A6.6. Fixed Effects Linear Models for the Impact of Spouse's/Partner's Transition to Flexitime/Teleworking on Parents' Subjective Well-Being.

Variables	Fathers			Mothers		
	(1)			(2)		
	Satisfaction with Life	Satisfaction with Leisure Time	Satisfaction with Health	Satisfaction with Life	Satisfaction with Leisure Time	Satisfaction with Health
Spousal/Partner Characteristics						
Flexitime	−0.0159	0.0529	−0.0625	0.0260	0.248+	−0.0399
	(0.169)	(0.171)	(0.202)	(0.110)	(0.150)	(0.189)
Teleworking	−0.256+	−0.266	0.227	−0.0822	−0.229	−0.0191
	(0.190)	(0.258)	(0.264)	(0.139)	(0.174)	(0.188)
Other Flexible Working Arrangements	−0.0643	0.0859	−0.0964	−0.0395	−0.176	−0.0156
	(0.106)	(0.103)	(0.110)	(0.089)	(0.106)	(0.122)
Employment Sector (reference category: semi routine or routine)						
Intermediate	−0.281	0.0954	−0.212	0.0721	−0.264	0.0946
	(0.227)	(0.265)	(0.268)	(0.212)	(0.240)	(0.339)
Management & Professional	−0.394*	−0.0215	−0.0847	0.0753	−0.0895	0.115
	(0.200)	(0.238)	(0.225)	(0.186)	(0.208)	(0.248)
Age	−0.0226	−0.0195	−0.0903	0.0592	0.0184	−0.0127
	(0.114)	(0.063)	(0.060)	(0.060)	(0.067)	(0.073)
Private sector	−0.0677	−0.238	0.0208	0.0204	−0.106	0.299
	(0.147)	(0.176)	(0.176)	(0.133)	(0.153)	(0.184)
Long standing illness	0.115	0.00897	0.0722	−0.0328	−0.0389	0.0879
	(0.108)	(0.122)	(0.136)	(0.087)	(0.105)	(0.112)
Job change	−0.0851	−0.102	−0.0618	0.0728	0.0372	0.0292
	(0.112)	(0.126)	(0.149)	(0.105)	(0.130)	(0.130)
Individual Characteristics						
Age	0.0293	0.0688	0.130*	−0.0733	−0.00397	0.00564
	(0.113)	(0.062)	(0.059)	(0.062)	(0.072)	(0.077)

Table A6.6. (*Continued*)

Private sector	−0.161	−0.0371	−0.379*	0.0119	0.0126	−0.0499
	(0.172)	(0.197)	(0.182)	(0.136)	(0.149)	(0.153)
Long standing illness	0.0811	−0.195	−0.274*	−0.202	−0.328**	−0.456***
	(0.115)	(0.119)	(0.134)	(0.123)	(0.112)	(0.135)
Job change	0.188	0.000434	0.0230	0.0289	−0.0598	0.0177
	(0.113)	(0.135)	(0.139)	(0.099)	(0.134)	(0.149)
Employment Sector (reference category: semi routine or routine)						
Intermediate	0.140	0.000538	0.434	0.160	0.298	0.185
	(0.242)	(0.299)	(0.299)	(0.219)	(0.226)	(0.276)
Management & Professional	−0.150	−0.243	0.478*	0.0251	0.0642	−0.285
	(0.233)	(0.289)	(0.218)	(0.205)	(0.217)	(0.285)
Number of Children (reference category: one child)						
Two	0.119	0.201	−0.347	0.189	−0.354	0.0900
	(0.204)	(0.275)	(0.270)	(0.146)	(0.209)	(0.191)
More than two	0.483	0.0824	−0.616	0.158	−0.706	−0.192
	(0.403)	(0.538)	(0.523)	(0.268)	(0.406)	(0.386)
Number of children aged 0–2 in household (reference category: none)						
One	−0.113	−0.267	0.227	−0.311	0.00550	−0.280
	(0.201)	(0.272)	(0.271)	(0.162)	(0.210)	(0.183)
More than one	−0.0332	−0.403	1.019	−0.199	−0.121	−0.0485
	(0.376)	(0.533)	(0.546)	(0.298)	(0.418)	(0.370)
Number of children aged 3–4 in household (reference category: none)						
One	−0.0644	−0.0516	0.264	−0.227	0.0391	−0.181
	(0.186)	(0.256)	(0.265)	(0.141)	(0.198)	(0.180)
More than one	−0.610	−0.448	0.414	−0.459	0.0684	0.253
	(0.438)	(0.440)	(0.674)	(0.471)	(0.564)	(0.452)

(*Continued*)

Table A6.6. *(Continued)*

Variables	Fathers			Mothers		
	(1)			(2)		
	Satisfaction with Life	Satisfaction with Leisure Time	Satisfaction with Health	Satisfaction with Life	Satisfaction with Leisure Time	Satisfaction with Health
Number of children aged 5–11 in household (reference category: none)						
One	−0.209	−0.231	0.204	−0.226	0.181	0.125
	(0.189)	(0.264)	(0.251)	(0.148)	(0.199)	(0.175)
More than one	−0.481	−0.313	0.202	−0.289	0.544	−0.00981
	(0.353)	(0.520)	(0.500)	(0.272)	(0.372)	(0.329)
Number of children aged 12–15 in household (reference category: none)						
One	−0.328	−0.354	−0.0724	−0.0758	0.372	0.0118
	(0.192)	(0.264)	(0.262)	(0.145)	(0.199)	(0.186)
More than one	−0.568	−0.612	−0.0466	−0.0671	0.617	0.00358
	(0.361)	(0.541)	(0.486)	(0.262)	(0.364)	(0.346)
Log household income	0.0156	−0.0309	−0.167	−0.418	−0.0508	−0.374
	(0.258)	(0.233)	(0.304)	(0.213)	(0.211)	(0.283)
Number of observations	2528	2528	2528	2814	2814	2814

Notes: The standard error value for each estimate is mentioned in the parentheses. + $p < 0.1$ * $p < 0.05$ ** $p < 0.01$ *** $p < 0.001$.

CHAPTER 7

WORKPLACE FLEXIBILITY, WORK–FAMILY GUILT, AND WORKING MOTHERS' PARENTING BEHAVIOR

Melissa Rector LaGraff and Heidi E. Stolz

ABSTRACT

Despite the important implications for families, limited research has examined how workplace environments influence parenting behavior. Situated within the Work–Home Resources Model, the purpose of this study was to investigate (a) whether workplace flexibility, a contextual resource, predicts positive parenting behavior, a home outcome, and (b) whether work–family guilt mediates this relationship. A sample of working mothers with children between the ages of 1 and 18 (N = 302) completed an online survey. Linear regression analyses indicated perceived workplace flexibility predicted overall positive parenting, positive reinforcement, and warmth behaviors in working mothers, but not proactive parenting or supportiveness. Ordinary least squares (OLS) path analyses indicated work–family guilt did not mediate these relationships, but was significantly associated with workplace flexibility, indicating workplace flexibility had a significant negative effect on work–family guilt. The results of this study provide preliminary evidence that mothers' workplace flexibility may influence positive parenting behaviors; thus, policies that promote flexible work arrangements could promote positive family outcomes and reduce feelings of guilt related to work and family life.

Keywords: Positive parenting; work-family conflict; work-family enrichment; work–family guilt; working mothers; workplace flexibility

Flexible Work and the Family
Contemporary Perspectives in Family Research, Volume 21, 201–228

ISSN: 1530-3535/doi:10.1108/S1530-353520230000021007

It is well-established, both in the popular press and empirical literature, that US work–family policies provide very little support to families as compared to other high-income nations (Trask, 2017). US parents experience the greatest parenthood penalty compared to 21 other Organization for Economic Cooperation and Development (OCED) countries (Glass et al., 2016). In fact, more and more Americans are deciding not to have children or delaying parenthood due to the lack of support working parents experience in terms of federal policy (e.g., paid parental leave) and provisions (e.g., affordable, quality childcare; Belluz, 2019). Working parents' ability to balance work and family life is influenced by work–family policies (Brough et al., 2009), and the absence of these policies is taking its toll on American families, particularly for working mothers, as it is "harder to be a working mother in the United States than in any other country in the developed world" (Collins, 2019, p. 1). The COVID-19 pandemic has only served to exacerbate these issues for US working mothers. Since February 2020, nearly 2 million women have left the labor force, in part due to a dearth of supportive and protective work–family policies that could keep mothers employed in the face of caregiving challenges experienced during the pandemic, like inconsistent childcare, school closures, and limited or nonexistent paid leave options or flexible work arrangements (Fry, 2022).

Three work–family policy areas have been shown to be beneficial for families: expanded family leave, paid sick leave, and workplace flexibility (Trask, 2017), with research pointing to workplace flexibility as the most beneficial set of policies to support workers and their families (Pitt-Catsouphes et al., 2009). Workplace flexibility is becoming a requirement for our modern workforce (Hill et al., 2008) and is a cost-effective policy that has been found to reduce turnover and increase productivity (Ruppanner et al., 2018) as well as attract better workers and reduce absenteeism (Trask, 2017). Workplace flexibility has also been found to reduce employee stress, encourage healthier lifestyles, and improve the long-term health of employees (A Better Balance, 2010).

Limited research has investigated how workplace policies influence parenting behavior (Kim, 2018). It is well-established in the literature that safe and positive parenting behavior, which includes warm and supportive parenting practices, is related to healthy child development and overall child wellbeing (Sanders et al., 2014; Stack et al., 2010), yet we do not know whether work–family policies like workplace flexibility promote positive parenting behaviors.

Additionally, the emotions surrounding the work–family domain that may explain the relationship between workplace policies and parenting behaviors have yet to be investigated. One such emotion experienced by working parents is guilt, but this emotion is not often studied within the work–family domain (Cho & Allen, 2012; Daly, 2001; Judge et al., 2006; Livingston & Judge, 2008). Work–family guilt has been defined as the "discrepancy between one's preferred and actual level of role participation at home versus work" (Korabik, 2015, p. 142) and stems from the inability for one to wholly fulfill the social roles of worker and family member (Livingston & Judge, 2008). Thus, the purpose of this study is to (a) investigate whether workplace flexibility predicts positive parenting behaviors for working mothers, and (b) investigate whether work–family guilt mediates this relationship.

LITERATURE REVIEW

Theoretical Framework

Work–home resources model. The study is situated within the work–home resources model (W-HRM; ten Brummelhuis & Bakker, 2012), an integrated model grounded in conservation of resources theory, which presents "work-home conflict and enrichment as processes comprising antecedents, mechanisms, and outcomes" (p. 553). The model posits that *work demands*, such as overtime, depletes one's *personal resources*, such as time and energy, which in turn negatively affects *home outcomes*. Conversely, *work resources*, such as supervisorial support, can increase one's *personal resources*, thus leading to positive *home outcomes*. Whereas this investigation is interested in the work-to-home process (as just described), the model also accounts for the home-to-work process where *home demands* and *resources* influence *personal resources* and lead to *work outcomes* (ten Brummelhuis & Bakker, 2012).

More specifically, a work resource is considered as a *contextual resource*. "Contextual resources are located outside of the self and can be found in the social contexts of the individual" (ten Brummelhuis & Bakker, 2012, p. 548). An example provided is that of job autonomy, a *contextual resource*, that allows an employee to schedule their work in a way that saves time, a *personal resource*. The time saved can then allow the employee to invest in other activities which may put them in a position to gain another *contextual resource*, such as a good marriage. In addition to attempting to explain how resources in one domain (i.e., contextual resources in the work domain) can affect another domain (i.e., personal resources in the home domain), the W-HRM was also designed to answer questions about how processes develop over time and under what conditions work–home conflict/enrichment are most likely to occur.

Contextual demands, or stressors, are defined as the "physical, emotional, social, or organizational aspects of the social context that require sustained physical and/or mental effort" (p. 549). *Demands* in one domain, such as work, diminish *personal resources* which leads to poor outcomes in the other domain, such as home. It is this process (work demands depleting personal resources used at home) that defines *work–home conflict*. On the other hand, it is *contextual resources* that are the "starting point for enriching work–home processes. In line with the idea of a gain spiral, resources can produce other resources" (p. 549). Therefore, *work–home enrichment*, as opposed to *work–home conflict*, is defined as the process of *contextual resources* from the work and home domains leading to the development of *personal resources*. *Personal resources* developed in one domain (work or home) lead to positive outcomes in the other domain. The authors state, "whereas *contextual* demands and resources are the causes of, respectively, conflict and enrichment, *personal* resources are the linking pins between the work and home domains" (p. 549). In other words, in order to have positive outcomes in the home or work domain, one's personal resources must be developed by either increasing contextual resources or decreasing contextual demands (see Fig. 7.1).

In the W-HRM, outcomes are organized into the following categories: *production*, *behavioral*, and *attitudinal*. *Production* outcomes center around efficient and effective performance in the work and home domains.

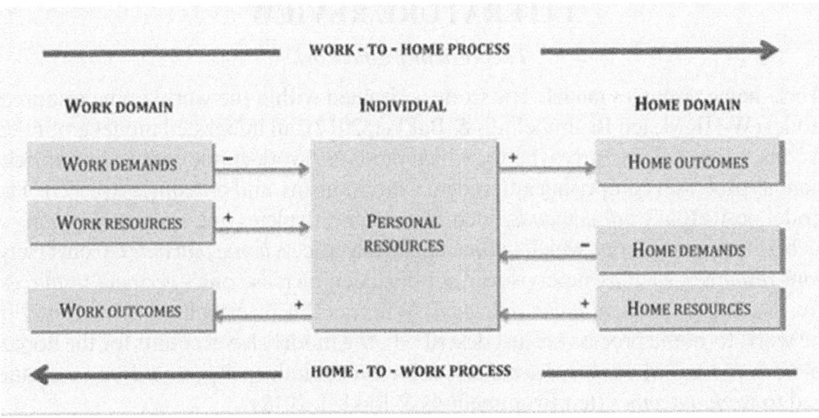

Fig. 7.1. The Work–Home Resources Model (ten Brummelhuis & Bakker, 2012). *Source*: Copyright © 2012 by American Psychological Association. Reproduced and adapted with permission. The official citation that should be used in referencing this material is: ten Brummelhuis, L. L., & Bakker, A. B. (2012). A resource perspective on the work-home interface: The work-home resources model. *American Psychologist*, *67*(7), 545–556. 10.1037/a0027974. No further reproduction or distribution is permitted without written permission from the American Psychological Association.

> Examples of work production outcomes are efficiency, product quality, and meeting targets. In the home domain, examples… are efficient performance of household chores, high quality of care for family members, and realizing leisure targets. (p. 550)

Behavioral work outcomes consist of behaviors that affect absenteeism, turnover, and work safety. Availability, accountability, and provision of a secure home environment are examples of *behavioral* outcomes in the home domain. Lastly, *attitudinal* outcomes in the work domain

> refer to beliefs and feelings that are valued by the employee and the employer, such as job satisfaction, organizational commitment, trust in management, and work-related well-being (e.g., work engagement or low feelings of burnout). (p. 550)

Examples of attitudinal outcomes in the home domain include family satisfaction, positive relationships with family and friends, family commitment, happiness at home, and home-related well-being (e.g., low feelings of stress).

Based on the W-HRM, it is hypothesized that a parent's workplace flexibility, a work/contextual resource, is influential in determining the home domain production outcome of positive parenting behavior. More specifically, it is expected that the resource of workplace flexibility increases a parent's personal resources by reducing negative work-related emotions, and parents' positive resources are, in turn, predictive of positive parenting behavior outcome.

Workplace Flexibility and the W-HRM

Workplace flexibility as a contextual resource. ten Brummelhuis and Bakker (2012) contend that autonomy is a subtype of contextual resources in the W-HRM as it is the ability for an individual to "decide how and when tasks are performed" (p. 550). As Hill et al. (2010) contend, individualistic cultures, like the United States, "are self-oriented and value personal time, freedom, and challenge" whereby workplace flexibility is seen as a work environment that emphasizes "'personal autonomy and self-fulfillment'" (p. 350; as cited in Osyerman et al., 2002, p. 4). According to Hill et al. (2008), workplace flexibility is defined as "the ability of workers to make choices influencing when, where, and for how long they engage in work-related tasks" (p. 152). The ability for workers to *choose* how to arrange core aspects of their work life is central. A worker's control or agency related to workplace flexibility is valuable in promoting optimal outcomes for oneself, family, workplace, and community. Perceived autonomy was reviewed by de Menezes and Kelliher (2011) as a key mediator in the relationship between remote working and job satisfaction, describing the potential role of job autonomy between schedule flexibility and job satisfaction. Flexible work designs enhance autonomy for employees with modern technology allowing employees greater control over their work. "This flexibility... provides employees with more autonomy to organize their work tasks in accordance with their preferences and to better coordinate their work and non-work activities," (p. 238) therefore, "workplace flexibility is associated with increased feelings of autonomy" (p. 241) and positively associated with employee well-being (ter Hoeven & van Zoonen, 2015).

Several external factors influence the construct of workplace flexibility. First, different types of workplace flexibility can be placed into five broad categories. The first category is *flexibility in the number of hours worked*, regardless of whether the hours are worked over the course of a week, month, or year. Examples of options include part-time work, part-year work, job sharing, and phased retirement. A second category is *flexible schedules*. In this category, workers might be able to alter starting/quitting times by request, shortening one's work week, working nonstandard hours, or having a choice for shifts. A third category is *flexible place* in which an employer allows options for locations for work, and employees may be able to choose to work from home or another remote location. The fourth category is *options for time off* in which an employer allows employees to take time off to attend to other responsibilities either for short or extended periods of time. Examples include paid leave for caregiving, extra unpaid vacation days, paid/unpaid time for training or education, paid/unpaid sabbaticals, paid/unpaid time to volunteer. The last category of *other options* contains options that do not fall into the previous categories. These include an employee's ability to time their work breaks and allowance to transfer to a job with reduced responsibilities for reduced pay, if desired (Pitt-Catsouphes et al., 2009).

Second, in defining and conceptualizing workplace flexibility, Hill et al. (2008) explained the construct should be considered on a continuum since some professions will be more conducive to flexibility based on "external organizational constraints related to the nature of the job, the needs of the business, and the availability of technology" (p. 152). Additionally, flexibility options originally designed for salaried, professional positions have been slow to adapt to hourly and shift-based jobs. In fact, flexibility options are currently disproportionally afforded to professional and salaried US workers as compared to hourly workers. Lower wage-earning, hourly workers in industries such as hospitality, retail, and transportation, have less access to flexibility policies than those in professional and managerial positions (Lambert et al., 2012; Swanberg et al., 2005).

Third, Hill et al. (2008) definition also highlights the interaction between workers and their employers. It is important there is both opportunity for flexibility within an organization, such as formal flexible work options, and the choice of the worker to utilize workplace flexibility policies. However, it is not enough for an organization to enact formal flexible work policies. The organizational culture must also be explicitly supportive of the use of flexible work policies (Hill et al., 2008). For example, supervisor support is important in implementing workplace flexibility policies since flexible work arrangements usually require approval from one's direct supervisor (Jaoko, 2012). Lastly, other factors, like parental status and number of children, are associated with access to flexible schedules (Swanberg et al., 2005).

Thus, due to these external factors (broad categories, job type, organizational culture of support, parent status), this study investigates working mothers' perception of their workplace flexibility. This intrapersonal perception also coincides with the focus on workplace flexibility as contextual resource of autonomy.

Workplace flexibility and home outcomes. Research has shown that workplace flexibility, or schedule control, contributes to positive home outcomes (Trask, 2017). Workers who perceived their work schedules to be flexible also reported greater work–life balance (Jang, 2009). In examining flexible work policies and life satisfaction in dual-earner parents, Minnotte et al. (2016) reported that having access to flexible scheduling policies did not predict life satisfaction in mothers or fathers. However, dual-earner mothers who used flexible scheduling reported greater life satisfaction while dual-earner fathers who used flexible scheduling reported less life satisfaction. Minnotte et al. speculated this finding may be due to gender expectations for women to fulfill childcare and home tasks more so than fathers and/or the lack of support for fathers to take advantage of flexible workplace policies. Schedule flexibility has also been associated with greater parental involvement, particularly in children's education (Earle et al., 2011). The impact of parenthood on well-being (lower levels of depression and anxiety symptoms) irrespective of gender was mediated by a sense of control for dual-earner couple parents one year after having a baby (Keeton et al., 2008).

The Results Only Work Environment (ROWE) is an initiative designed to improve workplace flexibility and parents' perceptions of time spent with their children. ROWE is different than other flexible work arrangements in that the employees can change when and where they work without notifying a manager; their work just needs to get done. It was found that mothers, but not fathers, under the ROWE initiative, reported an increase in controlling their schedule. The actual time spent with children did not change, but ROWE was associated with mothers eating more evening meals with their children (Hill et al., 2013). As Ladge and Greeberg (2019) describe, "many working mothers find the standard American workweek is out of sync with their children's and family's schedules" (p. 136). Workplace flexibility can allow working mothers to adjust work hours to better align with home and family responsibilities. In sum, work–family literature does point to the benefit of workplace flexibility for family life.

Parenting Behavior and the W-HRM

Parenting behavior as a home outcome. One example of a home domain production outcome is "high quality care for family members" (ten Brummelhuis &

Baker, 2012, p. 550). In parenting literature examining the quality of care for children, two parenting dimensions have consistently emerged. Barber et al. (2005) described these parenting dimensions as parental support, and two forms of parental control – behavioral control and psychological control. Parental support and behavioral control also correspond to Baumrind's (1971) typological framework and the parenting dimensions of responsiveness and demandingness, respectively. A substantial body of family science research supports that positive outcomes for children are related to high levels of nurturing parenting behaviors (parental support) and guidance behaviors (parental behavioral control; Stolz, 2011).

Drawing from these two parenting dimensions, broad composites of positive and negative parenting behavior have also been identified. The focus of this inquiry is on positive parenting behavior which can be "typified by warmth and affection, positive reinforcement, firm and consistent discipline, and active involvement in and monitoring of child… activities" (Parent, 2017, p. 1). The measure of Positive Parenting herein includes subscales of proactive parenting defined as "child-centered appropriate responding to anticipated difficulties"; positive reinforcement which is considered "contingent responses to positive child behavior with praise, rewards, or displays of approval"; warmth which is described as displays of affection; and supportiveness defined as "displayed interest in the child, encouragement of positive communication, and openness to a child's ideas and opinions" (Parent & Forehand, 2017, p. 2146).

Limited research has investigated how the work–family life context influences parenting behavior. One component of high-quality parenting in the United States is the amount and quality of time parents spend with children. Another component is parents feeling good about how well their children are developing and functioning (Milkie et al., 2010). Time spent by working parents in routine care of their children was related to less success felt in balancing work and family whereas time spent in interactive, engaging activities was related to an increased sense of success in work–life balance (Milkie et al., 2010). Furthermore, negative interpersonal work environments for mothers were significantly related to decreases in positive parenting and increases in negative parenting, but these spillover effects were not found for fathers (Costigan et al., 2003). Mother's report of work–family conflict and father's report of job dissatisfaction was negatively associated with parenting self-efficacy which was associated with an increased use of ineffective parenting behaviors and higher levels of problem behavior in children (Anderson, 2006). Job stress can lead to a decrease in engagement and withdrawal from children as well as lead to an increase in conflict and tension between parents and children (Repetti & Wang, 2014). However, when work benefits a parent's psychological well-being, it is associated with positive parenting behaviors (Repetti & Wang, 2014).

The Role of Work–Family Guilt

Definition of guilt. Guilt is an unpleasant emotion one feels when they have acknowledged a wrongdoing or have acted in a way that is perceived as violating norms of behavior. Guilt is "typically attached to a particular action and does not condemn the entire self" (Leith & Baumeister, 1998, p. 3). In most situations, the negative effect of guilt prompts one to "counteract the bad consequences of their actions, for example, by confessing, by apologizing, or by making amends" (Leith & Baumeister, 1998, p. 3). Thus, guilt is argued to be an interpersonal emotion typically arising in the context of relationships (Borelli et al., 2017a). In this regard, guilt has been found to benefit interpersonal relationships by encouraging awareness of one's behavior, moving focus to one's motivation on repairing the aspect of the relationship that is weak, and taking the necessary action to counteract the results of the behavior or action (Cho & Allen, 2012).

Work–family guilt in the work–family domain. Guilt is one emotion experienced by working parents, yet this emotion is not often studied within the work–family domain (Cho & Allen, 2012; Daly, 2001; Judge et al., 2006; Livingston & Judge, 2008). Work–family guilt may explain the relationship between work and home outcomes. Increased feelings of guilt results from both work-interfering-with-family (WIF) and family-interfering-with-work (FIW) due to the inability for one to wholly fulfill the social roles of worker and family member (Livingston & Judge, 2008). Working mothers transitioning to parenthood felt guilt prior to maternity leave due to being off work and potentially burdening coworkers as well as feeling guilt for returning to work following maternity leave (Millward, 2006). In Daly's (2001) inquiry into the notion of family time, "guilt was pervasive in the way both women and men in these families talked about their experience of time" (p. 292). It was inferred this feeling of guilt, expressed by both mothers and fathers, was born out of the stark contradiction between the ideals and high standards the parents held for family time and the reality of family time experienced. In fact, work–family guilt has been defined as the "discrepancy between one's preferred and actual level of role participation at home versus work" (Korabik, 2015, p. 142).

Limited research has examined the role of emotions in work–family conflict. Work–family conflict is defined as "a form of interrole conflict in which the role pressures from the work and family domains are mutually incompatible in some respect" (Greenhaus & Beutell, 1985, p. 77). Two common forms are time-based and strain-based work–family conflict. In terms of WIF conflict, time-based conflict "occurs when time devoted to the work role hampers the fulfillment of responsibilities in the family role" whereas strain-based conflict "occurs when stress generated in the work role inhibits effective performance in the family role" (Cho & Allen, 2012, p. 277). Those who experience work–family conflict, whether time- or strain-based, may consequently experience more negative emotions related to this conflict. Guilt is an *emotion* associated with work–family conflict (Judge et al., 2006; Livingston & Judge, 2008), as evidenced by the aforementioned qualitative studies. Cho and Allen state guilt is "especially pertinent to the context of working parents due to its interpersonal characteristic" (p. 278). It is expected increased feelings of guilt result from both WIF and FIW due to the inability for one to wholly fulfill the social roles of worker and family member.

Conflict exists between work and family life because one believes the demands of both roles cannot be fully met (Livingston & Judge, 2008). A parent feeling guilt due to missing bedtime because of an evening work meeting would be an example of WIF while a parent feeling guilt for missing a morning work meeting due to staying up late with a sick child would be an example of FIW (Borelli et al., 2017a). Family-to-work conflict experienced at work was associated with guilt at work and work-to-family conflict assessed at home was associated with guilt at home (Judge et al., 2006). Livingston and Judge (2008) confirmed FIW conflict is positively associated with guilt while WIF is indirectly associated with guilt. Again, as Daly (2001) suggested, work–family guilt has also been defined as the difference between one's preferred and actual level of participation in the domains of home and work. Work–family guilt is also often described as a result of one having to choose between work and family life and/or the inability to balance work and family life (Korabik, 2015). In their interview study, Aarntzen et al. (2019) found parents, but primarily mothers, mentioned feeling guilt in the context of their work–family conflict, and mostly in relation to their children.

Women and work–family guilt. Work–family guilt has also been characterized as one perceiving they do not adequately fulfill gender role norms (Livingston & Judge, 2008) or results from trying to manage the double standards placed on women in contemporary society (Korabik, 2015). In fact, Livingston and Judge identified the "mommy myth" as a contributor to work–family guilt. Parents, and perhaps especially mothers, feel they should be both an ideal worker and a good family member because it is perceived other parents and women are able to do so. Thus, guilt is felt when family renders one unable to meet the ideal worker standard or work prevents one from upholding the good family member (parent/spouse) standard. Furthermore, WIF conflict may affect women more due to the expectation that women generally have primary responsibility for care of the children (Borelli et al., 2017a). Additionally, working mothers tend to be held to higher standards in the workplace which puts them at risk of also experiencing FIW conflict. Thus, if in the face of work–family dilemmas one chooses to prioritize work over family, mothers may experience more personal distress due to the violation of traditional gender norms.

However, limited empirical evidence points to gender differences in work–family guilt. For non-US working parents, some women report significantly higher levels of "employment-related guilt" than men, yet both men and women had significant associations between work–family conflict and high levels of guilt (Aycan & Eskin, 2005), and both reporting high levels of guilt (Martínez et al., 2011). In the United States, after controlling for general guilt, working mothers of toddlers reported both significantly higher work–family guilt and WIF-guilt than fathers (Borelli et al., 2017a). Number of hours mothers worked was positively related to WIF-guilt, but not for fathers, and when mothers reported experiencing greater work–family conflict, their levels of WIF-guilt were higher than fathers (Borelli et al., 2017b). Collins (2019) found in her interviews of 135 mothers in Sweden, Germany, Italy, and the United States, that US mothers experienced "enormous guilt and tension between their work and family roles" (p. 202). These feelings were similar to those shared by mothers in Germany and Italy, but whereas mothers from those countries blamed external factors (outdated cultural norms and the government, respectively), US mothers "blamed themselves for not 'balancing' or 'managing' their responsibilities" (p. 202).

Influence of work–family guilt on parenting practices. Despite a substantial body of research acknowledging working parents experience work–family conflict and preliminary research indicating employed parents experience some level of work–family guilt, research into the relationship between these constructs and parenting outcomes is scarce (Aarntzen et al., 2019; Cho & Allen, 2012). Scholars have suggested work–family guilt may influence parenting behaviors, and these parenting behaviors stemming from work–family guilt could cause negative consequences (Borelli et al., 2017b). For example, work–family guilt could encourage a parent to regularly engage in permissive parenting practices which are associated with negative child outcomes, including behavior problems (Borelli et al., 2017b; Martínez et al., 2011). WIF-guilt was associated with self-reported permissive parenting behavior, but more investigation is warranted to determine whether WIF-guilt caused permissive parenting, permissive parenting led to greater WIF-guilt, or if another factor explained the relationship (Borelli et al., 2017b).

Conversely, Cho and Allen (2012) examined trait guilt, or one's proneness to feeling guilt, as a motivational factor in prompting working parents to engage in positive interactive behaviors with their children despite WIF conflict. Three different types of parent–child interactive behavior were measured: educational activities (e.g., reading), recreational activities (e.g., playing), and passive activities (e.g., watching TV). Two different types of WIF conflict were examined: time-based WIF and strain-based WIF. Time-based WIF occurs when time devoted to work prevents a parent from being able to take care of family responsibilities. Strain-based WIF occurs when stress felt at work hinders a parent from performing well in the family role. It was hypothesized that parents who are prone to feeling guilty "are likely to accept responsibility for WIF, which may result in compensatory behaviors, such as engaging in parent-child interactive behavior" (p. 278).

Parents who reported greater WIF conflict reported lower recreational and educational activities, especially for parents reporting high levels of strain-based WIF. There were inconsistent findings with regard to the passive interaction activities. Trait guilt was a stronger moderator of the relationship between WIF and recreational activities than with educational activities. Parents who reported low levels of trait guilt reported lower levels of both active activities (recreational and educational) than parents with higher levels of trait guilt for both time- and strain-based WIF. One exception to this finding was that trait guilt was not a moderator for the relationship between educational activities and strain-based WIF in Study 2. No relationships were found between passive behaviors, WIF, and trait guilt. Thus, high trait guilt may serve as motivator rather than an inhibitor for working parents under WIF-conflict to make concerted efforts to be actively involved in their child's life (Cho & Allen, 2012).

In two studies examining the consequences of work–family guilt via interviews with parents and a diary study, working mothers first shared they compensated for their work–family guilt in relation to their children through behaviors like giving extra hugs or reading an extra story. However, the working mothers with high levels of work–family guilt then reported making plans to spend more time with their children, but the diary data indicated they spent less attentive time with their children (Aarntzen et al., 2019).

Workplace flexibility and work–family guilt. Empirical research specifically linking work–family guilt to workplace flexibility does not yet exist, however, Collins (2021) argues US work–family policies reflect the ideal of intensive mothering and found that "work-family policy shapes which aspect of motherhood produce these guilty feelings" (p. 23). Thus, based on reviewed literature on workplace flexibility, parenting behavior, and work–family guilt further research is warranted. For example, Korabik (2015) described the lack of control over one's job predicted higher levels of WIF-guilt reported by American workers. Therefore, it can be posited that perhaps workplace flexibility policies, which give employees more schedule control (Hill et al., 2008), may reduce feelings of work–family guilt for working mothers.

Summary and Research Questions

In summary, workplace flexibility may have important implications for parenting behaviors. A mechanism that may explain the relationship between workplace flexibility and parenting behavior is work–family guilt, especially for working mothers. Specifically, the following hypotheses will be tested:

1. Greater workplace flexibility will predict more positive parenting behaviors (global measure as well as four subscales).
2. Greater workplace flexibility will reduce work–family guilt.
3. Work–family guilt will mediate the relationship between workplace flexibility and positive parenting behavior.

METHODS

Sample

The sample for the broader project consisted of (a) non-self-employed (b) adults (c) working for pay with (d) at least one biological or adopted child between the ages of 1 to 18 (e) living in the home at least half time ($N = 355$). The sample for the present study was further restricted to working mothers who reported working 30 or more hours per week ($N = 302$). Descriptive statistics pertaining to sample characteristics are provided in Table 7.1.

Procedure and Instrument

Recruitment. A convenience sampling approach was used to recruit survey participants. Personal email invitations with the survey link were extended to personal contacts who were eligible to participate as well as sent to two university department listservs. The survey link and a picture of the recruitment flyer were posted to the first author's personal Facebook page and to a "Work Outside the Home Moms" group Facebook page. Lastly, a snowball sampling technique was used, with a request for participants to share and/or forward the survey link to others. The first author's personal Facebook post was shared 54 times. Others shared the link to their personal Facebook page, the Academic Mamas Facebook group, Reddit, and Twitter.

Table 7.1. Sample Characteristics.

Characteristics	*N*	Percent
Age	*M* = 36.85	*SD* = 5.93
Race		
White	276	91.4
Non-White	26	8.6
Hispanic or Latinx		
Yes	8	2.6
Not Hispanic or Latinx	293	97.0
Missing	1	0.3
Relationship Status		
Living with partner/significant other	15	5
Married	255	84.4
Living alone; single/separated/divorced	32	10.6
Level of Education		
Some college or less	14	4.6
Associate degree	15	5
Bachelor's degree	79	26.2
Master's degree	140	46.4
Doctorate or Professional degree	54	17.9
Personal Annual Income		
$5,000–23,999	13	4.3
$24,000–35,999	29	9.6
$36,000–47,999	50	16.6
$48,000–59,999	66	21.9
$60,000–89,999	86	28.5
$90,000–119,999	38	12.6
$120,000–179,999	15	5
$180,000 and over	5	1.7
Total Household Income		
$12,000–47,999	8	2.6
$48,000–59,999	15	5
$60,000–89,999	60	19.9
$90,000–119,999	90	29.8
$120,000–179,999	82	27.2
$180,000–239,999	29	9.6
$240,000 and over	17	5.6
Missing	1	0.3
Focal Child Age	***N***	**Percent**
1 year	65	21.5
2 years	33	10.9
3 years	50	16.6
4 years	40	13.2
5 years	19	6.3
6 years	13	4.3
7 years	15	5.0
8 years	12	4.0
9 years	10	3.3
10 years	5	1.7
11 years	3	1.0
12 years	5	1.7
13 years	5	1.7
14 years	10	3.3

Table 7.1. *(Continued)*

Characteristics	*N*	Percent
15 years	1	0.3
16 years	11	3.6
17 years	3	1.0
18 years	2	0.7
Childcare Setting of Focal Child	188	
Center-based formal childcare	128	68.1
Home-based formal childcare	14	7.4
In-home care – Spouse/partner	13	6.9
In-home care – Family member or nanny/ babysitter/friend	31	16.5
Other	2	2.1

Instrument. Participants completed an anonymous online survey using Qualtrics software over the first half of March 2020. Following completion of the survey, participants had the opportunity to enter a drawing to win one of six $25 Amazon gift cards.

Measures

Workplace flexibility. The 5-item Work Schedule Flexibility scale by Jang et al. (2012) measured workplace flexibility and participants responded to items on a 5-point Likert-type scale from 1 (*strongly disagree*) to 5 (*strongly agree*). Examples of items include: "I have the schedule flexibility I need at work to manage my personal and family responsibilities," "I am given a lot of freedom to decide how I do my own work," and "It is easy to take time off during my work day to take care of personal or family matters." The following three items were added given the low reliability of the scale in past research and because the original measure did not fully encompass the broad aspects of workplace flexibility: "I am given a lot of freedom in where I do my work," "I can easily change the number of hours I work whether they are worked over a week, month, or year," and "I am given a lot of freedom in taking work breaks during my work day." Because items were added to this measure, a principal components factor analysis with varimax rotation of the eight items was conducted. One factor with an eigenvalue over one was found, and the visual inspection of the scree plot confirmed one factor (Costello & Osborne, 2005). The 8-items were averaged to create a composite scale score, with higher scores indicating a greater perception of workplace flexibility. The Cronbach's alpha for this scale was 0.89.

Positive parenting behavior. The Multidimensional Assessment of Parenting Scale (MAPS; Parent & Forehand, 2017) measured positive parenting behavior. The positive parenting broadband scale consists of 16 items representing four parenting subscales: warmth (3 items), positive reinforcement (4 items), proactive parenting (6 items), and supportiveness (3 items). Parents were asked to report on their behavior in the past two months and respond on a 5-point Likert-type scale from 1 (*never*) to 5 (*always*). The items for *warmth* are: "I express affection by hugging, kissing, and holding my child," "I have warm and intimate times together with my child," and "My child and I hug and/or kiss each other."

The first two items for *positive reinforcement* were slightly revised to make them appropriate for children four years of age and younger as well as the school-aged children for whom the items were originally written. The original language is provided in brackets. Example items are: "If my child completes a task [does his/her chores], I will recognize his/her behavior in some manner," "If my child helps clean up [cleans his/her room], I will tell him/her how proud I am," and "I tell my child that I like it when s/he helps out around the house."

Example items for *proactive parenting* are: "I give reasons for my requests (such as "We must leave in five minutes, so it's time to clean up."), "I tell my child my expectations regarding behavior before my child engages in an activity," and "I provide my child with a brief explanation when I discipline his/her behavior."

The items for *supportiveness* are: "I show respect for my child's opinions by encouraging him/her to express them," "I encourage my child to talk about her/his troubles," and "I listen to my child's ideas and opinions." Items for each scale were averaged into a composite score, with higher scores indicating a greater level of positive parenting behavior. The Cronbach's alphas for each scale are as follows: Broadband Positive Parenting $\alpha = 0.83$, Warmth $\alpha = 0.73$, Positive Reinforcement $\alpha = 0.77$, Proactive Parenting $\alpha = 0.76$, and Supportiveness $\alpha = 0.70$.

Work-interfering-with-family guilt scale (WIFGS). The WIFGS is a 9-item scale that asks parents to "rate the extent to which they experience feelings of responsibility for the actual or potential negative impact that working may have on themselves or members of their family" (Borelli et al., 2017b, p. 1736). Participants responded to each item on a 5-point Likert-type scale from 1 (*never*) to 5 (*always*). In previous studies, 5 items were reverse-coded, however, reduced reliability has been found when using reverse-coded items (Weems & Onwuegbuzie, 2001). Thus, the 5 items were replaced with their reverse equivalent (with the exception of one that was already stated in reverse). Examples of the eight items are as follows with the anchor "How often do you…": "feel like you really should be at home when you're away at work?," "feel guilty about being away from your child when you work longer hours than usual?," "worry about the impact of your work on your child?," "feel like working makes you a worse parent?," and "feel like work prevents you from contributing to your family?" Items were averaged to construct a scale, with higher scores indicating a greater level of work-interfering-with-family guilt. The Cronbach's alpha for this scale was 0.89.

ANALYSIS

In the control variable analyses, Pearson's *r* correlation tests demonstrated that age was significantly correlated with the Positive Reinforcement subscale, $r(302) = -0.15$, $p < 0.01$ and the Warmth subscale, $r(302) = -0.19$, $p < 0.01$. Thus, age was only controlled for in analyses for Positive Reinforcement and Warmth. A one-way ANOVA was conducted to determine if education level, an ordinal variable, was significantly related to the parenting variables. There were no statistically significant differences between education groups, and this variable was not controlled for in subsequent analyses. Lastly, independent samples *t*-tests were conducted to compare mothers with only one child to mothers with more than one child. Results indicated women with more than one child reported significantly lower levels of Positive Reinforcement, $t(300) = 2.32$, $p < 0.02$ and Warmth, $t(300) = 2.06$, $p < 0.04$ than women with only one child. Based on these results, number of children was entered as a control variable in the tests for these two scales.

For the first research question, OLS linear regression tests were conducted to determine whether workplace flexibility predicts overall positive parenting behavior as well as each of the four positive parenting subscales individually, controlling for relevant demographic factors as described above. The second research question was addressed using OLS path analyses for mediation (Hayes, 2017) to determine whether work–family guilt mediates the relationships between workplace flexibility and overall positive parenting and each parenting subscale. The relevant control variables were entered into the models as covariates. Model 4 was used to examine mediation (Hayes, 2017).

RESULTS

Descriptive statistics and correlations are provided in Table 7.2. The result of the OLS linear regression test to determine whether workplace flexibility predicted overall positive parenting behavior was significant, $F(1, 300) = 4.15$, $p < 0.05$. Workplace flexibility ($B = 0.044$, $t(300) = 2.04$, $p < 0.05$) accounted for approximately 1.4% of the variance in positive parenting behavior. Results of the linear regression tests for each parenting subscale indicated that workplace flexibility did not significantly predict Proactive Parenting or Supportiveness. Workplace flexibility did significantly predict Positive Reinforcement, controlling for age and multiple children, $F(3, 298) = 5.44$, $p < 0.01$. Workplace flexibility ($B = 0.075$, $t(299) = 2.35$, $p < 0.05$) accounted for approximately 5% of the variance in positive reinforcement. Workplace flexibility also significantly predicted warmth, controlling for age and multiple children, $F(3, 298) = 6.31$, $p < 0.01$. Workplace

Table 7.2. Positive Parenting, Workplace Flexibility, and Work–Family Guilt: Correlations and Descriptive Statistics ($N = 302$).

Variables	1	2	3	4	5	6	7
1. Broadband Positive Parenting	—						
2. Proactive Parenting	0.730**	—					
3. Positive Reinforcement	0.715**	0.371**	—				
4. Warmth	0.614**	0.223**	0.265**	—			
5. Supportiveness	0.736**	0.435**	0.332**	0.281**	—		
6. Workplace Flexibility	0.117*	0.044	0.104	0.089	0.116	—	
7. Work–Family Guilt	−0.042	0.021	−0.017	0.001	−0.120*	−0.463**	—
M	4.32	4.02	4.38	4.56	4.35	3.39	2.52
SD	0.344	0.495	0.513	0.461	0.499	0.920	0.725
α	0.83	0.76	0.77	0.73	0.70	0.89	0.89

Note: * $p < 0.05$. ** $p < 0.00$.

flexibility ($B = 0.064$, $t(299) = 2.23$, $p < 0.05$) accounted for approximately 6% of the variance in warmth behavior.

Given the significant direct relationships between workplace flexibility, overall parenting behavior, positive reinforcement, and warmth, OLS path analyses for mediation (Hayes, 2017) were conducted for only these variables. The OLS regressions tests were Step 1 for the OLS path analyses for mediation using Hayes' method.

For overall positive parenting behavior, controlling for multiple children, Step 2 of the mediation model analysis demonstrated that the regression of the mediator, work–family guilt, on workplace flexibility, was significant ($b = -0.36$, $t(302) = -9.04$, $p < 0.001$). Step 3 of the mediation process showed that work–family guilt, controlling for workplace flexibility, was not significant in predicting positive parenting behavior ($b = 0.01$, $t(302) = 0.24$, $p = 0.81$). Step 4 showed that, controlling for work–family guilt, workplace flexibility was no longer a significant predictor of overall positive parenting behavior ($b = 0.05$, $t(302) = 1.91$, $p = 0.06$). The nonsignificant indirect effect of workplace flexibility on overall positive parenting behavior indicates no mediation in the model (see Fig. 7.2). Additionally, a bias-corrected bootstrap 95% CI indicated that the indirect effect through work–family guilt was nonsignificant, $a \times b = -0.003$, 95% CI: [−0.03, 0.02].

With regard to positive reinforcement, controlling for age and multiple children, Step 2 of the mediation model analysis showed that the regression of the mediator, work–family guilt, on workplace flexibility, was significant ($b = -0.34$, $t(302) = -8.47$, $p < 0.001$). Step 3 of the mediation process showed that work–family guilt, controlling for workplace flexibility, was not significant in predicting positive reinforcement behavior ($b = 0.01$, $t(302) = 0.30$, $p = 0.76$). Step 4 of the analysis showed that, controlling for work–family guilt, workplace flexibility was still a significant predictor of positive reinforcement ($b = 0.08$, $t(302) = 2.24$, $p < 0.05$).

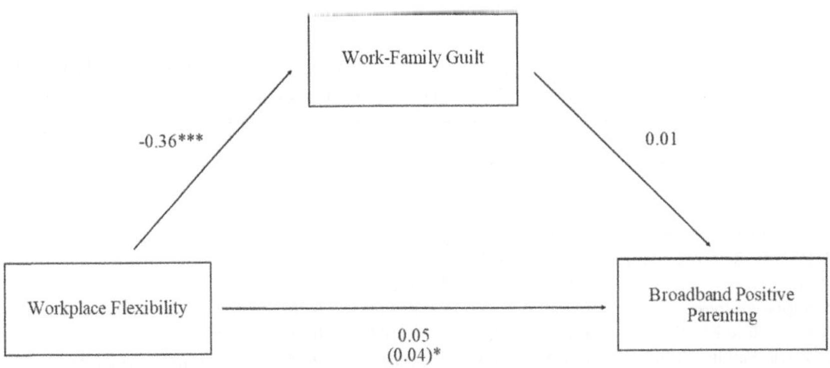

Fig. 7.2. Unstandardized Regression Coefficients for the Relationship Between Workplace Flexibility and Positive Parenting Behavior as Mediated by Work–Family Guilt. *Note*: The unstandardized regression coefficient for the relationship between workplace flexibility and positive parenting is in parentheses.*$p < 0.05$. ***$p < 0.001$.

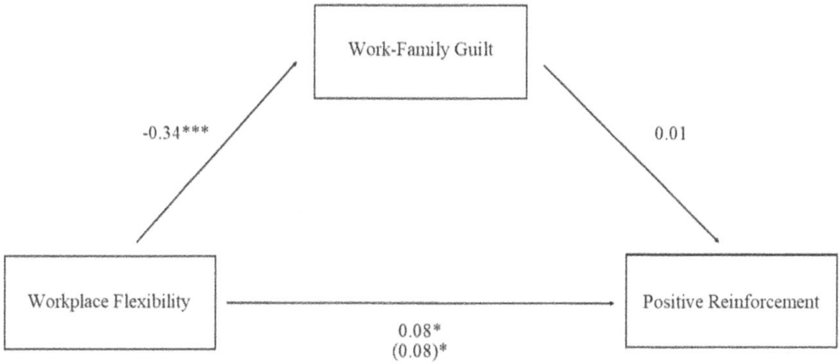

Fig. 7.3. Unstandardized Regression Coefficients for the Relationship Between Workplace Flexibility and Positive Reinforcement Behavior as Mediated by Work–Family Guilt. *Note*: The unstandardized regression coefficient for the relationship between workplace flexibility and positive reinforcement is in parentheses.$*p < 0.05$. $***p < 0.001$.

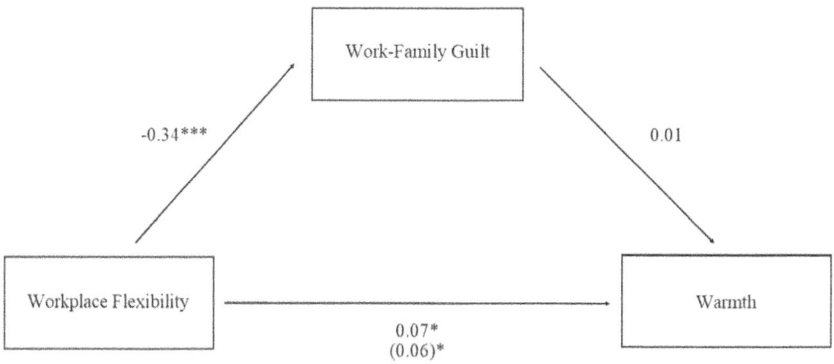

Fig. 7.4. Unstandardized Regression Coefficients for the Relationship Between Workplace Flexibility and Warmth as Mediated by Work–Family Guilt. *Note*: The unstandardized regression coefficient for the relationship between workplace flexibility and warmth is in parentheses.$*p < 0.05$. $***p < 0.001$.

Again, the nonsignificant indirect effect of workplace flexibility on positive reinforcement behavior indicates no mediation in the model (see Fig. 7.3).

With regard to warmth, controlling for age and multiple children, Step 2 of the mediation model analysis showed that the regression of the mediator, work–family guilt, on workplace flexibility, was significant ($b = -0.34$, $t(302) = -8.47$, $p < 0.001$). Step 3 of the mediation process showed that work–family guilt, controlling for workplace flexibility, was not significant in predicting warmth behavior ($b = 0.01$, $t(302) = 0.34$, $p = 0.73$). Step 4 showed that, controlling for work–family guilt, workplace flexibility was still a significant predictor of warmth ($b = 0.07$, $t(302) = 2.15$, $p < 0.05$). Again, the nonsignificant indirect effect of workplace flexibility on warmth behavior indicates no mediation in the model (see Fig. 7.4).

DISCUSSION

The purpose of this study was to investigate whether workplace flexibility predicted working mothers' positive parenting behaviors and whether work–family guilt mediated any significant relationships between workplace flexibility and positive parenting behaviors. This study sought to extend the literature by examining a potential link between workplace flexibility and work–family guilt. Empirical research had not yet investigated whether a work-related resource like workplace flexibility is related to the emotion of guilt felt when work interferes with family. This study also sought to expand on past research by investigating the constructs of workplace flexibility and work–family guilt and their influence on parenting behavior, examining specific positive parenting behaviors known to be beneficial to children. Although anecdotal evidence suggests work–family guilt may influence parenting behavior, and preliminary research found work–family guilt to be associated with permissive parenting for parents of young children (Borelli et al., 2017b) and less attentive time spent with children (Aarntzen et al., 2019), additional empirical research is necessary.

Workplace Flexibility and Parenting Behavior

As hypothesized, workplace flexibility was found to predict mothers' overall positive parenting behavior. This finding corresponds to the W-HRM in which a contextual work resource, like workplace flexibility, leads to positive outcomes in the home domain, such as high-quality care for family members. This finding is also an example of the work–home enrichment process, as described in the W-HRM (ten Brummelhuis & Bakker, 2012). Work–family enrichment is defined as "the extent to which experiences in one role improve the quality of life, namely performance or affect, in the other role" (Carlson et al., 2006, p. 132). Through the idea of a gain spiral, resources gained in one role can promote an improved performance in another role. A key requirement for work–family enrichment to occur is that resources gained in Role A must not only be transferred to Role B, but "successfully applied in ways that result in improved performance or affect for the individual" (p. 133). Accordingly, it seems workplace flexibility can provide resources for mothers in their role as worker that she is able to apply to improve her performance in the parenting role.

The work–home enrichment process involves contextual resources from the home and work domains leading to the development of personal resources, and it is these personal resources developed in each domain that play out in one's performance in the other domain. Personal resources are the "linking pins" between the work and home domains (p. 549) and are categorized as: *physical* (physical energy, health, sleep), *psychological* (optimism, self-efficacy, focus, resilience), *intellectual* (knowledge, skills, experiences), *affective* (mood, fulfillment, gratefulness), and *capital* (time, money). Thus, with workplace flexibility as a contextual resource in the W-HRM due to the autonomy it affords (de Menezes & Kelliher, 2011; Hill et al., 2010), it leads to the positive home outcome of parenting behavior through the increase of personal resources (ten Brummelhuis & Bakker, 2012). For example, it has been proposed that flexible work arrangements allow parents more time and energy, both personal resources, to participate in more caregiving activities (Kim, 2018).

For this sample of mothers, workplace flexibility predicted two specific aspects of positive parenting behavior: positive reinforcement and warmth, but did not predict proactive parenting or supportiveness. Although all subscales had sufficient variability overall, this result could be due to some of the items related to proactive parenting and supportiveness that might not be as relevant to mothers with very young children. For example, behaviors of explaining expectations and reasons for disciplining and listening to a child's ideas and opinions are potentially not as relevant for mothers of one-year-olds due to their developmental stage limiting understanding of explanations and one's verbal communication, thus parents of the youngest children may have had more difficulty in providing an accurate response to those items. Continued investigation into the specific sources of workplace flexibility and their influence on positive parenting behaviors is warranted.

Workplace Flexibility and Work–Family Guilt

Workplace flexibility had a significant negative effect on work–family guilt – as perceived workplace flexibility increased, mothers' work–family guilt decreased. This result was expected since American workers' lack of control over one's job predicts higher levels of WIF-guilt (Korabik, 2015). The sense of control afforded by workplace flexibility (Hill et al., 2008) may serve to reduce feelings of work–family guilt for working mothers. To the authors' knowledge, this study is the first to establish a direct link between these two constructs.

Workplace flexibility may significantly reduce mothers' work–family guilt because the flexibility helps bridge the gap between their ideal level of participation in their family life and reality of how they experience their family time (Daly, 2001). Perhaps it is workplace flexibility that provides mothers with the ability to better integrate their work and family lives such that expectations and standards are more fully met in both domains thereby decreasing the guilt felt. For example, mothers who are able to adjust their work schedule or reduce their time in paid work (Collins, 2021) to meet their needs and/or manage personal and family responsibilities, may feel less guilt about work taking her away from her home/family or worry less that her work is negatively affecting her child.

Work–Family Guilt and Parenting Behavior

Work–family guilt did not mediate the relationship between workplace flexibility and parenting behavior. It was expected work–family guilt would have a negative effect on positive parenting behaviors in the model, but this was not the case. Given that mothers reported overall low levels of work–family guilt and high levels of the positive parenting behaviors, it seems work–family guilt is not significantly affecting their positive parenting behavior.

Perhaps work–family guilt, while influenced by work demands or resources, may influence one's personal resources (as described above) more so than one's home outcomes, such as parenting behaviors. For example, lack of workplace flexibility may lead to high levels of work–family guilt which may diminish one's sense of self-efficacy which may in turn reduce the individual's ability to utilize their other resources in the most optimal way and in a way that promotes positive parenting behavior. In the W-HRM model, certain factors make work–family conflict and enrichment more or less likely. These factors include *key resources* which are a subset of personal resources. Key resources are the characteristics of a person and are the "management resources that facilitate the selection, alteration, and implementation of other resources" (p. 548). Examples include self-efficacy, self-esteem, optimism, and social power. Individuals who possess more of these key resources are better able to problem solve, cope with stress, collect new resources, and optimally utilize their contextual resources (ten Brummelhuis & Bakker, 2012). As such, it might be that work–family guilt plays more of a role in affecting one's use of their key resources instead of directly influencing one's parenting behaviors or other home outcomes. Future studies should examine the ways in which work–family guilt may contribute to the increase or decrease of personal resources via key resources or other paths.

Furthermore, work–family guilt may not be related to the parenting behaviors measured herein. The construct might be more closely associated with other positive parenting behaviors not measured, such as providing structure/routines for children, or specific engagement behaviors, such as recreational and educational activities. For example, parents' trait guilt motivated parents to participate in more recreational and educational activities with their children, like playing and reading (Cho & Allen, 2012). Work–family guilt may be more related to negative parenting behaviors, as evidenced by the link found between WIF-guilt and permissive parenting (Borelli et al., 2017b). Future studies should further investigate specific engagement behaviors as well as negative parenting behaviors, such as hostility, physical control, and lax control (Parent & Forehand, 2017). Perhaps a negative emotion like work–family guilt is more closely associated with negative parenting behaviors.

Limitations

This study has several limitations. Due to the cross-sectional nature of the data, it is not possible to make strong causal inferences regarding the relationships between the variables. Additionally, the use of self-report measures is not optimal. Although one's perception of workplace flexibility is more appropriately measured by self-report (Hill et al., 2001), there are concerns regarding the over-reliance of perceived flexibility. It has been argued that these measures are "problematic because it is not clear if perceived flexibility is measuring a modifiable attribute of the work environment or an individual characteristic such as sense of control" (Grzywacz et al., 2008, p. 200) whereas the measurement of formal policies and management/supervisor practices in following or not following the policies provide a more accurate picture of one's workplace flexibility and provides a more accurate understanding of the meaning of perceived flexibility because the extent to which perceptions of flexibility are shaped by specific practices can be determined. Social desirability poses issues as well for self-report measures, especially for the parenting items, with participants providing responses that reflect their desired parenting behaviors instead of their actual behaviors. In future studies, one could triangulate self-reported parenting behavior with youth or partner report of parenting behavior or using observational measures.

Although the MAPS (Parent & Forehand, 2017) measure encompasses central components of positive parenting, it does not include items related to the provision of structure and active monitoring, which are components of the behavior control dimension of parenting that have been shown to be beneficial to children (Stolz, 2011). Furthermore, this measure was designed for parents of children ages 3 to 17, so it is possible it did not accurately tap positive parenting behaviors of parents with children between 1 and 3, as discussed above. A self-selection bias may also exist in that the individuals who chose to participate in the study and have the time and opportunity or flexibility to spend an average of 21 minutes completing the survey may differ in some way than individuals who did not select to participate. The racial and socioeconomic breakdown of the sample is not representative of the diversity in the United States, thus the generalizability of the results may also be further restricted. The findings of this study are unable to account for the work experiences of low-income mothers who likely experience lower levels of workplace flexibility. Given low-income mothers have been found to experience greater benefits from workplace flexibility than mid- and high-income mothers (Kim, 2018), it is critical future samples be representative of the entire socioeconomic spectrum or focus on this vulnerable population that is not well-represented in the present study. Additionally, it is also critical future samples be representative of families of color, especially given working mothers from nonwhite backgrounds have identified alternative motherhood ideologies, such as Black middle- and upper-middle class working mothers who have expressed different cultural expectations for integrating work and motherhood that is not a source of work–family conflict, yet also experience tension between their personal mothering desires and cultural expectations (Dow, 2016). Although poor representation and generalizability was the case for this study, the decision to implement a snowball approach to recruit participants was made to attain a larger sample size and maintain the anonymity of study participants.

Policy and Practice Implications

Consistent with previous research, the findings of this study add further support that workplace policies that allow for flexible work arrangements are beneficial to family life. A strong public policy effort is needed to make flexible work arrangements become the new normal in the American workplace, especially following the pandemic and the significant increase in remote work (Robinson, 2022). A public–private infrastructure between key federal, state, and community partners needs to be created to incentivize, model, and market workplace flexibility. This infrastructure will allow the government to support flexible work arrangements as standard as well as support innovations in workplace flexibility by providing government-funded pilot programs and evaluations (National Advisory Commission on Workplace Flexibility, 2009). Furthermore, for local efforts to succeed, workplace policies must be framed as both an employer issue and a community issue. Involving local leaders in relevant coalitions can help define the community case for workplace flexibility (Galinksy et al., 2011).

Workplace flexibility also makes for good business by attracting better workers, reducing turnover and absenteeism, and increasing productivity which "translates into savings of up to $300 billion per year, or between $496 and $1,984 per employee per year" (Trask, 2017, p. 3). Still, less than one-third of full-time workers report they have access to policies that allow for schedule flexibility, including flextime and flexplace, with employees also expressing fear of negative job repercussions if they use the policies available to them (Trask, 2017). Furthermore, mostly lower-wage workers do not have access to basic flexibility policies, such as varying their hours or taking breaks or time away to deal with family emergencies (National Partnership for Women & Families, 2019), and this has been magnified during the pandemic (Wolfe et al., 2021). Other types of flexibility can be instituted for lower-wage jobs. For example, businesses could adopt job sharing policies or have a bank of substitute employees available for emergency absences (Trask, 2017). Federal, state, local, and private sector policies that afford workers with flexible work arrangements and establishes a supervisorial and workplace culture supportive of utilizing policies (Galinksy et al., 2011) can lead to beneficial outcomes for employees, employers, and communities.

Advocacy and research for other work-related policies that help families with caregiving tasks needs to continue as well. In addition to workplace flexibility, expanded family leave and paid sick leave are two other policies known to be beneficial to families (Trask, 2017) and would provide parents more time outside of paid work (Collins, 2021). In sum, American families would be better supported by workplace policies that decrease the discrepancy between their ideal family expectations and the reality of meeting those standards thereby reducing the possibility for feeling guilt related to one's circumstances or not fully meeting one's standards.

Intervention efforts can also help parents integrate work and family life. Parent education programs as well as home visiting and parent coaching can provide parents with the knowledge and skills to parent more effectively. Evidence-based, rigorous parent education programs have been shown to improve parenting practices (Stolz, 2011). Additionally, workplace policy-related interventions may also be effective. For example, a workplace intervention aimed to increase schedule flexibility for employees and found that participants of the intervention, particularly working mothers, spent significantly more time with their children following participation (Davis et al., 2015). A program or intervention that incorporates work-culture change, work–life integration skills, and parenting skills might be especially beneficial to families as parents can move toward meeting their standards for family life in the context of their particular work and family circumstances. Policy changes at all levels, and intervention/education programs might also serve to help reduce flexibility bias, the assumption family priorities are put ahead of work responsibilities and one's career, that women sometimes contend with when choosing to utilize flexible work arrangements (Ladge & Greeberg, 2019).

Summary and Future Directions

The results of this study provide preliminary evidence that working mothers' perceived workplace flexibility may influence parenting behaviors and work–family guilt. However, more investigation is needed in this area to better understand how workplace flexibility and work–family guilt affect parenting behaviors, and ultimately child outcomes. In the future, it would be ideal for studies to use longitudinal designs to examine the relationships between domains like work environment, family, guilt, and parenting. Longitudinal designs will allow for causal interpretations of any relationships found as well as parse out whether reverse causality may exist. Additionally, longitudinal designs are also supported by the W-HRM which proposes that

> long-term work-home conflict and enrichment reflect durable processes between the work and home domains, whereby structural contextual demands and resources from one domain affect long-term outcomes in the other domain through a change in structural personal resources. (ten Brummelhuis & Bakker, 2012, p. 552)

As indicated, further investigation is needed into workplace flexibility and work–family enrichment process. What personal resources might workplace flexibility produce to improve parenting behaviors? Does workplace flexibility allow mothers to more effectively tap into their key resources and better utilize their contextual resources to produce positive home outcomes? Collins (2021) contends one policy that can reduce mothers' guilt is giving them more time outside of paid work so does workplace flexibility provide mothers with specific energies, like time and attention, that can spillover into positive home outcomes?

The work–family guilt measure needs additional consideration. Is it only measuring moments of guilt? Future studies could use experience sampling methodology (Johnson & Swendsen, 2015) or daily diary methodology (Aarntzen et al., 2019) to measure work–family guilt over a period of time. This may provide a more accurate assessment of guilt and parse out the difference between brief moments of guilt that pass after a short time as opposed to pervasive guilt. Different influences on parenting might be found depending on whether a parent is experiencing acute guilt versus a more chronic guilt. It might also be worth exploring whether chronic work–family-related guilt could be an entirely separate construct, like work–family anxiety perhaps. It might also be pertinent for future studies to address and possibly control for the role of trait guilt or one's proneness to feeling guilty. It might be that those who are accustomed to experiencing higher levels of guilt are least likely to allow work–family guilt to influence one's parenting behaviors. Conversely, those who are not accustomed to feeling much guilt, or are surprised by new feelings of guilt, might be more vulnerable to its influence on parenting behaviors.

Fathers should also be included in this area of inquiry, especially since previous studies have found that fathers also report experiencing work–family guilt (Livingston & Judge, 2008; Martínez et al., 2011). It is plausible the relationships between the constructs might be associated differently for fathers as traditional gender roles compete with evolving cultural expectations for father involvement. This study only used a sample of women who worked 30 or more hours per week, however, part-time employment can be considered a form of workplace flexibility and is associated with increased enrichment interactions for mothers of young children (Kim, 2018). Future studies should consider including women/parents who participate in part-time work to account for their experience of workplace flexibility. Additionally, future studies should consider how workplace flexibility and work–family guilt influence parenting behaviors for single-parent households and families with children with disabilities. Time constraints and fewer resources experienced by single parents cause challenges for meeting the demands of work and caregiving (Kim, 2018). Parents, especially mothers, of children with disabilities experience increased levels of psychological distress, and flexible work arrangements can increase work–family balance and decrease work–family conflict for these caregivers (Brown & Clark, 2017).

Given other workplace policies, like paid leave, benefit the function of families (Trask, 2017), it is important for future investigations to examine whether they might be more relevant to working parents and predicting their parenting behavior. Additional research might also investigate whether workplace flexibility and work–family guilt predict antecedents of parenting behavior, like parenting attitudes, for example. Perhaps work–family guilt is more strongly associated with altitudinal constructs like parenting self-efficacy which in turn may influence parenting behaviors. This would be in line with the role of the key resources in the W-HRM model (ten Brummelhuis & Bakker, 2012). Due to the limitations of measuring perceived workplace flexibility (Grzywacz et al., 2008), future studies need to include the role of supervisor support, types of formal policies, and utilization of policies in addition to one's perception of workplace flexibility. It is also important to consider different types of jobs and the different types of flexibility afforded across industries since some jobs are more challenging than others in providing flexibility to employees (Hill et al., 2008). Lastly, it is recommended to more closely examine the autonomy workplace flexibility affords, as it may be autonomy that allows a parent to parent in greater accordance with their personal parenting values and standards, thereby reducing work–family guilt, and fostering positive outcomes for children.

In conclusion, it is important to situate this study in the context of the ongoing COVID-19 pandemic. Data collection for this study took place just prior to the time most of the United States was under stay-at-home orders, beginning around March 16, 2020, and although the findings of this study provide important insights into the relationships between workplace flexibility, work–family guilt, and parenting behaviors, they do not reflect the current experiences of working mothers. The pandemic has fundamentally changed society, and family and work patterns, in particular – from unemployment, to the gendered impact of school and childcare closers, to domestic labor changes between partners (Yavorsky et al., 2021). These changes have significantly increased the care burden placed on American women (Power, 2020), and have negatively affected the well-being of mothers (Calarco et al., 2020; Grose, 2021). Current social conditions are ripe for increased work–family conflict, work–family guilt, and poor family outcomes, thus underscoring the need for protective and supportive solutions that help women and families through the pandemic and after. Workplace flexibility is among several policy solutions that could help ameliorate the fallout from the COVID-19 pandemic, and it is pertinent investigation of these constructs and relationships continues in order to inform policy decisions and implementation.

REFERENCES

A Better Balance. (2010, December 1). *The public health case for workplace flexibility*. https://www.abetterbalance.org/resources/public-health-case-workplace-flexibility-factsheet/

Aarntzen, L., Derks, B., van Steenbergen, E., Ryan, M., & van der Lippe, T. (2019). Work-family guilt as a straightjacket: An interview and diary study on consequences of mothers' work-family guilt. *Journal of Vocational Behavior*, *115*, 1–15. https://doi.org/10.1016/j.jvb.2019.103336

Anderson, O. A. (2006). *Linking work stress, parental self-efficacy, ineffective parenting, and youth problem behavior*. [Unpublished doctoral dissertation]. University of Tennessee, Knoxville.

Aycan, Z., & Eskin, M. (2005). Relative contributions of childcare, spousal support, and organizational support in reducing work-family conflict for men and women: The case of Turkey. *Sex Roles*, *53*(7/8), 453–471. https://doi.org/10.1007/s11199-005-7134-8

Barber, B. K., Stolz, H. E., & Olsen, J. A. (2005). Parental support, psychological control, and behavioral control: Assessing relevance across time, culture, and method [Monograph]. *Monographs of the Society for Research in Child Development*, *70*(4, Serial No. 282), 1–147.

Baumrind, D. (1971). Current patterns of parental authority [Monograph]. *Developmental Psychology*, *4*(1, Pt. 2), 1–103.

Belluz, J. (2019). *The U.S. fertility rate just hit a historic low*. Vox. https://www.vox.com/science-and-health/2018/5/22/17376536/fertility-rate-united-states-births-women

Borelli, J. L., Nelson, S. K., River, L. M., Birken, S. A., & Moss-Racusin, C. (2017a). Gender differences in work-family guilt in parents of young children. *Sex Roles*, *76*(5–6), 356–368. https://doi.org/10.1007/s11199-016-0579-0

Borelli, J. L., Nelson, S. K., River, L. M., Birken, S. A., & Moss-Racusin, C. (2017b). Bringing work home: Gender and parenting correlates of work-family guilt among parents of toddlers. *Journal of Child and Family Studies*, *26*(6), 1734–1745. https://doi.org/10.1007/s10826-017-0693-9

Brough, P., O'Driscoll, M. P., & Biggs, A. (2009). Parental leave and work-family balance among employed parents following childbirth: An exploratory investigation in Australia and New Zealand. *Kōtuitui: New Zealand Journal of Social Sciences Online*, *4*(1), 71–87. https://doi.org/10.1080/1177083X.2009.9522445

Brown, T. J., & Clark, C. (2017). Employed parents of children with disabilities and work family life balance: A literature review. *Child & Youth Care Forum*, *46*(6), 857–876. https://doi.org/10.1007/s10566-017-9407-0

Calarco, J. M., Meanwell, E. M, Anderson, E. V, & Knopf, A. (2020). "Let's not pretend it's fun": How disruptions to families' school and childcare arrangements impact mothers' well-being. https://doi.org/10.31235/osf.io/jyvk4

Carlson, D. S., Kacmar, K. M., Wayne, J. H., & Grzywacz, J. G. (2006). Measuring the positive side of the work-family interface: Development and validation of a work-family enrichment scale. *Journal of Vocational Behavior*, *68*(1), 131–164. https://doi.org/10.1016/j.jvb.2005.02.002

Cho, E., & Allen, T. D. (2012). Relationship between work interference with family and parent-child interactive behavior: Can guilt help? *Journal of Vocational Behavior*, *80*(2), 276–287. https://doi.org/10.1016/j.jvb.2011.12.002

Collins, C. (2019). *Making motherhood work: How women manage careers and caregiving*. Princeton University Press.

Collins, C. (2021). Is maternal guilt a cross-national experience? *Qualitative Sociology*, *44*, 1–29. https://doi.org/10.1007/s11133-020-09451-2

Costello, A. B., & Osborne, J. (2005). Best practices in exploratory factor analysis: Four recommendations for getting the most from your analysis. *Practical Assessment, Research & Evaluation*, *10*.

Costigan, C. L., Cox, M. J., & Cauce, A. M. (2003). Work-parenting linkages among dual-earner couples at the transition to parenthood. *Journal of Family Psychology*, *17*(3), 397–408. https://doi.org/10.1037/0893-3200.17.3.397

Daly, K. J. (2001). Deconstructing family time: From ideology to lived experience. *Journal of Marriage and Family*, *63*(2), 283–294. https://doi.org/10.1111/j.1741-3737.2001.00283.x

Davis, K. D., Lawson, K. M., Almeida, D. M., Kelly, E. L., King, R. B., Hammer, L., Casper, L. M., Okechukwu, C. A., Hanson, G., & McHale, S. M. (2015). Parents' daily time with their children: A workplace intervention. *Pediatrics*, *135*(5), 875–882. https://doi.org/10.1542/peds.2014-2057

de Menezes, L. M., & Kelliher, C. (2011). Flexible working and performance: A systematic review of the evidence for a business case. *International Journal of Management Reviews*, *13*(4), 452–474. https://doi.org/10.1111/j.1468-2370.2011.00301.x

Dow, D. M. (2016). Integrated motherhood: Beyond hegemonic ideologies of motherhood. *Journal of Marriage and Family*, *78*(1), 180–196. https://doi.org/10.1111/jomf.12264

Earle, A., Mokomane, Z., & Heymann, J. (2011). International perspectives on work-family policies: Lessons from the world's most competitive economies. *The Future of Children*, *21*(2), 191–210. https://doi.org/10.1353/foc.2011.0014

Fry, R. (2022, January 14). *Some gender disparities widened in the U.S. workforce during the pandemic*. Pew Research Center. https://www.pewresearch.org/fact-tank/2022/01/14/some-gender-disparities-widened-in-the-u-s-workforce-during-the-pandemic/

Galinksy, E., Sakai, K., & Wigton, T. (2011). Workplace flexibility: From research to action. *The Future of Children*, *21*(2), 141–161. https://doi.org/10.1353/foc.2011.0019

Glass, J., Anderson, M. A., & Simon, R. W. (2016). Parenthood and happiness: Effects of work-family reconciliation policies in 22 OECD countries. *American Journal of Sociology*, *122*(3), 886–929.

Greenhaus, J. H., & Beutell, N. J. (1985). Sources of conflict between work and family roles. *Academy of Management Review*, *10*, 76–88.

Grose, J. (2021, February 4). America's mothers are in crisis: Is anyone listening to them? *The New York Times*. https://www.nytimes.com/2021/02/04/parenting/working-moms-mental-health-coronavirus.html

Grzywacz, J. G., Carlson, D. S., & Shulkin, S. (2008). Schedule flexibility and stress: Linking formal flexible arrangements and perceived flexibility to employee health. *Community, Work and Family*, *11*(2), 199–214. https://doi.org/10.1080/13668800802024652

Hayes, A. F. (2017). *Introduction to mediation, moderation, and conditional process analysis: A regression-based approach* (2nd ed.). The Guilford Press.

Hill, E. J., Erickson, J. J., Holmes, E. K., & Ferris, M. (2010). Workplace flexibility, work hours, and work-life conflict: Finding an extra day or two. *Journal of Family Psychology*, *24*(3), 349–358. https://doi.org/10.1037/a0019282

Hill, E. J., Grzywacz, J. G., Allen, S., Blanchard, V. L., Matz-Costa, C., Shulkin, S., & Pitt-Catsouphes, M. (2008). Defining and conceptualizing workplace flexibility. *Community, Work & Family*, *11*(2), 149–163. https://doi.org/10.1080/13668800802024678

Hill, E. J., Hawkins, A. J., Ferris, M., & Weitzman, M. (2001). Finding an extra day a week: The positive influence of perceived job flexibility on work and family life balance. *Family Relations*, *50*(1), 49–58. https://doi.org/10.1111/j.1741-3729.2001.00049.x

Hill, R., Tranby, E., Kelly, E., & Moen, P. (2013). Relieving the time squeeze? Effects of a white-collar workplace change on parents. *Journal of Marriage and Family*, *75*(4), 1014–1029. https://doi.org/10.1111/jomf.12047

Jang, S. J. (2009). The relationships of flexible work schedules, workplace support, supervisory support, work-life balance, and the well-being of working parents. *Journal of Social Service Research*, *35*(2), 93–104. https://doi.org/10.1080/01488370802678561

Jang, S. J., Zippay, A., & Park, R. (2012). Family roles as moderators of the relationship between schedule flexibility and stress. *Journal of Marriage and Family*, *74*(4), 897–912. https://doi.org/10.1111/j.1741-3737.2012.00984.x

Jaoko, J. (2012). An analysis of supervisor support of policies on workplace flexibility. *Journal of Social Service Research*, *38*(4), 541–548. https://doi.org/10.1080/01488376.2012.701158

Johnson, E. I., & Swendsen, J. D. (2015). Perceived social status and early adolescents' responses to negative daily events. *Journal of Child and Family Studies*, *24*(6), 1593–1604. https://doi.org/10.1007/s10826-014-9963-y

Judge, T. A., Ilies, R., & Scott, B. A. (2006). Work-family conflict and emotions: Effects at work and at home. *Personal Psychology*, *59*(4), 779–814. https://doi.org/10.1111/j.1744-6570.2006.00054.x

Keeton, C. P., Perry-Jenkins, M., & Sayer, A. G. (2008). Sense of control predicts depressive and anxious symptoms across the transition to parenthood. *Journal of Family Psychology*, *22*(2), 212 – 221. https://doi.org/10.1037/0893-3200.22.2.212

Kim, J. (2018). Workplace flexibility and parent-child interactions among working parents in the U.S. *Social Indicators Research*, 1–43. https://doi.org/10.1007/s11205-018-2032-y

Korabik, K. (2015). The intersection of gender and work-family guilt. In M. J. Mills (Ed.), *Gender and the work-family experience* (pp. 141–157). https://doi.org/10.1007/978-3-319-088914_8

Ladge, J., & Greeberg, D. (2019). *Maternal optimism: Forging positive paths through work and motherhood.* Oxford University Press.

Lambert, S. J., Haley-Lock, A., & Henly, J. R. (2012). Schedule flexibility in hourly jobs: Unanticipated consequences and promising directions. *Community, Work & Family*, *15*(3), 293–315. https://doi.org/10.1080/13668803.2012.662803

Leith, K. P., & Baumeister, R. F. (1998). Empathy, shame, guilt, and narratives of interpersonal conflicts: Guilt-prone people are better at perspective taking. *Journal of Personality*, *66*(1), 1–37. https://doi.org/10.1111/1467-6494.00001

Livingston, B. A., & Judge, T. A. (2008). Emotional responses to work-family conflict: An examination of gender role orientation among working men and women. *Journal of Applied Psychology*, *93*(1), 207–216. https://doi.org/10.1037/0021-9010.93.1.207

Martínez, P., Carrasco, M. J., Aza, G., Blanco, A., & Espinar, I. (2011). Family gender role and guilt in Spanish dual-earner families. *Sex Roles*, *65*(11–12), 813–826. https://doi.org/10.1007/s11199-011-0031-4

Milkie, M. A., Kendig, S. M., Nomaguchi, K. M., & Denny, K. E. (2010). Time with children, children's well-being, and work-family balance among employed parents. *Journal of Marriage and Family*, *72*(5), 1329–1343. https://doi.org/10.1111/j.1741-3737.2010.00768.x

Millward, L. J. (2006). The transition to motherhood in an organizational context: An interpretative phenomenological analysis. *Journal of Occupational and Organizational Psychology*, *79*(3), 315–333. https://doi.org/10.1348/096317906X110322

Minnotte, K. L., Minnotte, M. C., & Thompson, K. (2016). The life satisfaction of dual-earner mothers and fathers: Does flexible scheduling matter? *Journal of Happiness Studies*, *17*(6), 2365–2388. https://doi.org/10.1007/s10902-015-9698-5

National Advisory Commission on Workplace Flexibility. (2009, May 13). *Public policy platform on flexible work arrangements*. https://scholarship.law.georgetown.edu/pub_rep/2

National Partnership for Women & Families. (2019). *Flexibility for success: How workplace flexibility policies benefit all workers and employers*. https://www.nationalpartnership.org/our-work/resources/economic-justice/archive/flexibility-for-success.pdf

Parent, J. M. (2017). *Multidimensional assessment of parenting across three developmental stages*. [Unpublished doctoral dissertation]. The University of Vermont and State Agricultural College.

Parent, J., & Forehand, R. (2017). The Multidimensional Assessment of Parenting Scale (MAPS): Development and psychometric properties. *Journal of Child and Family Studies*, *26*(8), 2136–2151. https://doi.org/10.1007/s10826-017-0741-5

Pitt-Catsouphes, M., Matz-Costa, C., & Besen, E. (2009). *Workplace flexibility: Findings from the age and generations study*. The Sloane Center on Aging & Work at Boston College. https://www.bc.edu/content/dam/files/research_sites/agingandwork/pdf/publications/IB19_WorkFlex.pdf

Power, K. (2020). The COVID-19 pandemic has increased the care burden of women and families. *Sustainability: Science, Practice and Policy*, *16*(1), 67–73. https://doi.org/10.1080/15487733.2020.1776561

Repetti, R. L., & Wang, S. (2014). Employment and parenting. *Parenting: Science and Practice*, *14*(2), 121–132. https://doi.org/10.1080/15295192.2014.914364

Robinson, B. (2022, February 1). *Remote work is here to stay and will increase into 2023, experts say*. Forbes. https://www.forbes.com/sites/bryanrobinson/2022/02/01/remote-work-is-here-to-stay-and-will-increase-into-2023-experts-say/?sh=6b2b5aa220a6

Ruppanner, L., Lee, R., & Huffman, M. (2018). Do mothers benefit from flexible work? Cross-national evidence for work time, job quality, and satisfaction. *International Journal of Sociology*, *48*(2), 170–187. https://doi.org/10.1080/00207659.2018.1446119

Sanders, M. R., Kirby, J. N., Tellegen, C. L., & Day, J. J. (2014). The Triple P-Positive Parenting Program: A systematic review and meta-analysis of a multi-level system of parenting support. *Clinical Psychology Review*, *34*(4), 337–357. http://dx.doi.org/10.1016/j.cpr.2014.04.003

Stack, D. M., Serbin, L. A., Enns, L. N., Ruttle, P. L., & Barrieau, L. (2010). Parental effects on children's emotional development over time and across generations. *Infants & Young Children*, *23*(1), 52–69. https://doi.org/10.1097/IYC.0b013e3181c97606

Stolz, H. E. (2011). Parenting education. In S. F. Duncan & H. W. Goddard (Eds.), *Family life education: Principles and practices for effective outreach* (pp. 191–210). Sage.

Swanberg, J. E., Pitt-Catsouphes, M., & Drescher-Burke, K. (2005). A question of justice: Disparities in employees' access to flexible schedule arrangements. *Journal of Family Issues*, *26*(6), 866–895. https://doi.org/10.1177/0192513X05277554

ten Brummelhuis, L. L., & Bakker, A. B. (2012). A resource perspective on the work-home interface: The work-home resources model. *American Psychologist*, *67*(7), 545–556. https://doi.org/10.1037/a0027974

ter Hoeven, C. L., & van Zoonen, W. (2015). Flexible work designs and employee well-being: examining the effects of resources and demands. *New Technology, Work and Employment*, *30*(3), 237–255. https://doi.org/10.1111/ntwe.12052

Trask, B. S. (2017, January). *Alleviating the stress on working families: Promoting family-friendly workplace polices*. National Council on Family Relations. https://www.ncfr.org/sites/default/files/2017-01/ncfr_policy_brief_january_2017.pdf

Weems, G. H., & Onwuegbuzie, A. J. (2001). The impact of midpoint responses and reverse coding on survey data. *Measurement and Evaluation in Counseling and Development*, *34*(3), 166–176. https://doi.org/10.1080/07481756.2002.12069033

Wolfe, R., Harknett, K., & Schneider, D. (2021). *Inequalities at work and the toll of COVID-19*. Health Affairs Health Policy Brief. https://doi.org/10.1377/hpb20210428.863621

Yavorsky, J. E., Qian, Y., & Sargent, A. C. (2021). The gendered pandemic: The implications of COVID-19 for work and family. *Sociology Compass*, *15*(6), 1–13. https://doi.org/10.1111/soc4.12881

INDEX

Note: Page numbers followed by "*n*" indicate notes.

Printed and bound by CPI Group (UK) Ltd, Croydon, CR0 4YY

13/09/2026

14961062-0005